T0367446

John Shelton Jones

Awakening Kings and Princes Volume I

Sacred Knowledge to Nourish the Mentality, Support Spiritual Growth, Learning the Light, and Progressing to Become a Master Lover while Embracing Desire

John Shelton Jones

Awakening Kings and Princes
Volume I

Sacred Knowledge to Nourish the Mentality, Support Spiritual Growth, Learning the Light, and Progressing to Become a Master Lover while Embracing Desire

Administered to:

_____

By:

_____

Date:

_____

First and Far Most, Honors and Love to Adon Olam Yahawah and Adonai Christ Yahawashi.
I would like to give honors to my former English instructors from Ireland Drive Middle and Douglas Byrd Middle and Senior, and special thanks to former English professors from Fayetteville Technical Community College.
Honors to my Father and Mother.
Honors to Trafford Publishing and Author Solutions.
I would like to give honors for my kindred, friends, and the seekers of this book throughout many waters (p. 244 [for <u>many waters</u> meaning]).

Order this book online at www.trafford.com
or email orders@trafford.com

Most Trafford titles are also available at major online book retailers.

Print information available on the last page.

ISBN: 978-1-4907-7599-9 (sc)
ISBN: 978-1-4907-7598-2 (hc)
ISBN: 978-1-4907-7600-2 (e)

Library of Congress Control Number: 2016913308

Trafford rev.   08/30/2016

 www.trafford.com

North America & international
toll-free: 1 888 232 4444 (USA & Canada)
fax: 812 355 4082

$\mathcal{V}_1$

Contents

Prologue:
The Awakening

"Born legends; claiming your throne happens within, the prelude to the awakening of princes to become kings."

"There's a common missed ideology and framework on men of faith in that is the day you accept Christ you become a King and develop the gift of Priesthood."

If every male had the systematic knowledge of kingship within and embraced their royal destiny, the youth of the newly developed males would make possibilities of true kingship, gain confidence, become solid, strengthen vulnerabilities, and acquire the discipline to prevail. My goal is to use my gathered information as a guide to awaken the missing linkage that driven men apart from respect they deserved and the retribution to character. Many young male adolescents grow up without a **father figure**: *a guided king who uplifts the prince in kingship phase and elevates destiny.* Too many males become misled into darkness from what's righteous, healthy, strong, and true. Yet the pathway is very narrow. Every king understands a calling, but many don't know how to seek this calling out, many seek termination before determination, and many hide sexual desires, causing infidelity within relationships. Throughout this book I'll be establishing emunah with scriptures, empirical reality, and many other awakenings. Understand that this volume and the proceeding volumes is not just people of faith but light guider. In developing id, superego, ego, hypnosis, and many other important factors, an individual must first understand their rationalizing truths:

- ❖ Throughout this book, focus will be applied to awaken inner dimensions of your character, desire, light of knowledge and wisdom, and spirituality; harness strengths and vulnerabilities; become fervent to sincerities and investments; comprehend the concept of teleology; and much more.

To understand all of these rationalizing truths is a leap step forward to proper nurturing within to become royalty. Understand that these processes are acknowledgment of your own undisputed truths and are not a few minutes of processing but hours and days, maybe for some weeks or years. To gain kingship, one must not become a victim of influences and abuse persisted in the past but declare new sanity from within. After rationalizing truths, discover learning ways of leadership, self-helping arts of sexual counseling, and information on sacred sexual manuscripts practiced by kings and princes. Holistic formulas for sexual health will be given in this book to help accommodate certain desires; the real will only be included in this book. Knowledge is power; to become the power, one must feed the brain and hunger for more information.

The science of study doesn't create an individual; procreation does. No one can fully theorize a person nor can a study. Psychology doesn't create individualism, astrology doesn't create you, palmistry doesn't create you, and social construction doesn't create you. Only you create you, but God created your soul, and your actions in mind and body determine the repercussion of how you construct yourselves in this world. No one can fully determine who you are but yourself, and God knows the assets here on this earth are for you to utilize your guide and awaken who you are.

I've noticed the subliminal messages of how the new millennium fashion styles are okay to wear or piercings are justified on many areas or sexual enhancement remedies are designed to work when actually, they are failures in most advertisements or temporary fix. In addition, notice the social influence of television shows now adding in uncensored homosexual/transsexual scenes and sexual violence, provoking the thoughts of confusion to young men and projecting change to God's Word:

[27]So God created humankind in His own tzelem (image), in the tzelem (image) Elohim created He him; zachar (male) and nekevah (female) created He them. [28]And God blessed them, and God said unto them, Be fruitful, and multiply, and fill the earth, and subdue it: and have dominion over the fish of the sea, and over the fowl of the air, and over every living thing that moveth upon the earth. (Bereshis [Genesis] 1v27–28 Orthodox Jewish Bible)

Many males at ages fourteen and up imitate idols that illustrate gang violence, dealings with illegal merchandise, forsake faith and education, and abuse women just to be initiated unto penetrative evil. Many men lose their way because of women influences as well, portraying them tools for cash and influencing weakness thinking they can't function without the fruit, devouring a man's ability to become strong unless the male becomes king with persistent faith in Elohim (God) and Yeshua (Jesus) to overcome temptation. To become king, one has to learn the righteous and evil without becoming evil, submit to reality, secure ambitions and apprenticeship, unleash the animalistic behavior within, learn sexual and social intelligence, and awaken dimensional mentality.

I. Part I: The discovering of mastery within your subconscious while releasing truth within through knowledge and reason, thereby excelling development stages of strength using rationality and apprenticeship with the light to guide your pathway and submitting truths.

II. Part II: This part introduces the dimensions of soulful medicines, purpose of dreams and visions, the spiritual insightful things that various individuals don't acknowledge, and prayers.

III. Part III: Then awakening your healthy sexual Eros, truer lovemaking, and a reverence of embracing your inner personalities, along with your lovers' innermost desires. In addition, you'll be learning urban sacred sexual intelligence, along with biblical exegeses to awaken new dimensions of loving.

IV. Part IV: Conclusion, appendix I—Bible conspiracies, and appendix II—expanded portion of doctrines of honor, aggression, primitive arts, and added marital agreement contract.

This book is based on self-development, not history lessons but an awakening dimension to becoming strong in many areas. If you're reading this material for history, you will be disappointed, but if you

The Awakening

want to become superior from within, this material is for you. In this millennium, many men have not come to the awakening that were much more than man, but once your faith resides in the belief that you've been saved from sin by Jesus Christ, that's the day you become king and priest (Revelations 1v5–6 KJV).

Warning: Before readers begin further reading, family royal seekers you may need a notebook or journal to take notes or journalize to grasp certain concepts plus I invite readers to use the "Index" portion to your advantage along with "Contents" for directories. For this book will be intensive to certain individuals.

Part I:

Ark of Mentality, Hypnosis, Ra and Dolor, and Realism

The discovering of mastery within your subconscious while releasing truth within through knowledge and reason, thereby excelling development stages of strength using rationality and apprenticeship with the light to guide your pathway and submitting truths.

Chapter I:
Discovery Within

You never change things by fighting the existing reality. To change something, build a new model that makes the old model obsolete.

—Buckminster Fuller

Many men overlook their own individuality without discovery within, establishing protocol of developments. One must understand their rationalizing truths to prevail in mastery. There are many traits one must seek within self-consciousness, "a person's awareness of feelings, sensations, and thoughts" of how you function as a whole. Below is a chart of the four sections to understand:

Figure 1-1 Rationalizing Truths

Character and Meaning

Discovering character is the theory of your personality that makes you unique. Uniqueness is essential to character because you establish superiority without imitating everyone else. Kings are superior. We must seek the true character within ourselves to prevail—our certain existence or breathe nothing. Many men suffer reality because they try imitating other individuals without harnessing the special image and skills Jehovah Elohim has given. God (Jehovah) did not intend to make every person look the same, so don't stress yourselves with how you can imitate muscular image of others. ***Thy lie thou lives lies, but thee whom seeks truth prevails in truthful living may find better clarity.***

Young men lose their way because a lack of guidance in negative surroundings causes false confidence. ***Establish confidence within***, professionally, is one of my focuses to build true confidence, for there are two types of confidence: true and false confidence. Distinguishing the two, ***false confidence*** is built on the idea of always being dominant, assertive, liar, dishonest, and lack agape love through downsizing, manipulating, and mentally abusing others and not building investment in oneself. The purpose of false confidence is to gain attention from those around them. ***True confidence*** is built on ignoring people's perceptions of you and investing in oneself without causing mental anguish on others.

True confidence is a long-term solution for growth to true royal gentleman ways. The purposes of true confidence are to build models of true honesty and powerful connections toward women without false impression; build logical steps of true morality, royalty, and kingship; master true lovemaking; dominate with submission toward rationalizing truths; and master strengths and awareness of weakness. True confidence is driven by self-purpose and self-development and submission to vulnerability even in moments that may friction possibilities. Lean on your own understanding, not what is expected from others, for every man often walks the path alone to pursue their own desires with the Holy Spirit as our savior and hope *present*, *after*, and *before* all others banish us into the wilderness.

As human beings, we are responsible for our own lives. Our behavior is a function of our decisions, not our conditions. We can subordinate feelings to values. We have the initiative and the responsibility to make things happen. (Stephen Covey)

You must flow relentlessly regardless of what others may perceive about you to be free. People's negative perceptions and mockery will always be perceived as weakness, for they don't share the character you possess. Awaken meaning in your life without assumptions of others driving your direction. There's only one person who can walk you in this world, yourself, for the pathway is directed by your decisions alone. Holy Spirit is the light a king seeks, for he walks with you in every moment. Don't question your reason for existence as meaningless even if you were born into this world with limited circumstances. Change your existing reality for a healthier reality of living; reliving past generational curses doesn't establish meaning within your life but meaningless existence. Harness your own individuality; character defines your worth and royalty.

And that ye study to be quiet, and to do your own business, and to work with your own hands, as we commanded you; that ye may walk honestly toward them that are without, and that ye may have lack of nothing. (1 Thessalonians 4v11–12 Authorized KJV)

Desires and Sincerities

Discerning the proportionate utter realistic truth to who you are, then you'll discover your passion, and passion leads to discovery within meaning. Every one of us men has a desire in life of commitments to secure hope, its human nature and nurture to prevail. Desire is what drives our persistence above and beyond, but how sincere are you into putting that into action is the concern. Many males lose hope because of obligations of bills, family, and life contingency. The issue is sincerities. You may ask what the definition of sincerities is; sincerities are the driven will to persist on what's true to heart regardless of circumstances or past mistakes. Therefore, sincerities are based on self-discipline driven by desire. Desire is the flow of carrying on in life without such hope you're prisoner of your destiny.

There are certain **counterforces** that are *diversions preventing you from carrying out your destiny as a king.* Counterforces are social pressures, such as relatives, friends, associates, and strangers influencing misleading on a healthy pathway. You may ask what a healthy pathway is. This is the self-willing to pursue your own decisions without accepting fragile stupidity of others' perceptions on how you should breathe, "inferring a way of living freely and true acceptance of your nature." However, it's not a hindrance of counterforce if the intentions of desires are evil; thus, social pressure is argued upon you for its positive assurance to good gestures.

> *The man who succeeds above his fellows is the one who early in life, clearly discerns his object, and towards that object habitually directs his powers. Even genius itself is but fine observation strengthened by fixity of purpose. Every man who observes vigilantly and resolves steadfastly grows unconsciously into genius. (Edward G. Bulwer-Lytton)*

Nature nurtures; as beings, we must learn to harvest and supplement what's fulfilling, not what's gratifying on others' behalf but what's satisfying within oneself. Honor thyself in truth but don't forget to nourish family. Dreaming is essential toward living; to one day turn that dream into reality is what motivates our energy. Mental energy is powered by desire among men, a stage of greed looking to harness. Sincerities are the driven will to change procrastination into action. This action develops reaction, for there's a cause behind every effect as so for action to reaction. Never underestimate the human spirituality of your desire because you may receive all you've hoped for in time. Commitment to desire perceives sincerities. Remember that, for it's extremely important. To discover truth is to discover vocation. The Latin meaning of **vocation** is "to call" or "to be called," which means *a strong desire to spend your life doing a certain kind of work, establishing destined calling, discovering purpose within.* Some say it's the Lord's gift of intellect to us.

> *But let every man prove his own work, and then shall he have rejoicing in himself alone, and not in another. For every man shall bear his own burden. (Galatians 6v4–5 KJV)*

One of our respected biblical beings mentioned vocation in a unique way. Apostle Paul gave a meaningful message when he said, "Forgetting what lies behind, and reaching forward to what lies in front, I pursue my purpose, aiming at the prize of the high calling of God" (Phil. 3v13–14). His attention was not on materialistic matter but growth in spiritual knowledge and truth seeker within to define his purpose, his meaning, and his promised desires fulfilled by Elohim "Lord of the Most High." His past didn't provoke him, but his presence preceded him with purpose.

Learning and Processing

One must be aware of a disciplined pathway of learning without misguidance. If you feel misguided, meditate then seek the Yahawah and Yahawashi for guidance. No one can excel in life without education, for the brain must constantly be supplemented with knowledge to achieve intelligence in life. The world is advancing in career fields. High school diploma won't carry out your desire unless it's low wage you desire. Concentration will become a privilege when you exceed above and beyond intentions. Passive mode of learning is observance to what's beneficial and what's not. As men, we must learn causes to change our world. We must learn and administer the outcome of our causes by questioning rather the reason conveys a positive motion for agape and freedom versing the havoc and destruction to reach dissension on rather its actions will be a benefactor for a positive change to our world or if it's negative with leading actions of havoc. One must acknowledge the undesired before action leads to a disturbing fate. The world is a battlefield of minds, each one trying to harness what's desired. Learning from others' failures is a contribution to saving yourself from repeating the process of their failures. We're all apprentices. No matter what position we possess, we are never too old to learn new knowledge. Learning is the opportunity to fortify progression of change from within. Processing is the phase of transformation, the ability to change existing reality into a new reality. There's influence out in the world that tries to prevent us from acquiring knowledge to progress ourselves because some envy the drive of our success, as they didn't succeed. Learn those types of individuals for what they truly represent—jealousy and envy. Learn the conspiracies within this world by aggressive research and without being ignorant.

In Robert Greene's book *Mastery*, he formulated an excellent learning and processing phase called the Apprenticeship Phase (Figure 1-2) built on three principles.

Deep Observation (The Passive Mode)   *Skill Acquisition (The Practice Mode)*   *Experimentation (The Active Mode)*

Figure 1-2 Apprenticeship Phase Diagram

The passive mode is to *observe* and *absorb* reality in an ethical manner without positioning yourself above— "you first have to crawl before you walk." Wisdom is gained through experience, information, and elders who show established positions in life though that doesn't mean to absorb everything, for various things are beneficial for you not to absorb. Next is the practice mode, which is the **tacit knowledge**, grasping the feel of skills to hands-on application, thus increasing the ability to analyze oneself. Then the active mode is the action of using given information and applying it to real-world application with the possibilities of criticism from others to master self-vulnerabilities.

Strengths and Vulnerabilities

Clarifying your own strengths and vulnerabilities is the chance of progress within. Every man should be able to summarize himself if not meditate on it. If meditation doesn't work, review what throws you off-track. For most of us, it's women. But you must remember you're important just as much as her. Don't be discouraged by vulnerabilities. Be honest to yourself. Make a chart listing what you're good at and what you're not good at. Make use of your sense to achieve prowess. Sometimes this requires much more investment on what you strive for in truth. This is a primary difficulty to most individuals because ego gets in the way. Carry yourself in royal fashion without the acceptance of others who try to degrade you. Know that no one is perfect but reflects the idea of perfection. Below is a diagram (Figure 1-3) of building investment in you in matters of presumable strength within and knowing to privilege vulnerability and establish truth:

> *Be attentive to what is arising within you, and place that above everything else . . . What is happening in your innermost self is worthy of your entire love; somehow you must find a way to work at it. (Rainer Maria Rilke, M. D. Herter Norton)*

Cardinal rule to strength: *Never expose yourself into thinking you're bound because you are bound by nothing, for strength is inevitable.* Strength is entitled progression within oneself conscious to exceed beyond levels of dubious entitlement. Amending certainty of what's truly desired among within contributes to infinite possibilities. Condition the psychological and the physiological to royalty and disregard negative social influences. A way of conditioning the psychological is to feed the mind with positive psychology to inspire and give self-acceptance in oneself and condition the physiological to succeed in longevity, feeding the body healthy as deserved upon the self. Some individuals in the world want you to think of them as your master, but the only true master is Adon Olam (**Yahweh**) and Jesus (**Yahawashi**). Use vulnerability to your advantage through *inversion, an overturning process on what's troublesome into phases that no longer exist.* There are many types of strengths, such as *mental strength*—the intelligence gained through wisdom and knowledgeable materials constantly supplemented to the brain to invoke mental power within; *physical strength*—the inner strength of muscles conditioned to proportionate physical abilities and excel in power; and the *spiritual strength*—the inner being of intellect and faith to direct existence. Once we acknowledge our strengths and accept a change to our vulnerabilities, the sooner we will realize we are survivors and triumph above the darkest moments.

To awaken strength, you must identify hidden barriers within the mind, the part that causes doubts in what you're capable of without accepting counterforces that provoke your willpower. Every individual is capable of overcoming vulnerable offensive natures and stabilizing a strong mentality. Power is within the mind, which is the willing spirit to succumb in slave-free mind. Rights: Every man has the right to contribute a verse in their life span. Acknowledge a versatility within you. Awaken this power to travel at far distance and uplift the painful past you reminisce about to expand your horizon. Growth, in time, opens up a dimension of your solitude. You don't grow through loud noise but with silent and humble will. Meditation sheds light to your own questions and gives you answer's longed for through innermost feelings.

Abraham Maslow, the father of humanist[1] psychology, structured hierarchy of needs, which influenced each individual that to reach fullest potential, one needs to acquire their self-actualization,[2] which is the root of purpose. Maslow described the beginning roots are motivated through unsatisfied desires, though each stage must be satisfied before the admiration of self-actualization.

First stage is the *physiological* need, which is food, water, sex, warmth, proper sleep, and oxygen. Second stage is *safety*, the need to establish stability and assurance, the root to a secure foundation. Third stage is *love*, the benevolent feeling of being desired and receiving acceptance. The utter truth is that love is just a word, but you, your significant other and one's close to the heart give it definition. Fourth stage is *esteem*, the acceptance of you and becoming the truth of self-empowerment. The final stage is *self-actualization*, which is masterminding truth and desires without false vocation. In reality, the organized system may not apply to you, but it is essential regardless of what stage it is organized. That's the clarity of this hierarchy. Below (Figure 1-4) is a visual pyramid of the stages organized according to Maslow's theory:

---

[1] A psychologist focused on positive perception of free will and conscious control.

[2] I infer self-actualization as "rationalizing truths," but everyone has their different viewpoints.

Figure 1-4 Maslow's Theory

Sense the self-actualization within yourself, and you'll find another loving purpose as **Czeslaw Milosz** identified in his literature:

~Love~

**Love means to learn to look at yourself
The way one looks at distant things
For you are only one thing among many.
And whoever sees that way heals his heart,
Without knowing it, from various ills—
A bird and a tree say to him: Friend.**

Then he wants to use himself and things, so that they stand in the glow of ripeness.

It's more important to remain true than live a path of lies and falsify your identity. You're undermining your uniqueness and your solitude. You have to mirror your existence with empowerment and not seek your shadow but your radiance. In comparison, Japanese literature *wabi-sabi* is similar to what's previously reflected. The meaning of *wabi-sabi* is *"a way of living that focuses on finding beauty within the imperfections of life and accepting peacefully the natural cycle of growth and decay."* Conversely, the meaning can be used for owning up to your flaws and opening up to your identity, motioning your growth and preparing for discrepancies but keep flowing. Music artist **Bob Marley** was influential on this message from his album *Legend* (Marley 2002) with song "Three Little Birds" and many additional albums and songs.

Chapter II:
The Prowess of the Mind through Hypnosis

*"The lesson of hypnosis comes from within the
mind, and that directs the Spirit."*

Prowess of the mentality through hypnosis is about familiarizing yourself with the strong willpower to intellectually flow like water, and the vision and persistence to surpass any obstacles that seek to devour your strengths. Abstract the borderlines you believe are inevitable to rise above and direct your energy on persistence to achieve your prowess. Acknowledge all elements as essential for survival but on the contrary for mind hypnosis. When it's time to be solid, be a rock. When it's time to flow relentlessly be water. When it's time to drive with persistence, then let your flames burn strong and let no one put out your fire. And when it's time to fly, lift your mentality in the air instead of being suffocated in a vault.

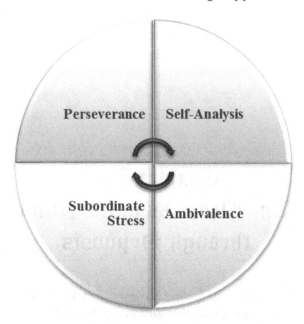

Figure 2-1 Four Acknowledgments to Nurture Prowess

Above in Figure 2-1 is a powerful acknowledgment of four important meanings to evaluate and understand because it prowess your mentality to nurture oneself. **Perseverance** is the continuous ambition to turn desire into reality. You've revoked all negative perceptions on what's assumed beneficial to you from social influences and kept striving for your ambition. **Self-analysis** is the providence of detailed understanding of your complex id "core of our being," an order to read your features. This is a thorough study of your id through investigating the problems and clarifying who you are through logical and rationalizing truths. **Ambivalence** is psychological attitude, approach, or treatment toward other individuals and yourself. Ambivalence through hypnosis is about awareness on your emotional response toward individuals you're agreeable with or disagreeable with. Our thoughts and emotions are our functions of how we conclude and make privilege discernment. It's important to acknowledge this before the response becomes regrettable through actions you've carried out.

Conversely, in reality, many individuals may spread the word wisdom is gained through experience and that experience is rooted in clarity to a more agreeable and intelligent outlet. This saying is true, but you can also feed your intelligence to avoid factors that possibly destruct your life goals and desires. Many young princes are naïve to the intelligent fact of what's possibly done may result to a worse outcome that may become irreversible in a world built on a judicial system that may not seem fair to certain individuals.

It's foretold that superior works are not adequately performed by strength but with perseverance as the key. The apparent agenda to question is can you pre-create the ambition to continue?

One of the most important hypnosis is faith. Believe in yourself, but above all, have faith in a higher power. This is an inducing process. Becoming receptive to your personal desires and bonding connection with "Lord of the Most High" is a very important principle. To subordinate stress, one should calm the mind from the common ridiculed mind that induces stress. Dwelling on uncontrollable events is anguish. Becoming intrapersonal with your feelings more rather than words is the inducing process of freeing one's mind. Subordinate a troubled mind with a more free-flowing mind even through your expectations. Instead of carrying so much on the mind, *journalize*. Construct written or typed documentations as reminders or reflections, such as messages, schedules, goals, expressions, and troublesome thoughts.

To prowess the mind through rational truths (see figure 1-1), one has to understand personality and build a strong conscious visionary without formulated toxins. Toxicity comes in many foundations— stress, environment, and heavy hearts. Consciousness is the awakened mind dealing with the present moment. Your hypnosis is your self-empowerment, and only you know the depths of your weaknesses and what's expected of yourself. You are your own placebo.[3] Meditation on the inner personality, which some often reject, is the German philosophical word "**angst**," meaning the "*inner sense of despair or dread*," which sometimes require attention to fix the problems that torment our joy. This is something I came across from the inspiration of Morgan Freeman, who played Sam in the film ***Unleashed*** (Li, Freeman and Hoskins 2005), when he said, "Sometimes people have to go back and fix the things that made them unhappy before they were happy." In the end, the character Danny (performed by Jet Li) found joy and relief during the musical tones of Mozart's ("Sonata Number 11") song, a heart reborn

---

[3]   I infer placebo as "your own testing subject."

with joy and rejection of a tyrant. Those types of influences are known as *confrontation*, seeking the means of clarity and relief from what anguishes persisted in your early mental stages of emotion, dolor, and burdens toward the individuals who were the cause.

Antwone Fisher film (Washington, Luke and Bryant 2002) was another message of confrontation through self-empowerment and self-therapy. It is a film based on testimony of enslavement and freeing thyself from burdens carried for years. It seemed like every time he tried to find solitude, the adversaries come and affect his mood. Antwone used the method of self-analysis to invoke perseverance. Fisher (Luke) lived a life of poor poverty with an unfortunate abusive foster parent, who was not a guardian but an adversary seeking to break his mentality, along with the foster parent's daughter, until a psychiatrist (Washington) and girlfriend Cheryl (Bryant) rescued a troubling past of abuse. Fisher inferred his emotion as living under a rock in the midst of constant rainy days. After he confronted the ones that made his childhood troubling, he found a relief of angst and became a man reborn.

Hopelessness is the biggest devastation anyone can ever go through, for it's the stage where depressing sanity takes place without indulgence of life. When we develop a sense of sanity, we begin to imprison ourselves to know meaning. Blaise Pascal (1623–1662) mentioned, "There are two equally dangerous extremes, to shut reason out, and let nothing else in." Sometimes we develop ambivalence. Every individual is mirrored in the eyes of another. Some can see right through you and you to them, and that's the time to inspire one another. Hope is essential, for it's your backbone when things don't go according to plan. Your inner prowess is the arch of a warrior within. You may feel it's late for a change when all your foes succeed then you reminisce a vocation you denied. The only positive provoking thing to excel is to continue where you left off. An incomplete journey is a journey with fear or avoidance because of shame. In addition, when you desire to excel, you'll receive social pressures, diverting your issue of reinforcement. Only because they've given up on there's a long time ago and developed a self-actualization of surrendering to a false vocation then they feed that energy on you. In the film **Town** (Affleck, et al. 2010), there was a similar experience through a thief named Joey who persisted with the ambition to leave his past angst lifestyle, while social counterforces tried to hold him from leaving to a harmonious living because they were afraid to lose him. Although in the end, he finally broke through the counterforces while unraveling the truth about his mother's death. It's important to formulate your plans on what you want to achieve out of life regardless of barriers. Positive psychology is the key to prevailing superior. This meaning can be reflected as searching for sensualism.

Sensualism

Persistent or excessive pursuit of sensual pleasures and interests.

-Merriam-Webster

You may ask what defines **sensual** living, which means *a devotion and relation to what you're passionate about or intimate pleasures*, and through this, you unravel your truth. In *Man of Steel* (Cavill, et al. 2013), Kevin Costner played Mr. Jonathan Kent, the adopted father of Kal Al aka Superman. In the moment, Mr. Kent gave a very important message. "You have to determine what kind of man you want to grow up to be" Know who you are in this world: Rather good or bad that person will illuminate a change. Those changes can either hurt and destruct you and others or heal and comfort you and others.

Intelligence Obsession

A wise man is strong; yea, a man of knowledge increaseth strength.

Proverbs 24v5 Authorized KJV

Knowledge is power, and wisdom leads to higher gains in life. Each time in life, you seek the meaning of understanding something foreign to your knowledge. You open dimensions of *transcendence* opening diverse systems of the self toward the goal of fulfillment and identity with all mankind. For instance, when you seek the depths of understanding someone, you favor of a different nationality, and you seek to gain stronger relations by their **persona** representing compromise between one's personality and true identity. This can be an act of sensualizing because you're taking time to show affection and respecting their social culture. Though rooted in faith become not sincere to another's faith (pious) but prudently ambivalent. Your mind is open to social intelligence. Social intelligence is giving social respect for the culture of others and giving the will to learn and communicate with exotic individuals with agape love or a higher type of love. For instance, if Rogue encountered an exotic female who he became infatuated with and decided he wanted to date her, but she spoke very little English and spoke Spanish fluently, Rogue will decide to take some Spanish classes or buy Sonia Gil's *Fluenz* language learning system to gain stronger connection. This is an act of sensualizing to another.

Become the Scholar, Not the Fool

Strengthen your intelligence. It's not all about physical strength, but the focus should reside more in mental strength. Physical strength is really an image of bodily definition and toning. Conversely, mental strength is the capacity to reach unlimited grounds of knowledge and success that support the spirit and capacity to expand your horizons. Mental strength supports the physical strength in time when you become successful and has established financial stability. Not to infer physical strength should be rejected, but more focus should be on mental first than physical. Mental strength is more superior to physical strength. Don't be ashamed to be more of a bookworm than a sportster. You don't have to bow to modernity influences but focus on your comfort ability and rationalizing truths. For instance, majority of the kings and princes back in medieval times were taught to become scholars first before physical fitness. In this millennium various males focus on physical fitness as a way of embracing confidence and attracting females while repelling knowledge.

Ontology

A science or study of being; specifically: a branch of metaphysics relating to the nature and relations of being.

- (Merriam-Webster)

Many people lost the consideration for ontology, which was considered the first philosophy discovering our problems and existence. The reason this is important is because it creates harmony to yourself and relation. People have become heartless with the beauty of nature and allow technology divert their attention when affection is calling. There are many parts of nature destroyed by men, for example, trees. The analogy is that every living tree when destroyed will lack the grasp for oxygen because trees bring oxygen and will lack shade in our hottest hours. Technology has advanced, and it takes over the nature of connection, thereby becoming the new subversive force of our living. Ontology is a systematic conception of existence, a deeper understanding of our existence and nature. As you seek more into ontology, you become more invested in your nature, and all that has meaning. There are perhaps a few people who lost study within themselves as beings and have become *nihilistic*,[4] *"a viewpoint that every traditional value and belief is unfounded and all existence is worthless."* These beings maybe considered suicidal. **The Sunset Limited,** a *2011* film, was a perfect example of nihilism when Black (Samuel L. Jackson) tried to persuade White (Tommy Lee Jones) to remain living, while White concluded that there's nothing worth holding on to. Our relations of being normally begins with the divine nature of freedom, the ability to make our own decisions; however, the Stoic philosopher believed that "as beings, we don't have the freedom nor can we change Urantia (world) to our heart's desire but have the willpower to make our own fate and assert actions because we are our own masters as men." The ideology of Aristotle is potentiality and reality, for nothing is in vain because you'll soon excel to your purpose. This develops a cause of closure to perfection of purpose and lively existence. Aristotle taught that everything has a **telos**, *a purpose or goal that clarifies its existence and provides its potentiality*; this is **teleological** (*purposeful*).

𝔑aturalism 𝔠onveys 𝔑ationalism

According to Pratt's book *Naturalism* (Pratt 1973), "rationalism" is primarily devoted to the logical and the analytical outcome predicted by the ideology; "naturalism" is conveyed by the physiological, vivid to the eyes and sound and earthily existence. Rationalism seeks the allure

---

4   *Webster's Third New International Dictionary, Unabridged, s.v.* "Nihilism," accessed March 10, 2015, http://unabridged.merriam-webster.com.

"of essence," while naturalism seeks realism of the living.[5] Naturalism consists of two drives—"the theoretical demand" to increase simplicity and "the pragmatic desire" to speculate things to increase simplicity toward "the practical" using theory to measure the intellectual on what accommodates.[6] For the intellectual is on what makes the appropriate sense and what seems true and justified on a personal measure. Basically, an individual who feels a certain way about true love or who gives sensualism discovers the theoretical demand for its use in the world; thereby, you've discovered your *telos* or *ontology*. An individual keeps flowing because it's what they love or what drives an individual to keep flowing is their love for it. It is faith itself into works, and in this, individual will be naïve to forceful lies within and the adversaries of construction that try to become a devil to an individual's pursuit. The essence is to free yourself through the embrace of your naturalism which conveys rationalism of our *ontology* along with our intelligent obsession for wisdom.

Discover Subliminal Personality

Discover your conscious of awareness on what's true in contrast to what's subliminal on your own deception. Heed perception on this personality, for it is extremely tricky. **Sublimation** is "rechanneling your impulse into a more socially desirable outlet" (Engler 2006). This discovery is brought upon a journey of your influencing thoughts, feelings, and manners by personality on how you outcast and unify yourself toward civilization. Empirical discovery is about capturing yourself in actions you portray through another's mind to understand your noetic prowess and use it for advantage. The masterminds of this subliminal personality are often pickup artists, salesmen, and politicians using this art as a deception to abstract reasoning, portray influence, or gain power. Discover how to use your subliminal personality to direct potential or what you're capable of without the feel of confusion or guilt for good purpose. The individuals who feel their inability act on emotion of intolerance may have developed a reaction of authoritarian persona. Authoritarian personages are people who seem to feel highly controlled and remain deeply buried to a

---

[5]   Pratt, James Bissett, "*Naturalism*," 13.

[6]   Pratt, James Bissett, "Naturalism," 21.

construction of power. In sublimation, you change fear and concealment into sociable and transcendent.

Finally, brethren, whatsoever things are true, whatsoever things are honest, whatsoever things are just, whatsoever things are pure, whatsoever things are lovely, whatsoever things are of good report; if there be any virtue, and if there be any praise, think on these things. (Philippians 4v8 KJV)

The scripture above is the process of transformation from the sublimation of conceit to naturalism of positive and using sublimation for a positive discernment only when deemed necessary. Remember *Philippians 4v8* for this is the discernment of *fair*; pure is judged upon what's deemed treasures, honorable, understandable, submitted to El Shaddai, and aesthetic rationalism (see *Aesthetic Individualism*).

Sublimation of a Girlfriend ~ 1996

Discovering good purpose through subliminal personality of Maggie

My first girlfriend was when I was in kindergarten. Her name was Maggie. We did everything together, including napping together, although there was this young prince who had hatred toward me. One day this hateful prince had a negative subliminal personality to project friendship. I nearly brought into it until Maggie used her intuition, thinking habits to project the hateful prince's perception with scissors. On that day Maggie told me that friendship with him was a lie. He's prejudiced because we're an interracial couple. **Don't become friends with the snake**.

Characterizing Sublimation

Maggie said he was prejudiced to withdraw me from friendship with the enemy as in act of love. If Maggie didn't use her subliminal personality, the hateful prince would have cut or stabbed me with the scissors. The hateful prince's subliminal personality was out of pure jealousy because he desired Maggie. Majority of this art is used through **supraconscious**, which means *functioning above level of the conscious* *without separating yourself from reality*. You're thinking above the moment with both sides of the brain by contrasting the cause and effect for personal or beloved's awareness and elevation. There are ministers out there who would say this is a sin to satisfy personal gains. The truth is if your intentions are evil, then this is true, but if it's to progress to positive higher position to benefit or save others and yourself, then it's not a sin. If it's still considered sin to individuals, then I advise others to use an act of determinism through theology to better characterize if it's completely sinful to use your subliminal personality for position. Every moment you've been conned, influenced, or humiliated is something of a subliminal personality from another individual for reasons of care or despising with discretion of hate toward you.

Throughout, subliminal personality can be an act of love or hatred; it's all how you use it. The sublimation is your self-defense against those who oppose you or others close to you, enemies with evil intentions that are looking for a way to make you seem like trash or unworthy. According to **Burton F. Porter**, your sublimation determinism can be used as both a social and ethical movement known as utilitarianism. This is known as *principle of utility* from his book *What the Tortoise Taught Us: The Story of Philosophy*. "**Principle of Utility** is the principle of approval or disapproval on various actions accordingly to the cause of commotion or judge remission of virtue with intolerance, although the pleasurable actions affecting the majority are better than the lesser when pleasure is virtuous" (Porter 2011). In addition, you can use your subliminal personality as a deception against social influences that try to utterly convince you of practicing or speculating something against your moral and personal ethics. For instance, if you're in the midst of devouring companies that convince persuasion on alcoholic beverages and drugs you vowed not to accept, but you convince them an insinuation of agreement, but in truth, you're completely against it and remain stubborn toward their persuasion, this is power of sublimation. In provoking this process, you may have made Yahuwah and Yahushua proud.

𝔇𝔦𝔰𝔠𝔬𝔳𝔢𝔯 𝔜𝔬𝔲𝔯 𝔇𝔦𝔰𝔭𝔬𝔰𝔦𝔱𝔦𝔬𝔫

The pessimist sees difficulty in every opportunity.
The optimist sees opportunity in every difficulty.

—Winston Churchill

Discovering your **disposition,** which is *your usual mood or attitude*, acknowledging what makes your temper rise and what gives peace, is a step to self-empowerment. Be honest with yourself in awareness that you can't travel back in time to fix the dispositions that were the cause of broken relationships and blessings that were withdrawn because of ugly attitudes, although you can understand what makes you react in certain manners and how you can withdraw from that type of negative disposition before you drive action to reality and regret your actions. Many negative dispositional mentalities react through discrimination of others or the fear of being manipulated. Reasons can be clear in disposition mentality when there are moments you have to be grounded in courage and bravery to let your issue be known to others or fight for what you believe in. Know that you're not wrong in this matter if it's what you strongly believe to be true. In the world we live in, not everyone find peace with compassion but with a fight because not all individuals who oppose them seek peace but havoc.

On the contrary, be true but be open-minded to your flaws and misunderstood direction. Sometimes you have to listen too in opposing viewpoint. That may be your enlightenment or considered assurance on your behalf. Don't let arrogance mislead you. It's important to be open-minded and strong-minded. Although sometimes disposition can be engaged in your addictions such as alcohol, sex, drug, or any other type, with effort and acceptance, you can withdraw from those triggers. Conversely, if you're a sex addict, it seems nearly impossible because sexual influences are everywhere, just as demonstrated in the film *Thanks for Sharing*. There's a saying "get with the program!" I believe this to be terribly infiltrated as something positive when really it's a negative brainwash to become what community wants from a citizen. Conversely, I believe this should be *"learn the program but don't dwell in it."* The reason for this belief is you have to learn the quality of life along with its people but shouldn't gravitate to what is influenced because social influences only accept this if you're comfortable in certain situations.

Life is a lesson that has to be understood. Obstacles will come and go, but the mind must remain internally strong, for champions come from within, battling the obstacles of temptations. Ambitions motivate our lives of prosperity. Willingness to make changes is the motion that obtains a new divine legacy. Time is limitless. The fate we make for ourselves is limited because it's about choice. What you make of your choices defines you.

Failure is the opportunity to begin again more intelligently. (Henry Ford)

Falling down is a chance to grow stronger morals, but staying buried is where we die with no opportunity rising! When life gives pain, improvise on the pain and turn it against the pain that drives you to sorrow. Become your dream, and your dream will become your savior. Peer pressure is nothing but jealousy among your current surroundings. Only the great can demolish a temple of envy. Be great. Furthermore, dreamers prosper without being accepted, yet still accomplish becoming the survivor who illuminated their name with aggression; they become the influence.

A vision on its own is not enough. Hard work & dedication is required to make that vision a reality. (Strive Masiyiwa)

Above is an influential message that we should hold to harness. Downfalls and ambitions are inevitable. Sometimes anger takes the best of us, especially when we lose someone we endured. The endured as a means of someone we really cared about and captured our heart strongly and given uplifting spirits to the point were not ready to let go. Endurance is internal because it brings out the aggressive ambition to make things better. —J.S.J.

Identity Revealed Into Your Eyes

Understand your personality through the Freudian concept. According to Sigmund Freud, our structured personality is a threshold of id, ego, and superego. **Id,** which is the "core of our being," is the natural instincts and drives along with our genealogy and reflexes and capacities to respond.

Ego is the driven will to realistically meet the desires and demands of your id in accordance to external world. **Superego** represents striving for mastery and internalizing values, ideas, and moral standards; superego is more moralistic than realistic, for it's the hope of going beyond limits (Engler 2006). **Superego** is perseverance to our core of being that supports our resolution to accomplish what's important to the heart and place that above other non-concernable things. Many individuals counter personality with defense mechanisms, blocking a way of being discovered through their conscious by others. This act is out of fear of what others forge against us, and this process is known as ***repression***, which involves blocking desire from conscious to balance sublimation. (Cultivate this—the Freudian concept will be reflected in Part III Chapter XIV: Art of Domestic Discipline).

In the Orthodox scholar doctrine, the *Philokalia* volume 4, "On the Inner Nature of Things and on the Purification of the Intellect: One Hundred Texts" – Number 35, **Nikitas Stithatos** stated,

> Know thyself: this is true humility, the humility that teaches us to be inwardly humble and makes our heart contrite. Such humility you must cultivate and guard. For if you do not yet know yourself you cannot know what humility is, and have not yet embarked truly on the task of cultivating and guarding. To know oneself is the goal of the practice of the virtues.

The king's heart is in the hand of the Lord, as the rivers of water: he turneth it whithersoever he will. (Proverbs 21v1 Authorized KJV)

The above Orthodox Christian text explains that we must first look at ourselves while remaining internally humble, that we substance ourselves with understanding and reflect the very nature of being a human being. In doing this, your mind is open, but with an armor of diligence to your worldly surroundings, you'll gain the humility of a type of super rational divinity, and suddenly, you'll repel all that seems to intoxicate your pungent heart and mind. People who accept slavery before they discover their humility intend on making themselves their own victim without taking responsibility for their own due diligence. Respecting yourself is a step to persevering in your faith and clarity. Since there are many that will try converting you to something completely obscene from your faith and morality, it's important to know yourself to support your armor.

Individuality is the naked eye looking to burst through the eyes looking at mirrors, waiting for the moment you discover its revelation. Your third eye is your eye of intellect, and through that eye, one would grasp the Holy Spirit's will, being the very nature of our purpose. Although this identity to discover is not easy, it's well worth the journey to reveal your truth. This is the journey to your self-realization, making a connection with yourself on a humanly nature and searching for divinity to understand your vocation. Perhaps when the charismatic kings start to acknowledge the ego within, we'll develop a more humane flow with YHWH and become a **Christian hedonist** (means *the pursuit of pleasure within the ego while having the superego to glorify, obey, and connect with the Trinity*) at heart, while the Adonai Yahawashi directs it.

The empirical truth from the majority of the people I met implies life like one big movie. Conversely, I completely revoke this theory because you can't rewind or fast-forward your entire living. The truth is life is considered a combination of playing a chess game and harvesting. Chess is about using your diligence to move in privileged directions but doesn't always work accordingly though when progressing against you're enemy, lines and dolor interfere to obstruct your vocation and drive. Harvesting in life is preserving humanity through humane love, privacy, unity, basic physiological needs, and breeding. There are times when you have to be a mountain, immovable to the flawed ills of every negative encounter. Many insinuate a mountain mentality as someone with much pride, but in truth, it's all about integrity, for it's important to not let others lead you to darkness or anguish. The higher your mountain is, the closer you are to the sun, and light diminishes darkness. What's below the mountain can be a shadow, and shadows are clones and darkness itself. It does an individual best to remain on the peak of the mountain, not the base.

𝔖𝔲𝔟𝔬𝔯𝔡𝔦𝔫𝔞𝔱𝔦𝔫𝔤 𝔖𝔱𝔯𝔢𝔰𝔰

"All things are lawful for me, but all things are not **expedient** (means *convenient and practical*): all things are lawful for me, but all things **edify** (means *teach in ways that improve the mentality*) not."—1 Corinthians 10v23 Authorized King James Version

Subordinating stress is about finding an opposing new outlook on what causes you to be stressed consistently and relieving those burdens that ache. Subordinating stress is not an easy process. The reason for this is because many things can't be forgotten or completely freed from even when it causes stress, and for that reason, reality strikes. Although there are things that can uplift your spirit, such as confessing problems to beloveds that are willing to listen, journalizing all your issues, seeking sensualism, and socializing, stop watching depressing films and shows in moments of depression, stop listening to depraving songs, and go out and speculate the beauty of nature. Some males I've spoken to subordinate stress through taking long walks and some take vacations. Various individuals prefer the nurture from their woman or go to strip clubs or meditate with music lyrics or journalize, and there are others who play a type of sport or instrument. In contrast to this, none harmonizes stress when excessively drinking alcoholic beverages or ingesting drugs because when they take those actions, they develop more problems than relief persist. Casual nights of playing pool, communicating with complete strangers at the bar while drinking in moderation, or simply praying and reading the Bible are some additional methods fellows discussed with me. Subordinating stress was mostly always best determined by how you self-perceive relief. Some subordinate stress with things science consider unhealthy.

ℰℂ

The lover of silence draws close to God. He talks to Him in secret, and God enlightens him. Jesus, by His silence, shamed Pilate; and a man, by his silence, conquers vainglory.

—St. John Climacus (AD 525–AD 606) On Talkativeness and Silence

ℰℂ

How Virtue Drives out Vice

Where there is charity and wisdom
there is neither fear nor ignorance.
Where there is patience and humility,
there is neither anger nor disturbance.
Where there is poverty with joy,
there is neither covetousness nor avarice.
Where there is inner peace and meditation,
there is neither anxiousness nor dissipation.
Where there is fear of the Lord to guard the house,
there the enemy cannot gain entry.
Where there is mercy and discernment,
there is neither excess nor hardness of heart.

—Francis of Assisi (1181–1226)

Provide Personal Meditative Therapy

Subordinating stress can be an action of meditation, for meditation harmonizes the Spirit and elevates mood while building a strong sacred connection in Holy Spirituality. From personal experience, meditation is a way of abstracting yourself from worldly cares to affectionate faith and superego. Meditations have to be around a peaceful environment, perhaps with incense and symphony music, to provide stronger harmony and connection to the Holy Ghost. Meditation is not chanting but tranquility and **intrapersonal** (means *speaking from within the mind*) to find better clarity. Apply the following protocols for meditation:

> *You have to look deeper, way below the anger,*
> *the hurt, the hate, the jealousy, the self-pity, way*
> *down deeper where the dreams lie, son. Find your*
> *dream. It's the pursuit of the dream that heals you.*
> *(Billy Mills, Oglala Lakota)*

Protocol I:
Choose a **tranquil** (*peaceful*) environment. Give an orientation of naturism or wear lesser clothing. Have near you only water or tea while opening to meditation and have humbleness, perhaps burn some incense

and play some sensual music. Meditation is great on rainy days, for it humbles the spirit and purges while creating a resting body.

Protocol II:
Stabilize your mind with a transformation from earthily cares, invoke by asking help from Adon Olam in this process, open yourself to sincerity on your reason and nobility, and then invoke vocation to Adon Olam.

Protocol III:
Revoke the reality of your dolor with replacement of evoking hedonist and aesthetic personality, channel desirable energy, and release your repression.

Protocol IV:
Reminisce good times and seek the cynical within yourself while asking Adon Olam and Adonai Yahushua intrapersonal to turn the cynicism to more humane and holy thoughts unless the cynicism is appropriate to your determinism.

Protocol V:
Pray from within your mind then give it voice to the Adon Olam and Adonai Yahushua then receive it to yourself and believe El Elyon has heard your hope. Then after you've finished, get up, count burdens a failed win, and count the coming blessings a forethought win.

You're in the process of meditation. You can relate it to sleep internally within physiological, but when you're disturbed, the physiological burdens the Spirit within. For instance, when you sleep and someone in your neighborhood drives by with their music blasting, it's a disturbance for you, so when anything affects you physiologically, you're affected by your resting internally.

Aesthetic Individualism

Eli Siegel logically explained that self-conflict is the defining reason of discovering our inner personage. Finding beauty in things is the predestination of finding what fragile, most important, and sensual consuming love for and vocation of the telos to give true senses of clarity and direction. In individualism, there's a cultivation of accuracy among the living. David Hume wrote something similar to this accuracy:

> Accuracy is, in every case, advantageous to beauty, and just reasoning to delicate sentiment. In vain would we exalt the one by depreciating the other . . . the genius of philosophy, if carefully cultivated by several, must gradually diffuse itself throughout the whole society, and bestow a similar correctness on every art and calling. (David Hume 1737)

Aesthete's philosophers are acquainted with Aesthetic Realism, which was founded by Eli Siegel (1902–1978), who created *three important principles*[7] in this philosophy:

1. The deepest desire of every person is to like the world on an honest or accurate basis.
2. The greatest danger for a person is to have contempt for the world and what is in it . . . Contempt can be defined as the lessening of what is different from oneself as a means of self-increase as one sees it.
3. All beauty is making one of opposites, and the making one of opposites is what we are going after in ourselves.

Aesthetes are *individuals passionate to art, nature, and beauty.* Aesthetic is an *ontology* and *naturalism* of the heart and *noetic* (*see Chapter VIII for meaning*). In the *Aesthetic Method in Self-Conflict* by Siegel, he expressed aesthetic individuals evaluate the conflicts that bring about opposition and provide the proper action of composition in beauty and nature to the living while holding on to the uniqueness of our id, ego, superego, and personality, thereby preserving liberation. An inner deep sense where art lies comes from Yahweh's creation and our centered individuality, and depending on your individuality, it can be the beauty itself shining brighter than others.

Being passionate to beauty is noted not fragile but clarity of sense to the conscious through what's most desired and the unconscious, which is a deeper sense of finding oneself of what becomes revealing as what we

---

[7]   Source of Three Principles: http://aestheticrealism.org/about-us/eli-siegel-founder/

desire that was thought not to desire. The conscious and unconscious beauty determines the treasure we seek and the acknowledgment of a cherishable vision. The analogy is that there's beauty in all of us, and our skin is reflected in the art of color, but an Aesthetic will realize all in union with nature, and our need to survive in nature is through passion and physiological needs. Harness that all matter is a cultivation of passion that we captivate in the very humane in us, flowing in passion for life, and all the living is an aesthetic philosopher, for that individual preserves the humane in them. All humans regardless of their nationality are all beautiful, capable of unique artistry, and the very dominion of nature itself. Each human is of blood, is of flesh, and is of Spirit, and this same beauty is the architecture from Yahawah. If Yahawah intended on every being to look alike, Yahawah wouldn't allow changes in skin colors. One explanation is of love, and that explanation is to see how well we can love someone of a different complexion from ourselves for we all have dissimilarities for its our opposition for uniqueness and those dissimilarities can have good value. Don't think when heaven calls. Yahawah is going to allow racial and discriminative individuals in his home, for Yahawah wants Ahavah (*see Chapter XII: Loveology Unfolds for Description of Ahavah*).

View on Knowledge

> *A piece of knowledge is never false or true—but only more or less biologically and evolutionary useful. All dogmatic creeds are approximations: these approximations form a humus from which better approximations grow. (Ernst Mach)*

Minds are often limited to a broader speculation among average individuals when it comes to wisdom, but wisdom can come from anywhere. For instance, I've heard many Buddhists give intelligent factors. However, I know my faith, so there's no need to feel a groundless attrition that I'm somehow breaking the rules when I accept some of their intelligent philosophy. Faith in a person is always immovable when it's true faith, so no skepticism should be a factor in knowledge.

Aesthetic View on Prejudice and Racism

An aesthetic philosophy on prejudice and racism from "The Equality of Man" (1923) by Siegel[8] argues that mankind and womankind throughout history have not had equilibrium of the mind in life to open up to their potentiality. Siegel's assertion to this was that if mankind and womankind were to use conditions placed at birth to potentiate their abilities, there would be equilibrium. Aesthetic Realism views prejudice and racism as an act of contempt and lessening of difference; but the battle against contempt, including ourselves, will gain clarity that others' emotions are equal or as real as their own, and harnessing this contributes an end to racism.[9] Thereby, aesthetic personality is more open to any ethnicity and interracial love.

---

[8]   *The Modern Quarterly Beginnings of Aesthetic Realism 1922–1923* (New York: Definition Press, 1969), 28.

[9]   Susan P. Smith, Hickory, SC Branch, NAACP, "Back to School Rally Offers Answer to Racism," *Hickory Daily Record*, Friday, 21 August 2009.

Chapter III:
Adversaries among Kings and Princes

Be sober, be vigilant; because your adversary the devil walks
about like a roaring lion, seeking whom he may devour.

—*1 Peter 5v8 KJV*

There are many faces of evil. Seek the truth among your companions before you make abundant assumptions. Personally, I love to hear more positive influences, characters, and lifestyles in a person's life than negative force of energy. You have to feed your spirit with positivity than drama. To many negative judgmental individuals, I rather surround myself with positivity than engage in a toxic environment with people who love chaos.

In the *Philokalia* text volume 1, St. Isaiah the Solitary, "On Guarding the Intellect," the scholars gave a very important understanding that we remain firm and rigorously practice the Lord's virtues without feeding our conscience[10] the cause to stumble. The conscience is called an "adversary" because it opposes us when we wish to carry out the desires of our flesh, and if we do not listen to our conscious, it delivers us into the hands of our enemies. Although desires of the flesh are natural and should be embraced, versatility is a must for good senses the fear of the Lord. We shall keep our minds humbled within ourselves until our conscience achieves its desired freedom and prosperity. This shall be our guardian, discovering what we must improve. We must support this desire with

---

[10]   *Philokalia* text volume 1, St. Isaiah the Solitary, "On Guarding the Intellect."

good gestures and intentions. The Lord messaged us on conscience condition. **"Agree with thine adversary quickly, whiles thou art in the way with him; lest at any time the adversary deliver thee to the judge, and the judge deliver thee to the officer, and thou be cast into prison" (Matthew 5v25, KJV).** People will say it's easier said than done. This saying is true, but that's the trail we carry by believing we can overcome these challenges that adversaries stumble us upon. Although sometimes we put ourselves in these predicaments, which are motivated by love, investments, and desires, yet we wonder how we'll prevail against those storms.

Unravel your shadow. According to Carl Jung, your **shadow** are *"those unsocial motives, emotions, and thoughts we precede with denial because of possibilities of rejection from others."* Conversely, we must come to agreement with our shadow even in possibilities of rejection. Jung emphasized that shadow is our need to acknowledge our animalistic impulses. Sometimes our shadow can be our enemy through being judgmental, prejudice, or any other type of discrimination, so you become your own adversary. In addition, that's why some shadowed behaviors are best left locked because you may harm another. Shadows are best brought to light when we're confessing to the Lord, trusted family members, or true friend, spouse, and younglings. Perhaps there are many royal snakes surrounding us, only waiting to push us to the limits of dolor, attempting to steal our love and joy. It's a terrible thing when some of those devils are the ones closest to you, who are looking to break you in secret. Those brothers and sisters are nothing but enemies of evil intentions. One should not accompany them but withdraw from them. The emotion of anger is in accordance with nature, and without it, a man can't attain purity. The confrontation derived from anger is a necessity to help the other or relieve yourself from burdens and confusion. Uprooting impulses are not all evil but sometimes a benefactor of fairness, unity, love, and freedom. Martin Luther King, Jr. amplified this when he was fed up with injustice and inspired the Christian anarchist movement while using faith. The reaction was the cause of anger from the injustice through unity and freedom. From his anger rectified a positive opposition to harvesting an aesthetic love of hope, unity, and more freedom. Because of this, Martin Luther King, Jr. will forever be an iconic legend that used his anger and dream to create a motion of fair justice.

Bringing truthfulness, I must confess that I'm not all loving and forgiving as the Lord, for I know I'm only human in the disposition who occasionally hold grudges, something that is not merciful. I reminisce occasionally the wrong when I should leave it in the past. Perhaps I remember these things to reminisce what I've been brought through and to take hold of my wisdom (making better judgements through experience). Though my heart is not pure as Yahawashi, I can learn to become more like him with a more proper love, such as his Gospels. The common brokenness a man can take inevitably is a heavy heart from women, not being loved back, brothers' betrayal, and loss from what you weren't prepared to loose. But through all this, the heart never cracks. So a heartbreak is a shim to a true emotion. The honest truth is that I, myself, may lack mercy and pure heart, and according to Matthew 5v7–8, blessings come further and greater when I become more merciful (forgiving). Then understanding strikes me. If I have a heavy heart toward a woman who had done me wrong, I should move myself away from her (Prov. 5v8) and brethren (Prov. 22v24). My part is to love, but if it's unreturned or scarred, then I remove myself from unhealthy company. Don't indulge the endurance of the unfortunate hurt but move forward. Many individuals would tell me I'm weak for not indulging in the company of the woman who was unfaithful and the brethren who was the snake, but the truth is you're actually stronger because various individuals would put up with the idea of accepting thy burdens, but you've chosen to free yourself without living in denial, and that's greater than false love.
—J.S.J.

Dolor and Ra

Misery won't touch you gentle. It always leaves its thumbprints on you; sometimes it leaves them for others to see, sometimes for nobody but you to know of.

*—Edwidge Danticat (*The Farming of Bones*)*

In Latin, suffering is given the name **dolor,** which means *pain, suffering, and grief*; something that we've momentarily or often experience in life. In moments of dolor, we break in positivity, driven will, and open-dimensional hearts and become defensive. There's not any type of help in the world to prevent dolor from touching you, but there's a reception on how you comply and overcome this touch. The dolor can make you enslaved or a rooted being of wisdom and strength. The manifestation of *dolor* and evil creates the response of emotional triggers that are responsible for the anguish and mired hearts. It's important to become prudent toward this to save yourselves if possible.

> *A prudent man foreseeth the evil, and hideth himself: but the simple pass on, and are punished. (Proverbs 22v3 KJV)*

Ra, which means by translators as *evil morals*, is the common evil we walk among this world not by mystical evil that brings out the reactions of the physical but evil intentions within. According to Randy Alcorn, a scholar author, **Ra** means *"calamity"* or *"disaster,"* the Lord's judgment inflicted to the evildoers. Because of our frustrations from the scars of our past, we sometimes allow evil morals to take the best of us, but when you seek grace, your grace is your blanket when you're cold on certain nights. When bad things happen, we survive and overcome the things that haunt us the most even when it seems everyone else has forgotten you.

The empirical truth is that there are some individuals who love deep but hate deeper. It's just genetic. Only Adon Olam can send forth love and cure that genetic, but until then, Ra may be inflicted toward others forming through the suffering of hate. The empirical truth is many people often go through the touch of dolor, and that can evolve into Ra. The only way to get through it is by remaining optimistic even when times are hard. My fellow brethren, *Tupac Shakur*, said, "You have to keep your head up." In the show *Breaking Bad*, even though drugs was a negative influence, there were some empirical realities within that show. One was when Walter was rejected by the ones closest to him and he adored the most, betrayed by his business partners on a foundation he built called Grey Matter Technologies, and betrayed by his apprentice and wife who both were involved in the business. Even through those matters, he kept his decency and continued to attempt to supply funds for his family. Honestly, many of us would hold grudges, something I'm familiar with yet love triumphs over *dolor* and betrayal.

Darkness cannot drive out darkness; only light can do that. Hate cannot drive out hate; only love can do that. (Martin Luther King, Jr.)

Types of Beings' Sufferings

Human beings individually can't change the whole world's suffering but can spark a relief of the sufferings in their lives and others in charitable giving when others struggle instead of abandoning them and the powerful purpose of cause, thereby providing inspiration. Sometimes our sufferings are needed toward a king and prince to make us better and stronger physically, emotionally, cognitively, and spiritually. The *physical suffering* is pain and abuse from the body. *Emotional suffering* is frustrations consisted from loss of hope and love and fear and depression. *Cognitive suffering* is lack of clarity and good sense of judgment and inability to theorize those surrounding them for understanding, such as associates, friends, relatives, and intimate companions. *Spiritual suffering* is the lack of faith and understanding what's true (Diehl 2009). In the film *Machine Gun Preacher* (Keller 2011) based on actual events, a boy confessed that Joseph Kony and Lord's Resistance Army forged him to kill his mother so that he and his bother may live, so he killed his mother. The boy inspired Sam Childers when he said, *"If you allow yourself to be full of hate, then they'll win. You must not allow them to take your heart."*

Give not over thy mind to heaviness, and afflict not thyself in thine own counsel. The gladness of the heart is the life of man, and the joyfulness of a man prolongeth his days. Love thine own soul, and comfort thy heart, remove sorrow far from thee: for sorrow hath killed many, and there is no profit therein. Envy and wrath shorten the life, and carefulness bringeth age before the time. (Ecclesiasticus 30v21–24, Apocrypha KJV)

In November 2014, I attended an Alcoholic Anonymous (AA) meeting. You may ask, "John, were you an addict?" The honest answer is no. I attended to support two nice women who ask me if I would like to attend to support them, then I thought these women may not have a family to support them, and me being a charismatic individual, I must attend. In the AA meeting, I observed the most supportive individuals who I've rarely come across. A spark of enlightenment happened within me, a vision of people making efforts for a change and completely vulnerable to their sins even to strangers. The biggest thing I noticed that I hope the world would reflect on is admiration and love for one another. I heard individuals recite the "**Serenity Prayer**" by **Reinhold Niebuhr** (1892–1971), and then I noticed it's the same admirable and true prayer that Kurt Vonnegut from *Slaughterhouse* narrowed down.

𝕲𝖔𝖉 𝕲𝖗𝖆𝖓𝖙 𝖒𝖊 𝖙𝖍𝖊 𝖘𝖊𝖗𝖊𝖓𝖎𝖙𝖞 𝖙𝖔 𝖆𝖈𝖈𝖊𝖕𝖙, 𝖙𝖍𝖊 𝖙𝖍𝖎𝖓𝖌𝖘 𝕴 𝖈𝖆𝖓𝖓𝖔𝖙 𝖈𝖍𝖆𝖓𝖌𝖊, 𝖈𝖔𝖚𝖗𝖆𝖌𝖊 𝖙𝖔 𝖈𝖍𝖆𝖓𝖌𝖊 𝖙𝖍𝖊 𝖙𝖍𝖎𝖓𝖌𝖘 𝕴 𝖈𝖆𝖓, 𝖆𝖓𝖉 𝖜𝖎𝖘𝖉𝖔𝖒 𝖆𝖑𝖜𝖆𝖞𝖘 𝖙𝖔 𝖙𝖊𝖑𝖑 𝖙𝖍𝖊 𝖉𝖎𝖋𝖋𝖊𝖗𝖊𝖓𝖈𝖊.

Personally, I believe this prayer reflects deeply on everyone, from the individuals who are presently saints to the individuals who lost faith to the one's still hoping for faith delivered to them and to the one's currently still looking for faith of their vocation. Often, I look around and see misery. Even in my own life, misery persists from poverty and dolor to a hope of wealth and true love. But then I keep in mind that true love can overtake wealth at any moment and that I have to remember what the Lord said you can't worship him and mammon. Then I've come to believe when I put the Lord always as my primary and everything else as my secondary—wealth, love, etc.—then a brighter spiritual light will shine. There's so much suffering in the world for me to explain it in one section, so I'll recommend one of my favorite books on this criterion called *If God Is Good: Faith in the Midst of Suffering and Evil* by Randy Alcorn to read to truly grasp the meaning of suffering and how it calls us to God, for I believe Alcorn mastered this criterion of Ra and dolor.

𝕴𝖓𝖊𝖛𝖎𝖙𝖆𝖇𝖑𝖊 𝕯𝖊𝖈𝖊𝖕𝖙𝖎𝖔𝖓

The art of inevitable deception is common among thieves, mockers, discriminators, agnostics, secular, and other pagans. "Be strong and of a good courage, fear not, nor be afraid of them: for the Lord thy God, he it is that doth go with thee; he will not fail thee, nor forsake thee" (Deuteronomy 31v6 KJV). You may encounter deceptive questions against your beliefs to mislead you or segregate you, such as,

- Where in the Bible it says this?

However, when a person doesn't accept what was shown, they refuse to accept or bound by growth of hatred. Don't ground yourselves worthlessly when another refuses to see truth because perhaps many won't believe the Word to be true.

- Can you prove He's living, or are you giving false hope? Where's your Lord, or has your savior abandoned you, or are you unworthy of the Lord? Am I?

"For we walk by faith, not by sight."[11] The film *God's Not Dead* was proving this point by justifying personal belief and the human spirit within to seek truth and guidance that gives us the right to seek the divine. Not everyone accepts Christ as our savior, but the important things is you remain faithful.

- Where in the Bible does it justify we should unite with others and can marry outside our tribe?

"Behold, how good and how pleasant it is for brethren to dwell together in unity!"[12]

- You are not allowed to position but are slaves to masters, and can you guess who your masters are?

"For we wrestle not against flesh and blood, but against principalities, against powers, against the rulers of the darkness of this world, against spiritual wickedness in high places."[13]

Men have no masters but the creator Yahawah and Yahawashi. Anyone who implies they're a slave is a slaver in his own mind. *The Matrix* trilogy, a few of the greatest philosophical films ever made, implied this philosophy, "prison for your mind," and that it's time to be free from the social construction of this world (not being brainwashed). Morpheus (Laurence Fishburne) said, "Everything begins with choice." Merovingian replied, "Wrong. Choice is an illusion created between those with power and those without." The philosophy of this is we enslave ourselves with proper way of going

---

[11] 2 Corinthians 5v7 KJV.

[12] Psalms 133v1 KJV.

[13] Ephesians 6v12 KJV.

about living but always had the opportunity to direct ourselves with our sanity and that threshold of Neo's (Keanu Reeves) response is "it was inevitable" before he sacrificed himself.

- Are you hallucinating to a belief that you may never encounter, and what's to say when we will all end up in hell anyway?

If an individual is a Christian and knows they've done the best they could, then they must realize our Father and the Son are very merciful and loving. Simply keep the faith and do the best you can to be vigorous to Adon Olam's Word. Let Yay be the answer for certainty that you'll meet Adon Olam and Adonai Yahawashi.

Attrition

Many of us kings and princes suffer moments of **attrition**, which *is sorrow for one's own sins that arise from a motive considered lower than that of the love of YHWH* (Yahweh). The mistakes some kings and princes make seem in a humanistic point of view to be unforgiveable. These occurrences happen through strong empirical guilt, violence among others, and rejection from many. Your assumptions of unforgivable practices are not unforgivable in the eyes of the Lord, for the Adon Olam forgives all sins with no restrictions attached. Disregard the negative influences that others make of you because your kingdom awaits you in heaven. All that's require on your part is supplementation of the Word, acceptance of the savior, faith, loyalty, and communication devoted toward Yahuwah (Elohim) and Yahushua. In Galatians 4v7 King James, it says, "Wherefore thou art no more a servant, but a son; and if a son, then an heir of God through Christ." The important questions you must ask yourselves in moments of attrition are the following:

- The question is can you forgive yourself, and can you confess your guilt toward the one you wronged?
- Did it feel good to commit that sin, and if it did, would you want to repeat that process?
- Do you seek redemption or momentary forgiveness?
- Are you aware that you're surrounded by spiritual love from El Elyon regardless of your condemnations?

- Do you have faith that all sins can be forgiven by redeemer Christ? Just believing, having faith, and repenting are all that are needed.

These five questions are very important in your self-assessment of attrition because sometimes the adversary is within yourselves. The process of forgiving yourself means you mostly have to accept the person you are and impulses act out, but seeking the means of confrontation toward the person you wronged can feel shameful on your part, yet it's a mark of repentance on your part. The hardest question to answer is did you enjoy the sin that caused attrition to your well-being, but the Lord knows your addictions. All you have to do is make efforts to confess and self-actualize your responses to withdraw from what triggers it. Attritions commonly happen from the emotion of feeling like trash and feels of contempt, but the truth is regardless of what anyone tells you, you're still worthy of Lord Jesus Christ as your redemption and entrance to heaven and worthy of going to a synagogue with other biblical saints without being treated as an outcast.

> God said, "The creative words remain on the side of the veil, but their echoes resound on your side. The real remains here, but its reflection is there; creation is My mirror, though it is not without distortions. I have created in spirit and in matter. My thoughts have ranged from the unseeable smallest to the incomprehensible largest. My greatest thoughts formed substance for the spirits of the sons and daughters of Earth. (*The Book of Gleanings*, Chapter II: Eloma, from *The Kolbrin Bible*)

My Moments of Attrition

I was born in 1991 into a world of sin and suffering, condemned as not suitable for royalty. In 1995, my early years, I developed an inflammation. The doctor called it chronic bronchitis or asthmatic. They explained to me that I wasn't suitable for neither military nor any aggressive sport. But deep down, that still didn't stop me, for I still pursued my most favored sport—marital arts. Once I begun a level of depression envying others who could progress in higher levels of sports-related or fitness-related activities. Then I became somewhat limited on how destiny would turn out for me. I felt for a moment that condemnation was justified.

In 1998, I felt abandoned by a father who decided a woman was a worthy replacement for a son. Perhaps Father was neglecting me for the fear of emotion that of my mother, which now I understand. My father took care of his dharma through supplying a decent child support check in times of emotional dolor through separation (divorce). I reminisced the times were family was absent without preceding guidance's to a path of proper enlightenment, for there were times when I was lost on proper judgement of principality, choosing of friends and women but then I noticed I've done well with enlightenment from Adon Olam. My influences came from associates, friends, and elders where I learn from mistakes made through empirical realities, not by books or false testimonies. I've learned that the many of the churches I fellowshipped proclaimed saints and often gave false testaments just to please eyes without a sacred healing and confession of truth or just in all empirical truth. My assistance in life was often limited perhaps because of my moderation of independence or pride, although walking into a world where demands of strength were required for survival is always a challenge. Strength is not necessarily from the physical but mostly the mentality and emotional stability in darkest moments.

In 2002, an oracle came to me with hope through faith and a guide to harness mastery within body and belief in Most High known as Adon Olam and Adonai Yahushua to nourish my mentality with salvation to the soul. Then persisted a constant journey for purpose, for I was born into the legacy of poor poverty, not a wealthy mansion and assurance but a constant hustle for prosperity. My biggest questions were "Can I make it one more night?" or "Will the Lord end my suffering?" The anguish was not overcome through mysterious treasures but through a strong mentality of hope and driven possibilities. Although one was constantly mocked and manipulated as someone who wouldn't succeed in his fortune and ambitions, through individuals who wasn't to liking of me neither, the driven will still kept moving forward because reliving the past is a waste of time.

A real good friend of mine was always encouraging me when depression struck. His name was Gabriel who died at age of eleven (same age as me at the time) from a transport driver while on his bicycle. Then I distinguish the primal reasons and truths that Lord Majesty enlightened me with, that I still have a purpose without the consent of others. Then I found remorse on self-actualization when I reminisced one of the most important things Gabriel told me. ***"You have to keep flowing regardless*** *of what misery strikes. Just remember you're still breathing."* Everyone has the moment of attrition. On September 24, 2014, I reminisced this when I was listening to songs **"Pray"** and **"Spun A Web"** from **Jeff "Ja Rule" Atkins** in his album *PIL2*. The songs reminded me of close reality, seeking an optimistic lifestyle from the dolorous lifestyles; the struggles a down-to-earth person goes through; Ra from others looking to fill a person with contempt; and webs of construction seeking to prison the mind.

Among many important things I've learned empirically is that a bad company is very *covetous, adulterous, conniving,* and an overall surrounding of *snakes* waiting to fill a being with *contempt, dolor, and Ra.* **"Be not deceived: evil communications corrupt good manners" (1 Corinthians 15v33 KJV).** In the reflection of this scripture simply means **"bad company corrupts good character,"** according to *New Living Translation,* second edition, can be spiritual beings that advertise disposition from a humble spirit and love the surroundings of drama, those particular types of company are worth withdrawing from. Simply meaning an individual that portrays to be humble but disguises themselves away from their true intentions, which is devouring a positive livelihood in another to something of havoc and evil deeds through true intentions. Many kings and princes lose the ability of faith and love because of false ministers persuading them to other routes according to their liking and fear. Conversely, they have no position over you when believe to perceive something justified by the Word of the Lord. They are not your idol. Yahushua is your idol, and it's you who must study vigorously when able to understand the meanings of His Word delivered, although various kings and princes procrastinate or don't study vigorously.[14]

An analogy for you: When it's judgment time, do you think He's going to call you with everyone you encountered in life that taught you to bank in your justification, or do you come to the sense that you'll be judged alone in front of the living Lord? When you grow in learning with a corruptible movement that is looking to target certain individuals to make them feel a moment of attrition, they are more likely built on a discriminative motion with evil intentions. It's best to leave that particular movement before you cause internal damnation of yourself and your followers.

---

[14]   I infer myself as well, for I don't always study vigorously but acknowledge my weakness of procrastinating.

~ 2014 *Spontaneous and a troubling spirit of influences of life* Journal

From personal experience, I can deeply relate to a troubling spirit with pursuing an ambition of making a dream into reality, not being concurred by the unconscious nor the subconscious but bringing forth a dream to conscious. The subconscious clarity wants a belief that all the desires are currently right around the corner, but the conscious knows that's not true or nearly completed. Puzzling thoughts reminisce of current strategies through asking one of the most important questions in life. "Have everything in your current pursuit made your life better or worse?" The unconscious stage of mind gives me a driven depth in mind to accept and decipher the boundaries. Humanist approach is always a reflection of nature with deflection, for every being is different, so we can't analyze others but discover similar intellectuals and instincts, which is also a reflection of being.

My time at Fayetteville Technical Community College (FTCC) has subjected me toward understanding emotional intelligence and fortified an outline of accommodations and positions. Embracing the arts of self-writing, such as a journal and/or monograph, to better nourish the troubling spirit and mental stages has better made me aware of knowing and clarifying thyself. There are many struggling situations in life from financial to health. Planning how to surpass aggravating and troubling circumstances gives me a more profitable cause on compensating something that leans toward joy even when events sometimes go spontaneously wrong. Look around at all the individuals in the universe who struggle to achieve a favorable outlook on lives just to consume enough joy to be satisfied in life. Notice the statement I've given, "consume enough joy," not consume enough money because money doesn't always bring happiness but brings stability and assurance, while love is an intimate bondage that brings comfort and compassion with unity, giving affection for your being. Understanding purpose for existence of humanity, nature, and other creatures gives a magnificent structure of idea, spirituality, and unity and gives a conscious reason here on Urantia. Understanding and structuring a challenge is critical toward prosperity with an attentive mind-set to master mental stages without being corrupted, which is reliable information. Everyone faces obstacles whether it's driven from a source of hate, pain, bad circumstances, cruelty, or discrimination. Reflecting on the outcome of obstacles defines or adjusts your mentality. Everyone has a theory of ethics, relationships, driven future goals, and religion yet never notice that important unconscious question I've given previously, which basically sums up to "Are you happy with yourself currently?" In addition, knowing yourself deeply relies on the pursuits of joy and gives a meaning of truth. Within, clarification of obstacles, joy, and mental stages concludes an individual's average pursuit epicurean. **Epicurean** *"is one who pursues luxurious pleasures"* lifestyle, contrasting an inevitable awareness of problems. —J.S.J.

𝔓𝔬𝔦𝔰𝔢𝔡 𝔅𝔢𝔦𝔫𝔤𝔰

Ask yourself how you can solidify understanding when you continuously progress in your heart practices of prejudice and discrimination against skin colors, bloodlines, and sexes. The film *American History X* (1998) made a prime example of this, blameful of everyone through discrimination until the important question sparked the brain. "Has anything you've done made your life better?" Bad karma comes to those who abuse others with hatred in their heart. Even the individuals who believe their supreme masters eventually suffer from hatred they provoked and/or committed against others. These supreme masters can be anyone who thinks they have charge of you, such as bosses, supervisors, dirty law enforcers, politicians, higher-up leaders, and any others who believe they have power over you that portray evil intentions or scornful behavior, although respect must be given to those who possess good deeds and a warm heart.

> *We are not enemies but friends,*
> *We must not be enemies thou passion may have strained,*
> *We must not break our bonds of affection,*
> *The mystic cords of memory will swell and again touch,*
> *And surely they will be by the better angels of our nature.*

> (*American History X* (McKenna 1998) film)

"Blessed is the man that walketh not in the counsel of the ungodly, nor standeth in the way of sinners, nor sitteth in the seat of the scornful."[15] Just because you carry the bloodline of a prejudice and bias family heritage doesn't mean you should sustain continuity of carrying that

---

[15] Psalms 1v1 King James Version.

poison in your veins. The ultimate courage in those circumstances is to fight against and rebuke those who provoke brainwashing with ideology of prejudice. Individuals among your presence may be stereotypical but don't even know the person, so it's best not to advertise compliance but make known your disapproval. It's always better to lead than to follow. Although discrimination may be justified in matters of biblical notions, where all living beings trying to persevere receive love and pleasure, understand purposes and truths, and exceed infinite possibilities, let that be your judgment. Although there are some individuals who "can't be brought or sold, some individuals just want to watch the world burn," those are the ones you have to speculate with a distance because their intentions are hardly ever good but built with evil morals.

Speculating my time on the transits and many other places, I've come to acknowledge a brief truth, which is no matter how decent of a person you are, various individuals will ignite dolor and hate upon you just because their spirit is down or how their livelihood suffers. Truth is people become poised on how they were mistreated and betrayed, feelings of unfair livelihood, or just personal vendetta on complexion, so they take it out on the people who may seem in outcast to them with a hidden envious personality. Even if you've done nothing to them to justify that type of treatment, the best foremost thing is to not indulge with forged anger but completely ignore them unless it gets physical, but sometimes even then certain kings don't always forge anger but simply walk away. In analogy for you, say it was a woman who bestows her anger upon you. Would you indulge in hurting her while she receives the joy of locking you up, or would the king rebuke her transgression by leaving and simply finding another? It's best not to indulge in scornful nature because they're below you, and kings should know legends are born but heroes are made. I've come to understand this when I was listening to **Citizen Aim** song "**I Am Legend**." He taught various individuals this and many other things before he died.

Awaken Armor

Your suit of armor is what you feed your spirit and clarity and how you train your body and mentality to succumb the evil morals and shadow of others. Jake Hoyt (Ethan Hawke) in the film *Training Day* said that the streets are about "smiles and cries. You have to control your smiles and cries because that's all you have and nobody can take that away from you." In the midst of armoring, when you feel a moment of despondency, first look to the Yahuwah to give you strength and remember to take positive action on relieving this tension. Sometimes the best thing to do is open up to someone who you trust and confess with prayer. You may ask how this helps. The honest answer is human beings are very social species, and without that social ability, we lost our being of sense. Seating in a segregated room with no communication will get to a person's mind eventually. Despondency develops through a stage of low spirit through the cause of losing hope or courage. Therefore, in moments of despondencies, it's important to think positive thoughts or broaden your environment for a better chance of breathing.

Never perceive limitation as it's all your capable of because in the end you can bring new definition, for limitation is nothing but social constructive ideology of devouring your motion to accumulate more: so make no limits and have faith that there's no limit to your horizons.

Brethren once told me you may shoot for the stars, but the bullet may greatly curve and land its place on the moon, yet it all depends on how persistent you are that you may aim to your purpose, so it's important to armor yourself. Helping yourself is not always easy, but it's an achievement you'll come to acknowledge. An article articulating the mentality we should possess called "Rhino mentality is your armor against negativity" by Chris Swenson announced the characteristics of Rhino mentality are "facing adversity, accepting failure, and embracing our fears but without Rhino mentality where chained by fear" (Swenson 2015). Rhino mentality is our armor through providing ourselves with positive personality and facing fears while rejecting negative surroundings that may create barriers and preparing to battle adversaries that try to implement limits along with your struggling poverty.

~ February 2013   *Overcoming Obstacles*   **Journal**

The meaning of the statement is that no matter how tough things get, you must resist temptations and peer pressures to implement prosperity in life. Individuals may ask how you can overcome obstacles when they maybe living in your home. This implement is called removing yourself and using your subconscious for a higher morality upon yourselves to find a more powerful force of good energy than you may find your *vocation*. Overcoming obstacles is the key to life's success of making wise decision and keeping what's true to the heart. Sometimes you have to be naive to what others say to follow your own heart on what you want in life. Obstacles are nothing but hindrances that attach themselves to us to keep individuals on modest level of an average living. To overcome this negative impact enhances possibilities of making something out of life. Enforcing our ambition from the negative obstacles is the way to flourish in life. When people can't do things themselves, they would tell me I wouldn't succeed, but overcoming the negative by not letting compromising overtake my intelligence gives the great meaning of potential excellence without return. Think of life as a horse race by not thinking of others ahead or behind who would try to plague contempt of possibilities. It's important to keep rising and follow the vocation destiny of what an individual seeks in life. Obstacles in life are nothing but jealousy and hatred of what's wanted to be gained of, which they've not earned or their imperfections of their decisions in contrast to various kings. Overcoming those obstacles keeps morals highly privileged. —J.S.J.

A cargo of lies doesn't benefit from truth. Armor can form from the inevitable, for there are so much foolish propaganda in the world saying how things should be and foolish violence that people influence. Armor is more so preparation and a quantum of wisdom. I, as a testament, now acknowledge that many elderly men will purposely provoke Ra toward a prince who's on his way to king often or occasionally face elderly snake kings who try destroying life or misguiding. I've personally learned that as a young man, many elderly males try persuading negative influences of drugs, liquors, and beers; instigating fights; and drawing princes to promiscuous women who are bound to break your mentality or transmit diseases. Snakes come from anywhere, your relatives, friends, bosses, strangers, and associates trying to purposefully guide you into their conniving deeds. The empirical truth is that these conniving deeds come from certain women as well. These types of women seem to indulge in corrupting prince/king's thoughts to create a fighting motive or invoke jealousy. When a woman or man invokes jealousy upon you, they're preying upon your mentality through their appeal to build envies.

Chapter IV:
Awakening the Royalty

"When you become to accept your royal throne, your shine will glow endless; royalty is bestowed by the Lord not by Men law."

Royal gospel soldiers you are, gentlemen, we're all descendants of the royal bloodline of Adam, in nature, we're all kings, so you're just as important as any other male that walketh this earth. Many kings and princes of faith feel suffocated in the world trying to abide by the Lord's laws. Listening to songs **"We Will Remember"** and **"Finally Arrive,"** from *Native Lungs* album by **Braille**, I've come to understand that the Lord altered my genes just as He has with you. No one resides in perfection, for we're all struggling humble beasts[16] harkened by Yahawah spiritual flow even when we fumble were saved through the acceptance of Yahawashi Christ. Braille gave the important message that freedom is a deception if you're running all the time, so remain solid to your purpose with a strong hold of faith. No one is perfect! From rarely too often, we all come across asking for a sign, such as rap artist **Earl "DMX" Simmons** literates in his song **"Lord Give Me a Sign,"** but without question, Jesus will take away all your sins even through the domestic violence as DMX literates on his song **"Blown Away,"** both from album *DMX Year of the Dog . . . Again*. Rebuke what is beneath you. This means anyone trying to provoke your positive mentality to something ill and suffocate your living.

---

[16] I stated beast because without any conduct from the Lord of the Most High, we're an uncivilized species. Some may say this has nothing to do with civilization, but truth is without the introduction to the biblical laws, the community may have been completely lawless and unhumble.

The most important kind of freedom is to be what you really are. You trade in your reality for a role. You trade in your sense for an act. You give up your ability to feel, and in exchange, put on a mask. There can't be any large-scale revolution until there's a personal revolution, on an individual level. It's got to happen inside first. (Jim Morrison)

Seek your inner human character to embrace and improve so that you might not be withheld from your crown. You may become somewhat arrogant though various individuals would consider arrogant as unappealing, though by definition, **arrogant** "claiming for oneself" means *revealing a better understanding of one's own purpose and/or potentiality.* So ask yourselves how is arrogant evil? Perhaps arrogant is not a word in the Bible in those ancient times but something fabricated as an act of control. Though arrogance that grows inner false confidence is an issue worth discerning for the betterment of the individual yet arrogance should not be the exterior of the individual but the frame of mind having hope and faith that the potentials of what's ambitioned is capable of. Exterior arrogance is an adversary. The essence of interior arrogance is to value what seems fair, prudent, true and faithful within oneself while in silence, humbleness or sobriety, not the outburst of attention or revile. (cf. Romans 12v3) "Arrogancy of the proud" and haughtiness (Isiah 13v11 KJV) is the portion that God despise because the individual has removed altruism, edifying one another with love and grace (cf. Ephesians 4v11–32, Thessalonians 5v11) and sensibility from their heart.

Lies to Purge

Adon Olam established in His Word that prudence is very essential to humility. "The wise in heart shall be called prudent . . ."[17] This was a symbolic meaning to way of living, for the heart is depended upon for survival, and if the heart is deficient, we may surely die. **Prudent** individual means *a cautious individual who seeks to sustain and obey*

---

[17] Proverbs 16v21 King James Version.

the divines conduct. It's important not to become self-centered but rather think of yourself with sober judgment with direction of faith that your deeds are good.

> For I say to all who are among you through the "unmerited favor, grace" (chesed) given to me, that you should avoid a false sense of superiority in your thinking; rather exercise "self-control" (shlitah atzmi), thinking with "discernment, good sense, wisdom, understanding" (seichel), as God has measured to each a measure of "faith, truth, fidelity, stability" (emunah). (Romans [Rome] 12v3 Orthodox Jewish Bible)

Prudent Sons and Daughters

The common ideology that many ministers convince younglings is when the Old and New Testament says, "Honor thy father and thy mother,"[18] that you're obligated to obey, but the truth is in the commandments, said **honor** means *deep warm approval for their position*. Keep in mind that a commandment is conduct, and Yahawashi sacrificed Himself for redemption of sins for He knew we would break conducts given, for not everyone agrees with Deuteronomy 21 and a few other chapters or verses, but we try persisting with prudence. Let me ask you kings, princes, princesses, and queens something. If you were told by your guardian to sexually enslave yourself for finance, stability, or their personal pleasure, would you accept molestation or allow the fiery Spirit within your humility to fight for what's right while honoring your body for you're not heirs to your guardian but a blessing for your presence? If you're constantly exposed to a sadistic guardian who enjoys brawling on you, do you think you're supposed to submit to this act or stand a strong soldier and have stronger love for your health? When a parent persuades you to sell narcotics or ingest narcotics, will you obey or rebel? There's purpose for rebellion. Normally, it's considered a sin; conversely, it can be prudence, strength for positive freewill, and a journey to wisdom. El Elyon was specific with his commandment of honor because he knew there were snake guardians in the world. The younglings who experience this while fighting for the humane honor within prove to royal and the individuals who don't are still yet proven to be champions. The word does *imply* examples of obedience from guardians because normally, a parent

---

[18]   Exodus 20v12 King James Version.

has your best interest, but when the interest is not out of love, then it's not from Yahweh, for Yahweh's Word is to obey His Word above all. Many individuals grow on the acceptance that guardians should make arrange marriage but spoke freewill, not the will of others, so it's blasphemy to cling to your parents' marital arrangement. Living from the heart is better than living from pragmatic loving decisions of others (see chapter XIV for pragmatic love).

Prudent Soldiers

Awakening royalty is first about honoring yourself instead of receiving yourself to misery, havoc, and abuse, for you owe yourself love and serenity, but many times, you may have to fight for it. Previously, I encountered some Christian brethren who had the ideology that Yahweh holds against soldiers and law enforcers the crimes of killing, for thee maybe damned for this sin. My reply was that no human is perfect. Some will lust, thereby committing adultery; breaking the laws of the judicial system; and committing "murder, theft, rape," but in all, the Lord is merciful, and the advantage is repentance. Then Christian brethren communicated with me that killing is the worst and more appealing to be done intentionally when someone enlists in the military, though I asked, "Do you not know that there was references in the Old Testament mentioning momentum of battles, some even the Lord demanded?" and "Do you think it was through effective communication, for many were possibly killed for creating serene kingdoms. A fight is worth having when you're fighting for great cause and *prudence* for love for others. The fights throughout history has caused the Word to be preserved, for many throughout history, presently and in future, have done whatever they could to destroy Yahawah and Yahawashi Word. Because of the soldier within ourselves, we've fought to sustain truth, and some of those fights come with death and sacrifice. The original word ratzach (רצח) means murder, not harag (הרג) meaning kill, certain English translators chose the word kill but originally as in the Torah "guided laws of the first five books of Moses," states "Thou shall not murder" (Exodus 20v13) which is quoted in Matthews 5v21, that actually means refrain from murder. Killing is an act of defense but murder is an action of hate, jealousy, envious covetousness, prejudices, and militia strategy of producing fear to further cause. God clearly prohibits murder but not a defensible kill that will save the lives of ourselves, kindred loves, and strangers that maybe coerced to be murdered based on ethnicity, faith, heritage, and other none sensible acts.

In **Sons of Anarchy** *Season 5 Episode 1* "Sovereign," Jackson Teller gave an outlaw influence of strength not through the common saying "what doesn't kill you make you stronger," for the truth he gave was killing you internally only increases dolor and Ra, but strength comes from good nurture of the ones you hold close to heart, for that's what's worthy of holding on to when hurting. A royal admiration was given in *Season 6 Episode 13* when Jax volunteered to imprison himself for charges against his wife, Tara, for the sake of love before she was murdered by Gemma Teller (Jax mother [Kate Segel]). In *Season 7 Episode 13*, Jackson "Jax" Teller (Charlie Hunnam) made the ultimate decision, for the people he cared most about yet in the end despondencies persisted from his brethren, Abel and Wendy. Jax decided to sacrifice his life for his younglings to change the poisoned legacy of criminality for his young princes and end the tribulation he unfortunately bestowed upon his brethren and younglings than use his death as the closure.

A warrior named "Spartacus." Spartacus gave outlaw influence of royalty when he addressed every slave should have the freedom to choose their own path, a true historical legend. According to the Spartacus series, Spartacus purposed that one is just as important as one with position, and if you don't remember that, then none have worth. Help who you can to better course of living. Spartacus fought and died believing in his cause for freedom among those condemned to slavery for the cause of freedom with reminisce of his departed wife's sufferings because of injustice forgery to slavery. In addition, the Romans did everything they could to break him by first separating him from his wife, condemning him to slavery. Legates foretold they grouped raped his beloved wife then portrayed a lie that she was safe while secretly assassinated her by forcing him to kill his only best friend (whom he adored as his younger brother), forcing Spartacus to fight to the death, killing many that Spartacus considered brothers, and being deceived by those he once titled foes, Spartacus carrying the weight of sufferings from those that hold him in high position to protect them and doing what's right. Everyone matters regardless if we favor them or not.

Question for all the saints is do you think El Elyon invokes men to be gentle, compromising, and soft or solid to your purpose and prepared to fight for something greater than yourselves?

𝔊rounding 𝔚orthlessly

Grounding worthlessly has nothing to do with grounding others, but you're enslaving yourselves into grounding by devouring yourselves with stress and contempt through others centric beliefs, for the centric only wants to brand a charismatic individual with angst. The attacks toward Christianity are nothing but fallacies, opinions, biases, and stereotypical judgments bestowed from individuals who are centric, secular, and heathen.

> *All universal judgements are weak, loose, and*
> *dangerous. (Michel de Montaigne) (1533–1595)*

All is best not to dwell on how others report and record you but accept the possibility of prosecution, for all people of the covenant of Yahawashi go through this. Many have already received and come to program themselves to loving disapproving of God. Acknowledge judgment from mankind, and womankind is all useless because no purity of the tongue can match Yahawah and Yahawashi. All individuals on this universal can be possessed with both evil and love. Deception is all people, and they're capable of being imperfect. All their tongues of negative judgment should remain silent to your ears because they simply don't have the rights of pure justice to forecast negative judgment on anyone regardless of how close they are to your bloodline. Fallacies are nothing but individuals fabricating measurements among another, but there's only one true individual who once walked this earth shall return, and that's Christ, for Christ means "measured." Only Yahawashi Christ has the right to measure! Oppression may become persecuted upon you, telling the ways based on their knowledge "how a man should be" or "how a woman should be," but there's no one definition of "how you should be" for it's your eminence of knowledge, prudency, *ontology*, reason and rationality within that defines "how you should be" not based on the prospective of others unless it's prudent or advocated from your lover, then it's worth considering or discerned measure.

𝖲𝗍𝖾𝗐𝖺𝗋𝖽𝗌𝗁𝗂𝗉

As young men develop in life, we have to be rooted to stewardship, which is the ethics of self-management and care for being(s) or something of cherishable possession, of environment, nature, health, theology and information. Stewardship is a responsibility, a devotion and a prudence of will to discern sensibility. Young princes must understand the royalty of this because it clarifies a teleological position of holding on to something without treating it as waste. These things can be a little value or of great value. For instance, when an individual believe they've found a breakthrough job and sacrifice much to attain the job, your rooting yourselves to a better outcome with a hope that it was all worth it, similar to the film *The Pursuit of Happyness*. The hardship of it is standing devoted to it. This can also be inferenced to family, relationship, and marriage, committing to a dream, and overall, be true to yourselves. The truth is when this is implemented, you become a loyalist and person of strong integrity. Stewardship is sustainable faith with hope of perseverance but devout even when hope in somethings or cause has become a disappointment or distressed.

Chapter V:
Empirical Realities

*"No one can substitute your reality with theirs, for they
haven't lived it. Regardless of scientific psychology, another
may diagnose. They only can fabricate their understanding,
for reality is not a film but a remolding of realism."*

mpirical realities are *the based on experiences on how you and
others went through in life and observances.* Many of us males
as young princes went through a life of continuous *dolor* from
preceding legacies. Empirical reality evolves into a culture reflecting our
value ideas; the ideology has become segments toward our perceptions
of values. These influences are mostly through real-world situations and
mass media. There are imposing arguments that mass media is the key
behind mental programming, not through the reflection of modernity
but construction ideology that represents subversive information of
social, belief, and political influences. This is one of the **core** substances
of *brainwashing*—a strong division of actions and reactions, what's
considered natural and valued, what's acceptable and ethical from
traditional to modernity, and hidden or exposed truths and falsities
(Thomas 2010). The empirical reality of poverty is often misfortune to
individuals who struggle, for individuals who are poor for significant
periods of their lives precede a legacy of poverty toward their younglings,
fighting that existing poverty of dolor is difficult, but anything is possible
with a strong mentality and faith.

> *Humankind has not woven the web of life. We are but one thread within it. Whatever we do to the web, we do to ourselves. All things are bound together. All things connect. (Chief Seattle, Duwamish [1780–1866])*

The triple Academy Award film *Crash* (Bullock, et al. 2004) gave vivid scenarios of empirical reality through suffering, hatred, and poor poverty. On each side, most are victims because of hatred and discrimination, but through that havoc, some discovered an unraveling truth or an awakening in strength. A few reflective scenarios of empirical reality, one scenario demonstrated how citizens discriminate Persians from overseas and other citizens, judging them with hatred and fear. Another scenario is a decent African American man going through *emotional suffering* by an adulterous prejudice cop molesting his wife right before his eyes, while he tried to persevere in decency. Later, the prejudice officer hoped for forgiveness after he rescued that same woman from the car explosion. In addition, there was a scenario of a Latin American hardworking father who became a workaholic to preserve stability, and his work brought danger to his place through a Persian man who became brainwashed on biased activities in America and became discriminative. The confused Persian found his residence then pointed his gun at the Latin American father, while the daughter (Latin American's youngling) ran to him to protect her father from the bullet. The Persian man fired with regrettable timing, yet the daughter didn't die, and his eyes were enlightened that there was a guardian angel shielding his misjudgment (although the revelation was that the bullets were fake because of the Persian daughter's judgment). There was also a demonstration of two African American burglars trying to survive by stealing and distributing, yet one encountered an influence from a stranger advising him to preserve his decency, while the other was murdered by a Caucasian cop who developed skeptical biased generalization. The film *Crash* reflected the nation on how injustice it can be, and if we don't learn to love one another, havoc will continue in those matters, an urban thriller that is very much provocative.

In reality, there are some, maybe many, individuals who have very few loyal people around them, and the few that are loyal sometimes separate or depart ways, leaving you to survive on your own. Some unfortunate events leave individuals alone, then they question themselves on how they make it through the storms hurting them. A touch of true kinship and love is out there somewhere for you. For those who felt abandon, I believe your season of good blessing and passionate love will come to you. Any dream of hope is a dream worth holding on to because you may make it reality. Nightmares and dreamscapes forever may haunt certain individuals from the acts of war, abusive childhood trauma, lost beloveds, and other fears; this is you being touched by empirical reality. The question is will you stand strong to fight against your haunting memories? Will you own up to receiving benevolence from someone who care about you? Many individuals become discouraged believing they can't accomplish (meaning something internally aimed for). Give yourself time to rise even when it's hard to savor patience. Sometimes it's necessary to gain better results.

You don't always necessarily know where you're going in complete certainty without experience. Not everyone was born wealthy nor in a stabile home, nor had loving parents; some cycles of life are unexpected and sometimes those unexpected empirical realities can purge the mind with dolor but the one's that fight against the nightmares become stronger.

Hustling Kings

In every moment of our lives, the majority of us men have the ambition for more power, wealth, and affection and the hope to maintain or gain prowess. The two main wisdom of hustling are the common **stealth**, which is the ability to preserve privacy while remaining resilient toward intruders who may want to steal your possessions, and the other is becoming **unpredictable**, which is the ultimate deception because your rechanneling everyone's theories of you. Nobody is aware of what you're thinking or the actions you're going to take. Through these Pairing with stealth and unpredictability, you bundle with *observation, selective, social intelligence* with sublimation. The clarity of these bundles is that observation is the empirical knowledge that benefits the conscience. Selective for making decisions that on a personal level, the individual believes is justified. Social intelligence is in accordance to theorizing your surroundings to accommodate charismatic character with versatility to communicate in a humane way without changing your character. In addition, bundle with removing from toxic individuals, led to your purpose, but humbling yourself against *covetous* (means *demonstrating strong desire to possess belongings of others*) and repel from *revile* (means *individuals who like to criticize with abuse*) and become *noble* (means *demonstrating higher moral principles and ideologies*).

~ June 2015   ***Unfortunate Homes***   **Journal**

From empirical realities, I've come to understand that not everyone has shelter, then nature calls a forceful hustle to do whatever it takes to nourish the physiological. Individuals of higher authorities would say there are plenty of opportunities in America to make a difference, but the analogy is "how are there many opportunities when jobs, houses, and apartments (although the only apartments available are within the projects of murders, thieves, rapist, persecutors, and contentious individuals) seem isolated to expand horizons?" The economy in certain places is so unfortunate in opening up opportunities. Surely, the Lord will make the difference to certain individuals and me. Then I received a revelation from some of my friends confessing that they've been homeless once. I looked with shock and wondered what became of the shelter with their parents. When I asked, they said their parents disowned (some for just being a Christian), abused, and/or raped them. Then I researched what actually the word "parent" means in Latin. It means "bringing forth." Fellow older friends who I call M and Mr. Jones told me that "having your blood child makes you feel like your newborn is greater than you and that you'll behave illicitly liberated to protect, guide, and love them and create possibilities for their future or die trying. This is the moment where you put your youngling before you."

A parent would do what they must for their children, but with prudence to the Lord's Word and anything that breaks that liberation, they'll accept punishment from Adon Olam to support their youngling(s). Princes and princesses without parents are sometimes blessed to have good guardians that Yahawah touched to have in place when abandoned. Many orphans, I'm sure, hope to inherit a life like in the film *The Blindside* featuring Sandra Bullock. However, the ones who behave illicitly and break Yahuwah's conduct will still be forgiven for their sins, for love covers a multitude of sins. That's an example of what a loving parent is or proportionate to real loving parents. —J.S.J.

Humane mammon, Matthew 6v24, Luke 16v9–13, has often been a difficult task to break because of the high value of money needed to have what's truly desired or a liability or pay for certain expenses that we're responsible for. Believe me, brethren and sisters, I feel the hustle for being delivered from poverty.

> Wisdom is even better when you have money.
> Both are a benefit as you go through life.
> Wisdom and money can get you almost anything,
> But only wisdom can save your life. (Ecclesiastes 7v11–12 NLT)

This scripture gives the importance of wisdom. It should be the primary protocol because wisdom gives direction to the soul, body, heart, and liberated decisions and overall proper direction. Money can be sustained with liberation or create a formality of evil and cause individuals to lose their way.

Gang Reality

Understand that gang violence in our reality is the rise of tribulations through hatred, greed, poisons, abuse, and destruction. First, we must classify the reasons for creation of gangs from the very origin. The reasons are to help the people in poverty, have a sense of belonging, gain reputation and respect, and retaliation (Pacheco 2010). Many princes and princesses have become abandoned by relatives, some their own mother and father. Not everyone grows up in a respectable home but a home of dolor. Individuals may join gangs because of traditional family legacies, money, social pressures, and curiosity. There are some princes that are constantly rejected with no food at home. The only food they receive is from school or a friend's house. Various individuals are born in a world where they feel as if it is cursed with dolor, so they carry out the initiation process and brand themselves for the gang they represent and union with. The 2007 film *Freedom Writers* expressed a strong empirical reality of reason though it was mostly singled out on hatred, poor poverty, and vengeance. People often forecast judgment before they even know the gang members; some went through so much dolor they don't know love.

Second, there are princes and princesses in this reality who try to depart from gang life for a healthier living but are not always able to succeed because they're receiving death threats on behalf of gang affiliations, threatening their lives and the lives of those closest to them. The common issue why they won't let them leave easily is because of their philosophy. *When you join the family, loyalty and commitment is required on your behalf, and in return, they help provide your needs and affection.* Although the unity may have seemed to perceive affection, security, sex, and money, blindness persists on princes' and princesses' behalf through danger brought upon them and their beloveds. In the union of these gang affiliations, Ra touches them.

Construction Ideology

You may ask what subjects to a construction ideology. It's an analytical system of implementing your behavior to become agreeable to its construction. For instance, often, you'll see news media suggest a more appropriate behavior; building appropriate behavior is what they agree upon. But alternatively, individuals may think it's most valued because it's broadcasted publicly to invoke that idea. Construction ideology happens often in music videos and songs, films, news, books, magazines, segregated groups, politics, advertisements, and television shows.

> *Security is mostly a superstition. It does not exist in nature, nor do the children of men as a whole experience it. Avoiding danger is no safer in the long run than outright exposure. Life is either a daring adventure, or nothing. (Helen Keller from* **The Open Door** *[1957])*

From *The Matrix*, Morpheus explained constructive ideology:

> The Matrix is a system, Neo. That system is our enemy. But when you're inside, you look around, what do you see? Businessman, teachers, lawyers, carpenters. The very minds of the people we are trying to save. But until we do, these people are still a part of that system and that makes them our enemy. You have to understand, most of

these people are not ready to be unplugged. And many of them are so inured, so hopelessly dependent on the system, that they will fight to protect it.

Construction ideology is everywhere, and because it's everywhere, people program themselves into thinking that's the modern way, or a placebo study is scientifically proven to work for everyone, or you have to take all your vaccines. The same ideology influence a one world government or unity of all religions and eliminate those that choose to rebel. Higher authorities implement and prey on young minds as well as older minds to construct appropriate reason that may be built on webs of deception in the long run. Personally, one of the main reasons a proportion of results from the assumed empirical perception of studies from the administered higher-ups known as the wealthy and governing authorities, fabricate a majority of individuals have the tendency acceptance or become receptive to, or fabricate an opposition that the nation hasn't agreed to be true but is advertised to be accurate or modernity is actually inaccurate because once they question every living being, then it's proven to be accurate. For example, advertisements promoting that tight pants (skinnies) are the new men's fashion is a falsity because promoting that ideology doesn't mean everyone agrees, and various men would consider tight pants as effeminate. When various music artists symbolically or openly admit they're Illuminatis while creating a persuasion to the youth, idolaters consider it as natural because ideology is getting someone inspired by them to convert to their beliefs. When mass media segregate people based on their ethnicity to a cause, this is based on political and discriminative social constructive ideology. When mass media promote shaving private hair for both manhood and womanhood, they're using agreeable people to convincingly construct others' minds to do the same by insinuating it's more desirable and appealing among the majority. This is falsity because specific areas of beings do not give equilibrium to everyone's ideology, for not every being was questioned. For instance, laws insinuated as justifiably that prohibited from medical coverage procedures built on ideology of acceptance through ages while preying upon minds of becoming agreeable to their ideology. Meaning certain medical procedures not given to everyone based on a system of theorizing if an individual is worthy of treatment based on income, based on age, based on health chances certain insurers won't even cover individuals that insurers and medical administration theorized to be not worth the expenses, mammon has become greed in healthcare systems than altruism. Gender movements (feminist and meninist) influencing that if you're a woman, you're a feminist, and if you're a male, you're a meninist is another falsity because labels segregate us, but the human over exceeds all gender movement labels. In addition, cultivate that labels segregate more than unite. To be human means you'll have different ideologies, beliefs, pursuits, and behaviors, and no one can change that, but just because certain individuals are not fond of it doesn't mean there should be an evented gender label something segregating (such as feminist and meninist), but mass media often construct this with a psychological or critic propaganda. Human is far superior than labels.

𝔐𝔢𝔯𝔢 𝔇𝔞𝔯𝔨𝔫𝔢𝔰𝔰

~ 2006   *Calling for Wings*   Journal

On a fall night, sitting up from the suffering of insomnia, I often reminisced being granted with wings by Adon Olam while I was listening to **Tupac Amaru Shakur**'s song "Until the End of Time" from the album *Until the End of Time*, then I would pray to the Lord for a rescue from dolorous poverty, seeking for a better circumstance on things, but I've come to an understanding that a person can't fly without putting in some efforts. Surely, the Lord hears the prayer, but I would have to walk on faith by looking forward with a willpower of persistence that if I really want it, the Lord will greet me there when I've reached a partial of the sky. Some of the elders I've encountered told me that "faith without works is dead." At that moment, I looked at them with confusion, but now I know the message. Just keep moving forward without the courtesy of worrying about what others may think of you. If you feel it's justifiable to move in that direction if an individual is in the wrong path and belongs to the Lord, He will graciously lead the individual back to the right direction. A man who thinks he's fully sanctified is in for a grave error, but the one who honors imperfections and knows he's capable of sinful deeds gives more of a truthful living. —J.S.J.

Shadows of kings and princes sometimes come through reminisces of things we've ran from in the past that our hope is to not encounter ever again and dolor. The truth is many experience mere darkness through dolor and past evil morals *(Ra)*. Sometimes the evil morals are not even your own but afflictions of trauma from others. Those who utterly regret or felt they were the fault of losses or abuse, those who once thought of suicide, and those who wish they could fly from the suffering.

Timing various when I reminisce thoughts of how I could gain wealth so dolor doesn't persist, then I get the negative influences of associates and relatives persuading me to sell drugs, but the pride in me fights for another day to do what's right. The Adon Olam I feel doesn't intend for us to sell drugs that are responsible for provoking the angel of death, destroying lives of children under violent and nonaffectionate parents all because of drugs. How can the world persist on selling drugs to damage others who have someone who loves them so much? The world is not a world without people living, nor is a living being alive if they're poisoning their veins often. The empirical truth is that there are often many kings and princes who have lost their way because they're filled with anguish of wealth for their sons, daughters, themselves, wives, and relatives who they can't contribute to a medical bill, field trips, and lunch for their younglings; can't take their wives and girlfriends out somewhere; can't contribute to travel expenses; and so much more. How can a world expect everyone to live decently when the world is selfish in offering opportunity? Occasionally, I reminisce all the wealthy individuals who rarely give charitable donations, but then I think to myself perhaps they've done charitable donations or perhaps they just don't. Nation is broken when the people suffer in healthy living, people who keep their hearts enclosed to the possible thought that someone maybe suffering but chosen not to help them.

Personally consider these three income levels: down to earth, serenity to earth, and mammonist to earth. A few individuals once told me down to earth is the ghetto. I believed this to be failure to living in hope. The **ghetto** actually means *an isolated or segregated area* that was founded in 1516. Ghetto is enslaving the mind to discrimination and slavery. Down to earth to me means a person who has no other option in the given moments but to adapt and make a change from the dolor of their poverty and hope that efforts will soon give serenity. **Serenity** means *the psychological stage of being calm, peaceful, and untroubled from dolor*. Down-to-earth individual often hopes for miracles for serene livelihood that they always hoped for, and when there's a possible breakthrough, they'll often fight through hell to get to a heaven on earth. There are two types of hell just as there's two types of heaven, and this is followed by the three trinities: earthily and heavenly (three trinities are discussed in Chapter VIII). The two types of heaven and hell are the earthily and the spiritual. Our flesh resides in the earthily, but our spirit ascends to Yahawah the light or descends to Lucifer the darkness; but Yahawashi can always left our spirit back to him even when we deal in anger for our dolorous living. The conscience is a part of our trinity for it's the mind itself in its actions and knowledge feed; it's the dominance of spiritual warfare and pursuit of good deeds.

When I was watching *Law Abiding Citizen*, at the very end of the film, I was somewhat inspired on what Nick Rice (Jamie Foxx) said to Clyde Shelton (Gerard Butler):

> *That we can't retract the decisions that we've made, we can only affect the decisions we're going to make from here.*

Personally, I found this to be entirely real. No individual can replicate the retraction when it's found adversary to our path and teleological; however, there can be a discovery of the reason to forward a positive redemption to our decisions. Although mere aggravations of our dolor can cause Ra within us, sometimes it is essential to a learning process we have yet to reconcile, a self-hypnosis on how we can substantiate the problem for a grasp of virtue. Experience is the process of learning from our actions even when we regret some of those actions. This can give a mere darkness, but the light is when we evaluate the negative into something beautiful than an individual can recover a light that comes from within the Spirit of our core. "*Experience* is remolding us every moment, and our mental reaction on every given thing is really a resultant of our experience of the whole world up to"[19] the present.

---

[19] William James, *The Principle of Psychology*, "The Stream of Thought," 152.

Life's Mirror

There are loyal hearts, there are spirits brave,
There are souls that are pure and true;
Then give to the world the best that you have,
And the best will come back to you.
Give love, and love to your life will flow,
A strength in your utmost need;
Have faith, and a score of hearts will show
Their faith in your work and deed.
Give truth, and your gift will be paid in kind,
And honor will honor meet;
And the smile which is sweet will surely find
A smile that is just as sweet.
Give sorrow and pity to those who mourn;
You will gather in flowers again
The scattered seeds from you though outborne
Though the sowing seemed but vain.
For life is the mirror of king and slave,
'Tis just what we are and do;
Then give to the world the best that you have
And the best will come back to you.

—Madeline S. Bridges

Chapter VI:
Life's Formulas

"What you learn becomes a formula of how you can use your intelligence for the betterment if you're willing to apply those formulas."

L ife's formula is the intake of wisdom and knowledge to interpret meaning, in-depth meanings; to gain *prudence*; and to preserve the *emunah* within morality, spirituality, and mentality.

I. For who sows *dolorous attrition* and *Ra* to others shall eventually reap what they sow and make no foolish belief that condemnation will remain secret, for they'll soon seek absolution to relieve the cursed fate.

II. Beauty is creation of *emunah* toward another, for *emunah* is beauty. Beauty is a precious substance, and when you find it, and beauty remains *emunah* to your vessel, it's worth holding on to internally in exterior horizons.

III. Refrain from walking in everyone's pathway, for if you do, you'll trip on each other, causing the other to fall with you and them to you. Soon, if you keep following the majority, you'll be buried, but if you follow your prudent mind, you'll walk a narrow valley to perseverance.

IV. Rebellion is not at all bad, for rebellion can be sharp as steel purging through the webs of social construction and deceptions to declare truth and *liberation*.

V. Persistent pursuit to Adon Olam requires risks and sacrifices, for the boondocks may become your home, and trials are inevitable. You'll begin to notice a decline in collaboration with others like sealed walls looking for a hole to collaborate as you fuel persistence to Adon Olam.

VI. It's wiser not to fuel the Spirit to Lucifer's institutions, for he preys on the moment he can destroy or fill you with contempt and *Ra*, so be wary of strange social gatherings filled with liquor, narcotics, and firearms and be vigilant of disturbing crowds. Luciferian institutions can be classified as certain clubs filled with liquor and narcotics, brothels of prostitutes, sorcery, tyranny and terrorism, fueling your vessel with large quantities of alcohol and narcotics, Satanism, following idols and gangs, following moralities that's not prudent to God's Word like *The Book of the Law* by Aleister Crowley and all other deeds that your Spirit and conscience feels are of Lucifer and not of El Elyon; your convictions will be God toggling at your Spirit for acknowledging conviction on involvement that is not of Him.

VII. Privacy shall preserve an individual in the face of thine devils, for anonymity to internally valued and treasured possessions creates perseverance to sustaining it.

VIII. Cultivate that there's always a snake looking for you to fall in a deep well so they can conquest your kingdom and all your possessions. Common snakes portray falsity of love and family to learn your vulnerabilities. Be discreet, and trust no man to the fullest.

IX. Sustain the *emunah*. Hope and love toward Yahawah. Don't fill the mental chambers with complete conscience but with *prudence*.

X. A strange woman can be exteriorly gorgeous, but this doesn't mean the interior is gorgeous; however, she may have a gorgeous appeal, but if the interior is a rotten egg, she'll misguide you into an abyss. Your only rescue is the touch of the heaven trinity, YHWH Word, and surroundings of agape love.

XI. Enjoy every earthily part of your queen's flesh and feel not defiled but undefiled. Let no higher authority take away your delight, for it's your heir when vowed. Let lovemaking be unrestrictive in prudence.

XII. A submissive who chooses to become an heir is far more valued to an Adon, for even with her liberty, she appointed to keel to an Adon and his persona. It's wise to hold on to this treasure and bestow your honor.

XIII. It's encouraged to have an abundant amount of friends but few counselors. Thorough analysis is required, for many would flatter, "but their hearts are full of poison." Although having friends is socially desirable, don't trust anyone as a friend nor brother fully, for all living beings on this earth are capable of deceitfulness so discern with caution to discover a serpent's tongue according to "Do Not Trust Anyone as a Friend" (97, 18–98, 8) from *The Teachings of Silvanus – Nag Hammadi Scriptures*. All beings are capable of *cognitive suffering* for a momentarily phase.

XIV. Don't buy into the stereotypical lies that you can forgive easily. The Bible says forgive, but forgiveness comes within time. You're not programmed like a machine with an on or off switch. The empirical truth is once heartache and mental ache is so deep, it takes longer to forgive, but in time, when you do, you'll breathe spiritually, exhilarating for the first time in a longing.

XV. The unconscious has evolved to realism. What once was an invigorating journey can become a mere darkness, and the ones we called friends sometimes grow smaller while becoming a shadow when broken loyalism becomes a deception, brutal, betrayal, contemptuous, and angst.

XVI. Friends will stray away, and those are the times you need friends for strength, but the real strength can be reflected in your mirror, and that's when you realize the greater friend. It's up to you to discover the inner id and nature that's reflected from the mirror. Seek admission into yourself what's beautiful and let that be your strength.

XVII. Sometimes it's typical to think you found what you desire, but then the opposition can happen, causing reevaluation on your options. Conversely, when you find beauty in something that holds treasures, you may have found beauty to your heart's desire that harvest love or pain through it. The harvest is inevitable, but your senses redirect for proper discernment and perception.

XVIII. The mind is the root of the soul, for the mind controls the entire body, so what you feed the mind, what you motivate to, is coordinated from the nerves of the mind. In all, it is how you feed the mind that heightens the soul or despairs the soul. The rest of the body is just living off what's impulsive to the mind. Only the foundation (sexual appetite) has an eager mind of its own, so let no social construction fumble with your mind into thinking it's only capable of one sex because man and woman are compatible in this.

XIX. The miscellaneous waste of corrupted individuals who seek the framework of blathering you from crown is not worthy of true friendship but worthy of a prayer for their corrupted framework. Waste follows to the sewers as in all wastes. Let them repurify their deceptive deeds while remain unattached availing in prayer so waste doesn't grow on you.

XX. What's foreseeable in the eyes can't grasp the full dimensions with a simple look. Sometimes you have to look deeper to reveal the truth, reason, and purpose.

XXI. Purpose only becomes a purpose when it becomes a founder without manipulation.

XXII. Earthily justice is an error with a conscious rationalization that there is no true justice, but the true justice, which comes from heaven, is true and fair above all propaganda on earth.

XXIII. Human is part of nature, is part of the trees, the ocean, the lands, the rivers, the atmosphere, the oxygen, the plants . . . When no respect is given to the parts of nature, the human that is part of nature will soon lose its proper habitation because of polluting and destroying it.

XXIV. The exteriors of human are not entirely the same, but the interiors that keep us functioning are the same, for those are the main roots that solidify the humane in use, for we all possess blood, Spirit, and water, so we're human.

XXV. A delirious person would think there's only one way, and that way is simple, but the truth is no way of living is simple, and there are many ways like there are many roads, but one must think above the system, and the individual must work strong to avail enough to be satisfied.

XXVI. Cultivate that mankind and womankind often love drama, so cumulate the warning of not sharing everything, or you'll give an opening to dramatic nuance, for snakes feed off drama!

XXVII. Desiring Adon Olam more always leads to more blessed means in the end. Everything else can sometimes be a temporary.

XXVIII. Don't follow that which is not true to the heart, for what is true to the heart administers the Spirit. Compromising the heart gives the Spirit a fowl impression that will harvest sorrow for choosing the untrue direction.

XXIX. Know that the signature of God is in the hearts, not in the flesh, so what's a multitude of discernments is true to what the heart covers. Through this, you'll become substantially obsolete and realize that humanity has a comparison of God's signature, then love for all will follow.

XXX. Learn that not everyone has the same definition of love. Discernments will follow on the propaganda of love, but what few fail to realize is love is the verb, for love rectifies the actions of lifestyle, not the subject of noun.

XXXI. What's foreseeable is only foreseeable in the Spirit. What's seeable is only seeable in the eyes, but sometimes the eyes can be a deceiver. The foreseeable has to be speculated to understand its character before the seeable.

XXXII. To dispute the original is to become extraordinary, for there's a true id in core of beings that's disputing the originals, because they don't follow worldly construction but are unique in their own way.

XXXIII. It's best to pardon yourselves from contentious individuals, for they only want the moon in the moment you want the sun. Don't allow your character's light dim to satisfy another. Happiness often gravitate envious personalities from others. That's the time a pardon is needed unless you have enough spiritual strength to support their dreadful contention and envy.

XXXIV. The weight of sins is carried on Adonai Yahawashi Christ's shoulders, not your own, for your acceptance of him makes you "made free from the law of sin and death.[20]" Fair no matter on what sins have been done, this scripture must be engraved in their hearts for an abundant living while disregarding the disdained. Others will have dissensions and bring upon contempt, but when you engrave that scripture, you're free from karma of wages of sin and death.

XXXV. There's a structure of atmospheres in us that forms emotions, but the challenge is breathing and rejecting certain atmospheres that maybe a hazard to the Spirit.

XXXVI. Emotional attachment is a natural phase in all humans, so don't burden yourselves with stupidity in thinking you should have solid hearts, for if you do, you'll be a caged being who's alien to the human.

XXXVII. The covenant is who you let in to your harvesting heart that brings the difference on rather leaves will fall or leaves will spring. Leaves are the Spirit, the emotion, and the love rapturous. This is a mystery for everyone, it's like Proverbs were you have to figure out how it relates to you. The clue is the covenant is your emotion and Ahavah.

XXXVIII. Suffering sometimes can bring an individual close to God, for that's the moment individuals often become more devoted, but that's the time the individual may suffer more for forgetting God. Focusing more admiration to God is a step to a more claim of therapy.

XXXIX. A laundry of filth needs a new detergent, and that detergent comes from a changing in the environment. Changes don't come hypnotically but in conscious action.

---

[20] Romans 8v2 King James Version.

XL. Natural cure comes from nature itself, and this nature is the doctorate of God's framework. Framework is the cultivation of reason, purpose, and existence (ontology).

XLI. Not everyone has the same temperament, but the temperament within itself if proven adversary is worth interrogating their own persona to discover the depths that make it adversary to develop a personal transformation.

XLII. Learn the propaganda but don't let that propaganda become your agenda, for spiritual liberation is your agenda, and the divine rights to free from construction.

XLIII. Compromising often against your liberation leads to internal arcanum of anger that will soon burst its way to mantle.

XLIV. Even though earth shatters from the uprising of mantle unequivalently in struggles, havoc, and sufferings, there's still beauty from a discernment of thanks for presence of Ahavah, living and Adon Olam. Mantle is a temporary heat that will soon cool of, this is symbolic to shatters and earth is within us, for were made of blood, water, and Spirit, we are earth's elemental and that's a discernment of fair quality within the Lord's (Adon Olam) temperance. The important thing is to keep moving forward against the shatters with faith and hope but the greater is love. Love is the discernments of the greater seeker and challenge to comprehend but it begins within the individual that will prowess vocation, telos, and overall individualism. (cf. Ephesians 3v17-19). Shalom.

XLV. Love is in the air, and every air that is breathed in by the living is capable of love. Just know that some minds are fractured, so it may be harder for air to circulate in some areas of the living.

XLVI. At certain times, you have to travel to strange lands to find a significant love that always been craved for, so we have to keep in mind not to get too comfortable and grounded on one destination for lifetime but journey.

XLVII. Discerning your passions with prudency fairs the soul and vessel; to help guide your spiritual vessel vigorously study the **Holy Scriptures** as the key to soul and heaven, the **Philokalia** volumes as the inspiration of the vessel, and fervent prayers to grasp Ahavah, for these are all aesthetic through love for love, beauty for discernment and art for aspiration, naturalism and inspiration.

Part II:

Christianity and Church, Yahawashi Anarchism and Spirituality

This part covers the discovering of the importance of purpose of dreams and visions, the spiritual insightful things that various individuals don't acknowledge, and prayers.

Chapter VII:
Intro of Soulful Medicines

"As kings, we need to reverence the art of soulful self-healing without manipulation of the secular, then you'll harvest direction from the light."

Soulful medicines are about the faith beyond what is speculated to a conscious of spiritual healing of the soul and body connecting to Yahawah. Some individuals experience tragic events, some experience dolorous sickness, and some experience heartaches. Christ taught symbolic meaning of the candlesticks. The candlesticks are resemblance of our vessel, and every candlestick is capable of receiving light. Some candles don't light up so quickly because they refuse the light but seek darkness; however, when the candlestick is lit within an individual, it must be strived to hold on to that light to receive good spirit (Luke 11v33–36). Certain individuals don't believe there is a soul, just a cynical (such as Atheist) belief of scientology but the ones who believe.

The Adon Olam said in **Yechezkel (Ezekiel) 11v19,**[21] "And I will give them a lev echad, and I will put a ruach chadashah (new regenerated spirit) within you; and I will remove the lev heaven (heart of stone) out of their basar, and will give them a lev basar;

Unfolded version, **Yechezkel (Ezekiel) 11v19** means Adon Olam "will give" us "a one and complex unity" "chest, heart, mind, will, opinions, spirit, understanding"; and Adon Olam "will put a new regenerated spirit

---

[21] Scripture taken from Orthodox Jewish Bible.

within" us; and Adon Olam "will remove the heart of stone out of" our "flesh and blood and will give" us "flesh and blood" "a chest, heart, mind, will, opinions, spirit, understanding"; therefore, what was old becomes new.

The *Nag Hammadi Scriptures* ([The True Testimony (44, 30–45, 6])[22] clarifies when an individual understands their identity by knowing themselves and knowing Yahawah, this individual will have become a savorer to themselves and crowned with an infinite crown without diminish.

A strong and long root doesn't break but has the possibility of curving or bending, but no matter what, if constantly nourished with living water, the root continues to grow. We are the root, and YHWH is the spiritual living water that we harvest, and that's the very foundation of development. The bending or curving is an adversity trying to counter block the Spirit from heightening. **Brother IG** mentioned similarities on his song "**Walk with Me**" from *Soul Searching* album and song "**Once of the Same Minds**" from *Off the Crooked Path* album.

Family people take into consideration that someone out there is suffering, looking for answers, because they've been touched with so much bad doctrine, dolor, and Ra from others. They've begun to lose love for the Yahawah. For one thing, majority of the world will be against the ones who follow Christ, but the world would be dimmed if Christianity is taken away, for civilizations need a torch; otherwise, they'll be lost. Therefore, it is the world that needs Christians, not the other way around. Signature of Yahawah resides in everyone regardless of the ones rejecting the Yahawah; Yahawah is there. Listening to one of my favorite songs from **Earl "DMX" Simmons**, "**A Minute for Your Son**" expresses the realism of calling to Adon Olam when thankful for keeping a Spirit under the Adon Olam's covenant and seeking consistent strength through rough times.

~ 2014   *A Letter to the Charismatic Princes and Princess*   **Journal**

Adolescents and college students, I can relate to times being tough, especially when trying to preserve your faith. Personally, I've come to

---

[22]   The *Nag Hammadi Scriptures*, page 622.

notice my past surroundings of how some of the princes and princesses have a hard time fitting into a community in your age-group when you're charismatic. Many hype persuasions come toward the youth, for that's one of the main things the adversary preys upon, the moment to seek to devour or convert the youth toward their error of ways. They attack youths, preying on charismatic youths to change their ways by becoming an atheistic and agnostic, joining Luciferian occults, converting to Muslim, or joining movement that you're against. Believe me, princes and princesses, your trials are not only your own, for many charismatic individuals have been up against such persuasions, including myself. The power is resilience and faith, which gives the individual liberation. Many parents are probably not even aware of all the trials you go through. Many probably don't even realize that the professors (who some pose as Sunday schoolteachers and Christians) can give these persuasions intelligently to alter charismatic thoughts on Christianity doctrine by professing authors of the books were not the actual saints, government authorities created a false doctrine to store order, and persuasions of certain Gospels are in vain, trying to intelligently withdraw charismatic youth from Yahweh's conduct and persuasively create a more diverse belief through other religions against Christianity and other clever deceptions professors or students try to alter.

The medicine is to sustain the faith of Christ within your hearts, the very willpower of rejecting all doctrines that try to pull you from the fundamentals of Christianity itself, such as faith that Christ is the Savior and Atonement for our sins, preserving his Word to remain truth to the heart, investing in becoming a Christian theologian, and remaining in a gathering of Christian brethren and sisters who share the same faith when your mind is loud (procreating migraines or aggravations or confusions) from the social pressures of heathens. Elder snakes prey on the youth to withdraw individuals from the faith. Personally, I believe music artist **Andy Mineo** had similar experience just by listening to his songs "**Young**" and "**Pressure**" in his album *Formerly Known*.

Princes and princesses, think not that you're alone, for many will persecute because Christianity itself holds greater value; that's why there are so many attacks toward Christendom itself. But think not that you're alone, for there may be some like-minded individuals who are your neighbors that you're not even aware are Christians. Civilization is engraved subconsciously with markings, signatures, cultures, arts, and communications of YHWH (the Father, the Son, and the Holy

Ghost). Christianity itself is subconsciously and consciously of Ahavah is surrounding you. Christianity is symbolically surrounding Western Civilization; when you go to certain hotels or motels the Bible is sometimes (or often) right in the room, when you attend various stores theirs crosses, in work place's there's sometimes an individual that's a Christian that share a daily Word from the Bible or glorify a testimony, when attending a hospital and you pass by a room theirs sometimes prayer groups or Ahavah in the midst, magazines broadening in the Christendom faith, news of Christianity spreading global from masses of media, from television shows or movies there's subliminally symbolisms of Christianity. Subconsciously, Christology is communicated often; some are just not aware of it. For instance, films like *Man of Steel, Notorious, Fast and Furious, Book of Eli, The Matrix Trilogy, Star Wars Saga, The Best Man Holiday, Blade Trinity*, and many other films have a subconscious part of Christology. In addition, even shows like *The Walking Dead, The Leftovers, Ray Donovan, Lost, Sons of Anarchy, Vikings, The Americans*, etc., and certain major characters in comics (DC and Marvel) as well subconsciously or consciously have a piece of Christology. You're not alone in Christian spirituality! Perhaps even some of you, princes and princesses, want to turn your faith into Christianity. Just know if it's in your heart to want this than Christ has already pulled you into the covenant. An individual may be in the situation with parents who don't approve (or may abandon or harm a child just for turning to the Christian faith like in the film ***God's Not Dead*** as a visual example). There's no need to feel like you're lying to Christ if you've already accepted him as Savior. You can just subliminally channel their beliefs but know within yourself that truly, your love is for Christ, for He knows your heart. —J.S.J.

𝔐𝔢𝔡𝔦𝔠𝔦𝔫𝔞𝔩 𝔗𝔯𝔢𝔢 𝔬𝔣 𝔏𝔦𝔣𝔢

Diagram created by **John Shelton Jones**
Inspired from the Kabalistic Tree of Life

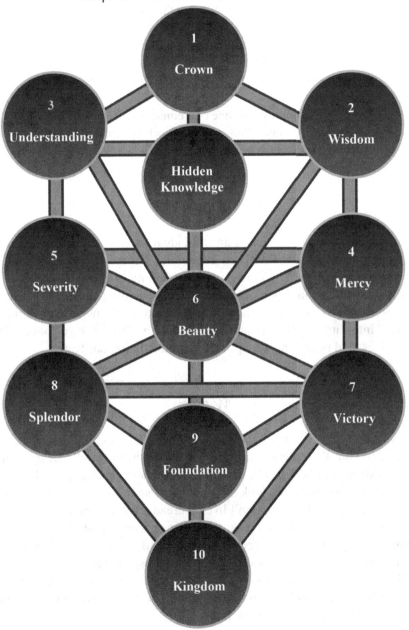

Medicinal Spirit, Inside Mirror

Therapy becomes a harmony, and that harmony is built on levels,
No one knows how to upscale another, for it has to come from the inside grails,
Striking inflicts at the mirror and hatred to the being of creator,
Causes hate in mirror too and abused flesh to the author,
Changes come from its prudence and rationalism liberation,
Not its pardon,
A mirror is but a substance of a conscious,
But identity says "let me fly" when journeying from the subconscious to the conscious.

Crown

The stage is the crown, which an individual receives from Christ once the individual has accepted Him as savior; thereby, they'll be ordained as kings and priests. The crown is the beginning of the cycle of how an individual finds sainthood. The challenge is holding on to the royalty within the conscious even when devils seek to break them. What shines is our integrity, loyalty, redemption from Yahawashi, love, honor for ourselves, and becoming strength while rationalizing our truths.

Wisdom

In wisdom, we have to cultivate that there are light and darkness in each one of us, but the determining essence is which one you'll let gasp the Spirit. Many individuals will proclaim to be fine counselors, but the only individual who can really look after another's soul is the wisdom of itself cultivating vigorous study. Can't live on bread alone for thirst follows; the question is which will you drink, the water or soda? Wisdom only comes from seeking the truth from adventuring into life itself. These adventures can come from theology, loveology, positive psychology, sociology, and a little scientology. Scientology, however, I don't say have a belief in this as a religion but simply as an understanding in rationality, humanity, and individuality, not for religion or faith.

Brethren and sisters, don't acquaint yourselves with ologies of "astrology, the stargazers, the monthly prognosticators . . .,"[23] for the essence of wisdom builds in strength, come from wisdom, for wisdom builds the conscience for stronger intelligent direction but it's the strength of the mind that is relied upon to make a surpass on what's trivial in misery to better substance a positive liberation and when this wisdom has gained a positivity to the conscience it is wisdom but if it gives negativity then nothing much was learned so it can't be wisdom but an internal suffering. On the contrary, it's important not to worship or associate yourselves to what's unliberated to the conscience and soul. Brethren and sisters, don't be naïve to what intelligence can be substantial, for the intelligence may lead you even closer to your faith in Christianity (or denominations of Christendom). The factor is to utilize what peace of information can be beneficial, and throw the others as spam if they seem withdrawing from faith (* I even expect an individual to do this with my book if it seems unliberated by your conscience and soul).

Understanding

In understanding, we often look for truth, but times of the conscience can be headaches or mind traveling to the truth. A simple mind that doesn't seek complexity will often remain subtle and don't articulate more of its meaning; but the individual who seeks complexity is a rolling stone closer to the divinity. The only way to truly have an understanding of something is to search the root of the studies, and it will lead you to a place of understanding. Change is consumable in understanding. The only reason to prohibit certain counselors is if it causes an individual to adapt a changeability in the faith of Christendom and disturbs the Spirit's liberation. A rooted dictionary is from the consist longing of understanding the reason, the meaning, the purpose, the chronological order, the hidden manuscripts, the unstable mind of construction, and the correlations on how it relates to realism and the heart, and that, my brethren and sisters, is the rooted dictionary, for it's in our minds and the materials we utilize to bring forth understanding.

---

23 Isaiah 47:13 King James Version.

Mercy

Mercy is not always easily given nor forgiven, but the concept of mercy can be looking for an outlook on things before having touchy conclusion and permitting its closure without discovering its realism. Someone can say, "Please forgive me," and the other can reply, "Okay, I forgive you," but majority still have the continuity to reminisce their mercy in error on should they really forgive them or merciless on thoughts of reason for grudges. Mercy is a human element that all is capable of, but the logic is will you forget? And the analogy is if you've forgotten, then you've learned nothing. In truth that the Bible says to forgive one another, but that doesn't mean forget. Forgetting and forgiving are two distinguished words. Forgiving is letting go of the harshness they've victimized another with to free yourselves. Forgetting is perpetrating like it never happened and learning nothing from it because of naiveties.

Severity

What's crucial is the character of who you are and how you connect with the world and how your reality is separate from the reality of the worldly. Pain, suffering, grief, and evil all in all are inevitable. The trick is to look at the substance of how it made you stronger.

~ 2003–2006   *Physiological Suffering*   **Journal**

Beginning at the age of twelve, I begun suffering chronic stomachaches. Personally, at that moment, I didn't understand why, and then I asked God why He let this happen to me. Since I suffered for three years with chronic stomachaches, it became so severe that I couldn't process food and could barely walk sometimes. A few could even walk to open the door when someone was knocking, so I made effort by crawling. During those moments, Zantac Extra Strength for acid reflex was my friend up until 2006. So finally, my primary doctor referred me to a radiologist for a scan on my stomach and found that I had three stones in my small intestines in size of marbles. The primary doctor referred me to Duke Hospital to perform surgery, and then I died for a few seconds. When I woke up, they notified me that I had about one thousand small gallstones in my gallbladder when they removed it with laser surgery along with the three gallstones in my intestines. Then I said to myself, "I'm amazed I got through that." Soon, as I took the pain medicine they've prescribed me, I noticed having an allergic reaction until the Benadryl cured it. —J.S.J.

This was just one of the many things I've went through, but the point is many of us go through a moment of severity to make us stronger. Now not all severity is just, for sometimes it's in act of an adversary, but the point is you've made it through. The touch of dolor, contempt, Ra, and pain has in some momentum touched every individual, I strongly believe. There's no way of getting out of it. The majority comes from people, for they've tried to convert another to the faith with force, or caused sufferings (cognitive, spiritual, physical, or intellectual), or out of matters of jealousy or enviousness, or economic struggles from poverty.

Hidden Knowledge

What's hidden is within us that very momentum of fiery looking to overtake being caged. Hidden knowledge is God's signature of your distinction from everyone else. Don't allow segregation of your hidden momentum. Hidden knowledge is also the grasp of faith and the spiritual dimension that's illogical to the conscious. What is hidden is within.

Beauty

In nature surrounded by beauty, sometimes we just don't pay attention to the beauty that surrounds us, but the essence of beauty is the discovery of how it communicates to your spirit. That determines its beauty. Beauty is nothing but fortifying and solidifying the appropriate determinism on how it remains true to you, true to existence; how it perceives your aesthetic personality; and how it captures your hedonistic portion of your emotion and overall, the clarity of faith in itself giving the possibility of abundant discovery. Beauty can be a calligraphy of ourselves from the physical features, the loving features, the household, the view of outdoor nature, the insects, the animals, the children given divine inspiration and happiness, the martial arts, the body embracement, the natural talents, the social gatherings sharing good times and communicating in laughter, and the *epicurean* of physiological and psychological.

Victory

The surroundings of victory come from prosperity. The essence of not giving up in the moment of feeling down is victory and how the mentality correlates the positive ambitions that meet its needs. Not victory based on war but victory based on perseverance that proves genuine to its cause. Whatever personal cause you have is your vendetta, and that precedes the liberation of victory when the causes are measured clarity of the relief of vendetta.

Splendor

Splendor is your luster in life, not fully on appearance alone but the fullness of Spirit, which others who lack will envy. Something of grand is difficult to find, but when you've leveled into that dimension, life seems all the brighter. But this is the level many will try to deprave your grand. Don't let another steal your joy, as thieves in the night seek what's not earned of theirs but disregard the foolish contradictions for purity to the duty of that splendor.

Foundation

Foundation is the loving in its nature, the portion of heaven from sexual liberation and procreation of younglings. The very foundation is a genesis repeating itself in newer proportions. The primitive of foundation is the embracement of its innate propensities without the regard of compressing it. On the contrary, the foundation can be one of the most dangerous of life. Dangerous because sex can lead to misery, contempt, induce real traumatic rape, promiscuity, and addiction which can give unwise decisions and direction. The reason is because sex can lead to earthily heaven when negative behaviors of fornication and adultery can lead to earthily hell. There needs to be an opening on what some individuals go through. I'm going to give many inferences. I decided to keep it real.

Certain individuals go through forced prostitution from sex trafficking to being pimped, and the ones responsible or the ones paying think this moment of darkness is okay because they're providing a service and pleasure to another.

Certain individuals are being molested and raped at early ages by the ones close to the family, the individuals who are family. Certain guardians are pimping them and raping them.

Certain individuals are being sold from arranged marriages that they're not even given the opportunity to make their own divine decisions.

Certain individuals are taking wives and daughters by force and making them sex slaves, and doing this, they're physiologically hurting the body and creating a broken spirit.

Certain individuals are looking for brutal ways of the sexual with a pairing of pain and violence, inflicting contempt, and treating another as a worthless being to something of an animal.

These are the problems of how a good-spirited individual remodels the minds into thinking it's a natural action. There's a problem with this because every individual who goes through something similar or worst of this sometimes feed into thinking it's okay, but the turning point is proving to yourself that you're capable of being better than the adversary once you've delivered yourselves from them and not create a repetition of what was done to you to another. This is the power of turning a foundation into something positive. Don't follow behind bogus viewpoints that trauma went through in the past somehow validates rights to make trauma a tradition.

Kingdom

The kingdom is your earthily heaven looking to ascend to Yahawah and Yahawashi in the moment of near death. This comes with a mysterious award that's something to look forward to from all Christian brethren and sisters. In its very moment is when there will be Christendom of union among all who follow Christ.

Chapter VIII:
Our Kingdom, Our
Vessel, One Church

Our vessel and the church are one union. When you begin to harness that understanding, you'll realize the church is our soul and mentality, not a building.

W e must all build ourselves through with the mentality of Yahushua to make one sense, for the path is narrow. We must focus our senses in a biblical worldview, which is founded by the Christ to guide us. Following the worldview of everything is not justified as biblical worldview, but it is a rule that we should abide from the law of the humanity. Although I do believe Yahushua also inspired the Christian Anarchism movement, obeying the righteous Word of the Lord, we are fused to one church—Elohim. A transformation phase is vital to the Holy Spirit given this message through Romans 12v2 scripture:

> *And be not conformed to this world: but be ye transformed by the renewing of your mind, that ye may prove what is that good, and acceptable, and perfect, will of God. (KJV)*

Jesus said, "Renounce the whole world and the whole matter therein and all its cares and all its sins, in a word all its associations which are in it, that ye may be worthy of the mysteries of the Light and be saved from all chastisements which are in the judgements."[24]

Keep that scripture, Romans 12v2, in your mind because there's a strong meaning in it. As physical fitness is important, so is spiritual fitness, but spiritual fitness is far more important because it determines where the soul will reside in the afterlife. Like all hard work, we must remember that spiritual fitness is not a simple task mastered overnight, for a kingdom is not built in a day but a long process of time. In the *Philokalia* volume 1, "Evagrios the Solitary" on prayer text, number 86, describes how spiritual knowledge is essential:

Spiritual knowledge has great beauty: it is the helpmate of prayer, awakening the noetic power of the intellect to contemplation of divine knowledge.

You may ask what in the world is a **noetic**. This is spiritual enlightenment, reason, and knowledge. A *noetic thinker* is an individual of reason, knowledge, and spiritual touch of powerful intellect. Some people consider them prophets or oracles. They are above average conscious thinkers and pass an average individual's understanding because an average person thinks in logic, although some individuals use this gifted talent to invoke control and deception while casting evil deities, such as spells and rituals. In the *Nag Hammadi Scriptures*, faith and love go hand in hand—one to receive, the other to give. Our origin is Hebrew, which Lord messaged inferring one church, one vessel, and one kingdom. There's no such thing as not being a fully accepted Christian because of birth origin, for we are all His children. Don't be deceived by modern worldviews. (**Important:** *see* **Appendix I: Bible Conspiracies** for what many are not aware of is the attack on the bibles though changing the doctrine)

---

[24] *The Gnostic Bible the Pistis Sophia Unveiled: The Secret Teachings of Jesus Recorded by His Disciples*, Third Book, Chapter 102, 454.

Nag Hammadi Scriptures:

> ## Faith and Love (61,36–62,6)
> *Faith receives, love gives. (No one can [62] receive) without faith, and no one can give without love. So to receive we have faith and to love we give. If someone gives without love, that person gets no benefit from what was given.[47] Anyone who receives something but does not receive the Lord is still a Hebrew.*

Theology in Everyone

Deep down, everyone who is in faith of the Reformation (such as Christians, Protestants, Jehovah's Witnesses, Presbyterians, Baptists, Lutherans, Jesuits, Seventh–day Adventist, Calvinism, Anglicans, Apologetics, and Mormons), Orthodox Christianity, Coptic Christians, Cathars, Encratite, Rastafarians, Nestorians, Melkites, Amish, Mennonites, Ebionites, Catholics, Hebrew Israelites, Nicene-Constantinopolitan Creed, Familists, Puritans, Judeo-Christians, and Judaism are theologians, and the ones who don't follow the Holy Bible are still theologians to a certain point of clarity. Theology can simply mean seekers of the holy doctrines and spiritual philosophy to solidify understanding and truth. Although keep in mind that kabbalah, alchemy, angelology and demonology, and Christian Gnosticism are not branches of religion but a cultivation of knowledge, practices, and/or mystical arts. However, despite theology, not all biblical faiths and alternative cultivations are on the same pathway, but all have similar doctrines with different philosophical speculation. Your faith is your primary, and your alternative (which is the helping tool or add-on interest) is your secondary. The reason most individuals seek an additional cultivation in faith bases is because of the fiery spirit of willpower to grasp more knowledge and arts on faith tradition so not everyone has the same philosophical speculation. The previous scripture, *Faith and Love (61,36–62,6)*, lets everyone know that you are still part of His creation, and there should be no segregations as others would segregate in accords to the twelve tribes of Israel and everyone. There are people in this world who will try to make you and others feel they don't fit and not capable of entering Heaven, but that is falsity (Galatians 3v28, Ephesians 4v32, John 13v34–35, Colossians 3v11,

Titus 1v12–13). According to Yahawah and Yahawashi, we're all Hebrews and are all capable of being written in the book of life regardless of what others say.

According to *Karl Barth*:[25]'

Theology is science seeking the knowledge of the Word of God spoken in God's work—science learning in the school of the Holy Scripture, which witnesses to the Word of God and science laboring in the quest for truth, which is inescapably required of the community that is called by the Word of God.

Charles Hodge[26] defined theology as:

The exhibition of the facts of Scripture in their proper order and relation with the principles or general truths involved in the facts themselves and which pervade and harmonize the whole.

My Definition of Theology   Journal

My proverb of **theology** is a doctrine study of overall foundation of biblical notions, *transcendence*, an scriptures relativist, researcher and conservative of the Word of God with sensible and measured pursuit of infinite growth, a marriage of the spiritual knowledge (Gnosis), and unutterable love for the faith in constant pursuits and mission for truths with devoutness to prowess faith and love from faith's vocation and *noetic* that's flamed within that gives us the calling (*vocation*) of *theologian*. For *theology* pursues an endless journey of the Lord's knowledge while maintaining the faith and is the strength hold of creed that manifest purpose, *ontology* and guardianship of the soul and wisdom, in a relation, a sound mind for divinity. For the sound mind is *Yahawah's farming* ([Farming (79,18–32])[27]: faith, hope, love, and knowledge. Faith is the elemental earth which is the root of life. Hope is the elemental water of purging and nurturing substance that surpasses or mitigate burdens and severity with providence and fortitude. Love is the elemental air which crowns, splendors, and is growth. Knowledge is the elemental light which is received from ripeness. —J.S.J.

---

[25]   Karl Barth, *Evangelical Theology: An Introduction* (Grand Rapids: Eerdmans, 1963), 49–50.

[26]   Charles Hodge, *Systematic Theology* (Grand Rapids: Eerdmans, 1952), 1:19.

[27]   The *Nag Hammadi Scriptures*, page 182.

Many individuals precede a process known as *determinism*, the doctrine of natural intellect by determining the belief of what is truth to individuality, free in the sense of being uncompelled. The other is *libertarian*,[28] the one who upholds the principles of faith tradition although an advocate of the doctrine of free will. However, God doesn't say be a *libertarian* because advocate of free will is not always prudent but often compromise, instead God systematically evolve *sensible* beings, which is the course of declaration or deed that's in agreement with wisdom and prudence, not the subject of sensitivity no matter how the word sensible is fabricated.

From The Doctrine of Infinite Growth

Lead us up beyond unknowing and light,
　　up to the farthest, highest peak
　　　of mystic scripture,
　　where the mysteries of God's Word
　　　lie simple, absolute and unchangeable
　　　in the brilliant darkness of a hidden silence.
　　Amid the deepest shadow
　　　they pour overwhelming light
　　on what is most manifest.
　　Amid the wholly unsensed and unseen
　　　they completely fill our sightless minds
　　with treasures beyond all beauty.

This poem is what I consider in theology as measured pursuit of infinite growth.

—Dionysius the Areopagite (sixth century)

Awakening to everyone, doctrine is extremely important for it's the top ark of the Yahawah and Yahawashi testament to us. Many individuals lose their faith because of following ministers, rabbis, apostles, evangelists, and so forth and translators tarnishing the Bible. The true doctrine, which is accuracy of the King James Version and Orthodox Jewish Bible, utilized in our understanding without removing, adding, and changing the Word of God. Yahweh, in the book of Revelation, chapter 22 verses 18 to 19, said,

---

[28] *Webster's Third New International Dictionary, Unabridged, s.v.* "Libertarian," accessed March 10, 2015, http://unabridged.merriam-webster.com.

For I testify unto every man that heareth the words of the prophecy of this book, If any man shall add unto these things, God shall add unto him the plagues that are written in this book: [1]And if any man shall take away from the words of the book of this prophecy, God shall take away his part out of the book of life, and out of the holy city, and from the things which are written in this book. (KJV)

The Lord said that specifically, the book of Revelation (because it said book and prophecy "which is singular" in that particular prophecy), to not tamper with His Word in any way, and if you do, you won't enter the Kingdom of Heaven. *This puzzled me!* If you fear God, you'll be mindful of Revelation, especially if you're a translator. Be mindful and use a journal to solidify your understanding of Revelation, but don't add or remove anything in the book of Revelation. Journalizing is the only way to utilize it for Jehovah wants His Words preserved.

Union

Union actually means "religion" from the Latin word *religare*, seeking divinity while bonding a connection with our Adon Olam and fellowshipping with human beings. "For through him we both have access by one Spirit unto the Father. Now therefore ye are no more strangers and foreigners, but fellow citizens with the saints, and of the household of God" (Ephesians 2v18–19 Authorized KJV). The union of individuals having faith in Christ and the Father are on one union just differences of *theology* and therefore are considered neighbors, and should be treated with love is the true loving union with Lord of the Most High, not through segregation, for the individual's that are followers of the Father and Christ are the *Christendom* church.

~ 2001–Present *Charismatic Fellowship: from Corrupt to True* Journal

The footsteps of my journey visiting many buildings that are insinuated churches, an individual may ask what's an insinuated church from a real church? Churches that portray unity of Christians in a building is not actually a church but what defines church is Christendom itself uniting spiritual direction to Yahawashi only, for an individual is a Church for the body and Spirit is a temple but it's how an individual administers it that obtains divinity. In addition, discovering many deceptions or bad doctrine, I begin to ask the question "What has become of church fellowship when it's vexed with wrongful doctrine and prejudice?" The few churches I've visited were driven by greed of money rather than love for saints. One church I visited asked for seven offerings (love, food, minister, rent, choir, God's and gas offering) and two tithes (tithes to the prime minister and donation). In that moment, I perceived enlightenment that this is not the Lord's way and that this church is surely vexed with greed. Then I traveled to other churches that revealed the love of creating commotion. This was surely not of God's love. Through my observance, I've come to notice that various ministers not only teach the doctrine to invoke prejudice remarks but also teach saints to an undermined understanding of the scriptures, for some ministers see words they are unfamiliar with (or saints) and insinuate an interpretation that's the opposite of scriptures because they don't use theology nor seek the origin of the meanings. For this issue various Christian individuals become non-denomination Christians for they'll attend many different denomination Christendom synagogues for the appropriate one, many join Christian Orthodoxy; there's a book on this analogy called *Everywhere Present: Christianity in a One-Storey Universe* by Stephan Freeman. For instance, a minister or saint can see a word like fervent and completely overlook its meaning. In 2005, when I first attended Manna Church, I felt a truer unity for diversity as beautifully complex. No biased remarks, service given a moment for everyone to greet with agape love, and there was order in the church. Conversely, I learned something truer about church, "for church is but a vessel connected to Yahawashi," then I become compulsive to doctrine, religion, and humane passion. Then I discovered Christian theology. Through this, I discovered essences of doctrine, religion, and humane passion. Various saints would imply many regulations of what's improper, what's heathen, and what's the proper reformation, but I've come to realize many fights against one another but don't acknowledge they read the exact Bible they do but all have different philosophical differences. It's important to unite, not segregate, an essence I've come to invest deeply. The reason I became a Christian theologian is to preserve my proverb of *theology* and measured pursuit of infinite growth as a progressive scholar for unbounded pursuit to the YHWH, and harmonize clarity. —J.S.J.

It's time for all the Reformates (such as Christians, Protestants, Anglicans, Jehovah's Witnesses, Presbyterians, Baptists, Lutherans,

Seventh–day Adventist, Jesuits, Calvinists, Apologetics, and Mormons), Orthodox Christianity, The Salvation Army, Coptic Christians, Rastafarians, Catholics (however, there are errors with Catholicism because in Christianity flagellation, vain repetition, confessing to priests and praying to Mary is prohibited), Hebrew Israelites (know that most Hebrew Israelites are dogmatic about the twelve tribes and distinction of ethnicities. Certain ones come off as prejudice, but not all, and prejudice is not of YHWH and rejects the Talmud), Judeo-Christians, Cathars, Encratite, Nestorians, Melkites, Amish, Mennonite, Ebionites, Nicene-Constantinopolitan Creed, Familists, Puritans and Jews (Judaism doesn't except the doctrine of Christology; however, one day faith and truth will give vocation to their hearts and minds; and Christianity doesn't obey the Talmud) to unite with the understanding that we all direct our study to the **Christendom** (means *a worldwide community of Christians*).

Throughout Christendom, I've realized people are losing the union more and more because of bad doctrine, feeling concealed as if everything is a sin, and many other things. Just when I thought I was the only one recognizing this, listening to **Flame**'s album *Forward* particularly songs "Knowing the Times" and "Moving Forward," then I knew I wasn't the only one thinking the same thing. Personally, I believe this is what YHWH spoke in Hebrews 9v10 about the "Restoration, Reformation," not the New World Order but a unity of Christendom.

Christian Spirituality

Christian spirituality is nature from the infinity Adon Olam. Through teachings of a sacred union, we broaden our capacity for understanding nature and provide a higher arch of hope and awards to come. Spirituality is not totally irrational but also rational in contributing a potential of meaning and knowledgeable wisdom to provide clarity of proper judgment, such as Proverbs. In the Bible, there are many laws, commandments, and histories on what I like to call **Royal-Kingdom Laws of Divinity**, a way of guiding us from the corruptible evil spirits, strengthening our clarity and substance to our morality.

> True religion is that relationship, in accordance with
> reason and knowledge, which man establishes with the

infinite world around him, and which binds his life to that infinity and guides his actions . . . and leads to the practical rules of the law: do to other as you would have them do unto you . . . Reason is the power man possesses to define his relationship to the universe. Since the relationship is the same for everyone, thus religion unites men. Union among gives them the highest attainable well-being, on both the physical and the spiritual level. (Leo Tolstoy from *Confessions*, 1882)

In Reformation spirituality, there's a dualistic of faith and hope to saving our spirit that makes us truth or if an individual doesn't believe is an error (1 John 4v6). Through acceptance of Adonai Jesus Christ as the propitiation for ours sins and love makes our spirit more at union with the Trinity, while we make effort to cast out fear (1 John 4v7–18). There are actually three Trinities:

The heavenly Trinity 1 John 5v7 "For there are three that bear record in heaven, the **Father**, the **Word**, and the **Holy Ghost**: and these three are one."

The earthily Trinity 1 John 5v8 "And there are three that bear witness in earth, the **Spirit**, and the **water**, and the **blood**: and these three agree in one." Blood and water creates flesh, while Spirit is gives eternal direction and providence or improvidence if not *prudent*. The three in one is called a *vessel*.

The redemption Trinity 2 Corinthians 13v14 "The **grace of the Lord Jesus Christ**, and the **love of God**, and the **communion of the Holy Ghost**, (be) with you all. Amen." (Matt. 28v19 confirms this through baptism.)

The Bible is not the religion but the Gospels. Gospels come with truths and guidance, history, testaments, and laws.

Essence of Faith

Now Emunah "faith" is the substance of things for which we have tikvah "hope." Emunah "faith" is the conviction of things not seen. —Yehudim (Hebrews) 11v1 OJB

The main essence of Christianity is through faith, and faith is beauty, which is part of the aesthetic philosophy of a nature greater than the conscious existence itself, visioning a higher power and treasure greater than ours. Faith is the food and hope of a living being's spirit for good judgment and graceful abundant miracles from Yahawah and Yahawashi, and the power of faith creates a psychical structure of *empirical* perception with a constant growth of *transformation* for providing clarity for following future *prudent* judgments. Faith and love have no measures, for its part of the human psyche, the psychical energy of awakening a communal elixir of spiritual champagne to evoke the *teleological* and the *aesthetic* prowess for power and belief greater than the cynical and secular. Faith is focused on belief stronger than oneself with no need to nullify reason but only excel to that faith chosen. A belief can be persuaded, but not faith for it remains solid, unmovable like a huge mountain. Anyone can believe in something but a few have faith, for belief is a temporary thing, but faith is an everlasting thing that's beyond other's perception of your persona because those without it just can't comprehend. "Faith emerges before articulate speech formulates it communicable symbols, thus giving rise to intellectualized belief," a process of faith that's uncertain on how the miracle will be provided from Yahweh but will be an intellect surpassing the superego.

> The faith, understood as an accumulative consensus of sensibility and valuation, giving quality and range to the psychical thrust of the culture, determines the dimension of depth in feeling and conception within the culture.[29]
> (Bernard Eugene Meland, from *Faith and Culture*)

Giving that, quality statement rectifies how faith can touch you and another like the reflection of the 2015 film *Do You Believe?* Faith is an essence of medicine for humankind that travels beyond the dimensions of the current world no visible human without it can comprehend, for its communed with a community that share that similar bond of belief through redemption, passion, and sacred union with a hope of healing and perseverance. Faith is a consistent journey for strong intellectual and driven complexities of *vocation* and *teleological* ambiguous psyche for optimistic complexities. Faith comes with the hope of miracles from the sufferings forced to endure while having that peace of internal hope that a change for better will come. From the motion picture soundtrack *The Prince Of Egypt*, the song "When You Believe," featuring Whitney Houston and Mariah Carey, gives voice to holding strong. This is the hope internally through belief to build up to faith. Everyone has a drowning point they go through in life, but when faith is unmovable, Lucifer loses. Lucifer seeks to drown our Spirits. Everyone goes through this point in time of their lives. when struggling, sometimes I listen to uplifting music, listening to the album *13 Letters* song "**Sound**," listen to *Tedashii*'s album *Below Paradise* and *Lecrae*'s album *Gravity*.

Essence of Love through Biblical Faith Fellowship

The seeking love that many I've encountered ask what type of love biblical faith individuals use to give love to everyone, in means of distinguish from different definitions of love that many individuals

---

[29] Bernard Eugene Meland. *Faith and Culture*, 12.

mistakenly confuse themselves with. This is a doctrine of agape. *Agape* is love that is more spiritual, heartfelt, and *noetic* in nature, the doctrine followers of Yahawashi and Yahawah. In addition, loving agape is internalized as *polyamory*, poly "many" and amor "love" = many loves. **Polyamory** is classified as practitioners of communion, love, desire, or acceptance for intimate and/or companionate relationships that are broad in loving with acceptance, ethical, and independent without commitment. However, the intimacy is withdrawn because of prudence of the testaments. *Agape* is more thriving in the heart and soulful to others. Polyamory bonded with agape is more of prudence than ethical, more communion than communal, more spiritual than physical, more attentive than affectionate, and more charitable than offering. The understanding of why more prudent than ethical is because an individual of biblical faith focuses more on the doctrine than the conscience. For instance,

> If you were driving and seen someone had a car accident, the ethical thing to do is call the police and leave it to the law enforcement, but a prudent individual would carry a stranger's important information (such as wallet or purse) and follow them to the hospital and pray for them while there in operation. The next morning would properly greet them spiritual love (meaning ointment, pray for them and/or provide wine/healthy juice that you'll best determine if healthy) and charitably invite the stranger to their synagogue.

The reason why more communion than communal is because doctrine teaches us our faith is sacred, not a political campaign but a communion for Yahweh. **Communion** means the action of sharing thoughts, spiritual love, doctrine and *theology*, and *sensible* union. This is *agape*. The more spiritual than physical is the threshold of accord to *Christian polyamory* to preserve your *emunah* to your spouse will inspiring Spirits to higher capacity. Meaning a growth for spiritual in sharing the Word of God in social gatherings, giving positive influences, being attentive while preserving more energy for perseverance of your consort in relationship. Basically, giving more emunah and Ahavah to your consort while having a limitation of giving out the energy outside the intimate union. Be more concerned for others' Spirits transcending to Yahawashi (Jesus) and Yahawah (Adon Olam) so we are *attentive* (means giving care or thoughtful of others) not affectionate for *affectionate* (means a fervent action of tender and loving feelings to another's physiology and emotions) is the love reserved for spouse.

Revelation of Truth through the Knowledge of Hebraic Translations

Do you believe that Jesus is our savior? Are you aware of his true name?

The true name of our Lord and Savior has been corrupted with misleading names and confusion of true names. However, the true names are derived from the proto-Hebrew language, not the *Matres Lectionis* and the *Masoretic points* vowel system. These below are revelation of truth:

Our Holy Lord names

YHWH = Yahawah יהוה (The ancient Hebrew name) "I AM," יְהֹוָה
The Alpha (Beginning) and the Omega (Ending) of old eternal everlasting father. Truth is no human knows how deep the dimensions of YHWH go but came before all existences.
YHWH = Yahuwah or Yahweh (the actual modern Hebrew name) "I AM"
YHVH (from the *Tetragrammaton*) = Yod He Vau He; Yahveh
El Elyon = "Most High God"
El Shaddai = "Lord God Almighty"
Jehovah = "The Existing One" or "Lord"
Adon Olam = "Master of All; Eternal Ruler"

Our Holy Savior names
Yahawashi (the original ancient Hebrew name) "I AM Salvation"
Yahu'Shuah *pronounced* **Yahushua** "I AM Salvation" (believed to be the real Hebrew name)
Ancient Aramaic the name of the Messiah is *Yeshua*. However, Yahu'Shuah and Yeshua are built on Masoretic Point System that was forced upon Asia and Jews from the Greeks, but the Proto-Hebrew had no vowels during the time of Moses (whom written the first five books of Testaments). *Yahoshua/Yehoshua* (other forms of Modern Hebrew names) "I AM Salvation"; those two names are built on the Masoretic Point System. These names are commonly used in the Orthodox Jewish Bible (OJB); however, despite the name in the OJB, they are highly respected as the true name from others.

Jesus (transliterated name of our savior, translated from Greek word "Iesous")

> According the **Nag Hammadi Scriptures**, *The Gospel of Philip – Jesus's names (62,6–17)*, his full name is **Iesous nazoraios messias**, which is the name Jesus the Nazarene Christ. The meaning of his name "Jesus" means "redemption," "the Nazarene" means "truth," and "Christ" means "measured." Gathering the meaning together, you have:
> = **Redemption truth measured.**
> In biblical Latin, Jesus is "Iesus."

Adonai "My Lord, My Master"

> Adonai is often used as a conjunction with the Lord's name to specify who you're calling to. For example, in loving matters, submissive wife can just say Adonai to her husband, but to our savior, you would give voice to "Adonai Yahushua my savior, I call upon you" is clarifying who. For evil spirits can assume you're calling upon them if you don't specify.

A Title not a name: Emmanuel "God with us"
A Title not a name: "Bright and Morning Star" which is actually "Bright Morning Star" (Revelation 22v17) as given in the Geneva Bible, Holman Christian Standard Bible, Amplified Bible, Common English Bible, Complete Jewish Bible and few others translations.
A Title not a name: "King of Kings, Lord of Lords"

> Since Christ has ordained the men who have faith in him as Savior, Christ gave the brethren the title Adon "King, Lord," and Priest, yet rules over all mankind for he has the highest title among Children of Men, and nobody can get to the father without him.

Discernable Revelation, Spouse of YHWH
Elohim "Lord of the Most High; The Mighty One" but is also plural "Half Man-Female God or Gods"
Jehovah is also an androgynous name meaning "Half Male-Female."

ASHRH *"Asherah"*; Ancient name **"Ahsharah"**

אשרה ASHRH = Asherah "Lady of the Sea" Revelation 22v17 KJV "The Spirit and the *bride* say, Come . . ." The Spirit and the bride are two divines because they're both greeting and the *and* conjunction. Clarity is the Spirit is the Father (John 4v24), so the bride is who? Some would say the bride is the church which is true, but if it's means that then who is the church greeting, the church is the one's that will enter into the Kingdom, not greet a non-existent, for the church is the individuals within the Christendom. In Revelations 22v16 KJV, Jesus spoke that he is "the root and the offspring of David, and bright and morning star," believed to be a idiom misplaced word and, in the middle of "bright and morning star," which is actually "And the Bright Morning Star." "Bright Morning Star" was Venus, the goddess of love, beauty, and sexuality (procreation), for *Asherah* was known as the goddess of procreation—Great Mother Goddess, consort of Yahawah. The reason "Bright Morning Star" is because Lucifer means in Latin "light-bringer; Morning Star," and Christ didn't come from Lucifer, for He overshines. $E = mc^2$ or $m = E/c^2$, from Albert Einstein, mass/matter/life come into existence by conjoining energy and light. Energy is equated with *Root* and *God* to signify *"masculine potential." Light* can be equated with *Bright Morning Star* and *Goddess* to signify *"feminine potential"* for procreation. Both require existence of both—YHWH *Father of all*, ASHRH *Mother of all*. Jeremiah 8v7–8 spoke of the scribes of vain for not adding the wisdom given, spoke her appointed times, which many reject. Asherah is mentioned as "Queen of Heaven" in Jeremiah 44v19. In Genesis 1v26, it says "us," so who are these us after our image? The answer is god and goddess.

Thorough point of view in Proverbs chapter VIII (8) clarifies that Asherah giving knowledge to sons of man that receiver her wisdom of prudence to the Father and fearing the eternal Father, her husband and receiving her as well works in sons of man favor. "[22]The Lord possessed me in the beginning of his way, before his works of old.[22] . . . set up from everlasting, from the beginning, or ever the earth was . . .[30] I was by him, as one brought up with him: and I was daily his delight, rejoicing always before him." Judging from the chapter, Asherah is completely submissive and subservient and full of love than all women on earth and desires to only guide sons of man to heaven and excel sons of man crowns from proverbs. In ancient times, Asherah signifies "(she) who walks behind." Hebrews called upon her as mother of all mothers, Queen of queens, and intercessor (however, Christ has the title to be intercessor). However, Asherah "Queen of Heaven" warns us that her husband, Yahawah, is a jealous Lord during Proverbs VIII. Before then, in Jeremiah 7v18 and 44v19, the women would often worship Asherah and reject his law, and this made him angry. In 1967, according to historian Raphael Patai (Viegas 2011), the time of the ancient Israelites worshipped both Yahweh alongside with Asherah, though in prudence God forbid His children to worship any other God. Asherah was edited out of the KJV and other version but some kept the actual name Asherah instead of changing "Asherah" to "grove". (cf. Exod. 34v13, Deut. 7v5 and 12v3, Deut. 16v21, Judges 3v7 and 6v25–30, 1 Kings 14v15 and 23, 1 Kings (15v13, 16v33, 18v19), 2 Kings (13v6, 17v10–16, 18v4, 21v3–7, 23v4, 23v6–15) and 2 Chronicles 14–19)

My purpose is not to cause protestation on the subjection of Asherah or to provoke a worship or even for others to pray to Asherah for this would anger God or cause confusion. The purpose I brought up Asherah is the existentialism that Asherah may very well be the spouse of Yahawah and for the acknowledgement thereof that Asherah exist within the biblical text that has been overshadowed from certain biblical translations.

Hebrew without Vowels Grammar System

La	Chaa	Za	Wa	Ha	Da	Ga	Ba	Ah
ל	ח	ז	ו	ה	ד	ג	ב	א
Ta	Ya	Ka	Tha	Ma	Na	Sa	I	Pa
ט	י	כ	ת	מ	נ	ס	ע	פ
Tha	Sha	Ra	Qa	Taza				
ת	ש	ר	ק	צ				

Table I. Hebrew without Vowels Grammar System

Table II below gives a vivid calligraphy of how Hebrew has changed throughout time.

Table II. Early Hebrew Writings to Modern

Permission by Kris J. Udd, 2010
Source: http://www.bibleplaces.com/paleo_hebrew_fonts.htm

~Meditation~

Lord, my heart is full of admiration and I want to talk with you,
For I am sure you understand me, in spite of my contradictions.
It seems to me that now I learned at last what it means to love people
And why love is worn down by loneliness, pity, and anger.
What can I do more, my Lord, than to meditate on all that
And stand before you in the attitude of an implorer
For the sake of their heroism asking: Admit us to your glory.
—*Czeslaw Milosz*

There's much all of us has to understand from God, not from man. Some of us has been deceived; some individuals have been corrupted into thinking they have faith when truly, all they had was belief. What's been advertised is not all glamourous even when construction portrays it such way. Meaning not everyone admits to their suffering and faults, or their deceptive ideologies but certain individuals reflect lies. When churches fall from a deceivable corruption, individuals start to downsize it, but really, they're relying on humanity, not God, and this causes a deceivable substance. Meditating the mind is about an association of the divine, not an association with everyone else, and this association can free an individual to a more abundant way of living. Certain individuals abstain from faith in Christianity or Christendom in general because of being threatened, segregated, abandoned, or forced from attempted social pressures constructing us to withdraw from the path of light, but, brethren and sisters, if you stand firm, God will grant us eventually after death if you've reside in faith and highly believe yourselves as liberated (meaning you've lived in faith of doing the best you could even when others disagree on your theology, outlaw, and actions).

Chapter VIV:
Christ Inspires, Christian
Outlaws, and Christ Heritage

For God so loved the world, that he gave his only begotten Son, that
whosoever believeth in him should not perish, but have everlasting life.

—John 3v16

C hristian outlaws (anarchism) is heavily based on the willpower to remain faithful to the teachings of Yahawashi without thinking of the traditional humanistic democracy but forming a party of the Gospel as an outlaws guide. We understand how to become the charismatic outlaws because of interpretations of Yahawashi personality and message from Yahawah, for his personality was distinctive because he was solid to his purpose, disregarding the negative heresies spoken against him all the way. Christ's personality mainly was extravagant and possessed introvert strengths with *noetic* thinking abilities along with many other abilities unordinary. Yahawashi is the perfection of personality, and as Christian anarchist, we strive to become more like him.

Hypothesis of Yahawashi Extravagant and Introvert Personality:
Extravagant:
Aggressive in his purpose, impulsive to the Word of Yahawah, optimistic through invoking the opportunities to become purged of sins, always active in the journey to spread Adon Olam's Word, testified to be Most High Priest of the Most High God and the infinite son of the Lord of Most High. In addition, Yahawashi is restless to everlasting love, passion, and spreading truth. Yahawashi was and is always responsive to false accusations; even in the moments of crucifixion, he's affirmative to his teachings and everlasting truth.
Introvert Strengths:
Yahawashi was and is always thoughtful to impurities of humanity by giving them everlasting hope through him by cleansing all sins in matter of faith and repentance. In this way, he provided mercy and taught mercy. Passive to the ones who caused physical abuse to him because of his passion for everyone. Ensuring his testament (gospel and truth) is not void while always remaining sober. Yahawashi demonstrated peaceful union with everyone regardless of their origin and impurities.

Yahawashi carried the weight of others past our understanding of sympathy (Mark 14v34, Matthew 26v38, Luke 22v44–46). He was deeply heavy hearted and carried fully all *dolorous* from every being. Our legendary outlaw Yahawashi was a very sociable Lord, for he feasted and drunk wine with the sinners (Luke 7v33–35).

The charismatic outlaw kings have to obey by which Yahawashi bestowed are two of the greatest commandments Yahawashi has spoken in Matthew 22v37 and v39:

First greatest commandment:

[37]Jesus said unto him, Thou shalt love the Lord thy God with all thy heart,
And with all thy soul, and with all thy mind.
Second greatest commandment:

[39]Thou shalt love thy neighbor as thyself.

For this is the golden rule, "Therefore all things whatsoever ye would that men should do to you, do ye even so to them: for this is the law and the prophets.[30]"

"A good man out of the good treasure of his heart bringeth forth that which is good; and an evil man out of the evil treasure of his heart bringeth forth that which is evil: for of the abundance of the heart his mouth speaketh.[31]"

Yahawashi left ten cardinal beatitudes from Matthew 5v3–11 King James Version, which indicated that blessings are the ones who are spiritually hungry; the individuals who are merciful, pure in heart; those that are humble peacemakers, and fight for a righteous cause. More likely, you'll have men and women who will try to persecute you but Christ said:

[11]Blessed are ye, when men shall revile you, and persecute you, and shall say all manner of evil against you falsely, for my sake.

Adonai Yahawashi Christ had a distinctive personality that is difficult for the many of us to follow in a multitude of times because perhaps many of us will develop a personality that psychologist Hans Eysenck (1995) calls *psychoticism* stage consisting of

- ❖ Impulsive
- ❖ Cold-hearted
- ❖ Egocentric
- ❖ Impersonal

These certain behaviors were contrasting from Adonai Yahawashi Christ, for Christ has a personality similarly to what Carl Rogers (1971) theorized called *unconditional positive regard* meaning the character of attitude of acceptance and honor on the observer's position (Christ) regardless of what others say or actions they take. Christ didn't care what others said negatively against another, for he's open to *humanistic approaches to personality*, meaning theories that id individuals' innate love, righteousness and desire to potentiate prowess of functioning, sensible to doctrine, love, and all the righteousness that can come from the human.

---

30   Matthew 7v12 Authorized King James Version.

31   Luke 6v45 Authorized King James Version.

The Love of God, Unutterable and Perfect

The love of God, unutterable and perfect,
flows into a pure soul the way that light
rushes into a transparent object.
The more love that it finds, the more it gives
itself; so that, as we grow clear and open,
the more complete the joy of heaven is.
And the more souls who resonate together,
the greater the intensity of their love,
and, mirror-like, each soul reflects the other.

—Dante Alighieri, Italy (1265–1321)

Understand, my Christians and Jewish brethren and sisters, there's a common mis-analogy (idiom) of loving thy neighbor as thyself or loving thy enemies as becoming defenseless. Adonai Yahushua said "But I say unto you, That ye resist not evil: but whosoever shall smite thee on thy right cheek, turn to him the other also" (Matthew 5v39 KJV). Cheek is symbolic and poetic for insult treatment or speaking with scornful abuse, and "right" is a literacy of saying "the discernably good works or liberated," meaning to make effort to refrain from retaliation of the insulted "spoken or treated with scornful abuse," scornful is to bring contempt or derision upon. Therefore, Christ Yahawashi is saying refrain being malice (cf. Proverbs 24v19, Psalms 37v1): but those that persecute you on your discernable liberation with insults or spoken language of scornful abuse refrain insult by sensibly creating opposition from disregarding the vindictive to progress discerned good works to give another chance, for their only two cheeks, as an action of providing mercy from will. Although the human within you will protect yourself and your loved ones because love is inevitable. In Psalms 149v6–9, Yahweh said children have the right to defend themselves against heathens who seek destruction upon us, (2 Timothy 1v7) Yahushua "hath not given us the spirit of fear; but of power, and love, and of a sound mind."[32] Ask yourself how you'll create a sound mind. The truth is through discernment of the sensible, wisdom, the Word as guardianship, outlaw liberation and humanistic approaches to personality, and *theology* (*see* Theology in Everyone). Ask yourself how you come to possess power. It is through the biblical Word, belief in the True Messiah, and prudence. Love is the

---

[32] 2 Timothy 1v7 King James Version.

sensibility of the Word and evolving ourselves to be Christ–like, not through prejudice of skin color and Islamic evildoers seeking to murder or persecute the Christendom, Jews and all other non-Muslims, known as *Kafirs*, certain Qur'an versions substitute the word *Kafirs* to *infidels*. Love is inevitable. It's up to the individual to discern and demonstrate its meaning, however Christ Yahawashi taught and live the grand Ahavah (*see pages 135-136*).

Brief Doctrine of Yahawah and Yahawashi Christ

YHWH: YaHaWaH and YaHaWasHi "I and my Father are one."[33]"I am come in my Father's name, and ye receive me not: if another shall come in his own name, him ye will receive."[34] The Yahawashi the Christ came in this world to free everyone from sin and death (Romans 8v1–2) who accepts him as the Savior so that we can gain living more abundantly (John 10v10–11). Christ is the intercessor (John 10v7) and propitiation (1 John 4v10). Yahawashi Christ as intercessor the Gospel of John verified that (John 14v6) no man can ascend to the Father without going through him. Yahawashi (Jesus) Gospel of John written that Christ is the bread of life (John 6v48), which is symbolic for strength given in Psalms 104v15, verifying bread, strengthening man's heart that Christ brought forth to human civilization from heaven written in John 6v32–40. Yet the bread is also symbolic for staff of life as expressed in Ezekiel 5v16, but staff is also commonly associated with our spinal cord, which consists of thirty-three vertebral columns that holds us together and if broken makes us disabled. The thirty-three vertebral is symbolic of the trinity for many things from God comes in three despite how others mimic it. Christ also died as the intercessor through our staff of life, scholars perceived that Christ Yeshua died at the approximate age of 33 because in ancient times, no individual was allowed to minister until age 30 (Numbers 4v3) and confirmed chronologically in Luke 3v23 after Christ baptism Yahawah his Holy Spirit went into Yahawashi Christ (Luke 3v21–22). Personally I believe Adonai Christ Yahawashi was tested by the Father Adon Olam Yahawah and after he past the trails with the fulfilment of baptism, his divinity of miraculous powers to heal the sick, raise individuals from

---

[33]   John 10v30 King James Version.

[34]   John 5v43 King James Version.

the dead, restore sight to the blind, and many other things; kind of like *Hercules (1997)* metaphorically. But who knows, he probably had those miraculous powers before then, though he definitely had *noetic* abilities in unexplainable logic.

Revealing the Doctrine about Christ's Nationality

There are a variety of individuals who refuse to accept Yahawashi's origin of nationality because of discriminative and prejudice purposes, but I'm going to give the real one. To clarify this would require a little knowledge about one of the twelve tribes of Yasharahla (Israel).

Yahawadah (Judah) = the Negroes, the Ethiopians, the Nubians, and the Egyptians "Gypsies"

Hebrews 7v14 "For it is **evident** that *our Lord sprang out of Judah . . .*" Revelations 1v14, v15 spoke of Christ's image. "His head and his hairs were white <u>like wool</u>, white as snow, and his eyes were as a flame of fire, and <u>his feet</u> like unto <u>fine brass</u> as if they <u>burned in a furnace!</u>" Because Christ had no earthily father, this would mean that Mary was from the descendent of Judah as Christ openly expressed in Revelations 22v16. Marry is confirmed a daughter of David from *The Queen of Sheba and Her Only Son Menyelek* (*Kebra Nagast*) (Wallis Budge 2000). King David is a descendant of Judah through Pharez (cf. Genesis 46v12 and Ruth 4v11–23). Revelation 5v5 "LION of the tribe of Judah, the Root of David . . ." The **LION** is symbolic for its origin, which is Africa. Tribe of Judah is considered the lion's (cf. Genesis 49v9) though all tribes from the descendent of Jacob in union are verified as "Great Lion," (Number 23v23–24) and all twelve tribes of Yasharahla are Israelites, which also went into Egypt with fertility of multiplying (cf. Exodus 1v1–8). Herodotus say during his adventure about 457 BC in Book II, "The Nubians, the Egyptians, and the Ethiopians have broad noses, thick lips, <u>woolly hair,</u> and they are <u>burnt of skin.</u>" Notice when it said woolly hair and burnt of skin. It closely reflects Christ's image and also correlates to Negroes. In one of the most captivating films, ***The Passion of the Christ***, which holds closely treasured as a reminder of Christ's crucifixion, the life events in film portray the truest of the doctrine according to the

Bible. The only misleading parts were Christ's hair was white (due to wisdom and stress), his complexion was dark brown, and he was crucified in Egypt (Revelation 11v8). Christ's eyes are a signature of the Father's throne, fiery flame as stated in Revelations 1v14.

Christ is a reflection of his Father, our Father Adon Olam Yahawah, and Yahawah's image is reflected from this tribe as spoken in Daniel 7v9 KJV.

> I beheld till the thrones were cast down, and the Ancient
> of days did sit, whose garment was white as snow, and
> ***the hair of his head like the pure wool***: his throne was
> like the fiery flame, and his wheels as burning fire.

However, because of limited resources, I will not go to deep into this material until I have more documentation and resources on the Israelite tribes.

Chapter X:
Spiritual Reading Truth

"Spiritual is above our understanding, but
the Spiritual can give direction."

S piritual reading is *the essence of spiritual dimensions as well as mental dimensions of understanding individuality and acknowledging the symbolic meanings and overall nature.* This is not an act of wickedness but a seeking means of intelligence and positive pathways. The Bible mentions spiritual reading that average Centric Christians believe is evil; such as palmistry, Christian Kabbalah, Christian Gnosticism. Various kings, princes, princesses, and queens have experienced spiritual readings above our understanding. Many are through dreams and visions before actual events occur. **Visions** are noetic abilities of an outer body experience in a speculative view. When you actually see events with your eyes before they happen, visions often give the true meaning of what's going to happen, then you'll experience a moment of déjà vu, which is a repetition of events. Carl Jung created a similar experience to visions called *synchronicity*, which is *a phenomenon of correlated events that connect together through simultaneity (as predicted timing or union of timing) and purpose.* These blessed gifts everyone is capable of receiving if they're in touch with divinity on a subconscious level, thereby developing noetic abilities. The common spiritual reading that almost everyone can relate to is dreams, for **dreams** are known to be lucid events of love, danger, imagination, sex, and unpredicted events that have a meaning. The usefulness of most dreams is prediction of the meaning. Dreams normally mean the outcome, symbolic, and opposite of something. During those visions and dreams, you may develop a **premonition**, which is a strong feeling that something is about to take place. A better understanding of this would be if you've ever experienced something that which was exactly the way you insinuated it to be. The film ***Premonition*** was a prime example of this. In Latin, it's spelled praemonere—prae "before" + monere "warn." According to Sigmund Freud, "The study of dreams may be considered the most trustworthy method of investigating deep mental process" (Freud 1961).

The journal given below, *Mind of Dreamscapes and Visions 2003–2005*, is me giving you readers some of my actual spiritual journey when I was of younger age. Some things may seem superstitious to others, but these are actual spiritual and true events that happened to me. I give these journals nakedly to the individuals who may have had similar experience or looking for similarities of visions, synchronicity, premonition, and dreams. Note some of things in my journals make no sense because I was really young, from age 11 to 14, so I didn't understand them myself, and yes, I wrote like this between those ages.

Mind of Dreamscapes and Visions 2003–2005 Journal

~2003   *Synchronicity, Premonition, and Vision of my Grandmother*

The *Dreamscapes and Visions* begun when I had a vision and turned into reality of my beloved grandmother's death. My life then started to change, for I begun to see more. A silent walk into my kitchen and hell framed me, and I framed hell. I knew that what I saw was real. In dreamscapes, there was a surround of darkness plague that came as 100-feet long black snake with red eyes that surrounded me in my bed. There was a sudden panic in me that burst into the living. That's what driven me to reading my Bible for understanding.

One day at church, God Jehovah has really moved me to see a vision of my beloved grandmother flash through my eyes. I told my mother. She smiled upon heaven and said thank you with relief. Then I saw one night, in the empty living room, images with a flash of visions of a bunch of demonic entities. That was one night I did not fear, but my mind was forced to believe what I did not want to see. I began prophecy with strong acts with God Jehovah and Jesus Christ, the world's two strongest elementals in life, cared with the global life stream, but sometimes I ask. Are you there? Do you care for me? And do you promise to supply my needs in life with support? Yes. I heard but wasn't for sure if it was the dormant side. I began to despise my prophecy and stop reading the Bible because it makes me feel like an outcast. There were times when I was talked or joked about by my brothers and sisters at school, but I still thought of them as family regardless. –J.S.J.

~2004   *Mere Darkness*

I was trapped in emotions of hate, deceptions, and evil. My mind brought back a frequent deception of my separated life of my father's family side and how I was abandoned by the clouded thoughts of thrive happiness. Long ago past sense stormed my memories through near death experiences, having the only best father figure that became incarceration for seven years, poverty and physical sufferings, and made me become treason of why these memories stop living. I began to trap my mind's memories to hate and evil, and breathe in sickness, and then I began to inherit chronic headaches and chronic stomachaches. There are certain periods at school I feel relieved and provided a little jubilation; other times, I was sick. Sometimes I got home and watched movies. They relieve my stressful symptoms. At this time the film *Tupac Resurrection* inspired me for an optimistic outlook. My mother seemed to think that the movies attacked me, but she didn't know that I had already been consumed and fought off attacks, so I no longer have to deal with possession of dreams or inherited illness.

The only inherited illness that I had was the vessels on this universe. I felt like I was brought here to confirm a message of revelation and reveal what the key of this message hold to prepare our future. One keyword is that technology will be the main gate to revelation. Out of the entire Bible, Christ, the Father, and Revelations fascinated me the most. There was one night in a peaceful sleep I've seen me standing on a rock surrounded by darkness with flashes of lightning. Someone gripped my ankle, saying, "Help me." Lightning surrounded me, and I grasped ahead with a flash of lightning and saw an ocean of blood and no land ahead and an infinite amount of people ahead screaming in an ocean of blood with demonic creatures abusing them, while I stood on the rock and grasped their pain. A spiritual reading, I had altruism through their sufferings with burden of hopelessness with hope in a sense I could save them. That day I begun to study the importance of these unknown images. It worried me with a thought. *Am I the one who would cause this suffering?* Then an oracle came to me, saying, "No, you're the one who will rescue them from the place of darkness. That's why they called on you for rescue." —J.S.J.

~2005   *Spare and Spoil*

Noise was in my ears from the voices around the house, provoking migraines from a rage of void arguments, jealousy, stress, and disobedience, with laughter of the devil driving us to be a separated family. A lot of people say spare thy rod, spoil thy child, or the reversal of that speech. I see the point of view of that speech; spare and spoil, that Jesus Christ already forgiven us for our sins and has been scorned and pierced with the rod of discipline. God's son has already took our discipline that's why he changed the law of spare, to spare us from the evils of thy rod, and spoil, to let us know to relieve our anger, that we must be dependable for obedience, and that we must prudently seek wisdom that is plausible to better serve best a personal liberation. Even adults are sometimes selfish upon others and hunger for greed. They yet need discipline but has been spared from thy rod of being scorned and pierced. The only time they become scorned and pierced is through experience of their own hand and choice of commitment. That is the act of God Jehovah's love on mercy, to discipline us through Him and not men. —J.S.J.

Powerful Energy of Hands

Many individuals are unaware that the hands have a strong spiritual persuasion, whether it's good or bad. Job 37v7 spoke similarities of palmistry as one of the marks toward understanding your parts of your vocation when it said, **"He sealeth up the hand of every man; that all men may know his work."** Also similar scriptures of palmistry in Proverbs 3v16, Psalms 8v3, Psalms 39v4–5, and Exodus 13v9, and because of these scriptures closely related to palmistry may not be sinful, due to Job 37v7 and the following verses, there's a possibility that Adon Olam left another guidance to us when "seal up the hand" is symbolic for knowledge and vocation for us to be aware of our telos and give direction but can also be literal, however this is left to your determination.[35] However, on the power of hands is the message we're going to focus on, for I wonder how many people are aware that spiritual level handshakes can be a ritual. There's a positive and negative side in everyone, and the theory is that one will outweigh the other in moments, but what others don't acknowledge is growing more spiritually rooted than the flesh your more prone to attacks. Meaning for if you act on the conscience more than without spiritual guidance than everything is permissible. For without Adon Olam's word there would be no morality. Being more spiritually rooted is the direct moral absolution of what's right or wrong that gives the direction to the Light (Adon Olam). Every handshake is a magnetic force of good and bad energy. Then causing an abnormal emotion, certain individuals wonder why the mood has dramatically changed without explanation. This is perhaps one of the main sources of why while the cynical and secular person would blame it on vitamin or hormone deficiency even when an individual is taking good care of their health, a spiritual person has the intellect that gives a deeper reason beyond logic. Many underestimate the power of the hands, although handshakes can be dangerous to your physical health because of possibilities of bacteria and viruses, this can also be damaging to the spiritual because of filling the spirit with *angst* and *Ra*. This is why I've come to understand one of the reasons why our Asian and Indian charismatic brethren and sisters give a polite bow. In India, Namaskār (Namastē) is practiced. Namaskār is a form of greeting where a slight bow is given with the hands caressed together, palms joined with fingers positioned upward while closely near the chest. Namaskār is one alternative to avoid negative energy, but the other is saying Yahweh intrapersonal or anointing yourself with extra virgin olive oil by rubbing the oil all over the body (or after washing with soap, pour the oil on a wet rag while showering to spread all over the body) every day and say, *"I'm under the covenant of Yahawah the Adon Olam and his son Adonai Yahawashi, and in their covenant, my Spirit, my blood, and my water are purified, and on this day, I ask Adon Yahawashi and Yahawah to shield me from error of my flesh and Spirit."*

---

[35] I don't want to mislead anyone, so I advise that you create your own scholarly study on this matter.

Power in the Tongue

Reminiscing my early moments in church, I used to wonder what on the earth is some of the saints speaking in an unfamiliar tongue, then I did some research of *speaking in tongues* called **glossolalia**, a vocal that is not familiar with heathens, Gentiles, nor Israelites, for it's a forbidden and sacred language transcended from the Holy Spirit (1 Corinthians 14v1–25). The word "abracadabra" is derived from Hebrew which means ארבא "I will create" ארבדכ "as spoken." Empirically, many Christians I've encountered speak of this word as evil. This word is actually used to ward off evil spirits and sicknesses. Centuries back, people were in the belief of this according to *Faiths of Man: A Encyclopedia of Religions or Faiths of Man Vol. I*; however, the case *abracadabra* simply means "*I will create as spoken*," so this means what you say is what you vow. Don't buy into that superstition that it evokes evil because it simply means a vow into action. "Death and life are in the power of the tongue: and they that love it shall eat the fruit thereof."[36]

Brethren and sisters, I've come to realize that often, we have been constructed to convict ourselves by saying "yes or no" in sentences or to conclude a honor of acceptance, but the hazard is when you actually say a "yes or no," God holds you accountable for what you say, which is why God gave a message of instruction so we won't be held accountable. If an individual say "yea or nay," there's an abundance in relief. Cultivate this language: "But let your communications be, Yea, yea; Nay, nay: for whatsoever is more than these cometh of evil."[37]

Address the Use of Incense Are Righteous

Before incense and stones were used for sorcery (witchcraft, paganism, Wiccan, and other evil deities), they belonged to Yahawah and the sainthood. It's time to take back our spiritual noetic abilities and transcendence, for there are possibly many centered Christians and other branch Reformations who are not even aware that there are scripture

---

[36] Proverbs 18v21 King James Version.

[37] Matthew 5v37 King James Version.

given for privilege and transcendence through the use of incenses that have great means for everyone looking to seek communion to YHWH. Incense was a way of availing prayers, worship, and communion to YHWH, but various centered Christians have their minds caught up in sorcery by the use of incense because what's centered in YHWH's Word the Lucifer will intelligently persuade some charismatic individuals. Certain Christians fear a repercussion of sin from the use of incense that they'll categorize it as evil or of the Luciferian occult. Then those certain Christians will persuade another with attrition that it's unjustifiable to the prudency conduct. Deeming incense as a form of evil ritual without looking into the roots of Judaism, Israelites, and Orthodoxy, non-usage of incense is way of withholding spiritual allure of the Old Testament from YHWH even though Lucifer never wins in the end. The message I'm giving on this criterion is take back all the help you can receive from YHWH, which is infinite, for the possibilities are deeper with the renewal of the mind. Now I'm going to direct you to many scriptures on *incense* along and trust you have your Bible to review these scriptures.

Exodus 30v7–9, Numbers 4v16, Deuteronomy 35v10, 1 Samuel 2v26, 1 Chronicles 6v49, 1 Chronicles 9v29, Luke 1v9, Numbers 16v16–18, 2 Chronicles 26v16–19, 2 Chronicles 29v7–8, Exodus 30v34–38, Exodus 25v6, Exodus 35v8 and v28, Exodus 39v38, Exodus 40v5, Leviticus 2v1–2, Leviticus 6v15, Leviticus 5v11, Leviticus 16v12.

Through these many scriptures given, you'll notice incense is very important in the biblical faith and is essential. One may ask what incense is. *Incense* is a combination of herbs and spices burned together for rituals and health. Empirically, many Christians I come across automatically assume rituals as something of sorcery, but *ritual* means a divinity of procedures or routines for ceremonials, prayers, and rites. Now let's review the meaning of certain common incenses.

- ❖ African violet is burned for protection and to promote spirituality within your home.
- ❖ Angelica is for protection, harmony, integration, insight, understanding, stability, and meditation.
- ❖ Basil is for concentration, assertiveness, decisiveness, trust, integrity, enthusiasm, mental clarity, cheerfulness, confidence, and courage to attract fidelity, love, blessings, sympathy, and wealth.

- ❖ Benzoin is for astral projection and purification, and it clears negative energy, promotes emotional balance, and eases sadness, depression, weariness, grief, anger, and anxiety.
- ❖ Bergamot is for money and prosperity and uplifting of spirits, joy, protection, concentration, alertness, confidence, balance, strength, courage, motivation, and assertiveness.
- ❖ Cardamom is for mental clarity, concentration, confidence, courage, enthusiasm, and motivation.
- ❖ Cedar burned for purification is to stimulate or strengthen the psychic powers, attract love, and prevent nightmares and for healing purification, protection, money, balance, grounding, clarity, insight, and wisdom. Cedar is another herb that quite often mentioned in the Bible. (cf. Leviticus 14 v4, v6, v49, v51, and v52, Numbers 19v6 and 24v6, Judges 9v15, Samuel 5v11 and 7v2 and v7, 1 Kings 4v33, 1 Kings 5v6, v8, and v10, 1 Kings 6 v9–10, v15–16, v18, v20, and etc.)
- ❖ Cinnamon is for stimulation, wealth, prosperity, business success, strength, and healing and to build Eros, attract money, stimulate and strengthen the psychic powers, aid in healing, and gain wealth and success. (Prov. 7v17, Song of Solomon 4v14, Revelation 18v13)
- ❖ Clove is for pain relief, intellectual stimulation, business success, wealth, prosperity, divination, exorcism, and protection, and it eases fears and improves memory and focus.
- ❖ Copal is for love, purification, protection, and spirituality and to attract love and uplift spirits.
- ❖ Cypress is for strength, comfort, healing, self-assurance, confidence, physical vitality, willpower, and concentration, and it eases anxiety and stress.
- ❖ Damiana is burned for facilitating psychic visions.
- ❖ Elecampane is burned to strengthen the clairvoyant powers.
- ❖ Frankincense—Take notice that frankincense is used often in the Bible, so you may ask what does it do for spirituality. *Frankincense* is used as spirituality, astral strength, protection, consecration, and courage, and it dispels negativity, aids in meditation, induces psychic visions, and attracts blessings. (Exodus 30v34; Leviticus 2v1–2 and v15, Leviticus 5v11, 6v15, 24v7, Numbers 5v15, 1 Chronicles 9v29, Nehemiah 13v5 and v9; Song of Solomon 3v6, 4v6, and v14; Matthew 2v11)
- ❖ Honeysuckle is for money, happiness, friendship, healing, good health, blessings, and psychic power.

- ❖ Juniper is for calming, protection, and healing and to increase psychic powers and to break the curses and hexes cast by evil. (1 Kings 19v4–5)
- ❖ Lotus elevates mood and for protection, spirituality, healing, and meditation for inner peace and outer harmony and aid in meditation and open the mind's eye.
- ❖ Mint is used to increase sexual desire and attract money. (Luke 11v42, Matthew 23v23)
- ❖ Musk is for aphrodisiac, prosperity, and courage and vitality and creates a sensual atmosphere or heightens sensual passion.
- ❖ Myrrh is for spirituality, meditation, healing, and consecration. During ancient times, this incense was used for protection, healing, purification, and spirituality. (Genesis 37v25 and 43v11, Exodus 30v23, Esther 2v12, Psalms 45v8, Proverbs 7v17, Song of Solomon 1v13, 3v6, 4v6 and 14, 5v1, v5, and v13, Matthew 2v11, Mark 15v23)
- ❖ Patchouli is for money, growth, love, mastery, sensuality to attract money and love and to promote fertility.
- ❖ Passionflower is for peace of mind. This sweet scent will soothe troubles and aid in sleep.
- ❖ Poppy seeds are burned to promote female fertility and attract love, blessings, and money.
- ❖ Rosemary is used for remembrance, memory, energy, and healing to purify and aids in healing, prevents nightmares, preserves youthfulness, and dispels depression.
- ❖ Rue is burned to help restore health. (Luke 11v42)
- ❖ Sage is used for wisdom, clarity, and purification.
- ❖ Sandalwood is for spirituality, healing, protection, and astral projection to heal and protect and for purification.
- ❖ Vanilla is for Eros arousal and mental alertness and stimulates amorous appetites and enhances memory.

Chapter XI:
True Essence of Prayer

"Fervency and emunah in a surrounding tranquil environment is what avails a prayer greater, not the false impressions of trying to impress."

Prayer is the movement of the heart toward Yahawashi (Yashiyah) and Yahawah (Ahayah). Prayer is the calling for connection toward our creator. Symbolically, it's the breath of our soul and provides hope for ourselves, along with humanity, keeping submission to His will. Praying is making feeling permeate itself toward Jehovah Elohim. Praying in front of the cross, prostrations, and icons is not a true prayer. The essence of true prayer comes from the heart, invocation of feeling to reverence Adon Olam. Glorifying and speaking humble emotions to the Lord through true prayer is signifying submission and gratitude for His blessing and is inspired to glorify Him regardless of circumstances. Preparation of true prayer is clearing your mind first from all worldly cares, giving Adon Olam your complete affection. Using prayer books gives a chance for cultivation of how prayers should go and gives a firm foundation and mesmerize them to become engraved in your hearts. True prayer comes from feelings to lingerer within your soul because it's derived from all dolor, love, and faith. The essence of true prayer comes with patience and open expression. You're not required to have a priest intercede for your connection with Adon Olam because with cultivation and heartfelt communication, you're already connected.

A common misconception is confessions, for some fellowship churches believe that your sins should be confessed to a priest only, and the priest brings your confessions to the Lord. This is a common deceptive deity, for James 5v16 says,

> **Confess** (means *admitting your wrongs*) your **faults** (means *unpleasing features*) one to another, and pray one for another, that ye may be healed. The effectual **fervent** (means *showing a passionate intensity*) prayer of a righteous man availeth much.

Keep in mind this is not the book of Revelation, so I can solidify this. There's a fine line between confessing you faults and confessing your **sins** (means **unrighteous acts that are unlawfully against God's Word**), for your sins are meant to be confessed to Yahawashi and Yahawah alone. In addition, you don't necessarily have to give voice of faults to a priest in particular but can be righteous brethren or, interpersonally, a trusted individual or wife. Many fellowship churches teach vain repetition. You may ask what this vain repetition you speak of is. This is the act of repeating words commonly used to grasp the Lord's attention in Matthew 6v7.

> But when ye pray, use not vain repetitions, as the heathen do: for they think that they shall be heard for their much speaking.

Invoking a sequence of our Holy Father and Holy Savior names are not qualified as vain repetition. What's qualified as vain repetition is chanting or reciting repeats of lines/sentences. The Lord does not adore chanting, for He knows what you say before you say it (Matt. 6v8). Matthew 6v5 explains that hypocrites pray to show off. That's the only reward they'll have. But Matthew 6v6 expressed for those who pray in secret, rewards are **more abundant**.

Humane Support

One of your sons from the descendant of Adam and Eve (*or daughters from the descendant of Adam and Eve*) calls to the heaven: the **Father**, the **Word**, and the **Holy Ghost**,
Spoken from the earthily trinity: the **Spirit**, the **water**, and the **blood**,
I (*full name*) humbly ask that you cleanse all my impurities so that my prayer ascended to you is not vexed,

Adon Olam Yahawah and *Adonai Yahawashi*, my faith resides in you in deliverance of dark valleys,

Deliverance of illness, a keeper to my heart, a keeper to my vessel, a keeper to my Spirit,

Sustain me when I may fall, for daily, I need heaven's wings for shield,

Help me provide for others in need, so agape can flow into the hearts of others to help one another,

Change the hearts of mankind and womankind that cause havoc,

Give intellect to our government to prevent unrighteous acts from becoming justifiable against your Word,

Remove those from counsel that seek to break your Word,

Let snow come to purify the vessel so that it may unthaw from sins,

Remold the minds and hearts from the feeling of constructive grounds and attrition,

Eloah Va-Daath "God Manifest" touches to humanity to motivate the humane in us to aid the poor, heal with affection, and provide Judeo-Christian leadership to others in positivity,

Guide our daughters, sisters, mothers, fathers, sons, brothers, grands, kin, friends, wives (*or husbands if woman*), and associates to your touch and covenant,

In the names of *Adon Olam Yahawah* and *Adonai Yahawashi*, let my prayer ascend to you, Great Holy Spirit *El* "the Mighty One," Amen!

An Ultimate King's Prayer

Brethren (full name) calls upon the heaven trinity: the **Father**, the **Word**, and the **Holy Ghost**,

Spoken from the earthily trinity: the **Spirit**, the **water**, and the **blood**,

Adon Olam, my idol, shield me through dark valleys that may corrupt my vessel,

Yahawashi and *Yahawah*, I thank you for your love and your sacrifice,

I humbly ask that you cleanse all my impurities so that my prayer ascended to you is not vexed,

Help me throughout my despondencies that's inevitable,

Grant me serenity to rationalize acceptance from the core of my being to all my egos,

But heavenly Father in your Word, let not my rational acceptance cause evil morals,

For if it does give me the courage to improve and tranquil and provide a transformation,

I plea mercy for not providing proper worship nor love to the heaven trinity,

El Elyon, I call upon your love to help the ones I've encountered and ones soon to come,

Let my light shine strong so that it may give vocation to their spirit,

Jehovah Elohim, may I humbly request intelligence and mercy bestowed with fruitful blessings upon me,

So that I may have greater knowledge and bestow charity to others and let me not forget brethren and sisters in time of blessings,

Adonai Yahushua, I'm internally grateful for my opportunity of redemption through your sacrifice on the cross,

I call upon mercy for my transgressions of (*Confess the commandments you broke and the sins you've committed discreetly to God only*)

Thy *Jesus the Nazarene Christ*, I open to you as my Savior,

The *grace of the* **Lord Jesus Christ**, and the *love of* **God**, and the *communion of the* **Holy Spirit**, (be) with me,

El Shaddai, I humbly ask that you bestow opportunity for financial stability for my position to my wife (speak full name [or wives]), my youngling (speak full name [or younglings]), my elders that I hold close to heart, and everyone else that I hold close to heart for the Kingdom you bestowed upon me as dominion,

Holy Ghost, purify my spirit to persist throughout my days,

And strengthen me against the devils that try filling me with contempt, a dolorous spirit, sickness throughout my body and Ra,

Allow me to persevere and subordinate stress,

Grant me powerful noetic abilities and help me become symbol literate,

Allow my spirit and body be saved from diseases and webs of promiscuous women,

Allow me to embrace only heterosexuality as you created it, for I don't want to be deceived from effeminates, for in thy holy Word, I rebuke evil spirits that cause these unholy persuasions,

In my lovemaking, allow my foundation to become

Virile, vigorous, fruitful, emunah (*see Chapter XII for meaning*) and unashamed,

While embracing both the Eros, Amorous, Ardent, and Thanatos nature to my wife,

For I now know my sacred marriage makes my lovemaking undefiled,

Allow me to fulfil power exchange (*given in 1 Corinthians 7v3–4*) and bestow loving discipline,

And bring about a transformation of my wife (or wives) if needed,

Bring out the submissiveness that's within the nature of my wife (*or wives*) as given in your Word,

Bring out the humane in me,

Jehovah, I call upon wisdom to give me proverbs to distinguish proper social intelligence and pathway,

Enlighten my eyes to become more aesthetic to your nature and not worship money,

Ask of *El "the Mighty One"* to provide companionable and passionate love from wife (or wives, if in a polygyny marriage) I desire so that my flesh don't commit adultery,

Eloah Va-Daath "God Manifest," bestow upon me strength, radiance, and splendor,

Preserve my Spirit to remain with you infinitely,

For your soldier is hungry for the *Holy Spirit*.

May voice be given to **Adon Olam Yahawah** and **Adonai Yahawashi**, Amen!

Part III:

Sensual Adon Lovemaking

Awakening your healthy sexual Eros-Thanatos-Ardency-Amorous loving, courageous truer lovemaking, and a reverence of embracing your inner personalities, along with your lover's innermost desires. In addition, you'll be learning urban sacred sexual intelligence, along with biblical exegeses to awaken new dimensions of loving.

Chapter XII:
Loveology Unfolds

"Love is at its simplest is the unlimited and heart-felt of inevitable forces for endurance is inevitably unpredicted, and sometimes those forces can Ahavah or grow dolor and Ra."

Ahavah "agape, love" truth unfold to something more earthily real rather than something out of romance film creating illusions of love is all happiness. Many individuals have a different philosophy on what love is, so I will give the biblical definition.

1 Corinthians 13v4-7 and 13[38]	1 Corinthians 13v4-7 and 13 Unfolded Translations
[4]Ahavah (*agape, love*) suffers long, Ahavah is kind; Ahavah does not have kinah (*dirge*); Ahavah does not brag, ahavah is not puffed up in ga'avah (*conceit, pride*); [5]ahavah does not behave shamelessly; ahavah does not in anochiyut (*selfishness*) insist on its own way, Ahavah is not touchy and vindictive, keeping a record of wrongs. [6]Ahavah does not find simcha (*joy*) in evil, but rejoices in HaEmes (*the Truth*). [7]Ahavah covers all things, believes all things, has trikvah (*hope*), even zitzfleisch (*patience*), for all things.	[4]"Regard with affection or love" suffers long, love is kind; love does not have dirge (mournful literacy in another's death, but rejoice for the end of suffering); love does not brag, love is not puffed up in "conceit or pride"; [5]love does not behave shamelessly; love does not in selfishness insist on its own way, love is not touchy (touchy is the adjective defining "taking offense with slight cause") and vindictive (seeking vengeance), keeping a record of wrongs. [6]Love does not find joy in evil, but rejoices in the Truth. [7]Love covers all things, believes all things, has hope, even patience, for all things.
[13]But now remain emunah (*faith, truth, faithfulness, fidelity, stability, faithfully, truthfully*), tikvah (*hope*), and Ahavah (*agape, love*), these shalosh (*three*). And the greatest of these is Ahavah.	[13]But now remain "faith, truth, faithfulness, fidelity, stability, faithfully, truthfully," hope, and love, these three. And the greatest of these is love.

Notice that this scripture says charity in the King James Version because translators assumed that agape can mean either love or charity, so they choose charity. They've done this throughout the New Testament, so actually, the word "charity" varies because the truth is the word could actually be love (or a type of love: agape). But if you diligently seek the truth, you'll notice that charity makes no sense to be greater than hope and faith, for the Lord is love (1 John 4v8).

---

[38] Scriptures taken from The Orthodox Jewish Bible.

We constantly live in a world where growing cultures are inspired from mass media and social pressure reassuring adultery as justified, although the Word encourages us to remain *emunah* with hope and love toward our significant other.

Loveology is equated overall to these words:

Ahavah, high-spirited, bonding, patient, mystery, romance, jubilation, fervent, emunah, forthright, compassionate, rapturous, infatuate, beatific, supportive, sex, sensibility, affectionate, healing, power exchange, charismatic, compelling, resolute, satisfying, sympathetic, honor, heartfelt, undefiled, profoundness, euphoric, marriage, desire, treasure, all-consuming, ecstasy, healing, mesmerizing, sensualism, Thanatos, Eros, amorous, affection, ardent, and enduring.

Chart 12-1: Loveology Acquainted Words

Novice of Ahavah

The greatest happiness of life is the conviction that we are loved, loved for ourselves, or rather loved in spite of ourselves. (Victor Hugo)

Connection through Communication

Before pleasure begins, the most important is getting to know another, and that values grander than without it. Learning the inner beauty before the outer beauty of a royal woman gives a more genuine love by making oneself knowledgeable of their significant other. To determine the connection, our bond must actually be more of the spiritual than the physical first. See Figure 12-1 below:

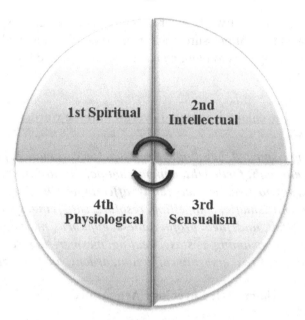

Figure 12-1 Flow of Attraction

Spiritual is the main direction us kings, queens, princes, and princesses should strive for first because it's the growth of strong relation since Adon Olam Yahawah and Adonai Yahawashi are before all. This announces the commitment to Royal-Kingdom Laws of Divinity as a teleology for an appropriate direction because it's liberated, and there's faith in the covenant of Ahavah. This determines a prolonged commitment in union to another for YHWH's is the primary. Servitude is given to Adon Olam Yahawah and Adonai Yahawashi before everyone else, and this determines a proper stewardship and speaks from a language of love that an individual possesses leadership, for they don't follow the crowd but stand their grounds. Being devout in YHWH Word is a way of harmonizing and domestic discipline. (*cf.* Romans 8v6)

The *Intellectual* is how you and the significant other have agreeable faith, agreeable likings, agreeable intentions, and agreeable motivation. The intellectual stage is very important because it determines bonding (magnetism), the mind levels, the stewardship, and the very thing that helps us warm up to another. Let intellectual be in high profile because it gives the capacity of relations and a deeper root of attraction.

The *Sensualism* is the full likings of each other, the very foundation of how you relate in the physiological and philosophical means. This is very important for the root of knowing how the relationship will survive in loving. This determines if the relationship can be embraced in emotion and sexual nature without the feeling of burden and rejections. The *Physiological* is the courtesy of understanding each other's health and approvals, the feeling of ardency and love, the sensationalism of intimacy, and the passionate and compassionate factors in intimate union. The physiological is always a factor in determining the depths of love. Perhaps many say it's the love itself, but the truth is it's the root union of how love itself relates.

Byrne's Law of Attraction

Social psychologist Donn Byrne[39] formulated mathematically the framework of attraction from reinforcement in theoretical empirical basis, the agreeable through rewarding to disagreeable through punishment:

$$Y = m \left[\frac{\Sigma PR}{(\Sigma PR + \Sigma NR)} \right] + k$$

The attraction stands for Y, PR is the positive reinforcement, and NR is the negative reinforcement. The *m* and *k* are just variables. Notice that more positive reinforcement gives the stronger the attraction. Negative reinforcement is still important to apply in certain occasions, but more negative will decrease attraction basis. Counter the negative with more positive to accumulate a longer lovable attraction, which becomes the seduction naturally. An individual can provide more rewarding things, which include making reservations in classy restaurants, buying gifts, communicating more, and more intimacy and all the things that endure more to their liking create a more prolonged cycle of loving affections. The individual who provides more negativity can be positive in matters of Domestic Discipline (*see chapter XIV*) though the more negatives of arguments, rejection in affection, an individual become insensitive and bitter and abusive and do not provide bountiful gifts and intimacy will eventually depolarize attraction basis that sustains the relationship. The relationship of attractive spark will soon depolarize (break apart), leaving more emptiness and cause disliking affections.

---

[39]   Byrne, Donn E. 1971. *The Attraction Paradigm*. New York: Academic Press.

Attraction basis can be relied through demographic and agapic love, but this is based on the individual. Demographic selection can range from ages, ethnicity, race, sex, financial statues, the structure of education, to economic conditions. Agapic love is fully upon desire, selfless love, and strong interest in another while disregarding the demographics mostly. Demographic selection can be the back burner to someone toward another who is truly interested in but perceives a value of demographic. These demographics in real-life scenario can be the following:

When an individual is in love with a significant other, but the family doesn't approve of their religious preference, or the color of their skin, or their stability conditions (perhaps this person is unemployed) or doesn't approve of them in a matter of judgments based on the other's educational backgrounds or history.

When an individual is older than the significant other they've chosen, social gatherings may be judgmental on the couple because they don't approve of the age difference or biased on nationality.

Another would be if an individual has strong love for another, but social pressure fills them with the contempt of being together from the propaganda of demographics and attempt to do whatever they could to destroy it.

Demographic selection can be out of fear, prejudice, unproportioned faith, enslavement, and biases propaganda. An agapic love overtakes all demographic selection because the individuals just don't care what others think but are more drawn to their heart, faith, and hope. The heart is the chest of jewels in submission for the one who finds it and opens it. This is the same on attraction, for one must search to find it. This goes for both mankind and womankind. Treasures are hard to find, but when it's found, the heart becomes wealthy, and fervency will follow. The selfishness comes in when you don't want to share that treasure, which is the way it must go to sustain your intimate treasure. The truth is many people would endure love when it's found, but sometimes we have to seek a transformation all for Ahavah, and there are no limits. The film **Love Actually** (2003) emphasized this from different demographics, positions in people's lives, nationalities, and ages. All is limitless when it comes to Ahavah, but it's a journey sometimes without rationality expected and amorous.

Love is undefinable because of its infinite potentiality. Some people live a plague of pain just looking for hope and love with an inspiration of faith, and truth told, the real-world life is not cinema. A friend told me life is like a movie, but this philosophy can be useless. When I look around, I notice many drained women and men who portray energetic love who are really drained as well. Propaganda from people sometimes seems more destructive than helpful because it's deceiving to reality of various individuals. Some are planning deception behind your back or attempt of breaking a covenant of Ahavah between couples; propaganda deceptions of instigations, covetousness, and many other conniving ideologies, waiting to break the covenant.

There are too many people looking to be free lovers that can possibly lead to ludic loving, thereby hurting one another. Media says it's natural for men and women to have sex for a certain amount of years then move on to the next. I've even heard many men and women say swinging (cheating) is natural and that everyone does; however, I refuse to accept the movement of darkness from sexual immorality. Ludic loving people treat others who preserve their emunah and liberation as objects for pleasure than holding on to one another. How can you fervently love of flesh and blood when another is treating it as emptiness vails? Is it right to have intercourse and then leave? The answer is no. Why is there consisting pleasure of betraying, filling with contempt, and captivity toward another? I've noticed the mass media construct the vindictive methods of infidelity, people marrying for money without the Ahavah in union and certain individuals speaking to their consort inhumane or some type of contemptuous formality. Men often do this out of fear as do women, the fear of betrayal, contempt, and lust as do women.

Empirically, I've noticed the cycle of this dolorous millennium, the cycle of one person hurting another, then causing it to spread like a plague of deception but not many compassionate people resilient but drowning dolorous. In a means not many compassionate people are strong minded but convert to the sexualized publicity of fornication without commitment; adultery. Certain individuals let the best of them develop evil intentions that someone else bestowed on them so they hurt another and spreading that pain to another that is more loving, because they've been previously treated wrong. Many say follow your heart when there's conflict between the mind and heart, but the heart is symbolic for the soul and emotional direction, not the blood pumping, so it's more verbatim to think of letting your emotion guide you. Empirically, I've observed the

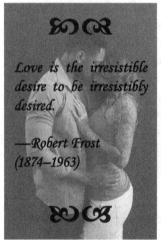

Love is the irresistible desire to be irresistibly desired.

—*Robert Frost*
(1874–1963)

different principalities on how others should love. Personally, if it's not coming from the Bible as my main guide, then all substantially decline what laws are given in reference to love life.

When I was watching in interview from Oprah Winfrey on how Orthodox Judaism lives in marriage, I said to myself wow (in a disappointing tune) on the fact some testimonials on mass media said sex is a woman's right; that during menstrual period, they remain abstinent; that they are not permitted to pleasure each other in public places; and that the greatest is they don't accept Christ in the doctrine. The one that said sex is a woman's right, I completely discovered is more inaccurate because of one powerful scripture. 1 Corinthians 7v3–4 clearly defines that its equilibrium or power exchange, husband and wife have completely given their body in vows when they repeat the scripture, so what was once the woman's body is now given to the man entirely, and what was once the man's body is now given to the woman entirely, so both rights were render to each other as spouses.

The Bible says have few counselors, why this is? Because any person can easily feel completely burdened by laws and prisoned by them and deceived by counselors. Looking for the hedonistic portion gives purity of the heart to transcend to Adon Olam's divine guidance, not by the counselors who enforce being captive to laws they created for the gratification of themselves or because of some political movements to gratify others' liking. —J.S.J.

𝕷𝖔𝖛𝖊𝖔𝖑𝖔𝖌𝖞 𝕰𝖓𝖉𝖚𝖗𝖆𝖓𝖈𝖊

An elderly brother in Christ told me that young love is not the same as real love, for real love is not about how happy you are but how long you can endure. The happiness comes before marriage, and in reality, often, sex can come before marriage, but what's overlooked is the Ahavah in union. For instance, a man can be in the military and a month after marriage could be called to go overseas to fight for their country, while a wife remains patient, reserving her emunah for months and sometimes one year straight, but the effort a wife makes can be virtuous when she's consistently making Skype calls, phone calls, and e-mails to keep the love companionate until the husband returns to re-inspire the passion longed for. Some wives and husbands would even take the time to write a letter because a letter can be very precious to another, for it signifies affectionate love that's patient enough to engrave a piece of them into their writing then seal it with the moisture of their tongue and pay the first-class expense to mail it for fast shipping so the significant other knows it's from them through their writing style for its more special than an autograph.

Another example of enduring love would be if your significant other was in a federal institute just for being at the wrong place at the wrong time, serving a sentence of five years. The question is how much emunah, hope, and Ahavah can reserve itself until it's time for release? Love can take place inevitably without logic. In the show *Orange Is the New Black* Season 3 Episode 13, Vince from the Christian Help organization fell in love with Lorna (Yael Stone) while she was locked up. Lorna proposed to Vince (John Magaro) before Vince could, and Vince married and consummated her in prison amorously. In the show *Power* Seasons 1 and 2 (Agboh 2014-2015), character James "Ghost" St. Patrick (Omari Hardwick) holds love for Angela Valdez (Lela Loren) since high school, and after reuniting with her after years of them being forced apart, they both fight through their circumstances for love that remains emunah to their heart. The problem was James had a secret lifestyle of being a drug lord she's against, but out of love, Angela hold outs from giving him to the Feds, while James strived to end the secret lifestyle for her and remain emunah to love within his heart for her. When your significant other has a traumatic accident (such as losing a limb, burned, etc.) or has sickness (such as cancer, Alzheimer's disease, heart deficiencies, diabetes, etc.), the question would be how strong is your love (Ahavah), hope, and emunah?

If a man was to ask himself if he's a lover or a fighter, this perhaps maybe a little difficult. Some men say if you're more of a lover, then you're weak, but if you're more a fighter, you're strong. The truth is this is completely false, and there's an inner emotion filled with pain. Thereby, the problem with that ideology is what lies within them, not necessarily you, nor should contempt of them attach itself to you. Deep down, some individuals have anger toward love because it crushed them internally, making them feel weak, so they give the illusion of strong through connection of being a fighter more than a lover. Although the basic human element is survival, our creator made love greater and more fundamental. Being the fighter is preserving your own individuality and protecting your physiology, but this all flamed from loving yourselves and others you'll keep close to your heart. So love is the greater keeper; fighting is the solidity to the identity. To determine if you're a lover or a fighter, answer these questions:

- ❖ If you had a choice, would you (A) rather die a king in a battle to be remembered as a hero or (B) die a king in sexual loving to be remembered as a fruitful master lover having your last sexual intercourse or spend ending moments with your family?
- ❖ If (A) a doctor told you that you couldn't have any sex for months for the sake of health, would you obey or (B) keep performing sexual loving and let that be your healing?
- ❖ If you are wealthy but there's trouble in business, would you (A) aid to the business when you don't need the money because your boss called you for extra hours to fix the problem, or would you (B) use your time to take your significant other out for an evening dinner with a purchase of expensive wine/champagne then forego sensual interest for the both of you and await dessert at night.

If your answer was (A), then you're more of a fighter, if you answer is (B), then you're more of a lover.

Loveology Virtues and Destructive Sins

Each man should so conduct himself that *fortitude* appear in labours and danger: *temperance* in foregoing pleasures: *prudence* in the choice between good and evil: *justice* in giving every man his own.

—Cicero, repeating Plato and Aristotle

Fortitude is the strength during pain, the person who remains resilience when times are hard for the betterment of providing sensible love. The temperance is the substance of remaining in sober judgment by not allowing ourselves to be overpowered with alcohol but dominant against drunkenness. The reason is to prevent undesirable afflictions and commotions. The prudence is the main essential, for it gives the clarity of proper determinism even when in an unfortunate predicament. The justice is not by being greedy or unfair to others but giving others the privilege of something worthy, when you already have your own, as well as the proper discernment of guide feeling to acknowledge the difference and self-determine if it's justified. Let those four be your reckoning for virtues.

The brilliant psychoanalyst **Erich Fromm** gave a Loveology framework on mature love through his book *The Art of Loving* (1956), for he stated,

> Mature love is union under the condition of preserving one's integrity, one's individuality. Love is an active power in man: a power which breaks through the walls which separate man from his fellow men, which unites him with others; love makes him overcome the sense of isolation and separateness, yet it permits him to be himself, to retain his integrity. In love the paradox occurs that two beings become one and yet remain two. (1956, pg. 17)

Fromm speculated that heterosexual desire is expressed as the basic need for love and union, a desire to break the barriers of the sense of separateness and create a fusion of union with another opposite sex. When there's a ticket of love, there's a ticket of life, and that life is the longing of a reason to exist, a reasonable pursuit of abundance, a reason to find God, a reason for a distinctive personality, and a reason to a covenant. Sometimes us mankind can have a beautiful woman right before our eyes while in a relationship with her. This beauty can cause harm to the heart, but the appreciative part is the beauty that nurtured our hearts for a moment even when we crave a longing consistency of the beauty for our own possession. The solitude is the appreciation for the beauty but the rejection of destructive that caused a ruptured heart in a moment.

Brethren, not every woman is of a faithful flesh even if they have a faithful heart, and because of not having the full dimension, we lose love for not consisting possession of both. This is the form that breaks our emotional motors, but it's also the form that strengthens our hearts to be more polyamorous and solid. It's not necessarily your fault for the inability to have a full open-hearted love to another woman from the last unfortunate mistrust of another, but we have the mandatory to allow another woman to prove her covenant of Ahavah, for loveliness is in a woman's nature. It's the emunah that has to be determined from her and that gives the faith in her to the king/prince. Loyalty, submission, and maidenhood are what are commonly hoped for from us kings and princes, and that's the mandatory protocol to your heart and rationality. Let loyalty of truth be your Loveology virtue.

It's important to cultivate that women are very important to us kings. Kings must realize that a woman can be our rescuer in certain times. She can rescue a king in the struggles of emotion that caved inside when a man is struggling. A woman can rescue a man with her umbrella when it's raining. A queen/princess can be a king's/prince's personal consultant if he let her have the opportunity of discernments. She can be a guardian in harsh situations and difficult decisions. In certain moments, it's the queen/princess who leads the man to faith in Adon Olam Yahawah and Adonai Yahawashi. Her beauty and loveliness can give insight that there's a Savior and creator who took the time to make that particular treasure just for that individual king/prince. For visual relation, the film *I'm in Love with a Church Girl* (2013) can inference this.

Many certain things in this world give destructive virtues, but Yahawah works in mysterious ways; some are felt as if a plague of dolor through the Ra of others because it's frowned upon in his conduct. For instance, there's a famous adulterous dating site called **Ashley Madison**, target specifically swigging while married or preying on married unions to fornicate with. Ashley Madison was specifically designed to commit adultery and fornication to satisfy lustful pleasures and not remain true to consort covenant. Women and men seeking sexual partners while there married creating a repercussion of havoc upon the covenant of consort Ahavah, this portion validates, *Prophecy, Reason Why I've Discussed Primitives* (*see Appendix II*). In United States of America, this is mostly a Christian culture, and Adon Olam would be deeply ashamed of thirty-seven million individuals looking to commit this adulterous act. People may portray having a site such as Ashley Madison as justified, but in *prudence* to YHWH's conduct, it's immoral and withdraws from *emunah* and brings upon shame when they're discovered. The hackers call this act *porn revenge*, a way of targeting women and perhaps even men to exploit their sins. Thereby, this can be a substitute for dolorous punishment to retribution for adulterous deeds.

Art of Spiritual Love

Spiritual Love (77,35–78,12)

Spiritual love is wine and perfume. [78] People who anoint themselves with it enjoy it, and while these people are present, others who are around also enjoy it. If the people who are anointed leave them and go away, the others who are not anointed but are only standing around are stuck with their own bad odor.

> The Samaritan gave nothing to the wounded person except wine and oil—that is, only ointment.[120] The ointment healed the wound, for "love covers a multitude of sins."[121] (From *Nag Hammadi Scriptures*, The Gospel of Philip)

Sideways (Giamatti, et al. 2005) in starting approximate runtime of 55 minutes and 30 seconds (00:55:30) to 59 minutes and 30 seconds (00:59:30), Miles (Paul Giamatti) and Maya (Virginia Madsen) demonstrated spiritual love session of wine in relation to a person. The aroma in wine generates an aromatherapy if a person takes the time to smell the incense. There are some studies insinuating that red wine stimulates women's arousal response. In reality, I've heard testimonials of this to be true. There's a predetermination of type of cologne a man should wear though being attentive on the types of aromas in the wines she tastes and smells indulgently by theorizing the relation. Surely, you can simply ask, that's a practical way, but she's fascinated when the man predetermines. Women are often turned on by musky, earthy, woody, coffee bean-like, oriental, licorice, and spice-like aromas. For us men, it's mostly vanilla-like, spice-like, licorice, orange, cocoa butter, lavender, rose-like, oriental, and ylang-ylang. A friend once told me that a good aroma smell is better than no smell. I believe this to be highly true and important.

When us men wear certain colognes and women wear certain perfumes, it is an essence of deep indulgence of themselves that somewhat reflects who they are, not necessary by scent alone but the scent of which it was harvested. Those aromas that captivate their senses become the piece of harvest of their personality, the very id of themselves in spiritual consciousness, for these are illuminated signature of themselves. The spiritual love of oils to anoint the body (from neck down) creates medicinal therapeutic effects along with natural aphrodisiacs to enhance love making, motivate ardency and eroticism, and to smooth thrusting; for ointment is like organic lubrication to increase intimate intensities.

The wine is the opposition of what another considers a significant fit on earthily spiritual significance (contrasting the divine is the heavenly spiritual significance). When a person takes the time to smell the wine before its taste, the other would know if they are allured by that scent or distinguished from it. For it's not taste that comes first to solidify who they're dining with, but it's the scent that predetermines them in their likings. For instance, a woman may not like the taste of the wine but indulge in its bold scent, thereby predetermining that she's allured to bold scents so her mentality may capture to a bolder man or bold scented cologne from a man. If the scent was earthier of scented woody with spice-like smells, she would be attracted to an outgoing man or a man who has an aesthetic philosophy for naturalism, hedonistic for nature and primitive sensualists. If the scent of cologne has a proportion of musk and the submissive indulges than she may develop intellectual behavior that he's ardent to carnal desire and okay with her naughtiness (a revolve of sensual atmosphere) and scent may purvey an appeal of masculinity. Another example would be if a man was allured by the smell of wine but eager to taste and discover if the scent was more of a vanilla-like or cocoa-like, and the taste was a hint of chocolate. This would predetermine to a woman what ointments and butters he indulges on his woman and predetermine patience through his eagerness by how fast he finishes the bottle or glass. Wines contain many scented notes like a person can contain many traits, but there are scents to everyone's liking, but a discovery is on your part so that you may read another's traits and likings. Spiritual love is spiritual reading of the naturalism to convey rationalism of what warms the heart and nature of the individual.

Submissiveness Blown Out of Context

Many men empirically use women's submission as a way of getting what they want. Surely, a woman who follows by the faith is supposed to be subservient to her husband, but this doesn't mean suffocating her in a condensed environment. Empirically, some of the brethren and sisters of faith I've spoken to told me some dreadful events. Somehow submissiveness has become naïve to the humility within. Say, for instance, when a wife strives to accomplish her ambitions to achieve a desired job she always hoped for, but the husband clutters her from succeeding and tries to do everything in his power to make her dependent on him. The royal way is to honor the wife. Honor means being supportive to her ambitions, not clogging the lungs so they can barely breathe (this goes back to chapter I: Discover Within). Submissiveness doesn't give approval to be deceived by a man with the only intention of fornicating then leaving her as if she was for rent, for that fills her nature with contempt, dolor, sexual immorality, and vengeance to the undeserving. A repercussion of *emunah* is required on a man's part. You may ask, what do you mean by vengeance to the undeserving? The rational answer is treating someone with Ahavah and *emunah* toward them as trash because of their previous experience when that person with Ahavah and *emunah* would have been more deserving of Ahavah and *emunah* in return.

Submissiveness in the Bible doesn't grant a man to brawl on her (Colossians 3v19) but love her. The last I checked, no man empirically enjoys being the brawling bag, and that same disenjoyment, "not being a brawling bag," is the honor that should be granted unto the wife (Ephesians 5v33). A woman or man that has been abusively brawled upon has the liberate right to divorce or leave or abandon the brawling abuser unto the wilderness (Proverbs 22v10), for they are scornful. *Scornful* means treating a person with contempt through hurtful language, abusive brawling on another, and making another feel unworthy. Yahawah's *Royal-Kingdom Laws of Divinity* says you have the approval to cease the strife and reproach of the scornful.

Arcanum, the Awakening Loveology

A human being is part of the whole called by us universe . . . We experience ourselves, our thoughts and feelings as something separate from the rest. A kind of optical delusion of consciousness . . . is a kind of prison for us, restricting us to our personal desires and to affection . . . our task must be to free ourselves from the prison by widening our circle of compassion to embrace all living creatures and the whole of nature in its beauty . . . true value of a human being is determined primarily by the measure and the sense in which they have obtained liberation from the self . . .

—Albert Einstein

Arcanum is a deep secret. The arcanum is to discover loving in a way that makes sense, capturing in essence of heaven in a sense feeling freedom, individuality in love, and prolongs endurances, and this is what God wants for us, to feel this Arcanum. In love, the ology "branch of study" comes through affection for another, and then that affection grows deeper. Of course, infatuations develop in this moment, but it's the strength of obligation to feeling the heart of the special person more than just the foundation (meaning sexual organs). This can be difficult for us certain men (and women), but it's a possibility that can give the arcanum of true love even when it's not always given back. We don't live romance films, novels, and comics, but we live realism, and realism can sometimes lead to an emotional ache. The path and telos of the arcanum is sometimes a difficult thing to find when it's about finding the truth of love. Some say it's a mystery, but the truth is the mystery is coming from within the heart of truth from the mind. If you're loving another when you're in a relationship, then Ahavah is not an arcanum in your heart, your heart is the aesthetical discernment of fair or one and complex unity (*cf.* 1 Samuel 16v7). Loving for money than Ahavah is not an arcanum in your heart, and if ludic play, then Ahavah is not an arcanum in your heart. Arcanum is a revelation of finding your true self. This true self of Ahavah is your light in love. What's been compromised is the theology of how an individual should act prudent but also it can create a shell if the individual is constantly feeling defiled from other individuals telling them how they should love. The love is in finding the flow of attraction and preserving faith in Adon Olam Yahawah, disregarding living for others but living for ourselves. Love is based on what's considered fair as the Song of Solomon pointed out. **Fair** means what's considered honorable or perceived sensible, trustworthy, decent, legitimate, favorable, tolerable, ardent, beautiful and attractive—the Aesthetic discernment and sensualism, emunah and or virgin. (cf. Genesis 6v2, Genesis 12v11 and 14, Genesis 24v16, Genesis 26v7, Samuel (13v1, 14v27 and 17v42), 1 Kings 1v3–4, Esther (1v11, 2v2–3 and 7), Job 42v15, Proverbs (7v21, 11v22, 26v25), Song of Solomon (1v15–16, 2v10 and 13, 4v1, 4v7, 4v10, 6v10, 7v6), Isaiah 5v9, Jeremiah (4v30, 12v6), Ezekiel 31v7 and 9)

Chapter XIII:
Awakening Arts of Domination
and Mastery Within

*Sex lies at the root of life, and we can never reverence
life until we know how to understand sex.*

—Havelock Ellis

Warning! This chapter may be inappropriate for certain ages.

T he arts of domination and mastery within us are the embracement
of yang, the power that drives our sexual ambitions. An individual
who tells you that lovemaking is all kind and delicate is lying
to you. Various individuals inhibit a moment of enclosed behavior or
repression to what's truly in their desire. It's time to be more in touch
with your **id** in a sexual nature and not sustain a moment of repression.
Social construction of other individuals' thoughts and the mass media
has caused many individuals to create sublimation to others without
pleasing yourselves. The truth is becoming an Adon is naturally in a
man's nature, while womanhood is submissive to our instruction of
lovemaking. Clarifying truth, sex is pure holiness granted to us by God.
It's what an individual substance it for that leads to evil deity, and I'm not
speaking of the sexual behavior but rather sex in rituals and other deities.
Awakening arts of sexology is actually all experimental and sensual. In
contrast to that, the rituals and other deities that practitioners, such as
Aleister Crowley, and evil deities, like Great Rite, are neither healthy
nor holy. Distinguished, **BDSM** is a variety of erotic practices involving

dominance and submission, role-play, restraint, and other interpersonal dynamic role-plays.

- ❖ **Bondage** = the tendency of a sadism behavior of sexual gratification through inflicting good pain, humiliation, and dominion toward a masochist with the practice of restraining them.
- ❖ **Domination** = the practice of seduction and Domestic Discipline toward the submissive, a directional path to becoming an Adon.
- ❖ **Sadism** = an individual who derives sexual gratification through good pain, Thanatos (see *Level to Master* below for Thanatos) nature, and humiliation toward the submissive.
- ❖ **Submission** = an individual who's willing to yield to an Adon/dominator through domestic discipline and love and accepting to the passive and receptive in the id primitive nature.
- ❖ **Masochism** = a sexual submissive that takes delight in the pleasure of being subjected to good pain and/or humiliation; the submissive who indulges in being dominated.

Out of the five practices, everyone should distinguish an acceptance and admit what ignites your very erotically fulfilling desires. Unless your desire is completely vanilla, which is the desire to keep sex sensual without the added substances of art and erotica, someone who don't want to try new things nor unlock their subconscious desires but remain attached to the original activities behaving subliminal in sex without worries of judgment.

> *Erotic love, enjoyed by the ignorant, becomes bondage. That very same love, tasted with understanding, brings liberation.*

> *—Āryadeva, Creating Purity of Mind*

Contrasting from Āryadeva, the *Nag Hammadi* holds ignorance the nurture of all evil ([Ignorance Is the Mother of Evil (83,30–84,14), from the Gospel of Philip]). Thereby, erotic love can't be indulged by the ignorant because you're caged in. In understanding erotic love savored with emunah, it conveys liberation. Breaking this meaning down, basically, it means living in denial to your sexual nature and *emunah* "faith, truth, fidelity, stability." You're burying yourself because of *repression*, but revealing your sexual persona sets free your burdens and oppression, thereby becoming **amorous** which means strongly seduced love and sexual desire that is without approval from others and unlawful to worldly laws. An amorous person doesn't seek consensual agreement from worldly cares but acts on agapic and erotic loving to what strongly seduces them (*see Chapter XVI, subtitle: Masterful Loving and Traits* [for lovers: erotic and agapic]). Various people of the Holy Faith believe that BDSM is the act of the devil. The truth is modern BDSM could be an act of the devil because many substances defilement and fill the submissive with contempt; however, Sensual BDSM is different because it opens your lovemaking to awaken your sexual persona of Eros, Thanatos, ardent, and amorous while striving for masterful artistic pleasures. If anyone was to type BDSM in Google Photo search engine, you'll notice a lot of inflicted violence that sabotage the art, but if you type Sensual BDSM, you'll notice more artful bliss than violence. Brutality is not Sensual BDSM nor is verbal degradation, for humiliation can cope but not so on degradation, its undesirable. Cultivate that indulging in Sensual BDSM is not sinful at all, for marriage sex acts are undefiled according to El Elyon law. Anyone who tells you different are speaking from their own conduct, not El Elyon conduct.

The interaction between tops and bottoms where physical and/or mental control of the bottom (submissive) is surrendered to the top (dominant/ master) is sometimes known as power exchange whether in the context of an encounter or a relationship. Sensual BDSM is about awakening the desire craved between couples (or harem), giving them a sense of belonging and satisfaction. The rest is ***artistic*** (means *done skillfully and tastefully, of art, creative, imaginative*). Nowadays, BDSM has been transformed into unpleasant and sick sexology. Sensual BDSM is the pleasant way of creating a spice in intimacy and Christian friendly art of lovemaking. In every Sensual BDSM sexual contact, each person must announce their *safety word*, the first cardinal rule each person must give to prevent accusations of harm. Honoring the safety word shows respect to the other. The second rule is **SSC,** meaning ***Safe, Sane, and Consensual***, or **RACK,** meaning ***Risk Aware Consensual Kink***, the important rule in this art. This is making another aware of your limits— hard, soft, and edge limits. ***Hard limit*** is letting another person know you're not tolerating or the ineptitudes. Basically, the receiver feels disapproving of the acts. ***Edge limit*** is letting another person know that their methods are on the borderline of pain and pleasure, making notice that the other is pushing their limits. ***Soft limit*** is giving notice to another that you're indulged in the methods bestowed, feeling it's completely sensual while giving a satisfying appetite. Letting the other become aware of your limits can be used symbolically as a body gesture or verbally as saying a word that establishes the limits. This is the **SSC/RACK**.

Level to a Master (Adon)

Master (Adon) lifestyle is another art similarly connected to the BDSM lifestyle but more disciplined and professional. The master lifestyle over time evolves to sexual arts of maturity progressed and higher levels of desires performed. Let's look into the definition of *master*.[40] *A person who is highly skilled, ingenious, or dexterous in some area of activity.* The Adon is a promotion above BDSM dominates. Master arts are more experienced than traditional BDSM dominates. Master is more disciplined and structured than the dominant. **Masters** (*Adonim*) explore the full dynamics of possibilities in sexual arts to his woman, the trinity of intimacy level to its prowess. The trinity of intimacy is the **Eros** (means *the powerful and mysterious sexual energy that savors in romantic love*) and the **Thanatos** (means *dark shadow of desire and aggression*) fulfilling both mirrors (your inner personality) of passion (Ferrer 2011) and the **Holy Amorous** (means a *strongly seduced love and sexual desire that is without approval from others and unlawful to worldly laws but prudent to the biblical Testaments*). Master is an instructor in the arts, so the analogy is if you teach your queen abuse, then expect it in return. If you teach her love and seduction, expect it returned in much delight—there is karma in this art. Conversely, if you teach her love and seduction, yet she doesn't submit to good gestures in return, then there's an affection problem on her part, and she may not be the queen for you. There's assumption that if a woman is really affectionate to you, she'll give you one or two of the pleasurable

A loving master performs amorously for his treasures submissive, going beyond proper for sanity to sanctify them both, and that becomes their internal and external healing, which becomes overall spice (their flavor & romance) of Loveology.

---

[40] *Webster's Third New International Dictionary, Unabridged, s.v.* "Master," accessed March 10, 2015, http://unabridged.merriam-webster.com.

appetizers, oral and anal giving to the King as a demonstration of an investing relationship and submission and are more trusted than ones who don't.

Although these assumptions are not necessarily all true on that part, these are optioned philosophy of various kings and young princes evolving in the world. In addition, some women won't perform any of these arts because of celibacy, the purified way of only giving dessert when investment is sealed with a diamond ring or spoken vows in biblical rites with the Bible as your right hand of a testament on promise through obligation and **dharma** *"duty."* Adonim (masters) remain obligated to their word and loyal unless betrayal is portrayed by the submissive/love slave. Master lover is the deep sense of opening up your lover's deeper secrets and supporting her fantasies, embracing the *Eros*, the *Holy Amorous*, and the *Thanatos*[41] (*see* Doctrine of Aggression) nature to fulfill satisfaction without the worry of publicity. Publicity will be judgmental to certain individuals who don't accept certain acts, but that's your own sacred desire and heaven. You don't need justification nor provide explicit detail on reason for your impulses. You only need to become the practitioner to become a master lover and harness while savoring your personal desires. Others' approval doesn't satisfy your urge but only prolongs the process of waiting momentarily until you're left with impulses to merge. Whether it's receiving oral, vaginal, and anal, you're justified by your own determinism and Lord when married. No shame should reminisce but only good gestures of embracement. The sexual hetero-animalistic you are is nature, not the subjection of an eccentric or ill-being. Remember some individuals project influence of persuasion because they don't like it, but it doesn't mean you have to withdraw from what's pleasing to you (this is your self-actualization you remain faithful to!), for there's another queen out there who can relate and accept your desire in whatever position. It's important to be masterful to become a master. The meaning of ***masterful***[42] is ***reflecting an imperious or domineering personality and actions.***

---

[41] When I infer Thanatos, I'm not talking about the supposedly God of Death, only the social science term.

[42] *Webster's Third New International Dictionary, Unabridged, s.v.* "Masterful," accessed March 10, 2015, http://unabridged.merriam-webster. com.

The *Adon* is sensible, a loyalist, discernably rational and honest, ardent, prudent outlaw, devout, aesthetic philosopher, guardian, knowledgeable or persistent in wisdom to persevere wise, inspirer, amorous, and embracer of the primitive persona and intimate arts.

Consensual Contract

Creating a professional consensual contract is a way of consensual understanding on what is acceptable in sexual desire and what is not. In private intimate union, Sensual BDSM, Domestic Discipline, and marriage contracts are very important to safeguard yourself and your significant other. Consensual contract is a matter of clear communication and protection without false proclamations that it was considered against will. A consensual contract is act of negotiation before the repercussion of role-play from your signature. Consensual contract is a signet (*see* Sacred Marriage Truth).

Sensual BDSM

No wife makes a great wife like a submissive wife, fully adore a submissive woman. Every king and queen possess a **love map**, which is the *"ability of connection and expressing their sexual desires in different, more passionate, primal, and creative ways"*; yet many are uncomfortable with the new millennium of BDSM because of the sanity of violence that lures to nothing of art but of sick sexual habits. The loving way is **Sensual BDSM**, which is *the desirable love map and role-play of making sensual loving arts longed for toward queen(s) from the Adon without infliction of bad pain and disciplined to power exchange Eros, ardent, amorous, and Thanatos in the bedroom.* Sensual BDSM is the true way to passionate lovemaking and considered sexually as aesthetic. Sensual BDSM is a mixture of *vanilla* with a spice of erotica and artistry. Vanilla only has the sensuality. Certain Christendom sites say that sensuality is evil because its embraced on desires of the flesh through becoming not prudent which leads the soul to death and sexual immorality, indeed, there's truth to this discernment though it seems certain Christendom sites have given discernments of all evil of the senses when truth is theirs a duality of the senses and it's what the individual substance it for that leads to good (cf. Galatians 5v22–25) or evil (cf. Galatians 5v19–21). Sensuality is thrived on the sensuous but the Spirit is connected to the sensuous because of the agapic love it shares undefiled when an individual is avowed and rendered unto the other individual with emunah, hope, and love, this is beauty of heart that clarifies a ministry of marriage. On the contrary, when I discuss sensuality I'm speaking of the sole purpose of emunah not promiscuity. Sensuality with the individual you're committing to or shared to if in a polygynous marriage, all of which is the essence of sensuality I'm discussing throughout part III and appendix II. For further discernment see *Sacred Marriage Truth* within chapter XVII. Sensual BDSM is built on a three-step pleasure system (Figure 10–1).

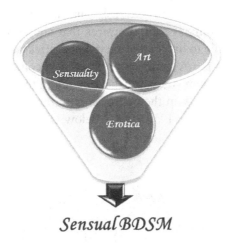

Sensual BDSM

Figure 10–1 *Erotica + Sensuality + Art = Sensual BDSM*

Erotica is built on seductive desires and innermost sensual sexual behaviorism. Erotica awakens the holistic nature of our impulses to discover and bring to reality as a nature of beauty and artistry. **Sensuality** is built on indulgence of sexual pleasure with a mixture of spiritual senses. Sensuality provides the connection of desires and pleasures into benevolence and affection, a peace of infinite love. **Art** is built on creativity and revelation. Art inspires the sensation of desire with opening to new dimensions of sexual awakenings. Art is the genuine of what's meet from the eyes that defines prepossessing. **Revelation** means a usually secret or surprising truth that is revealed into you and your partner's existence. Submitting to your true revelation sets sovereignty and rational truth. The *pleasure principle* is the tendency to provide immediate satisfaction through instinctual drives. Our instincts are our unlearned behaviors that have become more complex and hungered by our motivation to fulfill satisfaction. **Motivation** is the physical and mental abilities that ignites our drive of arousal, direction, and persistence.

The commonly used equipment in Sensual BDSM are collars, blindfolds, and either handcuffs or restraints or both. **Collars** *signify* ownership and acceptance similar to a wedding ring. **Blindfolds** *signify* revelation and naughty discretion. **Handcuffs** and **restraints** *signify* surrendering and receiving what is given without insinuation of rejection. **Blindfolds** are more known to be psychological play, intensifying the physiological reactions on the submissive while separating her reality to fantasy and fantasy to reality, teasing her subconscious while she's in nudity physically and mentally. You may ask what naked mentally is. This is the opening of a woman's sacred desires that she fantasizes about, and only her Adon is able to unlock the sacred pleasures while she completely surrenders because the Adon is committed to become her fantasy lover. Depending on the queen you have, she may tempt the Adon by wearing a blindfold while in nudity in the bedroom with the sheets off, waiting for the Adon to dominate her. Figure 10–2 below is a systematic approach to Sensual BDSM:

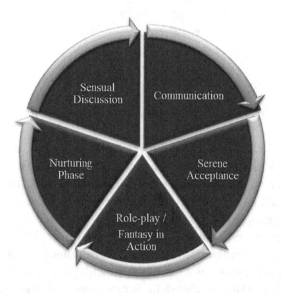

Figure 10-2 Clockwise Sensual BDSM and DD Process

Communication is the matter of discussion to what your partner is acceptable and disagreeable toward sexual acts, for its more noble to become benevolent without the intention to abuse. Communication builds trust and sexual intelligence, for communication can address your intentions and desires (such as sadist pleasure, emotional release, service satisfaction, or other notions). The next phase is **Serene Acceptance**. This is your partner becoming submitted to your acts while peaceful at mind because she's undisturbed more, for she knows your intentions (this perceives her conscious of revelation, while she's naïve to your art yet sexually enticed). The **Role-play/Fantasy in Action** phase is the actual act itself from the urge to the merge portion. A vivid example of Sensual BDSM role-play/fantasy in action is the *Fifty Shades of Grey* (2015) film theatrical version in approximate time of one hour and twenty-two minutes (01:22:00) to one hour and thirty minutes (01:30:00)[43].

> *Establishing Urge and Merge:* **Urge** is the performance of thought into action, the provoking impulse of uncontrollable desire (basically, you're thinking about what you're going to do to her before it's done). Your urges are your impulses, reminiscing what you're thinking about doing to her sexually with your Weapon of Love. In secret, sometimes your urge is what she fantasizes about, just waiting for you to merge. **Merge** is the action of performance with a controllable impulse in motion that sometimes brings out the uncontrollable. (This is you bringing your thoughts into action, the sexual intercourse in action). The urge to merge is called *impact play.*

The **Nurturing Phase** is the sensually art of therapeutic discipline, restoring energy with ointment, wine (or water), spooning, deserts, and food. The nurturing phase creates honorability. The discipline is withdrawn a lot more in the moments of *rough sex,* the *uncontrollable nature of aggression in sensual matters while connection of desire persists in the moments of power exchange.* In the film *A History of Violence* (Mortensen, et al. 2005) (approximate runtime of 01:07:20 to 01:10:13), the scene where Joey Cusack (Viggo Mortensen) and Edie Stall (Maria Bello) let their inner sexual urges loose on the staircase, merging roughly, was a prime example of rough sex. The reason I've given films to demonstrate a clear understanding is because in moments of rough sex, there's no logic, only virile and Thanatos impulses. Don't think sensual matters are soulfully slow, for this is not the meaning. The truth is sensual is taken with delight of what ignites your desirable cravings. Thus, you act on impulses while confirmation of your partner's intellectually acceptance through submission toward the performance. The clarity is reading your partner's acceptance of accepting sexual impulses, by your partner becoming receptive to it gives a psychological theory of acceptance from the sexual acts of Adon from the submissive. The **Sensual Discussion** is when intimate partners have the private discussion of what they enjoyed after that session of sexual art and what was unpleasant in the act. Sensual

---

[43]   Certain individuals may say this film is sinful to view as an example, but that's be honest, many things surrounding have sex in its nature. The telos of it is understanding.

discussion is the reconciliation for intimate relations, creating a fair bond and power exchange.

Power Exchange

Sexual lovemaking's overall core in *sexual awakening the physiological and emotional dimensions of sexual energy and power with connections to another being* is known as **power exchange**. Image gratified intimately by God clearly stated power exchange in the scriptures below:

Let the husband render unto the wife due benevolence: and likewise also the wife unto the husband. The wife hath not power of her own body, but the husband: and likewise also the husband hath not power of his own body, but the wife. (1 Corinthians 7v3–4 Authorized KJV)

Let the husband render the conjugal debt to his wife, and likewise also the wife to her husband. It is not the wife who has authority over her own body, but the husband; likewise, also it is not the husband who authority over his own body, but the wife. (1 Corinthians 7v3–4 Orthodox Jewish Bible)

Power exchange is a natural existence, a way of opening up and sharing willpower even when you seek to never reveal your inner natural emotion. It still eventually finds its way into opening through a companion. A man can be solid and unravel his deepest dimensions to the Lord and a living being whether it's pure or not; you release truth. Power exchange is a mixture of dynamics of two in one flesh, from physical, emotional, spiritual, and intellectual relations. The beauty of power exchange is that you're not always playing the dominant role but still in control; for instance, when your woman performs cowgirl "woman on top" position, she inverted energy of being the domineering, but the king/prince is still controlling her motion when your palms are on her hips, thereby you still have authority but allowing her sexual yin to invoke Eros and exploiting each other's love map.

Sexual ecstasy (*see* Section I: Loveology in its Nature) is primitive of sensual power exchange where the woman performs cowgirl position igniting the Eros and domineering nature while on top[44]; while for man, it's often the missionary position and doggy style position, doggy style is primitive because of the mammalian instinctual nature of resembling lordosis behavior from the woman while the man has the amorous sanctification of a *power play* (*see* Not Rape but Kink and Discipline) in the essence of the sexual carnal. *Lord of War* (Niccol 2005) demonstrated amorous and *power exchange* behavior from Yuri (Nicolas Cage) allure of affection for Ava (Bridget Moynahan) so his motion was not through forcing love but through honor of love for beauty during courtship with ardency, agape, and affection without time management, then sexual ecstasy thrived on the private jet for Ava had become seduced, then after an agapic marriage (starting approximate runtime of 28 minutes to 35 minutes). Rough lovemaking is commonly built upon *dolorous relief* and rage, and these impulses carry very little or no logic at all. The empirical truth is that no being is completely 100 percent dominant or submissive, which is why energy and power exchanges are between the lovemaking union, but the primary in men is yang, for this is our nature, and women is yin (yin and yang is explained in Chapter XV, subtitle: Becoming Lord of Sexual Roots).

Through power exchange, various individuals perhaps would fear the sexual behaviors brought into action because some fear their inner Thanatos nature or because possibly, an individual may have very greedy drive, very naughty, and strong aggressive sexual behaviors, bringing out a rough sexual nature, for these are the carnalities looking to taste the sensuous, so they suffer with *repression* through concealing it. Exposing your power exchange empirically mostly works when you have an intimate partner who is a down-to-earth individual with charismatic faith or type of belief who remembers not to be judgmental but be supportive and submissive in being rendered if it's endurable.

The Switch Philosophy

Forthright power exchange can become a switch if something unfortunate happened, or to explore primitive Eros, there are several BDSM books

---

[44]   The TV show *Strike Back* Season 2 Episode 15, starting approximate runtime of 37 minutes, could be used as a visual session of rough sex power exchange impact play where the woman demonstrated Thanatos and domineering nature while on top.

that imply that a switch is the man that was dominant becomes the submissive and the woman that was submissive becomes the dominatrix. Although this is a belief in their books, I have a different analogy of *switch* because men's primitive primary nature is the "sovereigns, masters, husbands, fathers, dominions." They're not submissive but just indulge occasionally to often having the woman on top because of sexual aesthetic thoughts (meaning the fervency to the view of their woman nude and thrusting as a *piquant-fruitful-sensualism* while aroused by her flesh, her facial expression and beauty, her feminine hairs, her gratifying gestures and motions, her perspiration, and her scent) or indulge in the feisty *Thanatos* nature of their woman or has unfortunate critical conditions. There's a common deceptive analogy that cowgirl "woman on top" position is a feminine nature of submissiveness in the man's persona. This is completely false, for cowgirl position is one of the most masterful ways to gain wisdom on how your woman savors coition so that the master may acknowledge satisfaction, while at the same, time it gives sexual aesthetic thoughts.

The matter of the woman playing the aggressor is more so dealing with the arousal of eagerness that formulates fervent response of becoming amorous and satisfied from the man. There's a common insinuation in mass media that the woman who plays the aggressor more likely have to be a spanker, brawler, or authoritarian, but this is not so. The truth is the desire arousal is the feisty momentum, eager, amorous, and aggressive coitus inner nature of a woman's sexuality unleashed and is what's mostly craved empirically from the dominatrix, not an abuser. The unfortunate critical conditions can come from injuries of serving your country whether it is from domestic violence to sports to government job to law enforcement to military or accident at birth. Thereby, for individuals who experienced critical conditions,

contempt may grow, causing dolorous emotion. *Contempt* means feeling worthless, despised, disregarded, and inferior. For instance, on the TV series *Hunted Season 1 Episode 4 Kismet* (starting approximate runtime of 00:36:24 to 00:38:20), Andrew (James Daffern) became disabled (unable to walk) due to an accident, so he's no longer able to perform missionary position so his wife, Zoe (Morven Christie), who performs cowgirl coitus position. After they've finished, Andrew begun a moment of *contempt* through reminiscing the past when he was able to dominate her, provide better for her, and overall provide better lovemaking for her, which gave him the fear of her leaving him, but his wife kept the covenant of *emunah* and *Ahavah*. She was strong for both of them and a loving enduring wife; the lesson is to appreciate the woman that's willing to be the stronghold for the *conjugal love* when going through unfortunate conditions. A switch can also be the provider for a self-cure for prejudice when two intimate unions connect and perform ardently with *piquant-fruitful-sensualism* to awaken the Eros and surrender amorously. For instance, in the film *Monster's Ball* (Addica and Rokos 2001), Hank (*Academy Award winner* Billy Bob Thornton) was a prejudice man who didn't like Negroes until he met Leticia (*Academy Award winner* Halle Berry). His emotion guided him to do the ethical when her son was hit by a car, then Hank checked up on Leticia. After Leticia communicated *avow* (for avowing, *see* "Domestic Discipline Philosophy and Psychology"), *power exchange* built up on them both then led to being *amorous* to communing a *love map* of *Eros* (starting approximate runtime of 01:04:28 to 01:18:45) shared between them. Both provided sexual healing and impassion. A person can be captivated by someone or something beautiful and recreate a transformation within themselves, thereby changing their outlook on what was once adversary to love, and that can be a switch.

Dungeon of Bliss

Find the whole **dungeon,** known as *"an erotic special room or place where you fulfill fantasy and keep your play toys and restraints,"* sexual orientation to be spicy scenery of desired environmental moods and variations. This type of scenery normally takes place in the master bedroom or secretive room, an artistic vision brought into reality with possessions of materials, such as, handcuffs, sashes, collars, liberators, scarfs and ties, spiritual love, vibrators, blindfolds and masks, Tantra feather ticklers, pulleys, chains, suspensions, aromatics, fantasy customs, or the embracement of nudism/naturism and gags. Warning. Using gags or pillows to restrain the mouth can be dangerous to the submissive; the bigger the gag is for the submissive the painful can be and perhaps difficulty in breathing and recommended to have a safety gesture. *Safety gestures* are *movement signals to make known you're uncomfortable*. It's also important that the Adon acknowledge the submissive's health, for she may have anxiety disorders, asthma, etc., or ill-health problems, so gags and any other materials that may give difficulty for breathing are not recommended. In Sensual BDSM, scarfs, ties, and sashes would sophist as a replacement for gags. Another thing to acknowledge is if you're using a flogger, it would be best to buy a quality flogger that's really soft on the skin (but keep in mind the Bible doesn't encourage flagellation, so floggers would come from an individual's own desire). Dungeons are examples of awakening fantasy into the conscious, embracing erotic themes that suit your gestured personality to deliciously naughtiness with your queen without feeling censored, for dungeons are uncensored. The dungeon can become your boudoir, "the private room" of sexual and spiritual love filled with wine, essential oils with olive oil to anoint the flesh, incenses or seductive candles, artistry sexual materials, deserts and fruits to feed your delights, music of your ladies choice, and a variety of therapeutic pillows and a comfortable bed (preferably among lovemaking, a king or queen size will suffice).

A *special formula* for the Instrument of Pleasure that will linger: combine red wine (empirically, I've noticed a good proportion of women enjoy Zinfandel or Sweet California Red, so one of these can be a good substitute to wine to consider in this moment) with a teaspoonful mixture of clove powder and Ceylon cinnamon powder. Apply teaspoonful of clove and Ceylon cinnamon powder in the mouth to linger for about fifteen to thirty seconds or longer then swish with red wine of your choice and swallow. This preserves a fresh-scented mouth while carrying on lovemaking for hours. Clove powder is for antifungal, antiseptic, antiviral, aphrodisiac, and a stimulate to blood flow. This formula can also be very good for the naughty women who *merge* to perform fellatio right after the man just finished driving the Hershey Highway and after she finishes fellatio. Keep your spices and wine nearby!

Contrasting Pains of Pleasure, Sorrowful Pleasure, and Abusive

There are two types of pain, **good pain**, which is *pleasant* and *desired*, and **bad pain**, which is *unpleasant* and *abusive*. A psychological terminology for this is algolagnia,[45] but don't misinterpret this as enjoyment of bad pain because it's meant for good pain only. Here's an analogy: Do you think a daughter of a real father will enjoy injuries with a look of sorrow and dolor on her face or a miniature bruise with a look of satisfaction and harmony upon her face? After you acknowledge that analogy, seek understanding of what is acceptable of good pain to your lady and comprehend the language of acceptability on her behalf, for every woman has a different sexual peak and comfort ability. The shocking question is "Is your queen a masochist?"[46] The role of sadism varies on rather your woman desires this type of infliction.[47] In reality, there are women who enjoy this act. This good pain desire is known as **sexual masochism**, means *intimate gratification from humiliation, pain, and suffering.*

In the Freudian theory, Freud expressed that a woman's nature is heritably a masochist through seeking intercourse and seeking to be mother's, which induces pain upon themselves. **Marie Bonaparte**, a follower of Freud, theorized the psychoanalytic position.

> Throughout the whole range of living creatures . . . passivity is characteristic of the female cell, the ovum whose mission is to await the male cell, the active mobile spermatozoan to come and penetrate it. Such penetration, however, implies infraction of its tissue, but infraction of a living creature's tissue may entail destruction: death as much as life. Thus the fecundation of the female cell is initiated by a kind of wound; in its way, the female cell is primordially "masochistic."[48] (1953, p. 79)

---

[45]   A fetish for pain.

[46]   See **Masochism**.

[47]   I infer infliction in this topic as "domestic discipline."

[48]   Marie Bonaparte, *Female Sexuality* (New York: Grove Press, 1965) (first published by International Universities Press, 1953).

Meaning, the woman's nature is the opening to a penetrator for deflowering virginity to womanhood of receptivity and passivity, opening in submission and to allow raw lovemaking to procreate motherhood or feel holistically the Weapon of Love, along with ejaculations. All of these come with inducing *masochism* from deflowering, submission of intimate openings, to nine months of bearing and laboring for motherhood, while men naturally have the prime nature of sadism (Hall 2000, 98) from penetrating.[49] Rainer Maria (Rilke 1962, 30) spoke of similar gesture, that pain and ecstasy, though may have different forms, the craving and delights are closely shared. However, there are pain sufferers out there in the world who are diagnosed with allodynia and hyperalgesia. They are more sensitive to pain infliction even the lightest touch (Thernstrom 2010). The initial sexual masochist process is to create awareness and negotiate the actions you're going to take rather than make it a surprise. Making aware and testing their capacity of tolerance gives the threshold. The empirical reality is that there are confused kings out there who believe beating a woman like they would with a male is acceptable, but the truth is this is not acceptable, for your infliction of bad pain is not even proportionate to love but lean more on *Ra* "evil morals."

There's an insinuation among some individuals who believe facial slapping is part of BDSM. Perhaps it is a part of BDSM but not Sensual BDSM. Boiling to reality, women adore their appearance and don't enjoy being bruised upon their body (a spanking on the butt will be admissible [*see* "Erotic Spanking Discipline," for disciplinary spanking]), especially disapproving if you're hitting their face, so if you do decide to facial slap, be mindful that she may look at you with sane and slap/punch you back and say, "Fool, you lost your damn mind," or she may grab a knife because she may perceive you're trying to abusively brawl on her, and she doesn't have to accept scornful behavior. Yeah, you read right. What you see in films and television shows is not how things often play out in reality. Abusive inflictions are mostly trauma from childhood, past relations that led to heartbreaks of a king, and social influences persuading bad pain as psychologically healthy to sustain relation while storing order. However, this doesn't validate your brawling afflictions toward your queen.

---

[49] Hall inferenced this from the book *The Development of Religious Toleration in England* by Wilbur Kitchener Jordan (1940) page 476–477. Note that "brutality and sadism are deeply rooted in a man's nature." In opinion, sadism is but not necessarily true on brutality.

In *Zalman King's Pleasure or Pain* (Morgan and Vasilopoulos 2013) film (starting approximate runtime of 01:10:45 to 01:32:19), Victoria (Malena Morgan) was tested by her husband, the dominant, Jack (Christos Vasilopoulos), who was so trapped in seduction phase. He lost his way by allowing Victoria to swing with another man that it broke the passion between Victoria and Jack. The wife is a treasure to the husband, and he has the need to own a treasure, but when it becomes shared, empirically, it's not as cherishable as it once was. Jack initiated that mistake by withdrawing from the passionate love infused through his absence of taking care of Victoria's sexual needs. Jack's sexuality with Victoria depolarized. Then pleasure became a <u>sorrowful pain</u> for Victoria. Victoria became the Pragma lover, for she tried doing whatever she could for Jack to regain the passion that they used to have; therefore, the love that was erotic, passionate, and agapic became manic to ludic (*see Chapter XVI, subtitle: Masterful Loving and Traits* [for lovers: erotic, passionate, agapic, manic, pragmatic, and ludic]). Individuals may ask why I reference a softcore pornographic film, the answer is because this type of voyeurism exist and it's empirically real from certain men according David J. Ley PhD. book, *Insatiable Wives: Women Who Stray and the Men Who Love Them*. Marriage is sacred not an open relationship (Mark 10v9), vows solidifies marriage purpose therefore it rectifies it's metaphysic description.

Below is table contrasting Sensual BDSM from an abusive individual:

Abusive Process
Process 1, abuser, is the individual who causes physical and verbal anguish and violence inflicted against their partner.
Process 2, guilt, the abuser concerned of exposure and consequences of his/her actions.
Process 3, manipulator, abuser will rationalize reason and avoid blame, provoking a natural cause.
Process 4, romancer, the abuser will portray an image of ideal lover and buy gifts and devote more time to pursue the one abused to ensure the abused one remains in the relationship.
Process 5, diligence, the abuser shows his/her true colors while creating a planning cycle in secret to regain his/her domestics.

Process 6, adversary, the abuser releases a devil again at their moment of determination when it's discreet.

There are some abusers who really make an effort to change by rejecting the things that make them trigger abusive afflictions. In vivid relation, the film *The Living* (Bryan 2014) portrayed a prime example of this when Molly (Jocelin Donahue) was <u>abusively brawled</u> on from her husband, Teddy (Fran Kranz), the *abuser* (process 1) through alcoholism. Teddy quested for absolution the next following morning and thereafter with the process of *guilt* but also contempt for undeserving, then he developed a plea of mercy (without process 3) by owning up to his afflictions by rationalizing and throwing away all the alcoholic beverages, fasting, and repentance to Molly and not avoiding blame while humble and sober. Teddy became a *romancer*, while Molly evoked shame upon him through his and her associates and friends in public places without makeup but a demonstration of her husband's bitter beatings, which manipulated Teddy. Molly evoked shame upon him to make him acknowledge her as his treasure (wife), not a brawling bag. Teddy became more so a *fervent* lover to Molly, and in the end, she granted him the honor of being her husband again. Molly also granted Teddy the privilege to drink one beer under her supervision from approval because of her judgment. She acknowledged that alcoholism doesn't change within a day, but a decrease in supplementation daily can soon become a sober supplementation. Notice three things Teddy didn't become—the *manipulator* (process 3), *diligence* planner (process 5), and *adversary* (process 6). When a woman goes through a brawling abusive process, she must intellectually perceive if the change her man portrays matches the process of Teddy. The process of Teddy is for the women whom live with a brawling husband that won't let go of their husbands because of hope and *Ahavah*, however hopefully these type of women will leave the scornful or the brawler will develop transformation and deliverance to brawl no more on the woman. Abusive process is known as *domestic abuse*.

The Tragedies Women Go Through Make It Difficult Love

Ultimately, a woman's nature loves the desire to be desired, a passionate and uncontrollable desire. Sometimes it comes with a sacrifice or greater investment than usual.

Women who have been abused are commonly the individuals who are supposed to receive love from others, such as husband, fathers, mothers, adopted guardians, brothers and sisters, and relatives. Women who have gone through abuse may find it difficult to participate in Sensual BDSM because of a legacy of violence that may always taunt memories. These women need more patient loving than domination but require an Adon. The Adon can provide a framework of a *Switch Philosophy* by allowing her to have more empowerment using an aesthetic *piquant-fruitful-sensualism* loving (discussed in *The Switch Philosophy* previously).

Even though their nature is designed to be submissive, it doesn't mean she'll willfully submit because she needs to build a personal intellectual that the king will not fill her with contempt nor abuse her but show ardent love and feeling that the king provides inspiration and affection rather than contempt and brutality. A woman who's been abused may act scornful toward her king even when it's undeserved. The Adon protocol is to develop a strong theory on her problems to help heal what has been abused in her. Humbleness is required on the Adon part too so that in time, her heart may reach a harvest of complete submission. Acknowledge she maybe bitter and difficult to compromise due to misfortune of trust from others, so a transformation would have to gradually increase on her part. Abused females would possibly have a hard time being submissive to the Adon all because of lack of *emunah* from previous malicious male encounter. Another empirical truth is that some women entrusted themselves to certain men in life that they were submitting to but were abandoned by dominants with seeds of child/children without being supportive and loving to their seed(s). Be aware that a dominant can be a deceiver, but establishing yourself as master, then you're residing in *emunah* and *Ahavah* because a loving master (*Adon*) doesn't leave his treasure but holds on to the treasure, preceding an act of stewardship and devotion. There are perhaps many dominants in life but few masters, for not many dominants stay in covenant with the queens but only have the intention to dominate them in bed a few times then leave. Masters will hold on to their possessions ardently, while dominants will treasure periodically then seek outside the covenant (relationship). Moreover, because certain women vessels—meaning body, mentality, and Spirit, have been pierced with *Ra* and *dolor* through dominants, defiling sexual assaults from the kindred or strangers, and harshly beatings. Faith and sensibility is required in process of companionship with intimate investment. The Adon must find a way to show true love! Cultivate that.

On the contrary, God warned queens and princesses of dominates within Colossians 2v8 KJV:

"Beware lest any man spoil you through philosophy and vain deceit, after the tradition of men, after the rudiments of the world, and not after Christ."

"Beware lest (is discerning caution and avoidance of) any man spoil (means weaken or destroy value or being too lenient to) you through philosophy (study of core of the nature of knowledge, reality, and ontology [*see* Ontology]) and vain deceit (means consuming or actions with excessive high opinion of one's visage, value, or skills, thereby creating a boastful character in another to seduce; flattery; deceitful to progress desire), after the tradition of men, after the rudiments (basic principles) of the world, and not after Christ." Furthermore, "after Christ" is not only saying faith in Yahawashi but the meaning of Christ "measured," so it's both faith and what's measured to be considered discerned *fair* (*see* Arcanum, the Awakening Loveology) of another. The spoilage is inevitable and often always good but Christ should be the center of *faith* and lifestyle. Spoilage to desires is capable within both mankind and womankind, for sexual urge can surrender itself to *impact play* and behave amorously defiled from dissimulated love, it's a natural sin. Forgiveness of the soul is at the hand's Yahawah and propitiation by Yahawashi, it's the cause of our actions that we have to edify and admit ourselves to providence. The heart is easily deceived, therefore easily spoiled upon, but God will search for malice of the hearts and bring upon vengeance of the one's deceitful in time (cf. Jeremiah 17v9–10, 1 Samuel 16v7). Deceit is dishonest and disloyal.

Certain women have invested in certain men that have philandered and those certain women discovered themselves spoiled in vain deceit and philosophy because of abandonment, scornful abuse or cause of *contempt* and *dolor*. Therefore, bitterness and adaption of courtesan tradition becomes a strategy to certain women to receive what they feel owed or deemed valued because the previous or current dominant(s) have given them fortune of descendant(s) though in reality some consider misfortune, then the dominate(s) is not willing to be accountable with stewardship and guardianship. Descendants' (children) are a beautiful grace and should be awarded with jubilation but there are many challenges a mother would have to go through but the dolorous portion is when she has to go through the challenges alone, without the man that shares the responsibility when he's the one that sowed the seed.

Therefore, the Word enlighten mankind to be Adon's toward *treasures queens* not the dominant. The truth is a Submissive (natural born woman) can become rapturous in majestic when she discovers reverenced desire within her king towards her gives stronghold of emunah, while not behaving furtively dishonest and disloyal, but the capacity to acknowledge what's his desire and remain steady and resolute to the devotion and desire, is deemed more crowned toward the man by woman because it represents focus, honor and stability towards her. However, this desire is not just on her but an ambition, a dream the king is looking to persevere, sensualism, and investments, all with remaining steady and resolute, are admired by the queen as a noble being. The man should only strategize behavior of hustle (*see* Hustling Kings) and reevaluate investment (*see* Intimate Investment) if discerning she may not be considered *fair*, a *devotee*, of *good works*, *sensible* and *treasures woman*. In Hebrew, the word "**husband**"[50] means *master, owner, lord, and possessor* (basically, it means **Adon**), which defines what Adon Olam strive us men to be. This would explain why Sara addressed Abraham as lord (1 Peter 3v6). While dominants are predominately princes, an Adon is predominately king, in addition, has the council of priesthood in those who covenant with faith in Christ and the Father; the Word ordains not the governing authorities.

---

50   Hayk Hovhannisyan, *Men and Women in the Ministry for Christ*, 9.

Chapter XIV:
Art of Domestic Discipline

Wives, submit yourselves unto your own husbands, as unto the Lord. For the husband is the head of the wife, even as Christ is the head of the church: and he is the saviour of the body. Therefore as the church is subject unto Christ, so let the wives be to their own husbands in everything.

—Ephesians 5v22–24 King James Version (KJV)

Warning! This chapter may be inappropriate for certain ages

Domestic Discipline is an art through the Adon creating and sustaining intimate relations union by psychologically restraining (the use of rules and punishment) toward the Submissive to *tranquilize* relations. Notice this is domestic <u>discipline</u>, *not* domestic <u>abuse</u>, before we begin. The approach of this chapter is strictly consensual lovemaking between kings and queens. Ephesians 5v22–24 scripture was meant for kings to claim dominion over women. You are king, but Lord is above all. You're all Adonim, which means in Hebrew, masters, "sovereigns, rulers." Domestic Discipline (**DD**), which is also known as ***Christian Domestic Discipline (CDD)***, is an ancient enforcement intended to help your queen overcome negative behaviors that they inflict upon themselves and their relation with you and others. Domestic discipline creates disciplined loving rules to the submitted behavior, physical correction, and a loving connection. *"For the woman which hath an husband is bound by the law to her husband so long as* *he liveth; but if the husband be dead, she is loosed from the law of her husband.''[51]*

Spanking is the traditional disciplinary protocol but not the only one, although the use of spanking is given by the dominant or master toward the submissive through proper levels of punishment given through her transgressions. Spankings are often performed through the use of a king's or prince's palm to slap on the buttocks when her transgressions are bad. The use of spankings should be used in a loving, caring, and masterful manner. According to Jules Markham, author of *Domestic Discipline*, **DD** can have benefits of both psychological as well as physiological factors through use of discipline. Before we begin on **DD**, know that the dimension to become acceptable to this lifestyle, you must preserve *anonymity*, for *privacy* is very important. Learn how to keep your mouth shut for you and your companion's sake unless you're both consented on being publicly open to it.

Abon Disciplinary Language

Many men perceive a false systematic disciple that they feel the need to speak to their woman harshly and abusive, but way too lovable language is a tone of pleasant, "pleasant words are as an honeycomb, sweet to the soul, and health to the bones."[52] Women respond more better in erotic spoken language. Say, for instance, in the film *Silver*, Zeke (William Baldwin) applied Domestic Discipline in a seductive act toward Carly (Sharon Stone) at the restaurant. He took the initiative of creating a game of intimate poker.

> Zeke provoked Carly, a daring seduction by asking about the luxury panties and bra, challenging her to take off her panties at the dining table to demonstrate she was wearing what he brought her, while she sipped on her wine. Carly became naughty, *humiliated*, and *submissive* to his challenge. While she smoothly slipped them off gracefully, smiling, she curled up her panties in her palm and tossed them on the restaurant dining table. Zeke

---

[51]   Romans 7v2 King James Version.

[52]   Proverbs 16v24 King James Version.

held on to the panties while leaving her nude under her dress, intently for easy open penetration later that night without the foreplay.

Speaking anguish (abusive tones: calling her words that feel contemptuous like hoe, fat, anorexic, and racial slurs and bring up past regrets that the Adon knows is harmful to the submissive queen's heart) to a woman is not the Yahushua intent on lovemaking to our women. The empirical reality is that occasionally too often, some men would speak to their woman like trash as something less than human, but the inner nature of a woman is more sensitive while kings/princes are developing more sensibility. There's a difference between speaking an Adon speaking to his submissive queen with authority and assertion and speaking to the submissive queen with anguish and hatred. The authority and assertion is what's needed sometimes for certain submissive queens like to test the Adon's yang, so it's a necessary to reinforce language with some authority and assertion. In practical street language, this is called smooth talking, but **DD** smooth talking is to currently sustain current relations. **Sensible** means persistent actions chosen with wisdom and prudence, sagacious, and or actions of discerning care and thought to another's vessel; **CDD** is *sensible*. Humiliation is one of the chastising arts of **DD**, for **humiliation** means *making someone feel guilty, naughty, and vulnerable, penetrating their dignity either in public or private.*

A form of DD along with Sensual BDSM called **writing erotica** is a grapy on language of what you're looking to fulfill your innermost desires sexually to your significant other for eventful artistry and arousal. Suppose you had a big project to study to pioneer the living of it. Thus, meaning the Adon will have to become a personal scholar of study their consort to reveal certain passions the consort craves, to perceive an intellect on what's craved with studying the consort symbolic loving gestures to better theorize what the consort wants intimately. Now think of that same project as studying the woman who's a treasure to you. You'll then comprehend how she'll react to certain things. This will strategize how to apply discipline to the submissive. The flaw of thinking every woman is the same is the greatest mistake an Adon can make, for not everyone is the same.

Not everything is in writing but a more symbolic nature of Sensual BDSM through the identity of the collars, scarfs, ribbons or sashes (are one of the more comfortable for submissive's, can be worn on neck like a scarf, tied thighs, or wrists) the submissive queen wears on her nude body or lingerie, for it's all symbolic with five distinctive colors: maroon (dark red), royal blue, beige (ivory), white sheer (white), and black.

❖ *Maroon* is symbolic for ardent love, erotica love, longing for long durations of lovemaking, a spice of aggression (Thanatos), vigor, impulsive, assertion of passionate love and deceasing foreplay because passion is already aroused, actions for a little forbidden lovemaking, behaving amorously, and primal.

❖ *Royal blue* is symbolic for desiring fulfillment of a novelty, looking to be a peaceful and divine naturistic atmosphere for lovemaking, amorous depths residing in emunah, and ensures fidelity.

❖ *Beige (Ivory)* is symbolic seeking humbleness, smoothness, warmth, detachment from the worldly cares, and therapy in lovemaking occasions.

❖ *White sheer* is symbolic for the desire to be treated as innocence and a mixture of spirituality, persisting intimate wisdom and healing, combination of agapic love and free love.

❖ *Black* is symbolic for something mysteriously forbidden clinging to, seeking deviant loving aggression in the moments and submissive seeking more authoritarian persona toward the master by being fully subservient (she wants to be told what to do, seeking the master to have his way).

Communication and Liberation in Disciplinary Notion

Communication of authority in the Bible says that the husband is the head, but the wife has the render of the Adon body just as the wife must be submissive to the husband because he has control over her body. Therefore, the truth is the Adon couldn't disregard the wife's opinion but still has the last say, but it's important to collaborate in agreement. For instance, if the Adon says I'm going out with the brethren to a bachelor's party, the submissive has authority over the Adon's motive to say, "No, you're not," then the husband has to be fair and render into the wife if it's liberated from the Bible. "[18]Wives, submit yourselves unto your own husbands, as it is fit in the Lord. [19]Husbands, love your wives, and be not bitter against them."[53] The important message to the Adonim is being

---

[53] Colossians 3v18-19 King James Version

not bitter, which means being affectionate, giving truthfulness, providing sensibility, and being inspiring and loyalty. Being bitter is being malign, untrue, disloyal, filling with contempt, and being harsh (means extremely severe). Though "every man is brutish by his knowledge . . ." (Jeremiah 51v17 KJV), therefore brutish is inevitable, which is why Yahawah gives providence that men be more rooted in the Spirit to purge brutish with doctrine of *theology* while the woman sublimates man with sensibility during his brutishness. The most common I've noticed that kings and princes in this millennium compromise often, but the analogy here is "if the Adon compromises on the majority, what is left to call yourselves the title Adon," for the man's position is Adon among the submissive, not the submissive.

Domestic Discipline Philosophy and Psychology

DD Philosophy in Mankind and Womankind

Various submissive women have the tendency to fantasize about becoming a *student, secretary, patient,* and/or *maiden* in the arts of intimacy, while she's craving a *mentor, boss, doctor, idol father,* and/or *officer* in the arts of intimacy. The **mentors'** role is the art of instructing the multitude of sexual positions or discipline, events and challenges of becoming skilled in creating seduction toward the submissive to create investment of the mentors will and inspire the submissive and sensible to her *cognitive sufferings.* The **boss's** role is to invoke order of proper sexual service and provide full-time hours to the submissive for strictly intimacy of affection and sex and allowing his consort in business and directing sensibly toward her *spiritual sufferings* to bring her into the high-spirited bliss. For instance, a submissive is constantly bored at home because the Adon is often gone working, and then when he gets back, he's brought groceries, cooked the food, and performed other household duties, but the submissive says intrapersonal "what's left for me to do if my Adon is doing it all, why can't he spend more time with me?" The boss's role is to provide more affection and sex and realize he shouldn't do everything, for she wants to be part of the Adon. Submissive wants a partnership, Submissive wants to drive the Adon to work, Submissive wants sexual healing, and then the boss Adon will create a full-time schedule. The main protocol of the boss Adon role is to give sensible honor to allowing the submissive to feel important and help meet partner. The Adon takes the 55 percent to 75 percent role in dharma and leadership, while the submissive takes the 45 percent to 25 percent role in dharma and leadership. The *doctor's* role is providing nourishment when the vessel is weak, sensibility to a submissive *physical suffering*, properly supplementing her with potent prescription, Serere Medicine to bring forth healings and provides the service she's craving or insinuating for and anoint the submissive body with holistic therapeutic remedies and providing loving healings. The *idol fathers'* role is to provide privacy and bring forth support to her desires, ambitions, and hopes and be sensible to her *emotional suffering*, dreams, and remind her of purpose in the tone of pleasant benevolence while creating commandments and addressing proper discipline for transgressions to heal her internally (for sufferings, see Chapter III, subtitle: Dolor and Ra). The *officers'* role is to provide sensual domination arrest with cuffs, sashes, and blindfold, addressing enforces on rules created, and gives the illusion of sexual captivity to allure a novelty, and promise of ensuring privacy and stability.

Many of us in the world are secretive in DD, Sensual BDSM, and sex. The truth is we desire privacy with a true urge and merge of sexual actions unrated, mature, and undefiled. An Adon and submissive must *avow emunah* of their sexual nature or be *repressed* and *suppressed* by it, but if they *avow emunah*, then it'll evolve into loving *liberation*. (*See below, subtitle: Adon Non-Spanking Disciplinary, semi-subtitle: Lack of Sex Discipline* for suppression effect). **Avowing** means to confess with honesty, open and unashamed, to awaken positivity for *liberation*. *Avowing* frees your sexual desire, awakening the naturalism of sexual lifestyle and perseverance. Sexual lifestyles can be DD, Sensual BDSM, naturism and nudism, private dancer . . . However, DD, Sensual BDSM, and sexual behaviors people have the tendency to not understand the empirical cycles.

Loving and Deviant Loving Cycles

The (+) is the loving that can be indulged by many individuals, for its more agreeable mostly but is not necessarily true for everyone. The (+/-) is the loving that's in between, some love and some disapprove, some consist of this behavior, and some don't. It all depends on who you choose for companion. The (-) is the disdain loving or not part of loving, and many individuals won't tolerate because it would bring a plague of dolor, contempt, angst, and/or agony.

> *Sin'ah (Hatred) stirreth up medanim (dissensions), but Ahavah covereth all peysha'im (sins, transgressions, rebellions). [Mishle (Proverbs 12v10 Orthodox Jewish Bible)]*

This scripture is important to the ones feeling like they're crossing borderlines in faith tradition, but the truth is love can be deviant, but that doesn't make it any less than love, just a different type of loving, not everyone loves the same. Let's identify man's loving and deviant loving cycles toward a woman, to better proportionate DD behavior. This diagram Figure 14-1 below gives acknowledgment on a man's behavior toward a woman, his nature, liberation, and prudence, and what he'll more likely become acceptable to give toward his woman:

Figure 14-1: Man DD Behavior

Notice that many women empirically are more so not acceptable to men who are alcoholics, brawlers, and insensitive men and men who are addicted to narcotics. The reason negative for exhibitionism is because just like men, women want to protect what's theirs without openly making room for another woman to tempt her man because of what the strange woman sees lustfully appealing. The reason is positive, for naturism is because the confidence a man inspires makes it a sexual turn on but even then can lean more too negative ineptitudes if it turns into exhibitionism because of protecting their relationships, "the covenant." The two reasons why emunah from a man to his significant other are disagreeable. One feels that he doesn't have her full submission sexually or the other is he's a complete deceiver built on only satisfying his pleasure; therefore, he's bitter because he doesn't desire to commit nor heartfelt so the communion; Ahavah and power exchange is empty. For creativity and humiliation, it is *negative* because the love map can be damaging resulting to uncomfortable positions, situations, and demands or *positive* for blissful comfortable positions, situations, and demands toward women (humiliation has to be with sensibility). The main logic in creativity is don't invest or accept in something unhealthy or dangerous.

For instance, in the film *Sex Tape* (Diaz and Segel 2014) (starting approximate runtime of 01:27:00 to 01:30:00 theatrical version), the moment they were following the *Joy of Sex* manual, one part was when Annie (Cameron Diaz) did a spinning flip to aim her Valley of Joy directly to Jay's (Jason Segel) Weapon of Love. You'll notice they both hurt themselves doing a dangerous sexual stunt.

Now compare and contrast the woman's loving and deviant loving cycles toward a man to better proportionate DD behavior. The diagram Figure 14-2 below gives acknowledgment on a woman's behavior toward a man, her nature, liberation and prudence, and what she's more likely to become acceptable to give toward her man:

Loving (+)

Emunah (+/-), Subservient (+/-), Honour (+), Serene Acceptance (+), Supportive (+), Sexually Eager (+), Submission (+), Nuturing (+), Ahavah (+), Advisor (+), Virtuous (+), Humble (+), Amorous (+), Sober (+), Eros (+), Receptive Hershey Highway Discipline (+/-), Passionate fellatrix (+/-), Realist (+/-), Sympathetic (+), Communion (+), Aesthetic (+), Ardent (+)

Deviation loving (+/-)

Masochism (+/-), Thanatos (+), Bondage (+), Feisty (+/-), brawling (-), Spanking (+/-), Humilation (+/-), Alcholic (-), Narcotics (-), Supporting edge-play (+/-), Bondage (+/-), Strap-on (+/-), naturism/nudism (+), exhibitionism (-), Sensual BDSM (+), seeking to be ravished (+), fantasy play (+), Dominatrix switch (+/-)

+ Positive Prowess

— Negative Ineptitudes

Figure 14 -2: Female DD Behavior

Withholding how you love is the pity of brainwashing how you should love, so you're suffocating yourself on your inner desire. Don't allow someone else to construct your lovemaking conduct on how it should be productive but free yourself amorously. Your emotions guide your senses of good judgment, so if you feel shameful within yourself, then you'll seek absolution within, but if it was pleasurable, then you'll feel ardent. Social construction often makes statements of deviant loving as something taboo and unnatural or make emphasis of something discouraging about it. The question is does everyone think vanilla loving is all original or healthy because vanilla just means something sweet and original; however, the analogy is who is anyone to construct an id of an individual to justify what is healthy and natural. Maybe deviant loving is healthier because a true love map has become uncompressed, unrestrictive amorous, and undefiled. Deviant loving is a combination of vanilla and the full embracement of primal nature that's unrestricted, uncensored, and *avowing emunah* to ourselves; therefore, the individual reaches above original because original is sublimation, while individuality is unmeasurably new and healthy because a true *love map* opened within the individual's distinction. The contemptuous portion is when an individual permit themselves to alcohol and narcotic abuse to make themselves guilt-free because of fear of oppression. Moreover, rationally various individuals like to play the victimhood role of insinuating it's all because of what's viewed in the media or consumed alcohol substances but innate truth is certain sexual deviances is already within their confidences, they're just using the blame of victimhood from voyeurism, narcotics or alcoholic beverage(s) to pardon themselves while attempting to gain empathy or approval from others. In diligence when individuals look into the moral relativism with films individuals highly invest in, such as, *Fifty Shades of Grey*, and other related films, individuals will acknowledge deviance within those films causing realism that there's a great relativism to deviant loving many invest in confidences. Without *self-analysis* (see chapter II) and *sensibility* to arcanum's *impact play* you're burdening yourself with denial, embrace and *sensibility* should be the factor not denial, so that the individual may edify themselves, the deviant individual would just have to find a compatible or amenable lover.

For a visual seminar of deviant loving, I will refer to *A Serbian Film* (starting approximate runtime of 00:09:33 to 00:14:00 from Blu-ray Unrated Version). When Milos (Srdan Todorovic) was viewing his past pornographic occupation, and his wife Marija (Jelena Gavrilovic) was aiming for his ardency, Marija slapped him (take note: he didn't brawl on his treasured wife), and he ripped her dress and performed deviant coercion Hershey Highway loving, the *Thanatos* thrived, then turned her over thrusting smoothly into Marija's Honey Pot with ardency which built a *love map* became a *power exchange* of *Eros*. Sex is more therapeutic in nature, "For some, sex leads to sainthood; for others it is the road to hell" as stated by Henry Miller. The controversial disturbing *A Serbian Film* proved to be the truest definition to road to hell but also vile affection. After runtime of 43 minutes to the remainder of the film, many individuals frown upon this film, but it's necessary to awaken the eyes of many of what's not to be done, how sexuality can become a horror or bitter, and how profanely defiling some individuals are in this world.

Erotic Spanking Discipline

Erotic spanking discipline is only between consensual adults, for erotic spanking stimulates a natural psychotherapy and a natural sexual response of eroticism and ardent loving (see chapter XVI, subtitle: Masterful Loving and Traits).

Vicarious reinforcement (VR) is *conveying the central behavior when appropriate through another to create arousal to determine delightful response.* This is a matter of observational learning to determine what is and when it is enjoyable. VR is the procedure on how the Adon will determine the appropriate method in discipline. Cultivate that this is no one else's business on how the Adon bring upon kink methodologies but the Adon's alone.

We're going to focus on three methods for this erotic spanking discipline, but keep in mind spanks should go nowhere else but on the bottom (buttocks), and the Adon is not required to use any spanking materials but his hands, for a submissive queen is more visually comfortable with a hand than noticing an object that her mind perceives maybe very harmful, so this will be a more holistic and ancient spank remedy.

Method I:

Original kink erotic spankings begins first by the Adon cuffing his hands (if the Adon hands is flat, the Adon may do harm than pleasure to the submissive. Cuffing the hand is like the form of an open C. This will validate as cuffing the hands) and spanking in an upward clockwise position, in a mildly to lightly aggressive spank. Spanks could range from one to ten spanks, but it's for pleasure, not for bitter beatings. In truth, spank can happen in any moment. When the Adon comes home speculates his queen bending over to pull out some freshly baked pie and apply *vicarious reinforcement* by ardently giving one mildly aggressive spank with a grasping hold on the bottom then stripping her to have her right in the kitchen or in the moment the Adon is having intercourse with his submissive queen. For every moment the Adon thinks his submissive is about to climax or if she's silent when he's thrusting in a doggy style position in her Valley of Joy or Trunk of Bliss, and she moans or breathes rapidly, the Adon would perform a spank to bring out a reaction from the submissive for blissful noise or pleasurable reaction. The switch can be when the submissive is performing the cowgirl position on the Adon, and during her thrusts, if she's slowing down or preparing to climax, the Adon can give her a mildly aggressive spank to keep her thrusting because a spank gives a sign for want of more or sexual fruitful cravings. Another switch can be the submissive giving spanks. When the Adon is in a missionary position, the submissive will provide an aggressive spank to intellectually and physically enforce to the Adon she wants more or to grab the Adon's buttocks forcefully and aggressively to her as a symbolic gesture "for more or to slow him down," a spank to signal "speed up." The reaction is the longing expression of this erotic spanking—the reaction spank to increase and decrease thrusting speed, the reaction spank to intellectually give another a symbolic understanding that the individual desires more thrusting, the reaction spank to give another in understanding of honor for enjoying it, and the reaction of hearing blissful noise while the submissive bits her lower lip.

Method II:

The *maintenance spanking* begins with the Adon binding his submissive queen over his knees or object and removing any bottom canopy she may have covering her flesh then cuff the hands and spank in a combination of clockwise mildly aggressive and counterclockwise lightly aggressive in maneuvering cycles on what's adaptable to comfortability to the Adon and submissive. This can range from seven to fifteen spanks in this particular phase of maintenance spanking. A *casual maintenance spank* can be just one mellow aggressive spank as a token of affectionate honor for the submissive queen's company, when she's done hospitality very well to the Adon's will for this act is symbolic for "job well done," cooked food and made desserts very good according to the taste buds or the appeal of being pleased with her in ways of the sexual, the Adon aesthetically beautified by his submissive's appeal, or her dharma of prudence (such as being supportive, good parental guidance, etc.). The other is a *negative reinforce maintenance spank*, which is the Adon's assertion of authority and sovereignty with a range from one to five spanks, cuffing the hands and spanking in a curve clockwise swing spank (for visual example, the 2002 film *Secretary* or 2011 film *A Dangerous Method*) because the Adon would spank his submissive queen aggressively hard to enforce a repentance within her for rebellious Spirit and actions or to assert ownership of the submissive when she's becoming temptation from gravitating another man through an act of lust or another religion through an act of confusion when she's supposed to remain in covenant.

Method III:

The *therapeutic spanking* begins when the Adon has the utilities of a little spiritual love nearby, such as the oil and wine. The Adon would have the submissive drink a glass full of her delighted wine. Then the Adon would lay her on her stomach, resting on a bed, while the submissive queen's eyes are blindfolded, mixing olive oil with some therapeutic oils.

Therapeutic Oils:
Angelica, Bergamot, Calamus, Chamomile, Carrot Seed, Clary Sage, Jasmine, Lavender, Nutmeg, Peppermint, Rose, Sage, Sandalwood, Vanilla, Vetiver, and Ylang-Ylang

These are the essential oils an Adon can experiment with on his submissive and blend certain varieties with the olive oil. First, the Adon is to anoint the submissive's buttocks, back hamstrings, and rheumatoid (back waist) with olive oil all over. Then apply three to five drops of the oils or oil of choosing to each cheek and rub in counterclockwise and clockwise rotations, for the submissive's indulge in variety. Do this for three to five minutes but avoid rubbing essential oils on the anal cavity but don't be afraid to go into the cheeks. When going in between the cheeks, the Adon should use his thumbs to gradually enter between them then bring both hands together (flat handed as if an individual was praying) and smoothly rub them from the between cheeks going upward to her rheumatoid then go back down and repeat the process of rubbing. After three to five minutes, the Adon would cuff his hands while rubbing (while the submissive wonders sensually), and then the Adon would spank in a lightly aggressive clockwise position for five to eight spanks then change rotation to spanking in a position of upward/downward motion for a rapid spank of twenty to thirty spanks lightly aggressive then give a pauseable one mildly aggressive spank with a firm fervent hold on the bottom and repeat this method again if she craves more, when she says "more, Adon."

Not Rape but Kink and Discipline

The Adon normally would train his treasures woman (if she's a woman who likes to be *scornful, contentious, or demanding*) that he's the source of power. Protocol: Adon must often have restraints on him or nearby. One thing that's often required is cuffing her wrist with handcuffs, sashes, tie, or quality rope, something to prevent her from fighting because it's unworthy to brawl on a woman, unless you're playfully fighting, then it's liberation (however, in reality, some brawling episodes are inevitably undisciplined. For instance, if an Adon was hit with a dangerous object, then *Ra* may awaken. The important is for the Adon to love the best he can), then bind her over your knees or object (such as couch, bed, etc.), use *maintenance spanking* method, then sensibly penetrate her with your Weapon of Love to assert your *yang* authority. The Thanatos (before you penetrate the Honey Pot or Hershey Highway [use lube shooter], apply spiritual love ointment, such as oil or water-based lubricant so you don't demonstrate unpleasant pain), it's important to provide sensibility for her pleasure and follow Protocol II in Chapter XV, subtitle: Artful Revelation of Thrusting. The empirical truth is there are treasures women who will act scornful or contentious for intimacy just so the Adon can satisfy them or reinforce that she still has the Adon ardency toward her.

Certain Adonim who are into *power play* do not intend to torment or be abusive but to assert dominance, restore his sensibility of power, authority, and personage. Certain submissives indulge in this power play, and to various submissives, this fulfills chest novelty. *Chest* can be simplified as something of a hidden personage that's secretly cling too discreetly, for it's the very arcanum of an individual's nature. However, before doing this kink, assert training a discipline of *SSC/RACK* to the submissive by addressing safety words and safety gestures so that the Adon can respond to the submissive with honor. It's important that this training discipline is acknowledged for future reference so the Adon doesn't have to worry about consistently asking or looking for consent because in reality, consent is not often asked but learned through emotion of another for submission.

The truth is much of mass media says consent, consent, consent but doesn't relate to a down-to-earth person so well nor an serene-to-earth person because certain individuals become drained of asking or become sexually turned off by a person asking "can we have sex," or "can I touch your breast," or "do you grant me permission to do this position," or "are you agreeable to this sexual act." The analogy is how an Adon would feel if the submissive constantly asking if could she touch or fellate the Adon. This consistent question will become not so arousing in time. The spark is the submissive's eagerness of initiative without question, not a questionnaire. Emotion gives the actual guide of consensual. Sometimes another individual (Adon or submissive) wants an individual to act on their impulses. They'll assert a hard limit if they're not comfortable. I've come to realization that there is an existence to an action called **nonconsensual consent,** which is the full agreement on the submissive's pardon to the Adon that she's going to fully accept what the Adon gives her in whatever holistic sexual penetration, fully allowing spanking, and fully unrestrictive lovemaking all without rejection. This *nonconsensual consent* is a Christian DD that certain individuals believe to be the true submission of a Christian woman, but the Adon must not be bitter, or God will hold the Adon accountable and inflict punishment. In *nonconsensual consent,* there are no safety words once the submissive vows to fully accept this contractual agreement, but there can be an honored SSC/ RACK if the Adon chooses to obey, but he's prudently liberated to not yield if he chooses. Cultivate that it's crucially mandatory for the Adon not to spank his submissive if angry, for he may give bitterness if he does so.

When Reinforcement Required

An example of *vicarious reinforcement* would be if the Adon was using the punisher method (negative reinforce maintenance spanking), but this didn't respond well for the Submissive for she had an irrational impulsive behavior, so the Adon would reinforce with his Weapon of Love, stripping her nude with forceful dominance from a *vicarious reinforcement* learning. The reason is because the Adon would know she's not in the mood for spanks but maybe craving loving internally rather than externally; for some women purposely do act impulsive irrational for affection. Furthermore, some vicarious reinforcement behaviors can rather be more amorous and disregard what negative perception others may think if your sexual actions are environmentally exposed. For instance, when I was working at Sam's Club Wholesale, I remember a married couple was sitting in the café, and the husband was masturbating his wife while their children were eating aside from them. The wife was briefly *humiliated,* but her *Eros* opened to it and became more *amorous* while enjoying it. Although this may have been disrespectful to others, the marriage is undefiled and virtuous in lovemaking, and being fearless in lovemaking is to become wild and natural in sexual loving, so no one really cared but the jealous ones and the ones who didn't carry similar strong sexual appetite.

When the Adon and submissive is in public, there's not much discipline that can be done except humiliating her with loving bliss, triggering reinforcement in the most pleasurable ways positive can be discipline. For instance, when the Adon notices his submissive having wondering eyes on other men, he can use his hand to gradually direct it to her Valley of Joy, rubbing her or masturbating her while in public, or the Adon can slide his hands inside her pants to grasp her tender bottom. Surely, this may humiliate her but also reinforces ownership and belonging and vice versa if the submissive was in the Adon's position. Another scenario would be say if the Adon left the restaurant table to use the bathroom then heading back to the dining table, the Adon notice submissive's eyes wondering or speaking to another man, the Adon could secretly sneak behind her and ardently grab one of her Blossomed Pomegranates while using the other hand to gradually coordinate her cheek gently to direct her mouth to the Adon and ardently give her a French kiss (however, the submissive's back head the Adon could use to coordinate, but the Adon must do his best to not mess up her hair. Empirically, women spend a lot of time doing their hair in preparation for casual eloquent dining and would be displeased for the Adon to mess her hair up and may cause a depolarization of the mood, especially if the Adon's queen is a beautiful chocolate woman. The film *Good Hair* also confirms this if you don't believe me. Chris Rock interviewed many well-known chocolate beauties, and they testified to this.

Submissive's Empowered Spanking Disciplinary

The submissive queens and princesses the Adon Olam loved so much that he provided a way where the submissives are empowered to accept sexual acts or reject them through a disciplinary called *Testicular Spanking* or *Testicular Grabbing*. Personally, I'm very sure that if Adon Olam wanted mankind to act like savages, he would've made mankind testes stronger and a lot less sensitive when an impact happens. Testicular Spanking and Testicular Grabbing is a way where if the submissive was forced into sexual activity that she rejects by an Adon, she could rapidly grab his testes strongly or give a brief spank to suppress his desire for sex. Testicular spanking and grabbing discipline is the one place where a woman can make man suppress if reasoning doesn't work. Two methods for Testicular Spanking and Grabbing would be:

Method one would be for the submissive to cuff her hands and very lightly to very mildly spank the Adon's testes for reinforcement of empowerment she possesses. The Adon will be focused on the pain from the spankings that he more likely would lose interest in sex. This is Testicular Spanking!

Method two would be for the submissive to give a lightly aggressive grab to the testes to create sensibility in the Adon with reasoning or protesting she's not interested. If the Adon tries overcoming the pain and becomes violent, the lightly aggressive grab will become a slowly stronger aggressive squeeze until the Adon submits. This is Testicular Grabbing!

However, if the submissive's wrists were restrained, she'll use her knees or some other maneuver to grab/spank the testes to discipline the Adon. Or she'll wait until the Adon is finished then intelligently portray like she wants more, then provide bondage (tying the Adon ankles and wrists) and spank/grab the Adon until he pleads for forgiveness. If the Adon is an abusive individual and decides to attack the submissive, a submissive has the right to defend herself from harm above all cost. Not many submissives will perform testicular spanking/grabbing due to sensibility and sympathy. Various submissives will become passive, receptive, and open to coercion sex, but the one's that refuse may apply one of these methods. A submissive can grab her Adon by the testes, creating a testicular truthful disciplinary. If she senses he's lying or keeping a secret, she'll gently aggressively grab the testes and make him testify or avow, and the Adon will confess to relieve pain (this is her feisty behavior for getting what she wants from the Adon when applies testicular truthful disciplinary). The submissive can use Testicular Grabbing to spark fire to the testes then smoothly masturbate the Heavenly Root during outside environments or social places to humiliate with bliss but also spark a fire of impassioned desire and establish her empowerment over the Adon's testes and assert that submission would be given only by her (she is reinforcing her position) unless in a covenant of polygyny (for *polygyny*, see Chapter XVII, subtitle: *Sacred Marriage Truth;* semi-subs: *The Polygamy Revelation*).

𝔄𝔡𝔬𝔫 𝔑𝔬𝔫-𝔖𝔭𝔞𝔫𝔨𝔦𝔫𝔤 𝔇𝔦𝔰𝔠𝔦𝔭𝔩𝔦𝔫𝔞𝔯𝔶

The non-spanking method is a way of reverencing the negative to sublimation. The common way is through humiliation and grounding. Grounding can provide a beneficial reactance to the Adon, for when a submissive is grounded from certain freedom privileges, she'll soon determine to motivate herself to freedom, then when she realizes she has no other way, she'll service the Adon's way to gain her privileges. In *Psychological Reactance: A Theory of Freedom and Control* by S. S. and J. W. Brehm, the studies stated, "In general, the theory holds that a threat to or loss of a freedom motivates the individual to restore that freedom . . . The theory stipulates what constitutes a freedom, how freedoms can be threatened or eliminated, and how the ensuing motivational state (psychological reactance) will manifest itself."[54] What endures to be the very important or pleasurable part of her privileges is the ones that can be used to substance restriction, those leads to reactive effects. She'll seek a plan because when threaten to be taken away, she'll seek to long for it because its position as worth, giving the Adon power, and soon, she'll aggressively provide submission and subservience to gain that value.[55]

Training Submissive to become Nudist/Naturist

For intentions to reinvent a woman to become a naturist or nudist, you use her rebellion to your advantage. Some would consider this nuances, but there are aesthetic kings/princes who savor their wife (or wives) nakedness. You're training her positivity of body acceptance and *fervent* to her vulnerability. The lesson is to teach your treasures submissive how to not be shameful of her nudity but evoke her mind on the beauty of her flesh and her personality, what you adore most about her distinction and the vivid artistry of her form and overall body itself. The Adon method for training a woman to become submissive nudist/naturist would come from grounding through the methods of curfew and esteem.

---

[54] S. S. Brehm and J. W Brehm, *Psychological Reactance: A Theory of Freedom and Control* (New York: Academic Press, 1981), 93, 96, 115–6.

[55] R. A. Wicklund, *Freedom and Reactance* (Potomac, Maryland: Lawrence Erlbaum Associates, 1974), 10–11, 86.

❖ <u>Method for curfew</u> would be, say, if the Adon establishes a time for the queen to be in the house, and she's late, the Adon notices the time, so he disposes all her clothes to locked room or closet except one pair he has on the bed for her, then she gets back, gives the Adon a kiss, apologizes for breaking her curfew, then Adon tells her, "I have some clothes laid out for you on the bed." The submissive queen decides to take a shower while planning to wear the clothes the Adon laid out for her. While she's taking a shower, the Adon quietly sneaks in to pick her clothes off the floor, then when she gets out, she notices her clothes are missing and enters the bedroom and notices the clothes laid out are put away. The submissive queen confronts the Adon (cultivate that she may protest contention, but the Adon's mission is to remain solid without compromising in this method. Keep in mind you're doing this for her health [see Chapter XVI, subtitle: *Untold Novels*; for naturist/nudist health] and demonstrating ardency and personal aesthetic persona). The Adon says, "Because of you breaking your curfew, you'll remain naked for fifteen hours or more hours (or days)." She'll look and notice the Adon has the keys, and the Adon says, "No type of covering will I allow you to wear on that beautiful body, not even sheets from the bed but only sleepers" (have a heater nearby during cold mornings, days and nights). However, if you both have kids, then Adon would only allow her to wear a robe and sleepers. The Adon must make sure the keys remain hidden (better hidden outside of the house), and then her mind will train itself to become more adaptable to being naked. Continue this process each time she breaks curfew.

❖ <u>Method for esteem</u> would be the spoken erotic tones toward your queen on what's visually stunning to the eyes of the Adon. This starts with playing a sexual game and testing her honor and respect by telling her to prove the honor and respect in a game. The trick is testing her ability to keep her word and excel in the rules of the game with actions of loyalist character. For instance, say the Adon and submissive were playing a pool table game, and each time, one says they're going to make the shoot and make it the other will have to strip. The Adon just have to make sure he wins if he's to succeed in having her stripped. Then after the Adon won, he'll instruct her to remain nude (on how ever long the rules was clarified in the mutual agreement). Be fair in the game. Another ideal is the couple (or harem) can create a bet and other ideals that come to mind.

Nudity can be an act of DD through a use of atonement because of the submissive's negative actions the discipline of humiliation that will soon form into the embrace of the body acceptance. In ancient times, the nudity was demanded as an atonement to inflict shame because of sin for repentance as demonstrated in *Game of Thrones* *Season 5 Episode 10 Mother's Mercy* (starting approximate runtime of 00:42:36 to 00:55:50).

Disciplinary Admission and Transformative Journal

The Adon can more so be *avowing* than a submissive; therefore, if she has trouble speaking to the Adon, the Adon protocol would be for the Submissive to write a journal *avowing* to relief her stress and be heard.

The Adon dharma would be to read what the submissive has to say rather in privacy (if she doesn't want to be there when the Adon reads it) or in front of the submissive (keep in mind there's no need to double confirm what the treasures submissive written. Just fulfill her language into action or suggest making effort for the transformation). In the journal can be disciplinary protocols she doesn't agree with, *writing erotica*'s (*see* Adon Disciplinary Language), what the submissive wants, what the submissive hopes for through the Adon, and the submissive's confessions. Certain submissives enjoy the role of being naïve with a sacred craving but just don't want to be filled with contempt as an Adon. The discipline is being knowledgeable, sensible, loving, and nonjudgmental. The Adon can agree or disagree, but the Adon should not fill her with contempt. This can be very helpful, even vice versa. The switch could be that the Adon has trouble avowing, then he'll *journalize* to his submissive, while she's reading it to him.

The protocol for a submissive with contentious behavior would be for the Adon to first direct her into room away from objects that may harm her or Adon and lock the door, then if the submissive only written a word count of 50 words or less, enforce her to write the same thing 3 times, the trinity of painful writing (for instance, if she written a word count of 50 for journalizing, then she'll have to write that same thing 150 times), then lock her in the room alone (make sure the room gives her access to a restroom in the house, out of respect for her) and follow up with the Contentious Relief Prayer (*see* Excelling throughout Investment). After the submissive is finished, you'll review it then burn it in front of her then take her out to eat at a nice restaurant or later supply her with a gift that the Adon knows she'll indulge (this is left to your determinism). If she doesn't comply with this punishment, then the Adon will establish grounding of what she indulges in the most.

Lack of Sex Discipline and Realism

In DD, some kings/princes suffer from not receiving intimacy from their queen/princess, so from reality from elders, I've learned that a man can persuade her to have sex through three steps; however these are only for consorts or individuals with intimate relationship, not for dating or courtship.

1. *Highly to Moderately Effective* - Use *positive reinforcement* to arrange something special or adventurous for having more time with your significant other. *Positive reinforcement* (PR) is conveying the central behavior with discipline of giving something desired for a better outcome, for example, when a queen offers Sweet Mouth loving for forgiveness for contentious behavior. In **Kevin Hart's** *Let Me Explain*, a stand-up comedy film (approximate runtime of 00:33:00 to 00:41:45[56]), he spoke of his own way of DD that's similar to PR from his ex-wife.

Or

Moderately to Less Effective - The arrangement of something special or adventures for her. You tell her you have cancelled it because of lack of lovemaking. For

---

[56] This demonstration is intended to be a seminar on what I'm explaining; however, if a Christian reader is sensitive to explicit language, then I don't recommend viewing this as a demonstration of PR. For some other demonstrations of PR, watch *Heaven Is for Real* (2014) film approximate runtime of 00:21:00 to 00:22:07.

some women, these adventures or special things happen to be vacations, restaurants, theaters and plays, concerts, festivals and carnivals, jewelry and shopping spree, not buying her possessions that she desires.

2. **Highly to Moderately Effective** - Provide PR: Sensationalize her with fervent pleasure of kissing, touching, rubbing, and spiritual love throughout her entire body to awaken the spice of desire to procreate seduction.

Or

Moderately to Less Effective - Tamper with stability, freedom, and finance that support her needs by not giving her what she wants to provoke her to submit to the Adon's will. These practices include portraying taking breaks from work telling her you're not working until she submits, canceling or temporarily suspending her debit/credit cards in your name, taking away her car keys, suspending cable along with Internet access and cell phone(s), and taking away certain foods and desserts she craves to eat in the house.

3. **Highly to Moderately Effective** - Puzzle her with the possibility of a new wife material. This makes her reminisce if stubbornness is worth of losing you. For example, when she resents giving you love, follow the first two steps above and tell her "because I honor you, I'm going to let you know I'm going out to search for another woman who can fully submit to love I desire. You wait in the house, while I find a real submissive who can handle this." Her thoughts will puzzle with "if he leaves, he may really mess with a promiscuous woman or maybe he has a woman secretly clinging to him." Then she'll think of logic that maybe her Adon may catch a disease, create a new family, or may fall more deeply in love with that mysterious woman through her beauty and/or skills and forget all about her. (Don't think I'm encouraging an affair because I'm not, but giving a trick of persuasion toward her; sometimes its tough love.) Conversely, if worst behaviors come into play (such as brawling woman, insinuated adultery, etc.), and arrangements of efforts persist negatively to be satisfied for sex or

affection, then soon, you'll rationalize it's time to separate, and *emunah* in the relationship has been sabotaged.

Realism

In ***Why Did I Get Married?*** (Perry 2007) film, Terry (Tyler Perry) and Dianne (Sharon Leal) had sex problems, and Terry influenced a *positive reinforcement* through creating a vacation and attempted to romance her then later broke Dianne's cellphone after communication failed then portrayed the action of leaving her while making Dianne believe he was having an affair with Pam (Keesha Sharp). On the contrary, she may threaten that she'll cheat if you cheat on her, but strength is to be solid and really mean that you'll search for another woman, and if she does cling to another man, you'll divorce her because the Bible gives you the right to do so. A man may deeply love his woman and want to hold on to her, but there's only so long before hunger overtakes you. Don't buy into the propaganda that "the longer a marriage last, the longer you can go without sex" because Yahawah didn't feel that way in 1 Corinthians 7v5, for He actually insisted sex often unless consent of time for fasting and praying before the devil attempt to break the union. For power exchange is essential and the Lord spoke demands in many scriptures that a queen to be virtuous must provide submission to her husband though the Adon should not have to starve in pleasure to receive sex.

Food is a physiological need, for a human won't survive without it, and if a human goes without it, the human will starve. This is the same with sex, for if the ***pleasure principle*** is not fulfilled in a moment of time, an individual develops a ***suppression effect***. When I was reading one of the true empirical psychology books called ***Monogamy: The Untold Story*** by **Marianne Brandon**, in chapter one, "The Monogamy Illusion," some women after they get married in time unfortunately lose their sex drive and men would have an affair. For men and women who are not satisfied through their physiological instincts tend to suffer ***suppression effect***, meaning *in internal craving that we make effort to delay but intensifies, thereby creating an obsession from the unconscious to the conscious.*[57]

---

[57] Marianne Brandon, *Monogamy: The Untold Story*, 10.

Conversely, if she doesn't submit, then you may have problems because if she really cares about you, then she'll willingly accept the lovemaking, and this goes the same from king toward the queen. Women who really love their Adon and/or rely on her Adon providing stability, love, and finance are more prone to willingly acceptance, but the women who are more demanding in their lives usually are scorned from violent past, financially successful, or stunningly gorgeous, thereby using their potentiality to do whatever they want (but this not necessarily true for all women). In ancient biblical times, this may not have been a problem for men because they had multiple wives, so when one didn't satisfy, the other would. The empirical truth is the sexual energy between two is best if compatible because sometimes one individual maybe satisfied faster than the other. For instance, a king performing coitus in the bedroom and suddenly ejaculates in five minutes while the queen craves for more can be difficult for her to be suppressed with insomnia and may, in time, seek satisfaction elsewhere from another man as demonstrated in the film *Addicted* (2014) or search for a woman (this is realism). Vice versa, a king performing coitus and within perhaps fifteen minutes while sex is continuous, the queen says, "Are you done yet?" and forces the Adon off her can ruin the sexual satisfaction and cause the king to be suppressed with insomnia, then suppression may lead to coercion sex (this is realism) or search for another as a concubine. The realism is some kings, princes, princesses, and queens can suppress, while others are reactive to satisfying the pleasure principle, and it all depends on an individual's body chemistry. No science can summarize everyone in this pleasure principle, but they can fabricate an understanding.

Reading quite a few books, I've noticed many authors (in their late thirties or above) write about soft lovemaking (meaning all gentle, long durations of foreplay, consistently asking for consent, polite, etc.), but the empirical reality is the more fruitful youth of a foundation (sexual chemistry) a man and woman has, the more eager and aggressive they can be. Chemistry is not adequate to everyone, so being real, it depends on the individual's sexual prowess. The contemptuous framework is when others try socially constructing the individual's mind that has a *stronger sexual appetite* (means longing for continuous erotic love while being amorous without suppressing it) in the relationship that they think may need to seek a therapist or they're someway abnormal or may use religion or revile movement to construct the mind. Empirically, I've overheard this quite often from feminist saying to another woman that she needs to establish ground rules on how often to have sex with their husband or boyfriend, and if a man, they say if the man really loves her, then he should submit to suppressing, or a feminist attempts to build a framework of contempt on the man. Conversely, the truth is they're trying to construct the individual to suppress their appetite, but what's needed is for them to reach the strong sexual appetite of the individual and distinguish their thoughts from revile and suppressive brainwash. Suppression can be a cage, but embracement and transformation can be bliss.

Sociologist Ira Reiss (1989) vaguely expresses the construction of segregations through researchers labeling what's normal or abnormal, natural or unnatural, ethical or unethical, and good or bad when he wrote,

> We need to be aware that people will use those labels to put distance between themselves and others they dislike. In doing so, these people are not making a scientific diagnosis but are simply affirming their support of certain shared concepts of proper sexuality.[58]

The problem is not the individual with the strong sexual appetite, but the problem is the individual who tries to confidingly fill the other

---

[58] Ira Reiss, "Society and sexuality: A sociological explanation," in K. McKinney & S. Sprecher (Eds.), *Human sexuality: The societal and interpersonal context* (Norwood, NJ: Ablex).

with contempt that needs the help of reaching a healthier sexual peak to be compatible. In life, sometimes the acknowledgement of being a workaholic can break intimate loving. This is where stewardship of dharma to the treasures queen transformation comes into effect when the individual realizes they're losing their submissive queen because of work. An inspiring film that gives this acknowledging criteria would be **Click (2006)** starring Adam Sandler and Kate Beckinsale.

Disciplining Lovemaking Duration Naturally

First, before we begin, I want to clarify the herbs I'm giving the Adonim are from actual personal consumption. Yes, you heard right. I'm a personal practitioner, and this is needed to be clarified before beginning. The way of disciplining lovemaking durations naturally is through spiritual love, which is conveying naturalism the true Adon DD way, even though there are other ways, such as the prostate message and testicle bondage (unhealthy and unpleasant), but we're going to focus on spiritual love. Below are the four consumptions for spiritual love:

Red Wine + Herbology + Consumption of Spices + Ointments = Spiritual Love

Red Wine

The red wine is the pre-elixir to longevity and vitality. "Drink no longer water, but use a little wine for thy stomach's sake and thine often infirmities."[59]

"And wine (yayin) that maketh glad of heart (levav) 'mankind, humankind' (enosh) and 'oil, ointment, olive oil' (shemen) to make faces (panim) to shine, and 'bread, food, crop' (lechem) which strengtheneth of heart (levav) 'mankind, humankind' (enosh)."[60]

---

[59] 1 Timothy 5v23 King James Version.

[60] Tehillim [Psalms] 104v15 Scripture taken from Orthodox Jewish Bible.

The sensual consumption of red wine can be a natural remedy to a stronger blood flow. The common substance in the real red wines with corks has a substance called resveratrol. **Resveratrol** can increase longevity, increase ORAC (Oxygen Radical Absorbance Capacity) scale, and increase the libido and consists of *ethanol* (alcohol), which stimulates a primitive function of the brain called **hypothalamus**. This portion of the human brain regulates the very basis of human functions: body temperature, hunger, hormonal levels, and sexual fruitfulness and induces loving attachment behaviors. However, this doesn't mean that red wines are full of potent resveratrol but only a little, though if a person wants to profit faster from the benefits of resveratrol to increase potency of resveratrol content, buy Trans-Resveratrol *98 percent pure Japanese Knotweed Root extract* and pour a half teaspoon of the extract into your glass then pour red wine of your choice. Have some fruits of your choosing nearby (sea buckthorn, noni, acai, pomegranate, etc.), particularly for natural health remedies. Below, I'll give two of my personal blends:

Heart Health Blend

Add some pomegranate (or I'll just buy Lakewood Organics Heart Health Juice), Welch's Grape Juice, and Cabernet Sauvignon

Sexual Health Blend

Add some pomegranate, acai berry, either 500 percent Concentrated Reishi Mushroom or Reishi Spores, choice of one or both of Panax Ginseng Tincture and/or Deer Antler Velvet Tincture, Welch's Grape Juice, and Cabernet Sauvignon

Herbology

Herbology medicine is the nature of God manifesting within His creation to give doctorate wisdom and medicine of its making toward (although some herbs can kill) the humans with the plants he have made born to manifest naturalism. Herbs give many rudimentary benefits, but it's all how an individual uses it. Below, I'll give the natural and potent herbs that produce a greater manifestation of truth to its reason of existing from my personal consumption:

Chest of Potent Herbs

These herbs I've personally have tested that works are potent in providing health benefits, and researchers and scientist proved they're very beneficial as well.

- Epimedium (known as horny goat weed)
- Reishi mushroom (known as lingzhi, Lachio Ling Chi)
- Cordyceps mushroom
- Deer antler velvet
- Polyrhachis vicina Roger
- Nettle root
- Saw palmetto
- Tongkat ali (also known as long Jack or pasak bumi)

- Ginkgo biloba
- Dong quai root
- Panax ginseng
- Bee products (honey, royal jelly, bee pollen, and propolis)
- Tribulus terrestris
- Fo-ti root (also known as Ho-shou-wu)
- Maca root

Spices

The most important spices for men to hold nearby are

- Cayenne pepper
- Ceylon cinnamon
- Clove powder

These three Cs are very potent healthy spices when you ingest them daily but must have eaten for ingestion of cayenne pepper (If using capsules, it's important to eat food before ingesting to keep the stomach from hurting.), for it's very potent for carrying nutrition throughout your body but a very hot spice.

Ointments

For your time, I won't list all the ointments but let you readers self-experiment with ointments and will give you the ones I've tried and are effective:

- Extra virgin olive oil
- Sandalwood oil
- Sweet almond oil
- 98 percent aloe vera gel
- Patchouli oil
- Rose oil
- Rosewood oil
- Vetiver oil

The safety precaution is to do some research before you apply these individual oils on your Heavenly Root then apply very small amount each different day, testing each one to determine if you'll have an allergic reaction or any type of reaction. I don't want anyone to have effects of any severances, so I highly recommend having consulted a practitioner before you test these ointments and the same for the herbs and spices. In addition, don't apply these oils if you're about to receive Sweet Mouth loving, except extra virgin olive oil and sweet almond oil (also, grape seed and apricot oil can be used as a lubricant and amplifier of the sensuous).

An Adonim Serere Medicine

Communion to Your Queen

In biblical scriptures, there are various implications of Serere "to sow" medicine (sowing seed and semen), urbanely called "White Honey." In the Bible, it's informed as living water and elixir. In Christology teachings John 4v10–16 KJV, a Samaritan woman questioned Jesus on living water. She was curious on the matter that water was already in the well, so she implied what is this living water he speaks of. Jesus said the water from the well she drinks shall continue to thirst, but the living water is within mankind.

[14] But whosoever drinketh of the water that I shall give him shall never thirst; but the water that I shall give him shall **be in him** a *well of water springing* up into everlasting *life*.

The Samaritan woman insisted on having this living water for herself. Jesus told her to call upon her husband. In Song of Solomon 2v3, Solomon's woman performed amorous oral sex outside under the apple tree. She reiterates she "*sat down under* his **shadow** with great delight and his *fruit* was sweet to my *taste*." Her being under his shadow reflects that she was on her knees (or butt), while Solomon was standing in front of her, and if you remember the Genesis, the El Elyon said be fruitful, and fruitful can imply vigorous, potency, virility, and loving. She implied that fruit from Solomon given a taste, so literally, she's speaking of performing Sweet Mouth lovemaking *(refer to Chapter XV chart for meaning of Sweet Mouth)*. Women who often indulge giving Sweet Mouth loving are called *passionate fellatrices*, for a woman in particular who indulges in this action is called *passionate fellatrix*.

According to Sally Robertson,[61] BSc, Serere Medicine contains fructose, ascorbic acid, zinc, cholesterol, protein, calcium, chlorine, blood group antigens, citric acid, DNA, magnesium, vitamin B12, phosphorus, sodium, potassium, uric acid, lactic acid, nitrogen, and vitamin C. In addition, Serere Medicine contains mood-enhancing constitutes—cortisol, estrone, oxytocin, thyrotropin-releasing hormone, prolactin, melatonin, and serotonin. Woman should only absorb Serere Medicine if it comes from a healthy host who doesn't carry any STDs; otherwise, her health would be at risk. However, various women don't enjoy the taste of semen; therefore, it's better to feed ourselves healthy remedies and ingest more organic fruits like pineapples, pomegranates, grapefruits, apples, and oranges, perhaps with a mixture of good tasting wine (not beer or liquor). Instead of smoking cigarettes, smoke spearmint for the sake of your health and her taste. Women who indulge in ingesting Serere Medicine call this *milking* or *Semen Therapy* as a daily supplement. There's even an invention called the *glory hole* (means Semen Therapy of Sweet Mouth loving to ingest a man's Serere Medicine through a hole in the wall in public places at booths to strangers anonymously), but I would recommend removing yourselves away from such *glory hole* events because of prudency and health because they're strangers. For serere health, consumption of Ceylon cinnamon, clove powder, peppermint leaves, and honey (or organic pure cane sugar) mixed with decaffeinated tea improves health and taste. Women who are aware of *Semen Therapy* benefit more, for it saves cost expense of buying nutritional supplements.

[61] Robertson, Sally. *Swallowing Semen.* http://www.news-medical.net/health/Swallowing-Semen.aspx. March 2, 2015.

This is why it's more important for kings/princes to give extra care to their health to give communion and regulate and strengthen internal health in them.

Receiving Sweet Mouth Loving

The moment of receiving fellatio from your treasured woman can be an act of domestic discipline because you're asserting dominion over her transgressions because she disobeyed your commandments or disrespected you. Conversely, you're supporting her longevity and nutrition, yet this becomes a benefit for her well-being as it's pleasure for the king/prince. There are four types of oral motions received from the submissive: *slow, fast, deep,* and/or *partial.* A master establishes the motions of what are most pleasurable. As a master, you must acknowledge that your woman is actually more empowered in this art because she has the control of your testicles and Sexual Steel, so in this act, you're entrusting her. Hypothesis: Although you empower more her health in this art because seminal fluid contains hormones and other biologically strong compounds, it prevents bone loss in women and progress osteogenesis through consistent exposure (Payne 2012). In addition, each time your woman performs fellatio and swallows Serere Medicine, she is supplementing herself with antidepressant and it possibly reduces breast cancer and ensures a woman's pregnancy safer and more likely successful through assumption of her partner's antigens (Payne 2012).

Women using the Instrument of Pleasure (oral sex) increase vulnerability and empathy in various males toward the female, so some males fear they may become somewhat soft. This effect causes kings to compromise more with their queens. This is why there's a common empirical saying that "he's addicted to that tongue," especially if she's skilled with the Instrument of Pleasure because she has the king into submission to her willpower, and the man is more vulnerable to her persuasions, for a Sweet Mouth is a power. "Power is in the tongue," and that power can favor persuasion, but the caution is favor can be deceitful unless she fears God and remain sensible for *good works.* (cf. Proverbs 18v21 and 31v30)

A *passionate fellatrix* can become dominantly empowered in this matter by persuading the Adon to be restrained with handcuffs or ropes, restraining both hands and ankles while under her power. A *passionate fellatrix* can discipline the Adon in Sweet Mouth loving for up to hours of continuous fellatio loving while ingesting Serere Medicine. Even when the Adon pleads for her to stop, she'll have the benevolence and *amorous* willpower to be disobedient and drain your well with pleasure or subservient to completely seduce her Adon. A passionate fellatrix can become so amorous that they'll perform Instrument of Pleasure outside environments or while her Adon is driving the car and many other innovative-eventful ideologies in her amorous mind (for instance, like the film **American Wedding** during the first five and a half minutes of the film, when Michelle [Alyson Hannigan] performed amorous fellatio to Jim [Jason Biggs] in the restaurant when his idea was to surprisingly give an eventful engagement). A *passionate fellatrix* literally and hypothetically have her king/prince by the balls. She'll discipline her king/prince with Sweet Mouth loving to turn things in her favor (such as turning a contentious/angry man into a humble and peaceful individual, persuading ideology, heightening spirits, or satisfying the *pleasure principle* to make it difficult for competitors to tempt her king/prince) and/or just for the pleasure of it (such as to provide healing and sensualism; elevate loving spirit, longevity, and good health; and stimulate arousal). A passionate fellatrix consisting love styles characteristics is more of pragmatic, erotic, agapic, and ardent (*see Chapter XVI, subtitle: Masterful Loving and Traits* [for lovers: pragmatic, erotic, agapic, and ardent]).

Important

> *For a passionate fellatrix to truly enjoy Sweet Mouth loving, a Adon must provide a desirable scent. A pungent scent that's unbearable for her will destroy the passion, but an aroma that's seductive to her nose is where the nose will inspire in savory with spiritual earthily loving, for the mouth will follow. Fellatrix often enjoys a king who is very well groomed on the intimate area as well.*
>
> *Deodorizing is vital for fellatrix lovemaking. Apply one of these methods for deodorizing:*
>
> <u>*Method I*</u>: *Wash the entire intimate area thoroughly with organic/ natural soap and apply a little of essential oil formula (or cologne) that fits your personality for the entire pelvic area (however, some women prefer a king's natural scent, so wear no aroma if this is the case) and wear no underwear because oxygen is a natural deodorizer, for the more oxygen flowing, the fewer bad odors you'll have, and in time that oxygen maybe your cure for bad odor.*
>
> <u>*Method II*</u>: *Wash the entire intimate area thoroughly with organic/ natural soap then apply mineral salt deodorant (Thai crystal is worth trying) for the entire pelvic area (don't use on testicles) then wait for it to dry and apply a little of essential oil formula (or cologne) that fits your personality for the entire pelvic area.*
>
> <u>*Method III*</u>: *Carry some wet wipes in a zip-lock bag and use the wipes before she begins performing.*

On the queen's/princess's end, various women enjoy *cunnilingus* in return. This is a part of **DD**, for the Adon is now disciplining the queen while the king/prince is performing the service. **Cunnilingus** is the Adon (husband) giving oral sex to the submissive wife's Honey Pot for her pleasure. Because this Sweet Mouth loving is very pleasurable to both mankind and womankind, a couple can often prefer the *congress of the crow* position. According to *Kama Sutra* on *cunnilingus*, "Some women of the harem, when they are amorous, do the acts of the mouth on the yonis of one another, and some men do the same thing with women. The way of doing this should be known from kissing the mouth."

Empirically, women love power exchange, the exchange to be empowered while they enjoy their king performing cunnilingus. Particularly, they can feel empowered by tempting the king while standing nude in front of the king while he's sitting, targeting his face to her Valley of Joy as a way of seduction, initiation, exhilaration, sensation, and communion, while she embraces her thighs caressing his head. In addition, performing the stand-in-front cunnilingus position in DD can be given as an act if she's been subservient to the Adon conduct; therefore, the Adon would give grace to her in this moment. In the KJV Bible, there's clearly condemnation of man-on-man sexual acts, in accordance, condemning woman with woman (lesbianism) there's a clarification that woman is made for man. To make taste more endurable for the ones not fond of *cunnilingus*, try warming some organic goat/cow milk (or almond milk) with a decent amount of wild/organic honey to sweeten the milk. Then once in comfortable temperature, pour gradually this mixture on her Valley of Joy (or just use honey without the milk). It's important to heat this honey and milk without the use of a microwave so you preserve the nutrition from the honey and milk. Another remedy is the use of chilled champagne or wine that suits a personal good taste buzz (or sparkling cider) by pouring a little on the Golden Crevice before performing cunnilingus.

> *Great love affairs start with Champagne and*
> *end with tisane. (Honoré de Balzac)*

Due to liberation, we're going to disregard the affairs and stick with the commitment, but you readers understand my point of the champagne ;)! "And the roof of thy mouth like the best wine for my beloved, that goeth down sweetly, causing the lips of those that are asleep to speak" (Song of Solomon 7v9). The "roof of thy mouth," is the symbolic to the tongue (cf. Job 29v10, Psalms 138v6, Jeremiah 4v4), which means Solomon performed *cunnlingus* to create arousal to his treasures woman, for "lips" is the Valley of Joy that was sleep, that awoken from stimulation that begun "to speak," is poetic for jubilation or aural sex (*see* Language of Love). Certain individuals will inference Song of Solomon 7v9 as a "French kiss," but the analogy is the tongue "goeth down" triggering lips to speak would be without obstacles (such as another's teeth and tongue) but more stimulate plus the scripture said "lips" to speak not "mouth" to speak.

€mbracing the Heterosexual
Fifth Base Intercourse

Biblical View to Driving the Hershey Highway

Heterosexual fifth base is classified as male-female anal penetration. There are opposing arguments on heterosexual anal penetration as something of taboo or sinful. The truth is it's projected this way because some individuals don't approve. According to Orthodox Jewish text **Mishneh Torah** (Isidore 1980):

> Since a man's wife is permitted to him, he may act with her in any manner whatsoever. He may have intercourse with her whenever he so desires and kiss any organ of her body he wishes, and he may have intercourse with her naturally or unnaturally (traditionally, *unnaturally* refers to anal and oral sex), provided that he does not expend semen to no purpose. Nevertheless, it is an attribute of piety that a man should not act in this matter with levity and that he should sanctify himself at the time of intercourse.

Various Christians believe hetero-anal intercourse to be a sin against nature; some consider it Sodom and Gomorrah from Genesis 19v1–8, but this scripture emphasizes male-to-male intercourse as the sin. The *Ancient Book of Jasher*, chapters 18 and 19, provides the full reason why Sodom and Gomorrah was plagued sinful through—man intercourse with man, swinging with wives and fornicating with virgin daughters from morning to night four times a year without marrying them, partying, murdering, starving the poor when they had abundance of food, and preying on visitors while stealing their possessions. (cf. Genesis 13v13, Genesis 19v4–7) The Book of Jasher is directly linked to the Bible. (cf. Joshua 10v13, 2 Samuel 1v18) Male homosexuality was so frowned upon that when the Benjamites attempted to rape a sojourn man, the old man that allowed the sojourn man to have shelter had unwelcomed company of Benjamites demanding to have the sojourn man for sex, but the old man offered the Benjamites his virgin daughter and his concubine so that they would not rape the sojourn man, so they accepted the concubine and sexually ravished the concubine from night until morning instead of raping the sojourn man (Judges 19). In accordance, the Israelite tribes raged for the fear of God's curse (Leviticus 18v22) which individuals believe is HIV/AIDs from penalty of disdaining (denying) sensibility and made the tribe of Benjamin (Benjamites) wait for women in Shiloh, Samaria (Khirbet Seilun) to have for spoils to prevent blasphemy (Judges 20–21).

Sodomy and sodomites actually come from the biblical language "the sin of Sodom," so the true term sodomites are Sodom's direct representations of sin but modernity pervades it as being an overall anal and oral sexual act as an act of constructive ideology that is falsity. In addition, the reason for this is because certain individuals disapprove, so they want others to become more agreeable on their ideology. If still not convince, hetero-fifth base not considered unnatural. Closely observe Leviticus 18v22 KJV, for it says, *"Thou shalt not lie with mankind, as with womankind: it is abomination"* and clearly explains there are only two penetration methods that male and female have in common, the Instrument of Pleasure and the anus, for womankind and mankind both have an anus and a mouth to perform sexual penetration. So the issuing clarity is Yahawah is openly expressing its senseless for man to seek a man in the desires of these sexual acts when theirs a woman around (or can search for a woman) that can perform openness to Hershey Highway loving and receptive to becoming a passionate fellatrix. A *physical penetrative intimate trinity* is more aesthetically systematic to the context of Yahawah, Yahawashi and the Word, and that makes perfection. According to *The Gnostic Bible the Pistis Sophia Unveiled: The Secret Teachings of Jesus Recorded by His Disciples*, Sixth Book – Chapter 147, page 555:

> Bartholomew said: "A man who hath intercourse with a male, what is his vengeance?" **Jesus said**, "The measure of the man who hath intercourse with males and of the man with whom he lieth, is the same as that of the blasphemer . . ."

A person may question, "What about the secretive/known individuals who are performing this action of male on male?" The truth is repentance to Adonai Yahawashi and pleading for mercy is a faith and hope that Yahawah considers for forgiveness through his son sacrificing himself for our sins because Yahawah is love. However, to truly mean it, you must preserve your *emunah* to him and vow to Yahawah you won't return to that lifestyle. Devastation weighs on the minds of young princes and kings who went through molestation or rape from men, for they may be touched with contempt and agony, but I pray that the brethren who experience this devastation be healed and know you're still royal men and capable of replenishing yourselves as heterosexual men and know you still possess your yang. Individuals that disdain prudency have given themselves to a reprobate mind so the ontology of prudency has been constructed to *brainwashing* of "do what thy wilt." For this YHWH is against therefore given them up to vile affections.

The dramatic film *In Hell* (Damme and Moir 2003), character Billy (Chris Moir) was a close friend of Kyle (Jean-Claude Van Damme), but because of his youth and being new to the prison institution, homosexual men targeted Billy and raped him. Despite that, he never gave up fighting back even to the death, and there is honor in that. Billy's last words were *"don't let them turn you into something you're not."*

Conversely, if any man has the secret desire to receive anal penetration, it's better for them to confess to the wife for assistance (asking her to take the dominant role with a strap on), then sin by fornicating with a male (remind her of 1 Corinthians 7v3–4 and Matthew 7v1–2) will perhaps be counted as nonhomosexual fornication in YHWH conduct (because it's not real flesh nor expelling of Serere Medicine) and pray to Adon Olam for guidance and transformation. Having your queen use a strap on for adventurous sexuality is far safer in spirit vessel, psychological and physiological health; this is a type of edgeplay in **DD** called *pegging* or *BOB* "Bend over Boyfriend," certain queens have this kinky aggressive nature to favorably give or assert edgeplay. However, this fifth base is left to your own *determinism*.

Primal Awaken to Hershey Highway Loving

According to Carolyn Riccardi, "More heterosexual couples become progressive in learning the indulgence of anal pleasure, for male-to-female anal penetration has been happening since the dawn of time." In ancient times, performing hetero Hershey Highway loving was a way of preserving chastity among women until marriage[62]; however, this is still as true in this millennium as in ancient times. This millennium calls it *God's loophole* (cf. Mentioned in explicit song "The Loophole,"

---

[62]   Paper 82 The Urantia Book, subtitle: The History of Urantia, semi-subtitle: Evolution of Marriage, page 918

from artist Garfunkel and Oates album *Secretions*) or **Saddlebacking**. Various beings consider Hershey Highway and Sweet Mouth as servile agape. *Saddlebacking* and Sweet Mouth loving is charitably a *love map* for loving while the queen maidenly preserve her Valley of Joy in chastity until the man is willing to become her Adon (*see pages* 158, 175, and 257) because the Valley of Joy is considered the great love of special treasure, this is the queen's discipline to the man for marriage as a way of her saying "if your fond and loving of me than commitment of conjugal should be aggressed." According to the statistics in 2006, the result given was that 38.2 percent of men from age 20 to 39 and 32.6 percent of women from age 18 to 44 engage in heterosexual anal sex. It is in contrast with Centers for Disease Control's 1992 National Health and Social Life survey, which conducted that only 25.6 percent of men ages 18 to 59 and 20.4 percent of women ages 18 to 59 indulged in it (Em & Lo 2007), and it continues to become in indulgence presently. Despite these statistics, the empirical reality is perhaps much more have indulged in heterosexual fifth base loving until everyone on earth has given their statistics, then it's a matter outlook that is not fully reliable but a construction.

Sex Educator Jamye Waxman addressed the common insinuate question: "Are you a homosexual?" She explained to straight men who indulged in Hershey Highway this is not so even though certain individuals don't approve of hetero-fifth base. Other testimonials are agreeable to Waxman. The only disagreeable ones are the ones that had a bad experience. Jamye briefly explains from her *Love Sex: Intro to Anal* video the reason why men and women find fifth base intriguing. It is because "it feels good, often seen as hot and dirty, and a little bit naughty." In Song of Solomon, there were indications of fifth base loving. "My beloved put in his hand by the **hole** *of the door*, and my **bowels** *were moved* for him" (Song of Solomon 5v4 KJV). Rebuke others who persecute this fifth base loving as immoral and unnatural between Adon and submissive queen because it is moral and natural according the biblical scriptures. Develop a renewing of the mind against subliminal biases. Surely, an Adon may notice mass media like a textbook, for instance, may have heterosexual couples having multiple positions but anal sex they'll have two men. There's a type of sublimation and construction when a variety of textbooks construct that anal sex is for gay couples when all other sexual positions are insinuated to be natural when truth is authors behind such work are only trying to convince an ideology of what they consider acceptable heterosexually or they'll use many testimonials that have agreeable intellectuals on the matter to construct a fabricated convincing on what's ethical to their standards. Scratch out this subliminal construction and awaken the primal.

The empirical truth is kings and princes are often visually infatuated with the beautiful nature of a woman's Blossomed Pomegranates, Valley of Joy, mouth, face, hair, body shape, hamstrings (or overall legs), and buttocks. Mainly what visually captivating is a woman's face and mouth, beautiful legs, Blossomed Pomegranates, Valley of Joy, and the buttocks. The loving of the Honey Pot, Hersey Highway, and Sweet Mouth is an intimate carnality of allure, homage, hedonism of sensuality, and sexual fundaments; while the visage, personage, buttocks and Blossomed Pomegranates is the seducer. All is a discernment of fair through investment and amenable charity to the Adon from Submissive (woman). A man's nature is a penetrator, so the eagerness rises to penetrate all openings (tunnels) of a woman. So what is between the woman's buttocks, a man is more likely eager to penetrate, while womanhood strives to make the Blossomed Pomegranates, Valley of Joy, body shape, hamstrings, mouth, face, hair, and buttocks appealing and desired. Therefore, in all speculation of *treasures woman*, it's natural to be fervently attracted to what is visually stunning to eagerly adventure into its openings, its primitive nature being true to itself. Take note that surely, there will be individuals who look for every reason to condemn fifth base loving through challenging its health. Use scriptures in hyperboles that are completely not literal to the meaning of the scriptures. Some will challenge its nature to fabricate why it's not justified, but in all your liberated in this fifth base loving, others just want to construct another or give their biases opinions on the criteria because they don't validate, so rebuke them.

Domestic Discipline to Hershey Highway Loving

Before you read this section, I want you readers to be advised that I highly recommend you consult your physician for administered care because of these remedies below and then properly self-administer.

In DD, there's a disciplinary use of enema for cleaning a woman's bowls and a preparation to Hershey Highway loving. **Enema** is a colon-cleanse and therapeutic treatment. An individual may have heard someone say, "She has no junk in her truck." This would be one of the most common explanations of a cleaner trunk. *Enema discipline* is considered a pre-preparation for women giving Hershey Highway loving to avoid embarrassing situations of feces seepage, constipation, and odor discipline. Individuals who often indulge in enema the fetish is called ***Klismaphilia***. Throughout history, many nobles, celebrities, and down-to-earth individuals used enema for detoxification, constipation, chronic fatigue, colitis, Candida albicans, parasites, bloating, etc., of other ill-health related issues. Home use of enema is best advised through a physician on how to administer treatment and aftercare because self-administered enemas can increase risk for bacterial infection that could lead to death or an allergic reaction when an individual doesn't know the safety procedures. Maintenance procedures would be to never share personal enema bag and nozzle. Perform aftercare treatment to personal enema bag and nozzle (making sure both are thoroughly clean) and make sure the enema bag is properly dry because residue from bacteria from the bowels can remain in the bag and prior to next treatment can cause infection. Below are the holistic methods to enema:

- ❖ Milk Enema – using 1 tablespoon of extra virgin olive oil and 16 ounces of warm milk and adding 1 tablespoon of honey and 1.5 quarts of warm filtered water. Add the combination to the enema bag to begin treatment.
- ❖ Salt and Soda Enema – using 2 teaspoons of pure sea salt, 1 tablespoon of baking soda, and 2 quarts or less of warm filtered water.
- ❖ Coffee Enema – using 3 tablespoons of organic coffee and 1 quart of filtered water. (Add coffee [not instant coffee] to filter water and boil for 3 minutes then reduce heat and simmer for 15 minutes.)
- ❖ And many other holistic enema methods. Consult your physician or practitioner to learn about these methods and proper safety instructions.

Another alternative consideration from *enema* as the essential disciplinary tool is in ancient times, enema didn't exist. It's the Weapon of Love and Spiritual Love, "the wine and ointments of herbs, spices, and oils," that provides the discipline. For primal nature, use the Holistic Special Formula below:

Holistic Special Formula Blend for Hershey Highway and Valley of Joy

Use first: Use as aphrodisiac, aromatherapy, and therapeutic (massage on Heavenly Root and pelvic area to penetrate Hershey Highway, though also can be used for Honey Pot):
Combination of food-based water diluted organic essential oils:
Sandalwood, peppermint, sweet almond, frankincense, myrrh (use very little), rose, and patchouli.
*acknowledge a little goes a long way, and cultivate that frankincense and myrrh were often enjoyed among the Song of Solomon.
Then use: Use as skin protector against toxins and nourishment (rub on Heavenly Root):
Blend one or both special food-based butters (for Hershey Highway and Valley of Joy):
Organic raw shea butter or organic raw cocoa butter
Use as a lubricant and purifier (rub on her Hershey Highway, Honey Pot, and a little on your Heavenly Root):
Organic extra virgin cold-pressed olive oil or 98 percent pure aloe vera gel or sweet almond oil or sliquid organics or coconut oil

*However, keep in mind this holistic special formula is not approved by the FDA nor medically endorsed. I highly recommend you consult your practitioner and take precaution by researching the oils, essential oils, and butters before you consider trying this and ask your partner about their medical history for precaution to prevent allergic reaction of ingredients. This formula is not recommended for oral sex, for it may induce illness or give an unpleasant taste, nor is this advised to use with a condom nor advised for women trying to conceive or pregnant.

Know that this Holistic Special Formula on the "Use first" and "Use as a skin protector" is often a momentarily usage, not necessarily a daily usage. The "Use as a lubricant and purifier" can be used as a daily usage. According to OrganicFacts.net and Mountain Rose Herbs, these special ingredients that make up this formula are insinuated to be an antiviral, antiseptic, and astringent, antibacterial, and antispasmodic; eliminates body odors; promotes cell regeneration and sustains healthy cells, cleans bowels, and ensures good health of the uterus and nerve tonic. In addition, it's insinuated to act as conditioner to the skin and a healing agent. In practical learning, there's a common insinuation for heterosexual fifth base loving in which driving the Hershey Highway while climaxing

Serere Medicine expels your lover's toxins (clearing her bowels, relieving constipation), an alternative lovemaking to your woman, thereby delaying children you're not prepared for and contributing to toning the buttocks on a female. During natural copulation, that's without a condom, within the Valley of Joy an Adon can discipline ejaculation to prevent possibility of children not ready for, through the Adon telling the Submissive (queen) to position herself in a rear mounting position when he has the uprising feeling of ejaculating within the Valley of Joy, the Adon will maneuver his member to penetrate the anus to initiate climax within the Hershey Highway. Jamye Waxman recommends for first-time heterosexual couples to use a Lube Shooter so the submissive queen has a better feeling.

Solidity Disciplinary

[4]A virtuous woman is a crown to her husband:
but she that maketh ashamed is as rottenness in his bones.
—Proverbs 12v4 KJV
(Remember this scripture when you read "Chapter
XVII, subtitle: Conscious Caution")

Liberation, Prudence over Feminism

Many men may have notice the propaganda of feminization as the insinuated belief of the new American institutions; however, truth is there's a brainwashing illusion of feminist control, but in reality, it's all propaganda. The truth is the most fearful opponent to feminism is the fear of men knowing their crowned and the potentiality of power and worth. Noticeably, there are many feminist books, reality shows, and many other masses of media covertly finding young women minds for the initiation of feminism and teaching of vain conceit to the uses of their sexuality to get what they want while subconsciously deeming themselves as courtesans. The most powerful discipline is when you say no when a feminist tries to alter a king's mind. A feminist can influence men to open to feministic natures by influencing an androgynous personality within men. Though sometimes saying no to her Honey Pot devalues her Honey Pot powers, it also lets her know the man refuses to be the beta but holds on the YHWH constitution of being only the alpha. A Golden Crevice doesn't make it polished of gold. Surely, it is part of her that makes it a treasure, but the man is the prize, and when more men acknowledge that, they become more of a Solid Alpha "the King." Scratch out the feminism propaganda and acknowledge that men and women are both human, but in Biblical faith tradition, men are the Adonim, and our great ancestral kindred, brethren and sisters knew this as well and honored this institution. Don't buy into that myth that "if you love women, you'll support feminism," for the Adon Olam didn't intend on women being the head but the companions nor is it rectifiable to be liberated based on feminist dissensions for man to be regarded on affection for a woman that he must degrade authority as Adon. (cf. Genesis 3v16)

[9]And man was not made for woman, *but woman was made for man*.[63]

In a way, **James Brown** was right on this ideology. *"It's a man's world but would be nothing without a woman."* A feminist activist attacks political, economic, and social rights for men by using victimhood as the main tool for gaining their social rights, forgoing actions of dominion over men as conveying information on how men should be to their favor and ontology. Feminism's primary focus is on the supremacy while seeking submissiveness from man and denying *liberation* and denying them a *harem* by their sexism, although denying harem is reasonable considering that a proportion of women love the sexual exclusive from their lover, an innate *manic* love, and protesting supremacy by the females' liberation while scorning men's supremacy, validating rights for abortion and subliminally promoting male disposability. The empirical reality is there are many feminist activists who reject spiritual liberated men because they want to be the head, but the Adon's obedience should only be relied on Adon Olam's conduct.

[3]The head of every man is Christ, *the head of woman is man*, and the head of Christ is God.[64]

A voice from Patricia Aburdene book *Megatrends for Women*, chapter titled "To Hell with Sexism: Women in Religion," page 119, clarifies that feminism is reevaluating women values and progressing for position of leadership through creating their own services, providing seminars of feminism, and reevaluating the Bible for feminism propaganda while

---

[63] 1 Corinthians 11v9 NLT.

[64] 1 Corinthians 11v3 NLT.

denying YHWH conduct and systematically creating a revolution through challenge of authorities to suit their agenda. In certain feminist worship, they've changed masculine prefix "Theo" Theology to feminine prefix "Thea" Thealogy credited by Naomi Goldenberg's book called *Changing of the Gods (1979)*. In addition, certain feminists have followed certain goddess spiritualties (movements).

- The neo-pagan tradition called Dianic Wicca (also known as Dianic Witchcraft, which is a female-centered (targeting all goddesses from all cultures) religion from the Budapest (founded by Zsuzsanna Budapest) lineage. Dianic is single worship of Diana and the predecessor goddess, Artemis, as the protector of women and wild nature.[65] Their covens are consistent on rituals reenacting religious and spiritual lore from a feminist philosophy, celebrating the woman's body (mostly the vagina while using it against men) and mourning of the abuses of women, and practicing spell work and hexing against men who abused them. Dianics bountifully welcome bisexuals and lesbians while in coven with many women. The goal is to open female sexuality and sensuality through rituals to affirm lesbian sexuality.[66]
- The reclaiming tradition is dynamic and versatile while rooted in core practices inspired by the Dianic and Feri traditions. Reclaiming tradition is for both female and male of lesbians, bisexuals, transgenders, and gays and testing others in persuasion. Reclaiming tradition practices magic to create change in political activism on oppressive systematics.

Feminism has become a religion and personally created a moral relativism masquerading system of ethics called Ethics of Care which was altered from a book called *In a Different Voice: Psychological Theory and Women's Development* and other added publish works by Carol Gilligan and other leading feminist, opposing the rights and wrongs but based on emotional system. An emotional system can be substance for good but can often be based on hate, conceit for wealth, suffering, deception and the lack of understanding through clouded emotion that may contribute to unfairness and injustice. However, when emotion is based on the

---

[65] www.templeofdiana.org/dwt.htm

[66] Barrett, Ruth Rhiannon. "Lesbian Rituals and Dianic Tradition." *Journal of Lesbian Studies*, 7.2 (2003): 15–28. Web. February 12, 2015.

character of love and prudency than dissensions' are often liberated from God (cf. Hebrews 10v22–23). Feminism has intelligently gained the ability to falsely accuse men of rape, discrimination, and assaults, and then when a man is proven innocent, his reputation is still tarnished. Seemingly, feminist advocate an epidemic of "Rape Culture" in the West but as beautiful antifeminist Lauren Southern pointed out during her interview toward the feminists' event called "SlutWalk," Southern written on her sign, "There is No Rape Culture in the West," unlike what's advocated by feminist; classifying a falsity of "Rape Culture" gives premised danger to a Culture's relativism. Lauren is a conservative to "innocent until proven guilty," not the scorn and oppression without evidence. Antifeminist woman, Phyllis Schlafly said,

> Feminist ideology about the goal of gender-neutrality and the absence of innate differences between males and females goes out the window when it comes to the subject of domestic violence. Feminist dogma is that the law should assume men are batterers and women are victims.[67]

The wise Mrs. Phyllis also wrote an insightful book called *Feminist Fantasies (2003)*, giving the destructive odds on feminism toward women's nature. In other words, women who built in institution of deception, promote whoring and adultery, revile, carry contentious behavior, brawl, and fill men with contempt are rottenness to a man's bones. Sisterhood can be very important to women, but feminism is not the necessity. Some women only join feminism to feel part of something. This doesn't make them rotten but only a lack of affection and the feel of inspiration from her Adon along with lack of contributing something of value that she may want to be part of. As others may know, if you're a college student, you're more likely going to be approached on feminism. One approached me on feminist studies, I showed them the Bible and inferenced this as my institution for faith, political, economic, social rights, and dominion. They had nothing more to say because it demonstrated faith and solidity. Women who plausible in liberation— meaning women that hold Adon Olam's Word credible and sensibly submissive to His framework, women subservient to God's systematics, liberated from Adon Olam's antifeminism and even notice empirically

[67] Schlafly, Phyllis. "Feminist Abuse of Domestic Violence Laws." November 28, 2007.
http://www.eagleforum.org/column/2007/nov07/07-11-28.html

women who are meninist are God-fearing women who have the mentality to obey His conduct and accept men as the Adonim. Those women are crowned according to Yahweh but also empirically more cherished by men.

When the adversary (serpent) attempts to break a covenant and systematic conduct of Adon Olam in humanity, he often begins with women just as the ancient time when it was Eve who was tempted by the adversary, then Eve was the persuader to Adam to bite the forbidden fruit (cf. Genesis 3 and 1 Timothy 2v13–15). The adversary can often use the female as the initiator of sin, to break the Spirit of man, persuading man to fight against their brother, persuading man to become an oppressor of Adon Olam's covenant, persuading man to allow her to have intercourse with other men from sexual fluidity, persuading man to break vows and turn against their children, persuading man to be effeminate, persuading brainwash for young man to be submissive while insinuating woman as the dominant, persuading man to sell narcotics for mammon, persuading man to betrayal of friendship, and persuading man for woman to always be right (she's not always right, fellows, but she can be the majority, perhaps?).

Comparatively, feminism seemingly is reflected from Adam's first wife which was actually Lilith, for Eve was the second wife made from Adam's rib. Lilith wanted to be the superior above Adam's position as Adon, so Lilith refused to be submissive and sexually servile for Adam. God commanded Lilith to be sensible to his Word but Lilith was rebellious and became evil (cf. Galatians 5v19–21). Lilith protested to cause sickness, kill children, and consistently provide oppression and malign against men, torment men with seductive lust and wicked dreams. Lilith became mistress and lover to legions of demons, all which transformed her into a demonic entity. Lilithians cult oppresses men, practices lesbianism, promote male disposability, and Lilithian women seek to be the superiors above men while rejecting sensibility. Whoring became Lilith when she shared her body with a multitude of demons, this is similar to feminism and ways of liberating unorthodox sexuality, fornication and adultery of sharing their vessel's with a multitude of people (many waters). Many Spirits are now following Lilith's ways and most commonly through feminism. (Lumpkin, 2011, p. 285–286)

Liberation of Women

In certain points of clarity, women have the rights to have equal privileges in education, jobs, and voting abilities. Personally, I've been raised by a single mother. Life was a struggle for her in salary, and maybe if the system paid a little more and gave her the ability to have equal pay as the men, she'll be able to support her sons and daughter the way she wanted. But me speaking for her, I felt she did well raising me and my brother and sister (still raising) as a single parent. Yahawah answered her prayers and increased her salary in her field of certified nursing assistant (CNA). There's an agreeable sentiment that women find it difficult to support their younglings alone, so it's important for men to understand women need child support to help raise the "our" child/children.

Tyler Perry mentioned in his play *Madea's Big Happy Family* that a man takes care of his responsibilities, "his children," even if the woman he was with turned out to be rotten. The child/children deserve support and a father. Reviewing the book, *The Feminine Mystique* by Betty Friedan (who certain individuals call the feminist prophet) did give a persuasive argument that women are capable of being more than joining motherhood and wifehood but can use their potential to do something important in the world (but also had persuaded a rivalry through patriarchy). Truth is the Adon's queen should have the rights to give in to her career dream but perhaps should be more of a part-time ambition. The reason for this is because there's an evil deity behind a queen who is married and has a child (or children), creates a broken framework of the Yahawah conduct, for the queen may become more of a workaholic, causing a process of developing resentments and lack of affection. Some regret having a youngling (this is realism! Though they still love them.) and regret marriage and revile against biblical authority of submission because of consistent search for their own independence. Part-time job would perhaps be more ideal for queens, not full time, for full-time work is part of the New World Order agenda.

Those who want to destroy the family will continue to urge mothers to leave the home and "become fulfilled in the workplace." When the mother goes into the workplace to become "fulfilled," or to increase the family's income, she leaves the care of the children to others. Those who warn against such practices will continue to be scorned by the feminists and others who have a hidden agenda: they want to destroy the family. (Ralph A. Epperson, *The New World Order* (Tucson, Arizona: Publius Press, 1990), 245–246.)

The understanding for women to be a part-time worker if they want to pursue their career is because Adon Olam gave them the systematics.

> [4]These older women must train the younger women to love their husbands and their children [5]to live wisely and be pure, to work in their homes, to do good, and to be submissive to their husbands. Then they will not bring shame on the word of God. (Titus 2v4–5 NLT)

Adon Olam's message is that all women with wisdom "builds her home, but a foolish woman tears it down with her own hands."[68](cf. Proverbs 24v3) However, it's important to cultivate that God made woman as a helpmate, so in reality if the Adon is unable to meet billing demands she can help if she desires to help. Even though I said part-time due to Titus 2v4–5, what choice does a woman have if she's alone in meeting bill demands or a single mother, reality is sometimes a woman has to be a domestic helper if the Adon is not meeting the financial demands or is struggling to find a job. However, laziness in a man is not permitted in Adon Olam's Word, for He conducted that men of faith in Him must work (1 Timothy 5v8). Hopefully the Adon's work is legal or striven will to work without putting his health in danger.

On the contrary, we have to look at the beauty of women that work—aesthetically, for instance, a man has a hard day at work than visits his accountant at the bank that's a woman accountant that brightens his day from the femininity persona of her voice, maidenhood-like character and visage she becomes a nurturer at heart and euphoria at mind to aid suffering from sweet character, "the helpmate." Another example would be the grace of a woman doctor or commonly nurse, for there's beauty in having a sensible woman aid, that's built on her perfection of nurture, which is the nourishing persona of "the helpmate," for many of us man feel comfortable with the femininity of a doctor or common nurse for their gentle hands, their altruism, and comforter maidenhood-like character. In addition, grace should be given to muses in the workplace, the muses (*see* Aesthetic Love for Muses) warm the hearts of the Adonim;

---

[68]   Proverbs 14v1.

without them we would have never known such potential of beautiful voices: Whitney Huston, Alicia Keys, Adele Laurie Blue Adkins, Mariah Carey, Celine Dion, and many others including the women that haven't been heard in the music industry.

Furthermore, muses in the workplace are seen as virtuous for honorable character of working with their hands in ways of caretaking to compassion while fearing Yahawah. For instance, in Proverbs 31, an honorable character is the *fair workers*—part-time or possibly full-time— if domestically demanded for household stabile income, are muses' skills of seamstress crafting for individuals that scarce for clothing including within household, and prudently charitable to individuals that scarce for food, drink, and *spiritual love* toward suffering individuals (*see* Art of Spiritual Love), manufacturing and producing her or others crafted or composed arts or literacies, *prudent* investors and intendants, professors or lecturers, beautician or cosmetologist, a gardener or vineyard grower, upholsterer, social worker, reporter, *prudent* event planners, chef, nature conservative, accountant, administrator and work related fields of—hospitality, science or medical. Correspondingly, a substituted *fair worker* is the queen birthing descendants and a caretaker (guardianship role) of the descendants until the descendant is of a proper age for public schooling unless parental guardianship(s) decides to homeschool. *Domestically submissive* queen(s) are subservient and submissive within *conjugal love*, stronghold of the household, nurturer, life-maker (motherhood), strongly impregnable to infidelity and disloyalty, prudently receive YHWH wisdom, and a *devotee*, which is the individual that faithfully gives enthusiasm, love, and loyalty toward the lover. (cf. 1 Timothy 3v11)

God has guided women to be workers similarly as men, and required to eventually marry and birth descendants to prevent them from adaption of *idleness*—the avoidance of working, living without *telos* or result, and lazy; wandering from house to house with gossiping and becoming busybodies from boredom—which progress sexual immorality, touchy gossip that creates conflict and exploiting other individual's confidences. (cf. 1 Timothy 5v13–14) The works of birthing, guardianship, devoutness, sensibility, *domestically submissive* to the Adon's domestics, spoilage submission and servility to Adon, *fair workers* and maidenhood of their household, are all **good works**, and non-idle. All of this is teleological and vocational to women with *aesthetic* visage, through *sensibility* which consist of being *devotees, fair workers, domestically submissive*, remain or progress *good works* are predominately called ***treasures women***, and called a ***treasures woman*** as an individual.

A Letter to Royals, Distinguish: Wanton and Treasure Journal

Dear Royals,

The philosophy of the rudiments of feminism at an early stage I learned could be positive regard for women but now has been corrupted and perverse as a systematic worship that's disdainful of prudency. Feminism definition on Merriam-Webster is different from realisms definition, because its defined by the feminist themselves. For certain women within feminism supremacy became consumed to be scornful, deceitful, oppress men, persuade changing laws of God's domestic discipline, adapting strategic knowledge of courtesan lifestyle to promote rivalry against men by allusion of philosophically convincing young women to join cause of assuming men are all presumed batters or disdained to women, plague *angst* to alter men persona, bring upon contempt or promoting disposability when they've achieved covetous wealth of certain men. In addition, certain feminist women have become haughty, wantons, malign, covenant breakers, maliciously spiteful, boasters, and domestically seek to be the Adonim. Feminism has promoted murdering child(ren) within their womb that was repercussion upon themselves when they've willfully participated in sexual fornication. The type of woman that a king possess will be able to tell if she's a sensible treasure or wanton by the way her council guide's the man: the two ways are either the path of sorrow or the path of grace. Grace is what's needed. (cf. Proverbs 15v13) The embrace of the woman's thighs can be either impassioned and ardent love, or a web of proceeding dolor from favor for deception. *Sensible* women (treasurer's) are keepers of impassioned and ardent love without limitation of servile pleasure for the Adon, for their more agapic, "the menpleaser," in accordance to the scriptures within Colossians 3v22–24 KJV,

> Servants, obey in all things your masters according to the flesh; not with eyeservice, as menpleasers; but in singleness of heart, fearing God: and whatsoever ye do, do it heartily, as to the Lord, and not unto men; knowing that of the Lord ye shall receive the reward of the inheritance: for ye serve the Lord Christ.

The servants are the Submissives, and the masters are the Adonim, this is why verse say "as menpleasers," and because of this scripture that the queens (natural born women) follow makes the Adon cheerful, from virtues of the *treasures woman* servile *good works*. A *treasures woman* provides a cheerful heart, in which a "cheerful heart is good medicine", though a wanton provides the broken spirit, for the "broken spirit saps a person's strength" (Proverbs 17v22 NLT). <u>Saps</u>, in this context means progressively weaken or destroy. The feminist that seeks to liberate adultery are often the ones of a serpent's tongue of deception and in their confidences will soon come into the light where there will be no shadow and those deceptions will break the covenant with sorrow and scorn when truth is revealed. *Adulterers* are the individuals that await the absence of their lover then in confidences prepare a place where there's no witnesses, behaving furtively, then when confidences are satisfied, webs are placed to allure sexual promiscuity, creating a brothel for each individual sorrowfully stuck on the web. The envy that proceeds certain feminist is the malice availed with spiteful ruination of another's reputation and blessings. A *treasures woman* counsels with *sensible* encouragement while crowning her king's nobility and dominion, and are of *good works*, establishes ardency, and gives providence toward the king. The courtesan and feminist seemingly gives the ways of pleasure based on knowledge that weakens men, that provides temptations of sorrow, contempt, and regret while guiding men to dissipation and improvidence while in search for new nobles for ruination, for they are often preying from envy on married, wealthy or devout men but married men are proportionally in fault for being sucked into her brothel when they have a treasures wife at home. A wanton is a common woman that shares her body with *many waters* (*see* Dimensions of Pleasure) while the *treasures woman* is a majestic, *fair, sensible* and of *good works*.

A *treasures woman* is partnered to a king's cares and a helpmate during his burdens (MPR [Book of Morals and Precepts] 16v14).[69] A *treasures woman* is comparative to "woman's empowerment," for majority of her ways are of loveliness: the helpmate, an ardent lover, a *devotee, Apprenticeship Phase* (Figure 1–2) in arts of love and sex that sustains the intimacies exclusive, a vocation to her aspirations with avows consensual to lover's will (cf. 1 Peter 3v5) and sensible to her younglings(s), a household builder and sustainer, and council wisdom from sensibility and mate's fondness's. "Women's empowerment" is not the ways of *feminist* currently but sensible beings without bringing *contempt* and disdaining to *prudency* upon men. Distinguishingly, *women's empowerment* seizes power within her good works and carries tenacious compassionate strength for both men and women despite age differences, while feminism protest victimization and tenacious oppression toward men. *Women's*

---

[69]   The Kolbrin Bible.

empowerment is seemingly council like the beautiful Tantra sex and relationship expert woman, Psalm Isadora, in the ways of sustaining relationship and edifying it and prowess in feminine potential, embracing naturalism and psychologically edifying sensibility and healing burdens of *disposition* from dolorous experience—the mere darkness's (*see* Mere Darkness), and learning the path of the chaste heart that becomes *aesthetic* and a Christ within Spirit (cf. Galatians 5v22–23 Orthodox Study Bible). For those ways of "woman's empowerment" regards why on the 103.9 FM Gospel radio station, Christendom women would announce "women's empowerment," and not "feminist empowerment" due to non-affiliation of wanton behaviorism and disdaining *sensibility* and *theology*, but lovers and investors of *sensibility* and *theology* and *good works*. Empirically, this is not just Christendom women but traditionalist, conservatives and other denominations of women who are against feminism that protest relativism *noetic* philosophy and sensibility all over *YouTube* or demonstrate their support on certain website, such as, "Women Against Feminism,"[70] and other websites.

Brethren don't allow the unvirtuous woman corrupt manner with malice toward all women based on certain women that disdain sensibility, behave wanton and carry deceitfulness; there a *treasures woman* among the *many waters*, just have to pursue with faith and hope for Ahavah and we must do our best to not let evil deeds take the best of us from regrettable misfortune of wanton women. Vengeance and malice seemingly gets the best of many men and women, thereby making another pay for the *angst* of another. Although I'm aware vengeance is inevitable when an individual is fulfilled with much *angst*, for certain of us men can love deep but hate deeper so we have to make effort to sustain sobriety in *fortitude, prudently* modulate our thoughts, and discern *justice*: all in this order. Christ and the Father understand the *psychoticism* so thankfully us Christendom individuals and others that yet have a chance to accept YHWH, are aware that YHWH has an *unconditional positive regard.* The corruption of the hearts has made certain men harsh with women but the treasures needs men to be more *philogynist* now more than ever. **Philogynist** means a man that ardently possess and shows fondness, love, and honor towards women; a philogyny man. Misogynist are differential from a philogynist. Misogynist are more bitter with women, disregarding the sensible for strong degradation much like the 2013 film, *Misogynist,* while philogynist regards the sensibility. Although both misogynists and

---

[70] http://womenagainstfeminism.com/

philogynists are all capably brutish when felt emasculated, infringed or dishonored upon, by oppressive women. —J.S.J.

Recultivate Your Mind

The humanity often tries to brainwash everyone's mind through persuasion, trying to make things seem unnatural and taboo or bring contempt upon. If an individual has interest in preserving their primitive nature, there's nothing strange about it. Social construction will make it seem this way, but an individual's peculiar self gives a true fundamental of id, your individuality, for cloning is sublimation. If there's a liberated love act an individual indulges in that's justified from the Bible, then nothing is taboo or sinful. Social construction labeled it taboo for caging in your sanity of how an individual should love and how an individual should conduct themselves, thereby proving an adversary to mind something of a serpent looking to cage an individual, all because of what disqualifies as modernity social sublimation. Humanity can cause destruction within itself, but the ape in the human that follows constructs illuminates destruction within themselves because they didn't admit to their persona.

If an Adon or Submissive likes a particular clothing style but wants to fit in with modernity style, why do you follow when you can be true to yourselves?

If an Adon or Submissive disagrees with a liberated revile of some type of political movement but chooses to compromise just because they want to fit in modern revolution, why do you follow when you can be true to yourselves and rebel?

If an Adon or Submissive has a sexual nature that's liberated to YHWH's conduct and the individual remains suppressed because of fear of judgment because the individual is nervous of rejection and wants to fit into modernity lifestyle, why do you do this when you can be true to your persona?

If an Adon or Submissive has the passion to preserve natural intimate hairs on their body but wants to fit with a social constructive persuasion that it's unhealthy or build shameful ideologies on the criteria, why do you lie to yourselves if this is what you desire and fits your personality?

If an Adon or Submissive has family that does not approve of a certain mate that they've chosen to take path in marriage but decide to fit their family's demographic desires, leaving themselves scorned, why do you lie to yourselves just to fit others' prejudice cultivations? Why not be true to your persona?

If an Adon or Submissive has love set on another but is going through an arranged marriage then thinks family knows best when truth is your id knows what's best, so why do you lie to yourselves just to fit another's construction?

If an Adon or Submissive has a novelty they longed to express why the individuals should live a lie and suppress from going to an adult shop just to please individuals who they fellowship with at the synagogue or ground themselves worthlessly with contempt because they believe it to be a sin, don't the Adon and Submissive know that love covers a multitude of sins? For sins are no sin when they are evaluated out of love—love from the Spirit, love from holding emunah within self's persona, love from the significant other's satisfaction as a demonstration of agape love, and love from passions of novelties craved.

Christianity is about being free from the laws of sin and death. Why reencounter this with worthless conviction if the Adon and Submissive have faith that they're undefiled? Truth is certain nobles that certain individuals look up to in church may secretly cling to similar desires but try to sustain from being caught and the social counters that come with that, that they'll order certain items online on Amazon and other online franchises. The charismatic individual who adventures into adult shopping places to fulfill novelties are more in true confidence and courageously amorous than the individuals who secretly cling to certain novelties.

There's such thing as freedom. If individuals recultivate themselves, they'll realize life can be a lot like for an Adon, an eagle flying around for the best environment and giving leadership while a Submissive is a dove in covenant with her leader. Remolding the empirical and adventuring new environments and being in liberation is a human's way. A person is a slave when they embrace themselves as slaves. Everyone has a fire deep inside them, and the fury will unleash arcanum if it feels constructed and prisoned.

Homework Assignment

For both Adon (man) and Submissive (woman): Create a written or typed journal of your Domestic Discipline rules and acceptance, avow carnal desires, document the study of your relationship, and novelties. Make this a mission statement and journal of dissensions and sensualists passions. Define your concept of love, of honor, and of family dharma. Reflect on your paradigms of scornful dramatic impulses and find a way to council an agreement to determine a better harmony for the relationship through creating a methodology for *new relationship energy (NRE)*, which means a receptive deep emotional bond that brings ardency and eroticism for a reinvigorating relationship. Admit in this assignment what's your philosophy of DD framework of ministry, BDSM prowess and ineptitudes, your sexual primitive behavior and *pleasure principle*, what you're looking for in your significant other, the essence of home to your Spirit and how you hope for it be conducted. Write what your acceptable to in the sensuous of intimate nature and what's willing to be compromised. Describe your motion of companionship and how you sincerely hope for it to be. Conduct a prayer schedule, a bible study and(or) theology study. How you like to be awarded and honored in the most rational ways. Preferable grounds of affection and profess your philosophy of power play, household governance and submission. Confess your sexual indulgence, demands, novelties, sadomasochism interest, arousing seductions and positions. Profess your ideology on monogamous and (or) polygynous relations in terms of fidelity, liberation, and sharing of wealth. Create and (or) use or add-on to "Adon Disciplinary Language," for a symbolical understanding in discrete secret between the Adon and Submissive. Create a doctrine on yourself of your aesthetic philosophy, naturalism, urbanism, traditionalism, and masterful and weakest portions of intimacy, and love styles (*see* Masterful Loving and Traits). Spiritual beliefs on intimate orthodoxies, how important Adon Olam's law is to you, and formulate *congruence test* which is the testing of tolerance, principality of the individual, emunah and veneration. Congruence test of *sexual ecstasy* and *provocative proclivities* toward the significant other and yourself (*see* "Section I: Loveology in its Nature," for *provocative proclivity* and *sexual ecstasy* clarification). Apply a drinking, smoking, erotic spanking discipline, curfew, public dress code and social gathering policy toward your significant other. Percentage of stability for the household and bills you're looking to cover, work ethics, and ambitions.

This entire assignment will be you and your companion's DD and sensual BDSM contract "signet." For as soon as it's finished your significant other would have to read and consent it through their full name authorized signature and (or) make a special note to the ineptitudes of their discernment from the journal and come up with a compliance or agreement than signature it.

Chapter XV:
Sacred Penetrative Roots
and Revelation of Ancient
to Modest Remedies

*"The deepest of lovemaking understands its nature
and how to grow masterful in its roots."*

Warning! This chapter may be inappropriate for certain ages.

Sacred penetrative roots and revelation of ancient to modest remedies provide mastery of extensive male sexual stamina, transformation of lovemaking, owning up to your nature and mastery of thrusting. It's a rhythmic coitus lovemaking system. The main focus of this art is oxygen mastering, identifying your sexual nature, rising to the apprenticeship of becoming a master lover, revealing the truth about PE,[2] and satisfying your treasures woman's erogenous zone physiologically and mentally. One of these ancient remedies is known as Imsak, which means to withhold or hold in, mastering retention toward premature ejaculators while satisfying a harem (Seeker 2014).

> *A man who says, "All women are whores" or "All women are angels" usually generalizes his experience of one woman. Misogyny and philogyny are two sides of the same coin, to use a cliché. (Dr. Joseph Suglia)*

You may ask what makes Imsak relevant to kings. The answer is within your desires of longed intensity—women proceeding sheer respect while craving for more of you, ability to give your woman multiple orgasms, and natural remedy to possibly cure premature ejaculation. *Comfort is critical within* this art, required to man up to your desires without worrying about the perceptions of mockery. Embrace your testicle craving and mind. Seek truth within self of what ignites your cravings . . . Short or tall females? Model? Chubby, curvy, athletic, slim, or thick-figure females? Older females, middle-aged females, or younger females? Skin colors—vanilla, cream, caramel, dark chocolate, or chocolate? Seek individuality within what's true to the heart and desire. This prevents deception of hurting another because you rationalized truths and prevented luring a woman you didn't accept but used her for pleasure.

Likewise, ye husbands, dwell with them according to knowledge (means *skills acquired by experience or education*), *giving honour* (means *deep warm approval*) *unto the wife, as unto the weaker vessel, and as being heirs* (means *legally entitled to her flesh*) *together* (means *one flesh*) *of the grace* (means *considerate blessings and refinements*) *of live . . .* (**1 Peter 3v7 KJV**)

The biblical scripture states that it's important to acquire sexual intelligence as a private study to become masterful and a *CDD* lifestyle of *sensible,* but keep in mind not all women are **angelic** (means *exceptionally kind and innocent*). There are possibly many who enjoy a different type of loving (the more aggressive nature), and the majority of us men are not angelic in lovemaking, and that's because of our sexual nature (for nature refers to *Becoming Lord of Sexual Roots* subtitle in this chapter). Don't think about traditional expectations from relatives, friends, associates, and strangers thinking or disapproving on who you choose, for it's better to remain emunah to yourselves. Various people will judge you for loving another ethnicity (race) because of cultures, society, and appearance features, but remaining emunah to yourself becomes careless on worldly cares and expectations from others because you've freed yourself a ghetto (go to Chapter V: Empirical Realities for meaning of ghetto), for it's better to be free to true heart's desire than captive to a heart's desire suffering *repression.*

Key Chart
Penis = Weapon of Love; Heavenly Root; Sexual Steel; Love Muscle *Vagina/Vaginal Sex = Valley of Joy; Honey Pot; Golden Crevice* *Anus/Anal Sex = Trunk of Bliss; Driving the* *Hershey Highway; Hershey Highway* *Oral Sex = Instrument of Pleasure; Sweet Mouth Loving* *Seminal Fluid = Serere Medicine* *Breasts = Blossomed Pomegranates*

Chart 15–1: Intimate Nicknames

𝔄rtful 𝔯𝔢𝔳𝔢𝔩𝔞𝔱𝔦𝔬𝔫 of 𝔗𝔥𝔯𝔲𝔰𝔱𝔦𝔫𝔤

Of the delights of this world man cares most for is sexual intercourse, yet he has left it out of his heaven. —Mark Twain (1835–1910)

It's time to bring back you're earthily heavens. Apply this five-step phase for preparation and coition process.

Protocol #: I

Acquire this focus that your mind should be rooted to the present. Don't let your conscious drift to fantasy of another woman nor anything else. Your presence is important in the moment of sex. It's wise to not let your mind travel miles away from the current moment of lovemaking because it's a turnoff to a woman's lovemaking, for women are jealous and envious beings, but that's a demonstration that she's seduced by you and desires your undivided time. Cultivate that lovemaking should be focused, timeless, and limitless. Don't allow your mind to be rooted to the need of a pornography film, for it'll give an insecure vague on pleasure shared. A position illustrated manual content something briefly vivid will do just find while your focus is rooted inside and outside of her.

For one of the best visual illustrated manual, I would recommend buying *The Modern Kama Sutra: The Ultimate Guide to the Secrets of Erotic Pleasure.*

The empirical reality is that lovemaking can happen anywhere depending on how adventurous you and your intimate partner is, so it's knowledgeable to unscrew the fixed mentality that the environment has to be musical or very quiet though the truth is a **tranquil** (means *free from disturbance*) environment is more precious and savored. It's important to release any burdens you have. "Free your mind" and concentrate on the nourishment of your woman.

Acquire tasteful thoughts. The sexual impulse can become acquitted with hunger on desserts and meats of what you indulge in. Allow tasteful thoughts to linger when she's nude before you. Demonstrate your fruitfulness with clean hands, clean tongue, and a nose lingering on her craved fresh/aromatic flesh. The empirical reality is that indulging in nakedness privately toward her, a queen/princess often indulges the king's/prince's eyes focusing on the Valley of Joy, Blossomed Pomegranates, and Trunk of Bliss (if she's turned around intentionally) with a fervent facial expression. Although if she demonstrates insecurity, she wants her king's/prince's eyes focused on hers. Keep in mind that not all women are naturist/nudist at heart, so those that are not appearing naked before you in seduction perhaps desire your initiative, for they may have some insecurities. However, when you provide privacy, she may feel more comfortable, and in time she'll become more induced to nudist/naturist sexuality openly to your eyes. (*For info on nudist/naturist, refer to Chapter XVI, subtitle: Untold Novels*)

Protocol #: II

Cultivate this second. It's important to acknowledge your penetration skills in a way where it's more blissful for you and your queen. Most females want you to insert your Weapon of Love in their meat slowly, not ignorantly blunt, especially if you're about to drive the Hershey Highway or if she's virgin. Spread her legs in a fifty-degree angle or greater for comfortability and easier penetration though empirically, a woman spreads her legs naturally for heighten pleasure and comfortability. Diving into the Trunk of Bliss requires starting smooth penetration, and depending on the female and your Heavenly Root, lubrication is influenced among this ecstasy (apply the Holistic Special Formula Blend, see Chapter XIV: Domestic Discipline). However, rather it's Honey Pot loving or Hershey Highway loving, this all relies on the sexual behavior of your queen and the king, for some want it rough in moments, while others want it sensually smooth in the beginnings. It all depends on the mood of you and her. Some women urge desires of deviance and merge sexual aggression stronger than others, depending on her and your sexual appetite for hunger; some crave the gentlemen of sensual behavior, while others crave the gentlemen of different loving or variously both depending on the mood. The practical honest truth that various books fail to mention is that often, various males, once the Love Muscle penetrates the woman, as men were more likely to not want to stop because our behavior is more focused on the thrusting and sensation. When sex begins, the mind is more controlled by the fruitful eagerness persisted from the Love Muscle, so acknowledge how you penetrate. Coitus is the root of passionate love or different type of loving, and it's flamed through feeding and nourishment, a power exchange for communion union. When a man penetrates a woman, he's savoring tension relief, holes of moisten suction as a place of Ahavah, heaven, sensualism, nurture, eagerness, healing, and sovereignty and high-spirited. When a woman opens to a man, she's savoring itch relief, a hardened sausage entering her while her openings is sucking it to grasp—Ahavah, yang, eagerness, desire to be desired, ejaculation of Serere Medicine, companionable love, and animalistic fuel. Both man and woman are providing communion of therapy and feeding and longevity to each other.

Protocol #: III

Next, acquire focus on every curve of her flesh and take much delight. Don't avoid giving her detail of the pleasure persisting. Many women desire connection emotionally with detail on how good we feel inside them. Women love your undivided attention, for it lets them know you're focus is with her, for various women are jealous beings. This provides reassurance that you're grateful, affectionate, and desiring only her Honey Pot, Instrument of Pleasure, Trunk of Bliss, Blossomed Pomegranates, and her company.

The salacious movement is to tease her when not expected during the moments of thrusting. When she is on her back, lift both of her legs performing the Pressing Passion position. Gracefully give shallow and slow deep thrust then withdraw some and repeat continuously for a few minutes or seconds. While performing, this you're spiritually reading her visually with longing eyes, directly viewing her eyes, interpreting soulful love then gratefully admire her Blossomed Pomegranates. During this movement, gradually move your eyes south until you're looking at your Heavenly Root, thrusting into her Honey Pot with smooth motion, then direct eyes gradually north until eyes facial beauty. This is building the versatility of intimacy, *Eros*, and *Holy Amorous*, then if so desired, bring out the *Thanatos* after the passionate moment. Depending on the **pleasure principle**, you or your intimate partner may suffer from the *suppression effect*, causing you to release the *Thanatos* before the *Eros* and *amorous* because of greediness or relief of tension (see *pleasure principle* in subtitle: *Dimensions of Pleasure*). When she performs the Instrument of Pleasure, grasp her head gently and slowly grab the starting roots of her hair. Ananga Ranga calls this "holding the crest hair of love," for the hair signifies potent sexual energy and strength hold, for this accumulates a strong sexual arousal. While grasping, don't be ashamed to create symphonies (*see* Chapter XVI, subtitle: *language of love*). After she finishes fellating you, delight her with a French kiss and perhaps cunnilingus in returning gesture. The sensible portion of sensual hair pulling is to not be ignorant by snatching her hair harshly when she's fellating or when she's in doggy style position for if you do distrust or skepticism will be her disposition, thereby making it in negative ineptitude and dissension. For visual learning of sensualism becoming ignorant by harsh hair pulling see *footnote*[71].

Protocol #: IV

Then acquire reading her impressions. Become aware of her motions and movements and gratifying gestures. Don't let your mind adrift from pleasure of her pleasure shared with you. She wants to see your impression of desiring her as she to you.

While performing this, breathe slowly, inhale, and exhale. This is an act of relaxing your body while completely concentrating on pleasuring her and feeling her pleasure—the Valley of Joy tunnel. In the moment you grow more aroused, think of her hair, flesh, eyes, and beauty as you begin to caress, stroke, and press on her sensitive flesh. Your imagination should be a vision of the current woman you're with. Focus on her penetrative openings as therapeutic smooth meat that sensationalizes the Love Muscle and suctions your Sexual Steel that creates eager meaty cravings for more

---

[71]   The film *Basic Instinct 2* (2006), edition of the: unrated extended cut. Approximate runtime of 00:38:35–00:40:50.

sexual loving. Sacred lust is the key imaginative arousal while performing hypnosis. Draw attention to her eyes while using your peripherals to smoothly stroke your hands on her erogenous zones—the throat and earlobes, breasts, nipples, inner and outer thighs, and pelvic area—and grasp the buttocks and hamstrings. Eyes focusing on her eyes, maybe, a little on her lips, depending on how her confidence responds to the gaze of eyes on her mouth.

Art of Revelation in Reflection through the Eyes

In lovemaking according to *The Modern Kama Sutra: The Ultimate Guide to the Secrets of Erotic Pleasure*, the timeless eye contact reveals "a potent sign of love and confidence," possessing revelation of "your innermost" identity, leaving your partner naked through their eyes (Thomas and Thomas 2005) to discover their heart and truth. Eyes observing her, taking delight in her beauty and her sounds is an open gratifying gesture while savoring her scent and perspiration. If a human being demonstrates difficulties to look in the eyes of a significant other for period in the art of intimacy, then they perhaps have secrecy of shame. The period can't be characterized on how long to stare, for this is fully understood by *noetic* abilities, emotion, and intuition. This shame can derive from not remaining *emunah* to covenant of marriage because of infidelity secrecy or emunah to personal repression because you may have hidden sexual desires that you're afraid may cause tension and suffering *suppression effect* or contempt for one's own splendor because you feel like you don't deserve that person or you're distracted from worldly cares or someone secretly lusting for or lost a sense of *honor* for them or feel *angst*. However, artful reflection of the eyes to gain emunah is removed when you're mating for the pleasure principle, Thanatos, and amorous. Amorous can still be used in eye reading.

Protocol #: V

After sex, communicate with her in languages of love by telling her you love her or show gratitude through sensual detail of what was delicious to you or just caress her. Insinuate a storytelling of her in your fantasy (adding a mysterious spice) while asking for a reservation to make that fantasy into a reality, and spoon with her naked while having her naked as well (this fuels animalistic lust and desire for more, an aphrodisiac that promotes an after spice in intimacy).

> *Full nakedness from the physical to the soul gives*
> *a fuel of Ahavah unfiltered and openings to raw*
> *depths of sensations, ardency, profoundness,*
> *bonding, warmth, naturism, effusive fruitfulness,*
> *romance, and sensualism.*

It's rude to screw then rapidly redress, leaving her in passion alone, emotionally cold. When you act in that manner, you're projecting to her your work is more important. It was all booty call or insecurity issues, or you fear attachment. She'll understand if it was a real emergency that cause this and forgive but only so many emergencies you can use before she becomes suspicious and frustrated. Various women want comfort with a masculine touch of sensual pleasure, talking or perhaps an acupressure message (although this may not be recommended for men with agitating rough hands because maybe more uncomfortable for her than pleasurable). This protocol is denied if you'll both made clarity that the intercourse would be a quickie because of obligations of stability or other focused matters but eventually will become intolerant and unsatisfied on either husband or wife if the action is frequently quickies.

𝔇imensions of 𝔓leasure

Remember a woman craves and loves intimacy and loves and craves pleasure.[72] Below are the areas of pleasure (see Figure 15-1):

Figure 15-1 The Four Pleasures in Human

Speak to her gently, in an explicit tone, based on her level of naughtiness. Instruct her on intentions and affections for her. Spirituality and desire must be opened in senses—her smell, her appearance, her soothing nature, her womanly figure, and other sorts of thoughts while you're kissing and undressing her and her pleasuring. Your special woman is your treasure and companion as the Lord intended. The heat of the moment of preparation defines your affection. Your woman is your treasure, and that treasure can be in endless currency of pleasurable living. Again, relaxing is critical, and breathing is the key to mastering tension. The moment of penetration applies breathing deeply and rhythmically, for proper oxygen intake is vital in any activity. Deep breathing is derived from the belly through the nose or mouth, although the deep breathing should be natural and relaxed. Healthy breathing

---

[72] Caressing and touching.

facilitates harmony and endurance, thereby developing ejaculation discipline. Sexual penetration is not about hitting it fast and deep but versatility of thrusting and longing sensation, for going deep is a natural tendency if you focus more on that you're a level closer to prowess. Pleasure is not about racing but endless moments of gratification and satisfying your own desire of novelty, thereby satisfying your significant other as well.

Foreplay is in the mixture of performing pre-satisfaction. The beginning of foreplay begins with a kiss, for sensual and physical pleasure both play a huge role in this performance. Go for the erogenous zones of her body as given in Figure 15-2. Focus is the primary of this art. Sex talk, affection, and moaning are the intellectual and emotional pleasure. Penetration is the whole package, but as the saying goes, *preheat before you stick in the turkey* may be vitally important to various women. Conversely, various males don't always do that because our sexuality sometimes hunger for the **Pleasure Principle**, which is "derived from buildup libido accelerating to uncomfortable level of tension and calls for immediate tension reduction," so vigorously, kings and princes become more assertive in nature and impulsive in a nonrational way (Engler 2006). Comparatively, queens and princesses experience this very same pleasure principle within their nature. Pleasure principle was later termed **Reality Principle**. Pleasure principle reflects back to the urge and merge motion, desperation from buildup libido waiting for sex longing to be satisfied while withdrawing from logic for physiological satisfaction. Pleasure principle is throughout *many waters* so we must not fool ourselves into thinking it doesn't exist or won't hunt beings but must come to rationalism of the *humanistic approaches to personality* and *unconditional positive regard* that it's inevitably undisciplined when *repressed* and *suppressed*. Moreover, **many waters** defined is the revelation Bible code for ". . . peoples, and multitudes, and nations, and tongues" (Revelation 18v15 KJV). *Reality principle* is primitive and because of this principle men and women are capable of amorous, devious, aggressive, unorthodox and rapturous sexual impulsive behavior. In accordance, this is why pleasure principle is liberated and ordained as *reality principle*. God didn't instore for beings to filter love life when it's undefiled, in the KJV scripture James 1v21 it says ". . . lay apart all filthiness and superfluity of <u>naughtiness</u> . . ." but actually this was altered by chain of order, the governing authorities, but actually the word as stated in the *1599 Geneva Bible* is "maliciousness," or "wickedness" among other English translations, instead of the fabricated idiom substituted word "naughtiness." Naughtiness is *good works* in undefiled.

> The Adonim purpose is not to embrace, become agreeable to, and worship feminism but to provide benevolence and love to women. Be wise to not construct yourselves on the ideology of feminism movement, but acknowledge you're an Adon, and the proper worship is to Adon Olam, not to a goddess, no matter what mass media and social pressure convince. Your perseverance in lovemaking is ensuring horizons of bliss continue to remain *emunah, amorous* to free yourself from *repression* and unleash the *Thanatos persona*, loveable with *Eros, agapic,* and *ardent* loving and honorably affectionate. It's wiser to seek a queen who's prudent to Adon Olam's dominant conducts, that husbands are the head (Ep. 5v22–24), and asserts conduct over their wives (Rm. 7v2).

Many kings and princes pride themselves on achieving muscularity and power and constantly penetrating women in hard and fast rhythmic cycles but don't always acknowledge some or maybe most women crave variety and a longing sensation of pleasure, so they hate when it ends fast. Although according to the seeker, fast and hard coition maybe desired by various women momentarily because they like the dominance from the psychological pleasurable moments, thereby craving your yang from power exchange, but the main arousal is lovemaking steady, rhythmic, and slow.

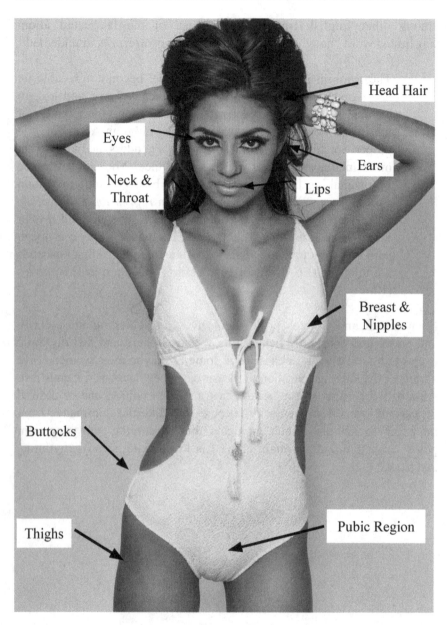

Figure 15-2 Pleasure Zones of Queens

Conversely, continuous fast and furious can cause *bad pain* to various women, from constant pounding on her pubic bone and buttocks, thereby ruining the physical and emotional pleasure persisting in the moment. A woman's intellectual and emotional pleasure in moments of intercourse is fulfilled in longing sensation. Some women want to let go of their conscious to the unconscious cycle during lovemaking. Fast and furious may dull the imagination and pleasure fantasied about because they want connection, and connection builds with undivided time and sensibility. For instance,

> Your woman may say, "I feel like you're somewhere else when we're having sex." This is because she craves your *emunah* and doesn't want to make love to your *shadow*. In addition, vice versa, if the man is experiencing this with his queen, for no one is satisfied in making intimacy in someone's shadow unless it's to feed the pleasure principle, and if that's the case, then it's all a booty call (an act of *"free love"*) or in a woman's case an itch relief call. Momentarily, men and women desire *"free love"* intimacy for strictly pleasure and nourishment (for *"free love,"* see *Chapter XVI*, subtitle: *Masterful Loving and Traits, Semi-subtitle: The Lover's Characters*).

Various women hope for more stamina and endurance for a more pleasurable experience. The subversive cause for most kings and princes thinking hammering women in bed is most desirable is because the influence of pornography or other males they considered role models who persuade them into thinking that's the way or mass media portraying this image, so some women become more invested in women than men. This was discussed in *Her Fantasy Lover Formula* (Stone 2013) performed by Krista Ayne and Leanne. The primitive lovemaking is not about hardcore or softcore sex but sensualism. People sometimes define sensualism as gentle love. That is not so. Truth is sensualism sex is about prolonging lovemaking performance in motions that feel more sensational and lasting without imitating what's been taught on pornography and influences but the individuality of id that gives your personal craving for more. In mankind predicament, it's better for men satisfy or over satisfy women in bed, but it has to do without time and sensuality. The reason without time is because women often don't project time in loving because they're focusing on sensation and pleasure and expect men to do the same. No woman wants a man to constantly look at their watch when romance begins, but women are sentimental sometimes with man's time management, but it's important to harvest that sensualism is more valued than materialism. In insightful film on this criterion would be *Sweet November* (2001).

I've come to realize that women are more literal, while us men are more practical. A fellow friend told me that "slow hands is the key," meaning once you begin any relation with a decent woman, you submitted yourself to a timeless dimension of endless arousal and stimulation. In time, with continuous rhythmic and thrusting, she perhaps may spasm ejaculation, aggressively and suddenly with orgasmic pleasure, relieving her tension of virtue. Orgasms are rhythmic waves of pleasure with contractions, toning the sexual glands and connecting the intellect, which your soul partakes on. According to the French language, *la petite mort*, called little death, particularly queens in tradition and modern societies experience similarities of dying pleasurably for a grasp of time. You may notice this if she passes out from orgasm or orgasms. Actuality manual stimulation of her G-spot through oral or fingers can induce a vaginal orgasm, but she still lacks that psychological dimension of real penetrative sex. In future reference, empirically cultivate in mind that not all women desire finger stimulation, for some are disgusted by this because they only trust their hands in the Valley of Joy or skeptical that she may be scraped or catch an infection from unclean hands or feel it's not as pleasurable as mass media would insinuate. During your motion of intercourse when you've drained your energy satisfying her and yourself, embrace the ejaculation of fueling her with your medicinal potency (Serere Medicine) wherever you may have penetrated. Your fuel is what relieves her starvation of wanting pleasures by feeding the physical, emotional, and sensualism. Then your dharma is to flood the Golden Crevice, Hershey Highway, and Sweet Mouth with Serere Medicine. Penetrative sex is her nature, the creative complementary opposites of male and female as the Lord created.

Revelation of Sexual Steel (PE²) Methods and Golden Crevice Strengthening Method

Majority of all the kings and princes in this millennium are researching for education on penis enlargement and enhancement (PE²); Out of respect I won't give the ingredients but will give you factors to expect. According to the Penis Enlargement Bible written by John Collins (Collins 2012), some of the very essentials for enlarging and enhancing your Heavenly Root are constant supplements of the following:

- Water and specific amino acids

- Human growth hormones (HGH supplement)
- Specific oriental medicines
- In addition, proper vitamin, protein-rich diet, and minerals intake is very important to harmonize the growth and health. Internally, you must make much effort to cleanse yourself of impurities residing in the body. If you're serious about this criterion, you may want to invest in John Collins e-book.

Collins's theory states that if you cause your body to regenerate puberty cycle, you'll cause new growth. The only side effect with Collins's formulation is that you may create balding on the head according to the testimonials. According to the book Natural Cures "They" Don't Want You to Know About (Trudeau 2004), your body should be supplemented with juicing or organic whole food multivitamins, for it is much healthier than chemically produced vitamins. Juicing with blenders, such as *Iomega, Vitamix* or other juicer/blenders, are a much healthier intake because it's fresh. For supplements, personally, I would recommend *New Chapter Organics* multivitamin supplements because of my personal supplementation of this brand. Conversely, this may not be for you, although there are other brands of vitamin supplements that offer great results and are organic, such as Host Defense and so forth. For HGH supplementation, Royal Velvet spray, Membrane Integrity Factor, and GenF20 Plus demonstrate excellent results according to testimonials, but I don't insinuate it's the best but worth trying. Collins recommends GenF20 Plus as the number one choice. Although Membrane Integrity Factor (MIF) and Royal Velvet spray testimonials are substantial (there are at least one hundred plus real customer reviews), I would recommend considering these two more because of the amount of real testimonials. The MIF was formerly called Find Longevity Now.

In correlation to the PE Bible, the Mayo Clinic established penile enlargement success is mostly derived from stretching (extender device or stretchers) or surgery (although many are not satisfied with the results and may become more harmful than beneficial). Collins's theory benefits perhaps greater with combination of a traction device to progress results. Mayo Clinic (Mayo Clinic Staff 2014) studies explain that pills, lotions, and exercises have not been proven to enlarge but give adverse effect that maybe harmful than beneficial. Vacuum pumps produce temporary results, but excessive usage can damage the elastic tissue. One of the most trusted pumps is the Bathmate Hydromax Xtreme Series. According to reviews, results are satisfied, although the enhancement is mostly produced in girth. Stretching exerts traction, creating natural *cell division* called **cytokinesis**. Various placebo studies acknowledge its "effective and durable lengthening of the penis" according to CBSNews.com (Livescience.com 2011). The traction devices most trusted are the CE Validated and FDA Approved and Medically Approved with clinical documents, such as Jes-Extender, Phallosan forte, X4 Labs, and Size Genetics. In addition, look for the better warranty, for a two-year to a lifetime warranty is always more worth considering. Although this information for you kings and princes is excellent for your benefactor, don't invest your last-in products and supplements when you're on budget. Rationalize your liabilities and expenses.

In empirical, reality is there are lots of subliminal opinions about penile lengths and girths from mass media through women's mouths subjected bigger is better and some giving an sizeable acceptance. The subversive analogy is that instead of measuring off men, they don't measure the anatomy of their own individual vaginal walls on what's acceptable but only theorize bigger is better. In addition, they don't often promote vaginal tightening oils, gels, and other remedies yet promote male enhancements that cause more damage than good, but subliminally, certain women subject rejection on certain sizes. According to Christine O'Connor, MD, a woman's Golden Crevice is "a very elastic organ which changes to accommodate whatever is going on," although there's indication that after natural childbirth, the Valley of Joy may become loose and less satisfying and because of this, various women practice Kegel, Kunyaza, and Pompoir exercises to strengthen and tone pelvic floor muscle (Worth 2011). On the contrary, before childbirth certain individuals prefer Cesarean delivery (C-Section) to preserve aesthetic appeal and possibility of preserving vaginal tightness, or perhaps voluntarily aggress to the Vaginal Rejuvenation, also called "Vaginoplasy," a procedure mainly used to tighten internal vaginal muscles and enhance sexual gratification for both partners and give aesthetic appeal according to Dr. Wesley Anne Brady.[73] Others women, prefer another holistic remedy, such as vaginal herbal sticks[74] or capsules for the vigorous strength, rejuvenation, and enhancement of the vaginal. Moreover, a proportion of women heal vigorously without the need for vaginal exercise's and surgical procedures. Correspondingly, intimate enhancements discussion of women and men are all capable of some type

---

[73] https://www.womenswellnessinstitute.com/vaginal-rejuvenation/

[74] Cf. http://www.vaginal-tightening.com/

of sexual dysfunction or vulnerable progression to prowess passion, so fairness is given not criticism, each individual has a voluntary pursuit to improve or embrace. In accordance, I'm not an expert on sexual dysfunctions, though I would recommend seekers of this knowledge to invest in author Helen Singer Kaplan's book, *The Illustrated Manual Of Sex Therapy Second Edition*. Cultivate, you're all royal men, and if you're not acceptable to certain females, then you'll be better off without her. Various women insult your manhood to degrade you and promote dissatisfaction or speak highly to make others envious and express satisfaction. Not all women feel the same way as mass media insinuate, so if John Collins's theory and penile extenders don't work accordingly, don't induce depression but search for a change from the common women in your environment and journey to new environments and get to know the persona of the woman before performing intimate acts that may depolarize because of not taking the time to learn her attractions of sensualism and physiological. Cultivate that not every sexual measure is put on man but a measure of the woman as well and neither sex can be physiologically built from force but prowess of the will, investment, and altruism. Certain men embrace without enhancement, or striven or strive to enlarge their Sexual Steel, while certain women embrace without enhancement, or strive or striven to make their Honey Pot tighter to feel the intensity of pleasure as if they were nearly in chastity.

Pompoir Method

Pompoir is another blessed method to strengthen and tone women pelvic floor muscles. Below are the benefits of Pompoir:

Stimulates sexual responsiveness and strengthens vaginal walls while regaining its vaginal tightness to better acquire more pleasure for her and male partner by harvesting control on vaginal muscles. In addition, it improves urinary incontinence and helps acquire female ejaculation orgasm, different levels of sexual enjoyment. It benefits men because women with healthy strong pubococcygeus muscles (pc muscles) make size doesn't matter from males. Another method, *Kunyaza Method*, corresponds nearly in the exact same methodology but with a longing patient coitus thrusts. Women who are skilled in Pompoir, which is also called *Kabbazah*, benefits vaginal toning. Although certain women prefer the Kabbazah method, which is when the woman gradually mounts the man and remains stationary while rhythmically nourishing the Heavenly Root with her Valley of Joy elastic organ, her abdominal muscles, and pc muscles; the rhythmic moves of muscular discipline is disciplined from the arts of belly dancing. Certain queens that are skilled in mounting the man Cowgirl style will innately harvest similar skill by thrusting smoothly up and down while the king's member is inside them, while she savors changes of the sensuous feelings from rhythmic cycles—moving her hips, back, pc muscles and abdominal side–to–side, back–and–forth, thrusting up–and–down.

Becoming Lord of Sexual Roots

The matriarch is to understand the nature of sexual roots to provide *emunah* of sexual roots to internalize healing within ourselves to give abundance of longevity and fruitfulness as a true lover. The individual who addresses their core roots with contempt will cause envious error to their Spirit while others free themselves from self-persecutions. Becoming one with primitive nature that nurtures foundation is the very foundation that is undefiled and perseverance of faithful roots. Before anyone makes assumptions about the word "lord," I know there's only one Lord above all, though I imply lord meaning someone having power and masterful over their lovemaking.

Sexual Kung Fu

Sexual kung fu, one of the factors, is preserving your **Ching-chi**, which is your sexual energy, preventing unnecessary ejaculation while optimizing multiple orgasms (Chia 1996). Your ejaculation derives from two phases, the emission and prostate contraction. In time the more of ejaculation, the more prostate can become enlarged, so to aid in this, personally, I would recommend ingesting *Saw Palmetto* & *Nettle Root* or boiling it into some decaffeinated tea. The Chi from sexuality can be acknowledged as of virtue or sinful intentions, for there's a duality of nature between male and female sexuality, and it is a union between yin (energy) and yang (power). **Yin** is *more mysterious and secretive, receptive, relaxing, soothing, and patient,* while **yang** is *more aggressive, possesses creativity, initiative, forthcoming, and focused.*[75] For males, the dualistic nature is that our primary energy is yang, and yin is the secondary

---

[75] Dunas PhD, Felice. *Passion Play: Ancient Secrets for a Lifetime of Health and Happiness Through Sensational Sex*, page 22.

energy, while female's primary is yin, and their secondary is yang.[76] The male remains active and erect, which is the yang, while the woman remains open, passive, and receptive, which is the yin. Kings are more similar to the fire elemental, which is quickly ignited, while a queen's nature is similar to the water elemental because it takes more time to heat up, although this may vary because some queens have a stronger sexual response than others. Empirically, not all women have more yin qualities than yang; a proportion are more initiative, aggressive, forthcoming, and creative. A variation of us men are fonder of the feminine nature of yang in women because they desire less foreplay, consist of a *power play* supremacy and feisty and enjoy making love undefiled. On the contrary, empirically, women who are more in touch with yin enjoy lovemaking undefiled when they intellectually grasp the pleasure of *emunah* from the king/prince, thereby gradually becoming feisty from the Ching-chi shared (one-flesh) and build up libido.

The Lover Is the Artist in Touch

Karezza in the perfect form is natural marriage—that clinging, satisfied union of body and soul, which true love ever craves and in which ideal marriage consists—and with every repetition of the act, the lovers are remarried, their unity renewed, deepened, intensified. (*The Karezza Method: The Art of Connubial Love* by J. William Lloyd)

Karezza Method is another method for sustaining from orgasms to prolong lovemaking cycles, a good book on this criterion would be *Cupid's Poisoned Arrow: From Habit to Harmony in Sexual Relationships* by Marnia Robinson, which is an excellent book on the realism of relations along with its Karezza Methodology. According to author J. William Lloyd in his book *The Karezza Method (1931)*, the transformation of this sexual method is not rooted on aiming for orgasm but soul blending without grounding in exhaustion for being goal-oriented to making an orgasm but sustaining a longing sensation of lovemaking to reach a touch of heaven, feel love in union with ardency, consisting of full sensualism aesthetically in creative passion, vigorous, high-spirited, and supporting longevity. In Karezza, in order for the queen to reach orgasm, she must completely give submission of love, ardency, agape,

---

[76] Dunas PhD, Felice. *Passion Play: Ancient Secrets for a Lifetime of Health and Happiness Through Sensational Sex*, page 24.

and eroticism to conscious to soul bonding her king/prince to create *magnetism* (meaning connection) from the emotion and intellect to give the reaction to the physical and sensual.[77] Meaning it's not all on the Adon to ignite the love fire but mostly her mind self-creating it, for she is human and has the capability of igniting her own love fire, not all on the Adon to ignite it for Adon nature is more yang, so the submissive has genuinely been created to become more *receptive* (means the capable of being prepared or will to receive favorably) in her nature. Submission is the yin, and that yin opens in magnetism to the Adon. I've noticed some counselors would instate that men must be very patient to a longing of foreplay, but this is not a primary in a man's nature, for it is yang, and yang is assertive in his nature with fidelity for her beauty gives discernment of fair and this grants honor of her (*see* Doctrine of Honor). Corrupting the natures disrupts the balance of its nature. However, if the man is more passive and seemingly a nice guy, the woman may act aggressive by purposely instigating an irritating behavior toward him to unleash a yang fuel of aggressive passionate, amorous and unrestrictive sexual impulses, she then has become a switch.

In man's nature the yang is fully permissible when the actions are evaluated *sensible*, yang is the very core of masculine strength in sexual nature. Woman's nature when yielded to embrace fully her femininity, she becomes yin, a great woman's empowerment, the portion that's potentially yin may become difficult for certain women that's shielding themselves from the potential oppression of the scornful (*see* Submissiveness Blown Out of Context), the philanderer, and the fear of dissimulation in a man that fake's love for her wealth.

Growing to Master Lover

Below are five cardinal principalities to be a master lover that must be acknowledged:

1. Transformation of how the mind conceals and causes that reformation within to become hedonistic and amorous, one must not be stuck on what everyone else constructing mankind

---

[77]   J. William Lloyd. *The Karezza Method: The Art of Connubial Love*, pg. 39–40.

loveable acts toward their queens but train himself to become a sovereign and elite.

2. Creativity must be artfully sensual, withdrawing the mind from what you learned from defiling pornography and using the liberation from the divine, ontology and your natural behaviorism. This very divinity and clarity can grow in your lovemaking but to do so must create a will of an Aesthetic personality and become fully primal to your truest nature.

3. Awaken to your naturalism in everything so you don't feel concealed but build yourself into becoming a personal psychiatrist and sociologist as a way of studying lovemaking, inspiring lovemaking, and training lovemaking to your submissive. Fully give her your sexual id and affection.

4. Honor your woman as your treasure, not rent. Know that being selfish for your woman's love is your given right. You shouldn't share your submissive with any other man. Affection is charitable by inspiration, libidinous action, sensuality and motivation toward your treasure and has to be provided often.

5. The greatest is providing the Ahavah, the emunah, the inspiration of hope, to her mind, body, covenant, and soul and accepting her individual nature while coordinating with her to edify love.

Chapter XVI:
Master Lover

"The only way to become a master is to cultivate the knowledge of another and yourselves with an ardency of techniques and test the forbidden. If you personally have faith, it's liberated."

Warning! This chapter may be inappropriate for certain ages.

A master lover is *a highly skilled performer of passionate affection for another opposite sex.* Becoming a master lover means you have to embrace all of you to your queen. Heterosexual relations should have no opposing argument on intimacy, for simple fact is women was created for men as companions. There should be no limit to sex when consummated to cherish each other in this world and the next. Master (**Adon** means **"Master"** = *Sovereign, Ruler*) lover sometimes breaks the rules of the world and its people to fulfill completion within the soul of desire. The behavior and action is the undeniable difference, and relations are the fire that burned in the union of love and continuously to burn if willing to motivate a **transformation**, which is "gradual improvement within your psychological and physiological factors." Your heterosexual desire and behavior is your divine right to fornicate when it's earned by your lover. These earnings mostly require marriage, affection, faithfulness, and communication. In worldview, many people characterize a person's appetite of desire as normal or abnormal. Utterly, the truth is everyone has different sexual variations, and there is no normal lovemaking. Desire is infinite without comparisons. People who speak of your heterosexual appetite as abnormal, only affirming their support of disagreement, which doesn't mean you should comply (not to compromise if it's what you desire). Truth is better than falsity. Sociological truth is that everyone has contrasting depths of desire according to their comfort. Sociobiological view is that females offer sex for love, while males offer love for sex.

King/Prince Art of Seduction is the process by which a royal male succeeds in persuading a royal female to become as devoted in him with Ahavah, sex, loyalty, and honor as he is in her. The most important learning is to build models for ourselves and awareness of our inner characteristics and embrace them, in addition, become morally open-minded. Time of mastery is not momentarily learned but a prolonged learning process over years of experience and not one book or teaching can change that in relation to true romance and Ahavah.

> *Women have evolved a sexuality that is more psychological than physical, and that psychological need is rooted in the need for security and connection. (Mark Manson,* **Models: Attract Women through Honesty,** *p. 30)*

Common Truth: A belief that men are naturally sexual aggressive, erect, and visually sensual beings and women are sexually passive, receptive, and open beings is mostly true. Although sometimes it can become a reversal performance, this is reflected as a power exchange; some women are more sexually aggressive than original men. Conversely, women are still built as the passive, receptive, and open beings to submit while being dominated or dominating. Although some would argue women are more receptive in nature of lovemaking. Master lover uses lovemaking as an additional benefactor to reduce contempt, fear, and anguish while soothing out the rough struggles in life and providing amorous inspiration and support from the exposures of suffering empirical realties with loveable healing.

Masterful Loving and Traits

The Lover's Characters

Sexual love is undoubtedly one of the chief things in life, and the union of mental and bodily satisfaction in the enjoyment of love is one of its cultivating peaks.

—Sigmund Freud

Now in this millennium, many individuals thrive on the need for "free love," a term used by philosophers meaning *allowed individuals explore acting on their sexual impulses without marriage, judgment, or contempt, basically an immediate satisfaction for lust.* In relation to free love, social science describes this as closely related to Ludus, a playful love; however, free love is not necessarily playful love but a free individual in the sense of lovemaking without added longing of patients (or "the preheat of the oven") but quick satisfaction in the moments of eagerness. Sociologist John Lee (Lee 1973, 1988) gave a framework of six styles of love: the ludic, manic, erotic, agapic, Storge, and pragmatic. **Ludic lover** is free loving without attachment, for there in for the pleasure which mostly satisfying lust without the repercussion for long-term commitment (commonly known as players). For a visual example, the film *Wedding Crashers* defines ludic loving. **Manic lover** is a *combination* of *Eros* and *Ludus*—type of people who romanticize strong with a repercussion of strong romanticism in return and if not honored then they'll desire a swigging (sex outside of relationship) on the side to reinforce affection when lacked because of drastic illusions of unfaithfulness or ineffectualness of *power exchange* from their partner, thereby imitating Ludus behavior; slight given affections give ecstasy for a momentarily time frame than the *manic* individual seeks side dishes of concubines unless given more affection. For manic lovers are obsessive, impulsive and possessive of their intimate partner with the mindset of feeling they need their intimate partner above all measures, jealousy is common within manic and an aggressive enforced love of seeing love as the means of healing, or reinforcement of honor in demand. Another is **Pragmatic lover**, which is the logic lover who seeks characteristics that individual desire in another individual, basically the one who seeks status of successfulness, though the benefactor **pragmatic lovers**, is there consider the lover who makes efforts to give love than just to receive because they make the efforts to prolong the love cycle; however agape has this benefactor as well. **Storge lover** is the love built between companions through friendship then deepening into a natural affection of intimate love. When love is despair, a returning love of only friendship will remain. Although empirically, despair can become a permanent closure of friendship, perhaps would no longer be friends depending on how deeply an individual has loved, the friendship may become unbearable (that's realism!). A visual seminar of Storge love would be the film *Love & Basketball*. **Agapic lover** is the person who romanticizes without logic but freely upon desire while sensible in Ahavah, a spiritual lover devotional to God (cf. Deuteronomy 6v5), in certain moments romanticism makes them amorous. The **Erotic lover's** mind-set is on the physical body, the sensual and sexual satisfaction to determine prolong commitment.

The Sacred Gnostic text *Nag Hammadi Scriptures*, **"On the Origin of the World"** describes *Eros (109,1–100,1)* means **"erotic love."** The word is derived from the god of love, for Eros is androgynous, the masculine is fire from the light, and the feminine is the soul of blood from substance of forethought, which is the virgin woman's Valley of Joy blood. According to *The Creation of Plants, Animals, and Heavenly Bodies (111,8–112,25)* from **"On the Origin of the World,"** *Nag Hammadi Scriptures*, Eros is often used in union of intimacy as symbolic to describe the type of loving craved after, for *Eros* is the love of beauty.

Once I received a fortune cookie that gave the statement "a good friendship is often more important than a passionate romance," then I looked at the statement like it was garbage and assumed that the individual who typed it was on drugs and throw it away like garbage. Although this statement may be true to other loving characters, it's different from an erotic lover, for an erotic lover is more consuming in physical and visual sensations. So the statement for an erotic lover would be "a passionate romance is often more important than a good friendship." An erotic lover can be momentarily a *free lover* to fulfill sexual ecstasy to sanctify desire, and an invested loyalist and possessive when sensuous and discernment of fair is satisfied. Companionate love would be more valued as a better replacement of good friendship to equally match passionate romance. **Ardent lover** is a person who has strong enthusiasm and devotion, providing deep warm approval, fervency, and sensibility toward another. An ardent lover sustains the ground of being a loyalist to their significant other and often speaks well of their significant other and are devotional to them. In ancient biblical times, which we have lost the understanding to, is that concept of free love affairs that men in this millennium call "whores," "gold diggers," "sluts," and other degrading callings, and women call them "players," "whoremongers," or "pimps," the scriptures refer to as promiscuous women and whoremongers; that your surrendering to anguish. Many heartbreaks from promiscuous females endanger your providence. God stated this many times in Proverbs. Preselection is very important. Just as a woman's fruit is special and sacred, so is the nectar derived from throbbing penis. **Proverb** means *"traditional saying expressing obvious truth."* God spoke about this special fluid in Proverbs chapter five along with privileged importance.

Evaluate yourselves, kings, princes, princesses, and queens. I know this is perhaps difficult to determine which certain loving styles proceeds within, but it's honesty among yourselves that will free you, and if you feel it's time for a transformation, then one must work at it. Mr. Lee expressed that an individual is better off knowing their love style to predetermine compatible mates. In biblical language, there's commonly a trinity, so below, you should pick up to three styles of love that is true to your persona.

The profoundest of all our sensualities is the sense of truth. (D.H. Lawrence [1885–1930])

For the **Adon** (Provide Initial Signature) Loving Style Truths:

Styles of Loving		
_____ =Erotic (Eros),	_____ =Ardent,	
_____ =Manic,	_____ =Ludic,	_____ =Agapic,
_____ =Storge,	_____ =Pragmatic,	_____ =Free Lover

For the **Submissive** (Provide Initial Signature) Loving Style Truths:

Styles of Loving
_____ =*Erotic (Eros),* _____ =*Ardent,* _____ =*Manic,* _____ =*Ludic,* _____ =*Agapic,* _____ =*Storge,* _____ =*Pragmatic,* _____ =*Free Lover*

Extra 2 for additional **Submissives,** if an Adon has a polygyny covenant (discussed in Chapter XVII, subtitle: Sacred Marriage Truths)

Styles of Loving
_____ =*Erotic (Eros),* _____ =*Ardent,* _____ =*Manic,* _____ =*Ludic,* _____ =*Agapic,* _____ =*Storge,* _____ =*Pragmatic,* _____ =*Free Lover*

Styles of Loving
_____ =*Erotic (Eros),* _____ =*Ardent,* _____ =*Manic,* _____ =*Ludic,* _____ =*Agapic,* _____ =*Storge,* _____ =*Pragmatic,* _____ =*Free Lover*

As I said, this may be difficult for you to decide, for empirical observation, I've noticed more individuals who are a little under twenty-one are often indulging in ludic love. Although I do believe in the theory that everyone is capable of free loving, meaning not everyone daily wants to discipline themselves to a foreplay but wants immediate satisfaction in moments. However, everyone is different, so to make you readers feel comfortable about choosing, I give my truth of my styles of love.

Styles of Loving
____*J.S.J*___ =*Erotic (Eros),* ___*J.S.J.*___ =*Ardent,* _____ =*Manic,* _____ =*Ludic,* ____*J.S.J.*_____ =*Agapic,* _____ =*Storge,* _____ =*Pragmatic,* _____ =*Free Lover*

A confession I must give is that I myself had a difficult time choosing because I consider myself on the borderline of *manic* love, so as it's difficult for me, it may be difficult for you. Don't imitate what I've chosen but be true to you as I am true to myself. What matters is the truth (emunah) in yourselves to clarify who you are. Perhaps one day you'll find an agreeable significant other. Out of eight of those loving styles, two are often empirically treasured from others, and that's the pragmatic lover and ardent lover; however, to others, the Storge lover maybe more appealing because some require more communication from months to years before they move up to intimate love.

Passionate Love and Companionate Love: Decipher and Connect

Passionate love is the longing intensity for intimate union, a possessive and obsessive trait for the other and high sexual appetite for the other. Passionate love is considered to be a combination of romantic love—the physical and companionate love—the spiritual (Jankowiak 2008). **Companionate love** is stronger emotional connection, portraying realistic truth, sexual variation in moments, and a lifetime of commitment. The fire of both must remain burning because when either one of those loves burn out, the lack of commitment, lack of appetite, lack of connection, or lack of realization along with affection, there's a higher possibility that an intimate relationship depolarizes. Although in some of the resourceful textbooks of social science clarifies that a relationship can remain sustained through companionate love, however, only individuality can determine the truth of this perception. A connection that *Kama Sutra*, means *"rules of love,"* one of the sacred texts derived from India now as of today's millennium went global provides principles to a healthy sexual habits and conducts and creativity of variations.[78] Vatsyayana manuscript should not be worshipped but only be used for insightful ideas. In many ways, Vatsyayana expresses connection of vital importance to maintain

---

[78] In my opinion, every male and female has the right to contribute their own sexual sacred **monograph** for personal use between husband and wife. Personally, I establish my own principles and conducts with guidance of Holy Spirit. The most beneficial ideal of this art is the creativity of sexual variations. The rest is not proven to be entirely accurate in today's millennium, but Vatsyayana gives some intelligent factors and insights that can be beneficial.

relationship satisfaction. This is very true in ways of affection, love, and spirituality. Vatsyayana explained that we kings and queens have an identical structure with a complementary nature, one open and passive, while the other is erect and active. The perfect bond, but yet we hurt each other in reality. A transformation of both beings must be proportionate toward invested frequency of prolonging intimate investment. In understanding the differences of infatuation and love, **infatuation** is moments of passion and persistent feeling for another, while **love** is the mixture of both passionate and companionate factors.

Passionate and companionate love is the matriarch of how a relationship can prolong, for loving styles only establish the truth on how intimacy flows through an individual, but passionate and companionate gives the connection and deciphers for appropriate compatibilities. No astrologer can match lovers' compatibility but only can give in optionated illusion of compatibility. Being real on love gives a clarifying factor on individuality and direction of where you best at through a percentage between companionate and passionate love. On the contrary, this doesn't mean even when you've figured out your deciphering and connection its finished for certain individuals may require spontaneity, ardency, and build of storge and erotic love for Ahavah much like the film *Couples Retreat (2010)*.

Establish your percentage divided out of one hundred.

For the Adon

_____ *% of Passionate love*

_____ *% of Companionate love*

For the Submissive(s)

_____ *% of Passionate love*

_____ *% of Companionate love*

_____ *% of Passionate love*

_____ *% of Companionate love*

_____ *% of Passionate love*

_____ *% of Companionate love*

The reason for this is because then as a relationship couple, an individual will be aware of what another desire more and their character. Making it short and simple, passionate love often is an individual who feeds on physical, sensual, and emotional love with an occasional reinforcement of intellectual, while the companionate love often feeds on the intellectual, sensual, and emotional with an occasional reinforcement of physical. Integrity is in both, but the passionate requires more physical affections, while the companionate requires more emotional affections.

Language of Love

Women favor more of romantic fantasies, while men favor more visual beauty. The two are complementary. Her life is like a form of a novel awaiting for her king to explore her depths and dip his Heavenly Root into her Honey Pot but first has to seduce her. The seduction guide is **first**, let her sensual delights be your guide on providing creativity. **Second** is providing a sincere and trustworthy personality that makes her feel she has the ability to open her heart while providing generous offerings. **Third** is providing mystery of id *"your inner being,"* thereby luring her into curiosity, for this creates salacious yearning. **Last**, this most important, is keeping your word or at least making much effort to. Women respond more to a heartfelt language of romance through songs and lyrics, love letters and poetry, undivided time, journalized thoughts of empathy, and personal artistry, such as drawings of her while she's completely entrusting you in her nude. Mood sets of love are commonly implemented in a peaceful and/or social environment with aromatics for aphrodisiac purposes. Most women in reality love a man who smells good and herbal while odorless free (this means washing yourself and clothes), for bad odor destroys the seduction. It's important to form a rebellion with what may be considered naughty from social influences and do it together without approval of social influences; this is called being *amorous*. Language of love cannot be forbidden if you're trying to explore naughtier things because it's your part of your heaven on earth. Naming your organ is an enticing arousal to yourself and your woman, depending on the name. Establish affection for you and your queen's sacred areas. Creating a name for your sexual organs and sexual masterful arts is an innovative way of changing what was common among everyone, to meanings more blissful and curious to your companion.

Naming Organs in Language of Love
Penis = Weapon of Love; Heavenly Root; Love Muscle *Vagina = Valley of Joy; Honey Pot; Golden Crevice* *Anus = Trunk of Bliss; Driving the Hershey* *Highway (Hershey Highway)* *Mouth = Instrument of Pleasure; Sweet Mouth* *Breasts = Blossomed Pomegranates; Dirty Pillows* *Seminal Fluid = Serere Medicine*

You savor it with confidence and may have a psychological effect on arousal in relation to your companion. Frequently, I've come to notice mass media often focuses on orgasms! Orgasms! Orgasms! Orgasms! But that can become draining just to hear it repeatedly. Perhaps in ancient times, lovemaking was much simpler, for the reason is they'd let orgasms come to them organically by sexual loving without the drainage of being goal-oriented. Orgasms will come, but the most important is enjoying lovemaking, not making lovemaking feel like a job title. The measures of orgasms come from artful thrusting, versatile motions, the mind fueled with salacious thoughts and language of erotic loving.

For women the best aphrodisiacs are words. The G-Spot is in the ears. He who looks for it below there is wasting his time. (Isabel Allende)

For men, *aural sex* is the pleasurable satisfaction of hearing your queen's melodies and dirty talking sexually. You know the "ochy, oooh, awwhiee, ahh or simply rapid breathing or speaking explicitly" as her to your performance as well as king to queen as an act of satisfaction and inner touch of your primal behavior because it's the soul flow of nourishing the Weapon of Love through the highly sensitive nerve endings. This can be a powerful aphrodisiac if you're creating sexual melodies toward your queen in the moment of sex, just as it's hot for the queen to make sexual melodies toward the king. In lovemaking, savoring to embrace noise (sounds) is reminisced as pleasure and bliss.

Sounds Is Love of All, the World

Sounds create soulful existence,
When the oceans tide, it is sound;
When fervency of love creates sympathy of sobbing, sighing, jubilating, and tears drops, it's a hymn of sound and presence.
When rains, it creates symphonies that therapeutic the body and mind, it is sound.
There is sound.
When sharing a glass of wine while looking at your significant other swallow its taste,
There is sound.
When night becomes morning, noise of the birds tweak, the dogs bark, pancakes sizzling on the pan, bees gathering for honey, it is sound.
There is sound.
When listening to music for a moodily Spirit, moving rhythmically to the music, it is sound.
When coitus makes quakes, it is sound.
In durations of lovemaking; the breathing, the objects banging, the thrusting, and the instrumental tones from the mouth, the kisses, the clapping and rubbing of flesh, it all surrounds the atmosphere, it is sound.
There is sound.
When love cuddles in your significant other sleeps, and hear breathing, heart beats, maneuvering, it is sound.
There is sound.
During intensity of love at its silence and loudest, there is sound.
As penetration of love goes deep and pulls out a sound of intensity opens and reactions follow, it is sound.
There is sound.
Beauty is the penetrating sound of the verses, the Psalms, the Proverbs, the Song of Solomon, the Gospels, and overall the Holy Scriptures spoken from a fervent tongue, power of thought, and sensible recovery from what aches, in all its sound.
Sound surrounds all ways.
It is sound.

Sound is therapy to the love and Spirit, a sound mind, in all, the world is sound.

The downside of aural sex is that some may find this aggravating and a turnoff if they feel uncomfortable with your dirty talk or symphony noises due to the distraction of her fantasizing, such as speaking in languages she questions because she doesn't understand it or extremely loud noises. You will notice her comfort ability with cultivating the focus of her emotional response and gratifying gestures. This is another reason why Protocol IV should be implemented (for Protocol IV, see Chapter XV: Sacred Penetrative Roots and Revelation of Ancient to Modest Remedies). Occasionally, a man's ego grows from the superego, and some men bluntly or aggravatingly ask if "so in so feel good," basically asking unnecessary question. The tip of advice is most of the time, you have to silence your mouth from aggravating questions. Think in this way, "if your queen was fellating you, would you indulge in her continuously asking questions, or would you be more sexually gratified if she continues fellating without pausing?" This is how she feels when she's trying to concentrate on the moment of pleasure, so silence your agitating questions and concentrate on her flesh, sensational meat, and give grace for her existence. Empirically, in aural sex, many charismatic people would insinuate words' like *fuck, and so forth* . . . are improper but the *amorous* and *Thanatos* inner nature releases this tension. Let's clarify the definitions. *Profanity* – speaking against God, swearing, something considered displeasing to acceptable morality or provoking anguish on someone; clarifying *cursing* – is calling to supernatural to inflict dolorous conflict. Now let's look at some scriptures.

Scriptures on Profanity and Cursing

"Colossians 3v8, Ephesians 4v29, Matt. 15v10–11, Matt. 12v36–37, James 3v10, Ephesians 5v4, James 3v6–8, Proverbs 21v23, 2 Timothy 2v16, Psalms 19v14, James 1v26, Psalms 127v3, Luke 6v45, Proverbs 4v24, Matt. 5v37, Psalms 34v13–14, Colossians 4v6, Exodus 20v7"

Notice on profanity defined portion of something considered displeasing to acceptable morality. The question here is "do you consider this unethical?" What's consider displeasing to others may not be so in your sexual union. So the clarity is "are these words really sinful?" and the answer is <u>no</u>. You're free on what to say in the arts of sex, but don't speak negatively about God, or it would be blasphemy and were not supposed to portray negative language when speaking on God's Word. Truth is when individuals do some research, they'll know these words were not even in existence in the time of Jesus walking the earth. Those so called profanity words in modern times are seemingly conveyed to be profane according to emotion of how it's used in language stance of favor or shame —derogatory, entertaining, or naughtily arousing, how it thrones the individual in a manner of intellect and sensuality, through feeling if the individual is educated or not, and traditional morality of constructions for appropriate manner. Filtering your inner bliss conflicts with the bliss undefiled let your hymns speak explicit (Psalms 149v5) where your *emunah* resides. ***Homework assignment:*** Research modern words considered profane and notice that majority of these words were invented somewhere in the fifteenth century or after, which is way after the Old and New Testaments in the Bible, then you'll acknowledge the words considered profane are nothing but the slang that's invented in this urban society not biblical stance.

Aesthetic Kings' Sexual Personality

Aesthetes are men and women who are natural beings, loving the beauty of what surrounds them, including creatures in humane gestures. Aesthetes are more tasteful to the art of creation, similar connoisseurs, and admiration to various cultural arts. Aesthetes are more humane in ethics by judging what's more attractive and beautiful to the eyes though critics to what's not appealing. (Remember the three main principles discussed in chapter III, "Aesthetic Individualism.") Mankind is more aesthetic. Certain individuals just haven't come into realism in this philosophy though it's true, the visual and muses rectify the earthily beauty. Mankind can't deny this, every moment mankind invests in infamous magazines like *Maxim, Playboy, Suicide Girls*, etc., or raptured by beautiful womanhood's form which in modern time is called "Eye Candy," or have admiration for creatures existing and overall complexity for stunning sites of nature, demographic regions, cultures, diversities, ethnicities, and architecture, while seeing and feeling fervency within giving a blissful or loving speculation and acceptance, becoming the union within it. Mankind itself is an aesthetic philosopher.

*Aestheticism is a search after the signs of the beautiful. It
is the science of the beautiful through which men seek the
correlation of the arts. It is, to speak more exactly, the search
after the secrets of life.[79] (Richard Ellman, from Oscar Wilde)*

Donald Kirkley made the statement that Aesthetic Realism is a
philosophic way of self-rationalizing conflicts within ourselves and
making these conflicts brought to clarity so that individual becomes
more correlated and joyful.[80] "Aesthetic sexuality" is amorous and
seeks "mastery" within to "intensify pleasure" of "bliss," persisting
effectiveness in potentiality to assist as a structure of communal
"communication and self-creation."[81]

Embracing the Nurture, Art, Beauty, and Nature of Blossomed Pomegranates Loving Nature

*Let her be as the loving hind and pleasant roe;
let her breasts satisfy thee at all times;
and be thou ravished always with her love.*
—Proverbs 5v19 KJV

A woman's breasts, "nurturing pillows," are like pomegranates when
blossomed for feeding, not necessarily only from the touch of the palms
but also the nutritional value of the milk and the fleshy tone of the breast
is a natural nurture of our arousal, a healthy instinctual habit. This habit is
healthy because it's God's intention of nurturing men. Just can't sleep on
the females beautiful nurturing dirty pillows, which would be the enticing
savory! Every moment of savory from a natural born female's Blossomed
Pomegranates is a connective pheromone of nurture and art.

Why? Because the female breasts consist of a cuddling hormone,
also known as "love hormone," called *oxytocin* that comes from
the hypothalamus region of the brain transitioning to and secreted by

[79] Richard Ellman, *Oscar Wilde* (Alfred A Knopf, Inc., 1988), 122.

[80] Donald Kirkley, "Poet Outlines a Philosophy," Baltimore Sun, August 2 1946.

[81] Byrne, Romana. *Aesthetic Sexuality: a Literacy History of Sadomasochism* (Bloomsbury Academic: 2013), 4.

pituitary gland released through; during sexual activity, arousal of nipples, childbirth, and lactation. According to Inga D. Neumann, oxytocin affects the emotion response through relaxing another, building trust and psychological stability. In addition, produces a longing relations bond, modulates social behaviors of care, sexual character, and aggression.[82]

> Oxytocin is of potential use in enhancing interpersonal and individual wellbeing, and might have more applications in neuropsychiatric disorders, especially those characterized by persistent fear, repetitive behavior, reduced trust and avoidance of social interactions.[83]

Oxytocin itself creates an *extroversion* character within self and the significant other. Extroversion means a seduction of opening up to another, opening to the ardent love from investing in another outside an individual's sensibility toward the self and the other; basically agape loving "romanticizing freely." Appreciation of the Lord's art of nurture is nothing to be ashamed of, only gratitude, for His creation of Eve's descendants. You can't hide from lust, only repentance for your sin, and let God take it from there. He knows our flaws. Embracing this loving nature is one of the most cherished from aesthetic sexuality, for it is beauty, it is art, and it is nature, and that's all worth savoring with *ardent loving*. In reality, males, there's a high probability you're going to sin because of the pleasure principality. Whether, you do it in secret or in the open, you're being recorded for your transgressions. The only thing that can be done is repent and admit you may lust again. Sex is a potent and powerful force in the eyes of men but acknowledge Romans 8, for if you've accepted Christ Yahawashi, then you are "made free from the law of sin and death."[84] "Live joyfully with the wife whom thou lovest all the days of the life of thy vanity, which he hath given thee under the sun, all

---

[82]   ID Neumann, "Oxytocin: the neuropeptide of love reveals some of its secrets," *Cell Metabolism*, 5 (2007): 4, 231–233, doi: 10.1016/j. cmet.2007.03.008.

[83]   Ishak W.W., Kahloon M., Fakhry H., "Oxytocin role in enhancing well-being: a literature review. *Journal of Affective Disorders*, 130 (2011): 1–2, 1–9, doi: 10.1016/j.jad.2010.06.001.

[84]   Romans 8v1–2 King James Version.

the days of thy vanity: for that is thy portion in this life, and in thy labour which thou takest under the sun."[85]

The Importance of Affection to Your Queen's Blossomed Pomegranates

When kings/princes consistently fondle, suck, and message her breasts, you're nurturing her health by keeping the breast from developing breast cancer, empirically when kings/princes consistently fondle and suck on her breast they cause them to grow larger or when they reach motherhood, this may not be so for all women but many queens I've overheard and encountered spoke the same, so it must be true on a certain level of clarity.

Lovemaking with the queen's breasts is ardency, the very internal jubilation of its existence. All that can be done is indulging continuously the perfection of God's creation. Thank God for beauty formed to therapeutic the heart in sensational nature.

Lovemaking with the breasts can begin with embracement of the king's/prince's hands smoothly as a message. Begin by anointing your hands with very little organic sweet almond oil (don't use if either of you is allergic to nut-based food) then use your tip of your fingers to gently rub in a circular motion, while your eyes are focused on her face, taking in notice of her reaction through her eyes and mouth and how she breathes. Then moving your hands on the lower breast area of your queen, then fervently maneuver your hands in a counterclockwise position and grasp it with fervency. After, begin the tongue-kissing phase, which is using the tongue to anoint the flesh, then warm it with a kiss. While doing this phase, blow air or use ice cube to create a shivering action all around her breast. Next, use the tip of the tongue to rotate around her nipples (the areola) and on her nipples and gradually use very little teeth to heighten bliss for her and suck with a mild suction, don't bite nor be aggressively bitter in breast lovemaking. After, anoint her entire breasts with organic sweet almond oil (or olive oil), and put her blindfold on. "Let her know that you're about have intercourse with her breast" and enforce that you will not harm her. Then after, breast lovemaking becomes blind to her performing **mammary intercourse**, which is a sexual foreplay of the Adon using his erect Love Muscle to thrust between the queen's immense

---

[85]   Ecclesiastes 9v9 King James Version.

or substantial Blossomed Pomegranates (breasts) while the breasts are caressed and squeeze together gently to mildly aggressive for a mutual lovemaking and orgasm.[86] Remember, Adonim, you don't suppose to worship your queen but love her, so cultivate in mind that this is not worship, for worship is given to Adon Olam alone, no matter how much mass media tries to cultivate the mind of worshipping women, for it's a feminist agenda, not of the Adon Olam's conduct. Love is given, not worship given. Blossomed Pomegranates is great sybaritic seduction, **sybaritic** means sensual gratification that gives great comfort and pleasure and voluptuous based on aesthetic approval and sensuous that provides seduction.

Embracing the Art, Nature, and Beauty of Vaginal Hair Loving Nature

A strong proportion toward many of us kings and princes, the earthily heaven and therapy of the majority comes from the Valley of Joy and the love a submissive woman gives toward the royal Adon; the Sweet Mouth and Trunk of Bliss still has great *sybaritic* position, but the most special *sybaritic* is the Valley of Joy. Although interior Valley of Joy gives fervency to the Heavenly Root, the exterior of canopy is fervency as well, for various aesthetic philosophers are considered to sexually embrace pubic hair fetishism, which is sexual arousal through touching or visual observance toward an individual with pubic hair. Conversely, because it's considered aesthetic, it's not considered a fetish but a natural beautiful art. For example, pubic hair in the nineteenth century Victorian Britain was considered a souvenir. A woman's pubic hair was worn on men's hats or carried in snuff boxes as a symbolic meaning of potency talismans or exchanged among intimate lovers as tokens of affection.[87] Embracing loving nurturing nature is a pathway to becoming an aesthete. Take delight on a woman's pubic hair for its a signature of maturity and a secretive covenant (Ezekiel 16v7–8; 1 Cor. 11v5–6 & v15) for the Weapon of Love awaiting to savor taste and feed the Honey Pot while the Honey Pot savors taste and feeding from the Weapon of Love, feeding itself.

---

[86]   Alex Comfort, *The Joy of Sex* (1972), 67–9 & 175.

[87]   "Secrets of the Great British Sex Clubs." *Slate Magazine*. Retrieved June 21, 2015.
http://www.slate.com/articles/life/welltraveled/features/2009/hellfire_holidays/secrets_of_the_great_british_sex_clubs.html

Throughout *Spartacus* the complete series in similitude to the history of the third century demonstrated many aesthetic philosophers who were very appreciative on women's mystery hairs through savoring observances of the Honey Pot hair. The visual pleasure of the differential colors, shape, styles, density, grooming, tone, and texture as an overall art and beautifies a signature of a mature mystery woman. Remember the hair signifies potent sexual energy and strength hold but also signifies virility of the animalistic tendencies and royal power. The mystery is how tight the vaginal walls are, how moist the inner Valley of Joy is, how she smells "either fresh or aromatic or pungent," how much blood of passion is flowing, what's the sexual behavior of the Honey Pot cravings and endearments, and how much sexual yin she possesses along with her distinctive personality.

In this modest time, individuals who indulge in pubic hairs is a fetish called **pubephilia** or **furvert**, but to a **primal aesthetic**, this is a natural beauty that signifies maturity, canopy, artistry, and mystery. In primal stance, Valley of Joy hair and Blossomed Pomegranates demonstrated a girl forming into a woman; therefore, it's considered more of womanhood. Mass media insinuates a stronger persuasion through consistent supporters that women are inspired to promote hair removal of the Valley of Joy covenant, in addition, persuade intimate hair on women as unfeminine, a false propaganda of social construction from Western narcissism. A woman

Love your queen's canopy, for it's there to provide a covenant for the king and warmth and signifies strength and virtue.

who rejects narcissism of complete vaginal hair removal gives a signature of strength, virtuously liberated, body acceptance, and more womanhood. The truth is a woman is born a feminine, "not feminist," but as time grows, she grows into womanhood, and sacred vaginal hair comes with that, and if Adon Olam didn't think it was art and beauty, he would not allow it on women. Nowhere in the Bible does it say our Mother Eve and Father Adam were waxing or shaving but were naturalist (*see* Naturalism Conveys Rationalism) and *naturist* (*see* Untold Novels). Intimate hair is also an excellent method for preserving fragrant oils on the Golden Crevice to produce a prolonging aromatic that will scent the environment during coitus while awakening deeper *ardent loving* through communion of organic or wild-crafted ointments and/or body creams, and depending on the ointments or body creams, it could have aphrodisiac benefactor as an aromatherapy. The grooming of a woman's intimate area is part of the DD, but keep in mind *grooming* doesn't *mean* shave or wax but *fashion eloquently stylish by preserving the naturally full or trim for refinement, and clean and hygienically fresh or aromatically alluring with fondness.* Eloquent can express perseverance of primal persona, a keeper—an aggression or vigorous action of naturalism and an expressive physiological, spiritual and mental flow to uncompromised intrinsic natural appeal. Intimate hair is predominately, modesty.

A Health Precaution

When kings/princes/princesses/queens are washing the intimate hairs, it's important to use a natural, wild-crafted or organic soap. However, soap can make the hairs brittle and strip away natural oils, so apply ointment or use a wild-crafted or organic body lotion, mist, or essential oil. Empirical overhearing, some women use Wen or other organic/natural cleansing conditioners to avoid damaging detergents from soaps.

In mass media, womankind will often hear to wax or shave their sacred area with illusion it's healthy for them. This perhaps is true for the construction of validating *ludic/manic love* because the fact is this is not so considered if an individual doesn't plan on swinging. Truth is shaving or waxing of woman's valley was constructed to prevent lice from fornicating with multiple partners influenced through pornography if women had that ideology of *ludic/manic loving.* The empirical truth is the canopy of hairs wasn't only signified as mature but also a disciplinary for patience. For instance, if a king/prince has difficulty finding their treasures woman's targeted vaginal hole as eager as they were it self-taught diligence and intelligence (learning her openings), a woman's empowerment to take the initiative of directing the Weapon of Love into her Valley of Joy opening (her tunnel) though she may briefly humiliate the king/prince in a language of love, but then she'll provide the honor (however, not all kings/princes have this difficulty, for others can directly insert instantly). A woman's intimate hairs create a natural protection from dirt, bacteria, and viruses. According to Health

Science at Columbia University,[88] vaginal hair is a natural pheromone diffuser from the apocrine glands secreting an odorless substance in combination with good bacteria from organic producing oil through the sebaceous glands. Pheromones remain within the hair follicles, creating a natural atmosphere arousal to the male.[89] Certain women become more artistry in the nature of womanhood Valley of Joy hairs that they'll apply coloring products specifically made for the Valley hairs, such as Betty Beauty and other products. There are various individuals who have their dissensions on intimate hairs, but the utter truth is it's a growth of the natural and becomes unnatural when it's completely removed. Locks (head and intimate hairs) have had greater importance than some may accept, but regardless of dissensions, locks have a beauty of existence and aesthetically seductive. All ethnicities of royal women consist a signature of intimate hair beauty when kept regardless of bias propaganda from social construction.

View on Realism Spiritual Love

Although as the stunning look of beautiful sacred hair is attractive to various aesthetes, so is a fragrant queen, for it causes attraction and nourishment as implied in Song of Solomon 1v13 when the fragrant lingered between her Blossomed Pomegranates as Solomon slept between them. A fragrant queen is the connection of intimate spirituality, for pleasant fragrances allures the sense to submissive nurture. Aesthete embraces natural nature to its potentiality. In sexual nature, when a woman sweats (perspiration) in lovemaking, it's considered something healthy and erotic, not to be disgusted upon but entwined as *sensuality* and *naturalism*. **Aesthetic science** is experiences that drive closely hedonic in responses to something of disapproval ◄——► approval and disdained ◄——► admirable and determining to avoid ◄——► approach. *Aesthetic science* is the study of the mind and emotions in relation to the sense of beauty (*Random House Dictionary* 2006). Aesthetic kings/princes sexual views exceptional taste is on natural beauty through a revealing of a woman's nakedness through the demands

---

[88]　Source: http://goaskalice.columbia.edu/answered-questions/whats-point-pubic-hair

[89]　Robert Burton, *The Language of Smell* (London: Routledge and Kegan Paul, 1976.

of the Adon artist.[90] Personally, as an aesthetic philosopher, I was also attentive to women artist of naturism/nudism, models, and muses and what's appealingly attractive to for sensual excitements in the blood that gives indulging company——portraits, sculptures, paintings, visual seeing a woman and drawings of beautiful women are collective also for indulgence, and real-life womanhood is aesthetic to manhood. For visual example, the *Titanic (1997)* film, spiritual love begun with Rose (Kate Winslet) becoming allured to Jack (Leonardo DeCaprio) for his persona of aesthetic individualism and profession of portrait drawings, that she became invested in Jack and in later time frame she opened to his essence of aestheticism and allowed him to draw her while she was bare (00:47:06–01:37:40).

Aesthetic king's first sentiment nature focuses on his diligent existence through preservation, then a new outlook on focus from the development of family, according to Rousseau's belief:

> The first developments of the heart were the effect of a new situation that united the husbands and wives, fathers, and children in one common habitation. The habit of living together gave rise to the sweetest sentiments known to men: conjugal love and paternal love . . . It was then that the first difference was established in the lifestyle of the two sexes . . . Women became more sedentary and grew accustomed to watch over the hut and the children, while the man went to seek their common subsistence.[91]

In spiritual realism, fragrance is important. Every man should have his own selection of colognes, but in reality, it's best not to share your knowledge on what you collect to anyone, not even your treasures queen. The reason is because this brings about distinction from every other man, leaving your woman in the illusion of mystery. Providing information to others on what a king wears, others will try to imitate his scent. Sometimes this can be a deception from snakes looking to harvest what's

---

[90] Johann Joachim Winckelmann, *Reflections on the Imitation of Greek Works*, pg. 13.

[91] Jean-Jacques Rousseau, "Discourse on the origin of inequality" [1754], in *On the Social Contract*, tr. D. A. Cress (Indianapolis: Hackett, 1983), pg. 140, 141– 3.

yours by using your individuality against you to still what's yours. No one needs to know what you wear as well as your treasure, but she can keep guessing, hide your fragrance collection in your secret chest for the sake of distinguishing the Adon's personality is to provide continuous mystery for her though she may test you by saying "how would I know what gift to give you if you don't tell me?" Your response should be "whatever cologne you think is best fit."

Aesthetic View on Homosexuality

Some individuals consider Aesthetic Realism as anti-homosexual movement or homosexual cure movement. Siegel believed that homosexuality derived from a person feeling they are beneath consideration and disregarded for the world that manifests itself as beneath consideration and disregarded as proper mates for women: And vice versa, for woman to seem fair to the man. A man may encounter this if someone negatively influences that another male is more of a man than you, or if they say you're attraction to mating of an opposite sex is not working for you, or someone influencing you to be gay or lesbian (if it's the woman in this position) so they can be the star. However, if this is you, I hope you'll preserve a strong mind to overcome these persuasions. Don't let them win because you're special like all others, and there's someone out there for you, but you may have to change your environment to find your significant other. For others the sexual chemistry has been misbalanced due to trauma from defiling sexual assaults from the same sex that was once filled with *yang* has become *yin* or what was once filled with *yin* has become *yang*. The opposition is for that individual to find power exchanged from the opposite sex that makes the other whole from the lack of yin or yang in oneself. This is a vulnerable complementary in certain individuals so in confidences a prudent couple may become practitioners of a *switch* to remold *Ching-chi* by having the woman as the dominatrix because of her strong yang nature while the man is deemed the submissive or slave for a momentarily time frame so that he may rebuild his yang through feeding off of her aggression while the dominatrix gradually communes passiveness and receptivity of yin from the submissive or slave man's yin, that feeds her yin. The switch exchange of *Ching-chi* to heal one another from dolorous past unfortunate defiling sexual assaults to therapy an individual's nature prudently is a form of transformation to reorient femininity in men to yang sexually.

Comparatively, this would be like the character Bunchy (Dash Mihok) and Teresa (Alyssa Diaz) from *Ray Donovan* season 3, Bunchy struggles to rehabilitate from molestation of a profane priest and gradually rebuilds his masculine lacks of assertion, forthcoming, focus and aggression, and a beautiful woman named Teresa, a dominatrix, becomes his complementary wife to domineer his lacks and love him. The regard of lesbianism in certain women that orientated masculinity to reorient submission to man is often the desire for mating to create family or the awakening persona of primitive cravings of real human penetrative sex with an embrace of masculine caress during copulations, prudency, ontological knowledge and tenacious will. A woman that reorient from lesbianism to sensibility is a seeker of an Adon. On the pardon of the Adon, he would have to sensibly cultivate that "bisexuality," theoretically will be within her nature so investments of polygynous relations would have to be measured or substantial measures of *sensuality* and sensibility given to the queen's satisfaction. Making one of opposite's is beauty, which gives measured connection and communion amongst one another. Aesthetic Realism is fond of opposition, God's systematics, that manifest *ontology* and *sensibility*. From Aesthetic Realism instructors counseling, brought upon a change in various men and women in 1978 as a homosexual cure through an advertisement with fifty signatures promoting[92] Aesthetic Realism.

Untold Novels

Supporting Her Fantasies and Lifestyles

Although most women would never tell men their sacred sins and fantasies because it's a defense mechanism for projecting innocence, queen-like, worth-keeping, and decent behavior. Women know the vulnerability toward males somewhat when she announces truths of the counts, durations, and anatomy sizes. A queen or princess doesn't want to project slut behavior but crave to be desired. Women's secrets are like mazes with barriers, each one with pad locks. In one of them, there's a locked diary of unforgettable memories, deceptions, and desires. On the contrary, certain queens often–to–momentarily become aggressive

---

[92]   Advertisement, "We Have Changed from Homosexuality," March 18, 1978, *New York Times, Washington Post, Los Angeles Times.*

in *writing erotica* of demands for adventuresome epics, or make their novelty become a lifestyle; the important thing is for the Adon to make discerning effort to approve their novelty and lifestyle. Cultivate this scripture when she confesses her fantasies because all you can do is approve or disapprove.

> *[1]Judge not, that ye be not judged. [2]For with what judgement ye judge, ye shall be judged: and with what measure ye mete, it shall be measured to you again.* (Matthew 7v1–2 KJV)

The loving nature of the fantasy is past our scientology because it's of a different loving that may be waiting to be explored for its erotic. Lovemaking is not scientology; it's aesthetic ology and a *love map* that awakens the *power exchange*. Women may be both receptive and passive in nature, and this was in female's very nature since dawns of time to be submissive, feel wanted, deflowered, loved, and developed life in their womb. Furthermore, certain women crave lifestyles and novelties through intimate languages and these languages are from the novelties of the persona seeking a naturistic lifestyle. In addition, certain queens in privacy or publicly wear these languages: ancestral—Victorian era that's descendant to *Victoria's Secrets* and Spartan or Grecian era[93] (similar to film Zack Snyder's *300*, or show *Spartacus* complete series; the type of clothing that's near bare), or Mayan era (this is the imitation of Pocahontas); and faith and personality—Angels that's influenced from *Victoria's Secret Angels* and the Gothic fashion which has become modestly common. Gothic gives a symbolic vampire novelty or individual's persona which is concerned with deeper shadows of life, introspective, romantic, creative personality, innate thoughts to Thanatos desires, spiritual, drawn to psychology and more philosophically inquisitive. The modest wear and novelty that has become a lifestyle for certain women is the Cowgirl western era. Another gradually modest wear and novelty is the adoption of tradition Indian artistry—the Lehenga's and Sarees. The novelty fashions are a deep persona freeing itself from bondage, for instance, cowgirl fashion women can innately crave the lifestyle of wildlife nature, testers of fearlessness within themselves, old-fashioned, animalistic intimate behavior—derived from confidence and domineering *love map* (p. 158) and *power exchange* (p. 164) from woman on-top *impact play* (p. 163), and passionate beings.

---

[93]   Some commonly found at: http://www.polyvore.com/ within the website search engine by typing "Grecian."

After reviewing many articles and speaking to quite a few women for confirmation, revealing novelties appeared that top fantasy women have according to Askmen.com (Snow n.d.), Womenshealthmag.com (Toglia 2014), and various other sources.

Naturism, Nudism, and Exhibitionism Lifestyle

Exhibitionism, naturism, and nudism is nudity expressed openly rather in home and outside of home. These individuals become more in touch with their nature, resembling their prime nature of eroticism. **Exhibitionist** is *an individual who becomes aroused by exploiting their entire or partial body naked in public to strangers.* Conversely, for exhibitionism, it is shameful to husband and/or wife and sinful if the king or your queen is in nudity to entice others. We're all born into the world naked, for it is neither shameful nor sinful to be in touch with eroticism as womankind and mankind nor shameful and sinful to embrace naturism and nudism. Taking in notice of her nudity supports her because it tells her she has your affection, and when you're aroused by this act, it signifies to her she has you in her power while provoking her confidence and proving her beauty stimulates your Love Muscle. An exhibitionist is commonly associated with naturist but is not equivalent, for naturist are nearly the same as nudists. **Naturists** are *practitioners of the naked arts. They're closely in touch with nature, occasionally often in nudity as an embrace of their bodies while earthily adaptable and opened. Their state of mentality is better harmonized and connected with nature*

while in nudity in environments and events. Nudists are practitioners who enjoy being naked occasionally to often without necessarily taking delight in being seen by strangers but only in her/his significant others eyes as so with a naturist. **Nudists** are *individuals who engage in practices of nakedness whenever possible and take delight in their flesh*. Naturists are more at one with nature, for if it rains, perhaps they'll remain *unclothed*, while nudists will wear *clothes* in demanding weather changes and environments. The empirical reality of women who are nudist, naturist, and exhibitionist is they're more completely natural in lovemaking. The philosophy is natural. Wearing condoms is not often embraced, especially if they know their partner is completely STD-free, for their nature is indulgence of a holistic lifestyle as Adon Olam intended, for they're more harvested in being naked.

In the garden of Adam and Eve, both were naked, embracing naturism and nudism:[25] *"And they were both naked, the man and his wife, and were not ashamed."* **(Genesis 2v25 KJV)**

Contrasting exhibitionist from the naturist and nudist is that the exhibitionists often use their nudity to intently grab attention from others, while naturist and nudist don't portray that image but strictly about becoming one with nature. Naturist, nudist, and exhibitionist orientation is to wear lesser clothing as possible. Furthermore, women that are preservers of naturism or nudism lifestyle prudently often wears no bra nor underwear unless menstruating for their persona is invested more in the Spartan or Grecian era fashion, or Cowgirl era that wears refined near bare clothing; for all is their eloquence. Naturist and nudist will embrace their nakedness discreetly or in front of their significant lover. Naturist and nudist in privacy take delight in wearing no clothes during day, bedtime, and in morning as part of their lifestyle, though sensibly they'll wear a robe, garment, or luxury pajama's for covering in presence of strangers and company. During outside nudity, couples will benefit sun bathing with a reduction of toxicity in the body through the sun because solar energy from the sun potentially cures diseases—depression, energy deficiency, insomnia, weight gains, immune deficiency, body odor, libido deficiency, PMS, and other abnormalities (Trudeau 2004), and enriching oxygen on the body improves skin health along with improving hygiene on all parts of the body. In naturism and nudism, it's important in faith tradition to preserve anonymity (privacy) in matters of social environments, for it creates lascivious behavior to others if you're not married or married. Strangers perceive lascivious and lustful impression, so it's always important to have a robe or some type of canopy nearby. In addition, there are laws against nudity in various areas; it's recommended to attend private locations or deserted locations to support these natures. Although in faith tradition, there are various biblical scriptures were in Christology taught to embracing nudism and naturism (Isaiah 20v2–4, and Matt. 6v25–34, and Luke 12v22–34 are verbatim). Embracing nudism and naturism demonstrates body acceptance, for this is a great confident potentiation so the individual grasp more admiration for themselves and their significant other, and through, this they become a wild-femina or wild-man at heart, mind, body, and (or) spirit. A **wild-femina (woman)** and **wild-man (man)** naturist, nudist, and exhibitionist is *an open earthily person who is primal, aesthetic, and affectionate to their nature and unashamed of their sexual nature and hedonistic to their nature.* These individuals are aesthetes, which are philosophers of aesthetic because they embrace nakedness, and nakedness can be an art, perhaps the greatest art. Naturism and nudism is a sheer form of naturalism and is considered lingerie.

Erotic Sensual Rape Fantasy

First will begin with the negative before the positive to acknowledge what's undesired before the desired out of respect for the women who have experienced trauma from real rape.

*Negative Nature – **Real Traumatic Rape***

Queens who have been involved in a traumatic experience of real rape can have emotional, psychological, and physical effects on a survivor, thereby creating a *post-traumatic stress disorder* by *increasing anxiety, stress, fear, and nervousness disorder.* Women who go through actual intrusion of their bodies, making them feel completely underpowered by someone and disgusted of their inside and outside body while drowning the spirit. Through this, she becomes less attendant socially by avoiding activities and losing interest, producing paranoia that is a troubled spirited mind having difficulty resting, and prone to sudden outburst. Don't assume because of the positive nature (see below) of statistics that it's pleasurable by the majority because this is not so. Some still suffer from traumatic rape that was completely beyond their control and was entirely unaware of those circumstances nor was it a fantasy of theirs. Not all women agree to this fantasy. In addition, because of this undesired affection from various women, they grow into hating men (not all hate men) and use feminism movement system to destroy men's lives because one or a few have made their lives miserable. Not only in America, but in the Middle East, India, Egypt, Africa, and many other countries and continents, women suffer from real rape trauma. Speaking with some of the women who originated and lived for some years overseas (off American soil) sympathetically expressed anonymously that "they constantly live in fear; the fear of rape, murder, and cruelty." The cause of this is a "matter of control along with the Islamic extremist, and spoken languages that's insinuated insulting, and that here in America women should be more grateful." Real rape is different from the media and fantasy. A woman once told me, *"It devours the body with devastation and creates a broken spirit while rupturing what hope and joy was broad."*

There are queens who seem to develop a type of programming in their real traumatic experience to become acceptable to this nature of rape. Those individuals are the ones who require greater affection needed in a more tender nature of loving regardless of how they provoke you. Those statistics on the positive nature below are statistics from American soil. This is not verbatim with all women universally, so please cultivate this. It's better to perform healing than feed her the nature of trauma. For those certain queens have developed a stronger defense mechanism of intolerance because of their abusive past, and it is a cause for kings and princes to nurture our queens and princesses. For some women, it's not only men who rape but also women who intrude, so they end up hating all adults, except the kids for they're the signature of purity and loving admiration. Unless the child reflects the intruder who traumatized them, then they'll neglect or despise them. Our companion queens and princesses who are suffering in darkest nights with a traumatic past that they've become enslaved to is looking for love, affection, and a reason to carry on living. Some of those suffering women tarnish their flesh by using their flesh for fields of prostitution (pornography and sexual slaving for wealth).[94] All kings and princes must acknowledge that there's a possibility that various women have suffered similarly to the film *Woman Thou Art Loss.*

---

[94] Although the empirical reality is that various men regardless of what field may not care much about women prostituting because they see it as a service but with hope may Adon Olam inspire us mankind to make a change.

Positive Nature – **Erotic Rape Fantasy**

Psychological studies conducted found that forced sex fantasy is one of the popular fantasies women desires by their kings. This fantasy from certain women is an open expression of a hidden personality of masochism, submissively subservient, unrestrictive sexual behavior, and a revelation of guilt-free loving. The indulgence of this fantasy may include a **Sympathetic Activation,** which *is the engagement of stress or danger, activating the fight or flight response by increasing heart rate, relaxing smooth muscles to intake more oxygen, and stimulating genital arousal.* In the article "Women's Rape Fantasies: How Common? What Do They Mean?" first we must understand that fantasies are desired through a woman's subconscious to conscious level. Placebo study "The Nature of Women's Rape Fantasies: An Analysis of Prevalence, Frequency, and Contents" by Jenny Bivona and Joseph Critelli conducted at University of North Texas (Bivona 2009) documented 62 percent out of 355 college women admitted they've fantasized about being overpowered/forced/raped by a male or female against their will. Particularly overpowered by a man, 52 percent indulged, although when the word "rape" was implied, only 32 percent indulged. The Journal of Sex Research described rape as coercion "the use of physical force, threat of force, or incapacitation against her will." Between one-third and more than one-half of women have indulged in rape fantasy (Saletan 2009). Rape fantasy is considered an innate stage of *sexual masochism* as a persona for passive love (Deutsch 1944, 251).[95] In the modern society, past researchers have performed *the woozle effect* known as changing the statistics in false matters to fabricate something they think is socially desirable without admitting the truth about, for instance, common rape fantasy. Felicia (Romeo 2010) conducted surveys of 1,700 females who were rape victims concluded that 57 percent indulged in their experience and 38 percent reminisce a repeat (Elam 2011). Another reason perhaps for the ones who fantasize to erotic rape fantasy is due to the propaganda of adversary novels, fictions, anime (the Hentai portion), and films, creating a *suppression effect,* thereby craving a *Thanatos* nature. This would be **Adversary Transformation** derived from romance novels of deviant male characters. Third reason perhaps is they secretly have experience power rape before and felt they were desired more or indulged in it. *Power rape* is a *power play* (see chapter XIV, subtitle: Erotic

---

[95] Deutsch, H. *The Psychology of Women* (vol. 1) (New York: Grune & Stratton, 1944).

Master Lover

Spanking Discipline). Basically, power rape is the Adon who becomes more aggressive with the un-intending desire for brutality, for power play doesn't abusively brawl on or harm another with dangerous objects but the attending desire to dominance, authority, yang, and full persona of unrestrictive sex.

Empirically, there are men and women who don't believe in marital rape because rape in marriage is not part of their vocabulary because the vows made of rendering each other as one flesh. (cf. 1 Corinthians 7v3–4, Colossians 3v22–24) Seemingly, the women that don't consider rape in marital are considered "traditionalist" or "orthodox" because of faith-based of preventing lover from adultery, ancestral lessons of wifehood dharma, empathetic rudiment "reality principle" of the husband, and empowered outlaw morale. It's expected to have sex whenever either woman or man chooses, but brawling would not be acceptable. Women, empirically, who feels this way only desire the depths of lovemaking without the *suppression* and *repression* but fully amorous sexual behavior, full natures of affection, being ravished, yang, assurance (devotee's eager longing to have her flesh), *emunah*, and love by their king/prince. However, certain women may ask for patience during her fortitude of pregnancy period or sickness while the man is pardoned to use **CDD** of *sensibility*, especially for the safety of *gravida* (cf. 1 Peter 3v7). *Gravida* means a pregnant woman or statues regarding pregnancy. Although in menstrual cycles not necessarily true, for the majority, if she's a sexual masochist she'll receptively allow copulation, and a sadist man wouldn't disregard affection but would perhaps have an arousing momentum or magnetism of sexual ecstasy. During a woman's ovulation creates an amorous behavior in a man through her hormonal release that the man may act libidinous. Erotic sensual rape is a sexual exclusive loveable deviance while the queen remains impregnable as a stronghold, against other men while remaining the *devotee*. In **RawStory.com**, David Edwards mentioned this in his article, "'There is no such thing as marital rape': Christian website says wives must yield for sex 'no questions asked'" (Edwards 2015). He explained there can be legitimate delay because of prudence if there's a proper reason for not wanting to have sex.

Although as a personal disagreeable *philogynist*, based on my *principle of utility* on Edwards title on the article, kings/princes must have honor for her in matters of pardon when she's ill—going through health problems, a king/prince must ask themselves "would you want to be bothered if you wear ill?" Then you'll have a little more honor for her in this manner and apply a measure of *DD doctor's* role. In **CDD**, when the wife is ill or has dolorous suffering the husband is compassionately kind and caring in languages of love and communication to show gesture of understanding so that the wife reverences her husband to mitigate her during her weaknesses to give her fortitude. This is *sensibility*. Although the *reality principle* will still make efforts to spoil her with philosophy and hyper-concupiscence influence. A private empirical theory for the Adon to see if his queen has this sexual fantasy would be the observation of noticing if she's often indulging in films or shows with coercion sex and consistently watching them, she may cling to an inner desire to coercion sex privately among her trusted Adon. Conversely, women who hold rape in marriage as part of their philosophy desire a little more submissiveness with *suppression* and *repression* from their king/prince. Sensual erotic rape fantasy that various women crave is closely linked to rough sex but a little more above rough sex. You may ask, can't I just ask for consent in the heat of the moment? The problem is this dulls the enticing arousal because various women want it as a revelation, that surprising merge. The mystery behind this is that these women desire in uncontrollable desire among the king, leading to animalistic behavior of shredding off her clothes with the constant urge to merge, but I don't believe in this nature she'll desire a complete stranger to ravish her. For visual seminar, in the film *The Little Death* (Lawson 2014), romance couple Paul and Maeve, Maeve (Bojana Novakovic) confessed a masochist behavior to Paul (Josh Lawson) that she desires a rape fantasy fulfilled (notice that she was reading a book, which goes back to *Adversary Transformation*) only by Paul (her *devotee*), but Maeve didn't want to know *when, how,* or *where* nor consent it. Maeve wanted to imagine it as a stranger overtaking her against her will spontaneously. She wanted it to be a revelation but only through Paul as the intruder (starting approximate runtime of 00:02:20 to 00:06:55). The first actual attempt by Paul toward Maeve (starting approximate runtime of 00:33:15 to 00:35:05), Maeve secretly indulged, but Paul stopped because he didn't sense terror in her, but Maeve had intellectual pleasure through Paul's scent, so she knew it was him. Paul became too sensitive but notice she wanted him to continue, for she completely submitted to coercion act. A woman that desires power rape is not disordered, only a healthy masochist and sensuous being. (*see* Section II: "Sadism and Masochism," for clarity of masochism and sadism.)

Attention Individuals

Don't think I'm validating an erotic sensual rape fantasy toward non-intimate relationships. This is why I chose **The Little Death** *as an example. Maeve didn't desire power rape from a stranger(s) that who's non-intimate with, but ONLY wanted it from her trusted boyfriend (meaning the one she's intimate with and committed to). Maeve really craved power rape, not stranger rape (meaning someone she doesn't know, non-intimate with, and gang of men), for the intellectual, she wanted identity of the fantasy adversary, and there's only a few ways she can have that through familiarities. By the cologne the Adon wears, by the tattoos she's aware of, by the Adon's real voice, and/or by an material (such as watch, necklace, ring, etc.), the submissive can identify it's her Adon. Intellectually, the submissive queen needs to know it's her ADON!*

Submission and Slave-etude Lifestyle (Sensual BDSM)

Sensual BDSM is a talented way of loving with the vanilla but also with an alternative way of loving that may prolong relationship. Various women fantasize about the idea of domination or dominating. This impulse is a natural desire, for it's opening up a new dimension of loving. Sensual BDSM is commonly determined erogenous, embracing the Eros and Thanatos that women may crave but don't want to publicize it. There are women who truly crave to be submissive as long as they have your loyalty. Various women love the idea of a man with sexual instructions and demands because it's a personal turn on of their nature. Submissive women are prone to the accepting desires of the king's will, but some can be rebellious with becoming acceptable to demands. Originally, a woman's nature is to be completely in submission to a man. **Submission** means *the action of agreement to superior authority of another*, and these women who become submissive are seen as keeping Adon Olam law (Colossians 3v18, Titus 2). Submissive women are like a crown jewel with instincts but even more treasured than a crowned jewel, for virtue is with them in the eyes of a king/prince. In various continents and countries, women are trained in this art of submission because of faith traditions and conduct, belief that the men are chiefs of the world and their **kingdom** (means *a territory ruled through a king with support of a queen when he's absent because of his dharma to his family*), and for stability in their marriage. Those that are entirely submitted develop a real slave-etude desiring personality. Women are commonly trained as an image of sexually submissive and **subservient** (means *obedient without questioning another*) (Sanchez, Kiefer and Ybarra 2006). Submissive nature from women has been happening since the dawn of time.

> Loveliness belongs to all women, for it is the heritage of womanhood. Beauty of face and form is carried away by the passing years, but the beauty of heart and thought grows as the waters and fall . . . Maidenhood, wifehood and motherhood, these are the phases of a woman's life. (**The Book of Scrolls**; *Chapter XXXI: The Marriage Song* verses III–IV, from *The Kolbrin Bible*)

The Book of Scrolls also gave an important message to men who are destined to become father and husband.

> Love belongs nowhere but beside your own hearth . . . which a man gives to his wife . . . remembering that the dart of love cannot penetrate a hard and inconsiderate heart . . . sustain and cherish your wife . . . He who sows seeds of discontent before his hearth reaps a full harvest of misery. (**The Book of Scrolls**; *Chapter XXXI: The Marriage Song* verses VII–VIII & XI, from *The Kolbrin Bible*)

A submissive allures the Adon into seduction to persuade the Adon to remain attached to her because of her subservient and submission to what his innermost desires crave, thereby the Adon is induced to her individuality. This submits the Adon to her power. In addition, her traits as with possibly many successful relationships is the fulfilled embracement of *yin*, tenacious will, uncompromised fervency of *good works*, empathic for her lover, and opened to versatility in the intimate arts. Another reason she gains power is because the seductive superego of fulfilling the *reality principle* of the Adon, so he'll know the differentiation of other women, thereby he'll often cleave to the submissive because of what she offers—infuses the amorous, wild femina, agapic, Ahavah, Eros, subservience, Thanatos, ardent loving, Sensual BDSM lifestyle and/or Arts of Domestic Discipline, and overall embrace the yin of her nature. Acknowledgment is that a wild femina is not always subservient but sometimes rebellious for lovemaking; for instance, if Adon told submissive to leave him alone because the Adon has to work/tired, she'll still tempt Adon for lovemaking regardless if the Adon says enough.

*Loving Slave Nature – **Real Slave-etude Desire***

Slave age fantasy, for there are various submissive women who desire role-play to please their king without objections. These types of women are commonly desired. In this millennium, they would be called *faithful love slaves* because their ***entirely submissive and devoted to their Adon***. These types of women are variously rare but commonly desired by kings. *Faithful love slaves* are subjected to a sexual maiden authoritarian personality—"highly controlled, rational, and deliberate"—thereby submitted by overall authority of her king sexually and maidenly. She has the desire to romanticize her king angelically and amorously naughty upon her king's command. A *faithful love slave* can become a great wife, but cultivate that it's important not to beat on her but love her to the fullest. If you're harsh with her, you'll psychologically break her submissive nature to something more controlling and sheltered because her trust and companionship have been corrupted with an ill nature. She'll no longer want to become involved with submissive nature because the Adon broke the trust in showing ardent love and passion toward her mind and body.

Faithful love slaves love to service and satisfy their king. They are not brought but submitted unto their desire of the one king who captures their heart and fear Lord Christ (Colossians 3v22–24), and the Adonim who mistreats *faithful love slaves* God will judge (Colossians 3v25–4v1). There's a common misconception that *faithful love slaves* are considered concubines. This is not true if it's based on her desire to become the faithful love slave, but if she's brought, then she is a concubine, and the king is whoremonger or sexual immoral, for a faithful love slave can be vowed as wife for mind and body, but the spirit is submissive to Adon Olam. There are many indications of forged women to undesired sex slaving in the *Book of Jasper*, *The Book of Jubilees*, *The Ethiopic Book of Enoch*, and Old Testament (Torah), such as Deuteronomy 22v28–29, Deuteronomy 21v10–14, and Numbers 31v18, can be inferenced as slaves or concubines. Conversely, concubines are not empty in heart but been filled with contempt and dolorous living, hoping for a turning point in their lives. Many become corrupt because of evil morals from others. In the film ***Pretty Woman*** (Lawton 1990), inferenced this when Edward (Richard Gere) was allured to a beautiful concubine named

Vivian (Julia Roberts), Edward paid Vivian for her service, but as time together progressed, her heart harvested for love and marriage. She had hope for transformation and faith of a king who would rescue her from her dolorous and contemptuous life, and in the end, her hope and faith prospered through being ardently loved back. For expanded portion *see* "Section I: Faithful Love Slave and Submissive."

Voyeurism Lifestyle (Remedy: Make a Sex Video)

Voyeurism is an individual who gains sexual pleasure from watching others engaged in intercourse. For instance, **Spartacus Blood and Sand** episode 3 – *Legends* would be a prime example of voyeurism (starting approximate runtime of 00:31:40 to 00:33:34). When you watch that part, you'll notice some of the spectators were aesthetic philosophers because they thought of it as art, beauty, and animalistic nature; while the others were analytical philosophers (making the prediction of strokes), but all their eyes were looking for pleasure. The problem with this is its creating spiritual transcendence because you're automatically engaging in **intimate spirituality** (*one-flesh; union*) through what is speculated (1 Corinthians 6v15–20) from **pornography**, derived from the Greek word *pornographos, "writing about prostitutes."* This may cause commotion through questioning the reasoning of why "he/she is not being treated as intimately or aggressively as speculated," then they'll begin a moment of disappointment or depression. One of the common voyeur practices is through the consistent watching of pornography, which projects often false lovemaking that inflicts lack of passion, bitter beatings, hatred, false confidence, promotion of incest and defiling language, and **rabbit animalistic behavior** which is the projection of *ludic loving, which is fornication with a variety of individuals who they're not intently marrying nor intently keeping commitment, thereby treating them as prostitutes or inhumane or rent.* These individuals are commonly known as **whoremongers**. Kings, princes, princesses, and queens are not prostitutes, nor should they be spiritually associated with prostitutes unless they're making efforts to help others find their way. No one should be treated as rent, neither should they be treated as toys. Many individuals would argue that watching a graphic sexual cinematic film is the same as watching pornography. The truth is it's closely symbolic, but cinematic films have a thoughtful propaganda, multiple genres suitable for moods, and storylines that create prolonged novelty, and depending on the movies you choose, they may qualify as something inspirationally meaningful, empirically educating or enlightening, and the rest is simply enjoyment, so if you feel like the communication is evil, then don't watch it but don't create judgment or contention on others watching it. Every being's spirit is different when they watch films with graphic sexual scenes, but pornography may be partially or highly responsible for bad deviant behaviors toward each other.

These bad deviant behaviors are hitting beauty on the face or undesired afflicted body parts such as breast, back (*not butt*), lower legs, stomach, genitals, ribs, head, and arms, abusing by hitting the companion with dangerous or very unpleasant materials, treating companions like trash and flagellating (piercing another with harmful materials, burning them with cigarettes or lighters, and hitting them with objects such as belts/whips/etc.). For the Adon also must acknowledge that their queen must not be treated as an animal but must be treated as human beings, so in reality pornography, the falsifying satisfaction of *coprophilia* (means sexual satisfaction from feces on the body) and *urophilia* (means sexual satisfaction from urine on the body) as something agreeable has given themselves a great error for the minds of individuals who think this is okay, for they have been deceived.

July 2015   *Faults on Pornography*   **Journal**

Confessing my thoughts on pornography, I used to think it was nothing but pleasure until my spiritual willpower unfolded my mind to withdraw from pornography films. In truth, I felt that *pornography* was perfectly fine to watch, and yet spiritual willpower withdrew me from certain films. Two of my favorites was *Nubile Films* and *FrolicMe*. You may ask what part withdrew me. Truth is scenes like portrayed *polyandry*, swinging, orgies, hardcore acts, and portrayed adultery; however, sites with scornful beatings among women, mutilation, effeminate, and other pornography films does not strike any interest of mine, therefore, I stray with repulse from any of those sites; for TV shows and films that unexpectedly consisted of those scenes I fast-forward based on my *principle of utility* (*see* Discover Subliminal Personality). Moreover, films and shows I have certain disagreeable speculations based on infidelities, effeminate scenes and languages, and portions of blaspheming God, from the revulsion and discernments of prudency, aesthetic philosophy and *principle of utility*; although the Christ Yahawashi said perversions will be encouraged, though the strength is to not let evil communications boast your manner but preserve prudency than you will not be burdened with *attrition* or subject to loathing and contempt. The truth I imply is that if you're watching a film or show, and there's a certain scene you don't approve of, either withdraw or fast-forward the scene, but don't cause arguments or contempt on others that feel no conviction. The gentleman quality is to use *principle of utility.* —J.S.J.

The truth of these scenes I've previously listed all have a major thing in common, and that is completely unlawful, sinful, and condemned in the Bible. Adon Olam's spiritual strength pulls on an individual's spiritual willpower more and more if it's wrong to withdraw, and you may not necessarily feel convicted of your actions. Adon Olam works mysteriously past our understanding, for He knows an earthily temple won't be rebuilt in a day, for what's a day to us maybe a year to Him, so timing is essential for deliverance. Forging someone to stop is ineffective in future because the individual is more likely to repeat what was forbidden to others stereotypical belief. It has to change from the inside first, and that's your spiritual willpower. You'll know it's wrong when you feel it's time for a change. Although you can let them dine alone and not support them if you feel the communication is evil for it's your spiritual willpower, but you've remembered the vows you spoken, and you've remembered the 1 Corinthians 7v3–4, then you'll make an effort to support them in watching or help them withdraw by giving an optimistic ideology (the choice is up to you!).

Adon Olam touched a few ex-porn stars to reveal the truth about pornography; for example, Shelley Lubben, author of *Truth Behind The Fantasy of Porn: The Greatest Illusion on Earth*, and few others confessed the lies that many perceived as delightful. **Robert Augustus Masters** book, **To Be A Man: A Guide to True Masculine Power** (Masters 2015) explained our need to withdraw from pornography in chapter 22. I'll give a brief summary, for viewers of pornography are creating a rational illusion that it's essential, while pornography is overly dehumanizing our inner nature of eroticism, self-creating the mind to the ritual of bondage of becoming one flesh with what's viewed, thereby amplifying the illusion to continuously watch through a chemical illusion than our natural, causing viewers to internally project their suffering. The chemical often always increases negative effects, while the natural balances and strengthens us so in all its better to make your own film. The utter most truth is the films shouldn't be given the credit for ludic (swinging) loving—courtesans, philanders, and free lovers (particularly, individuals without fidelity), but the nature of the viewer individual's persona that allow corruption of thinking it's okay to be a practitioner of swinging (sexually immoral). Viewing a cinematic film or show with sexual content doesn't deport you to hell (Sheol) but the basis of our actions of how speculative individuals imitate ludic play is the corruption of manner if the viewer individual is easily influenced to become ludic (cf. 1 Corinthians 15v33). Viewing cinematic films and shows is not the perversion, it's the works of the will that precedes the perversions, though positive influence is to repeal what feels condemn to the soul.

The creative natural remedy for this is making your own erotic sexual documentary and films, become creative with sex with proper equipment that specifically meant for you and your queen to make, and savor reminiscence. The recreative way would be *Coniugamorography* *"writing about spouse love"* (coniug- "spouse"; -amor "love"; -o "about"; -graphy "writing") is the proper prudent way of sexual recording. The benefit is you'll acknowledge your partner's gratifying gestures, Protocol IV (refer to Chapter XV: Sacred Penetrative Roots and Revelation of Ancient to Modest Remedies), and you'll experience a language of love if you completely open yourself to pleasure without focusing on the camera(s). Sacred lovemaking filming creates an admirable novelty that can be shared with your companion and at the same time make known hidden blissful truths. Private films are meant to be a revelation and arousing momentum, which keeps the spice in romance, and there's no sin in this act.

Erotic Private Dancer Fantasy

Erotic Private Dancer is an individual who moves rhythmically sexual, stripping off their clothes to nudity toward another individual to provoke sexual stimulation. The art of erotic private dancing is closely a behavior of sexual gestures and seduction to provocatively create eagerness and signifies her strength in energy (yin) and natural aphrodisiac. Women get off on this because it's their moment to provide a sense of domestic discipline and **goddess** (meaning *a woman who is adored for her beauty and existence*) behavior toward the male. Women are enticed with becoming the seducer because the aphrodisiac effect on the blood flow creates the **inevitable** (meaning *uncontrollable*) behavior, for this brings out the animalistic behavior she may crave while enduring savory of her **aesthetic** king. Various women who are practitioners of erotic private dancing become enticed with the idea of the king **masturbating** (means *stimulating genitals of another or yourself for sexual pleasure through what's pleasing to the eyes or vision in the current or past moment*) or being masturbated by her. It demonstrates aggressive sexual actions during her presence of this art without expelling Serere Medicine; a strong erection signifying greediness for their nourishment, flesh, love, and comfort, then she'll acknowledge your appetite for her and provide a servitude to your hunger, the service comes through her initiation of Sweet Mouth loving and (or) her instant assertion of the Adon's member into the Honey Pot or Hershey Highway of the Adon's choice or the choice of the queen of where she feels she desires the Love Muscle most in that moment, or the grace of the *physical penetrative intimate trinity*, modernly termed as "Three-Hole Par,"[96] a copulating ardency that utilizes the woman's Sweet Mouth, Hershey Highway and Honey Pot. For the queen wants to appeal captivating to her king's eyes, and having his affection in the moment of erotic private dancing compels her. Normally, erotic private dancing that comes with music can be sensational to the mood because it's a part of her loveliness toward her Adon. On the contrary, erotic private dancing from the queen toward the king is not always the woman's empowerment even though if she initiated it but can be the Adon's empowerment as well when he asserts smooth demands of telling her to dance slowly and remove her clothing until bare and summons her to perform intimate favors for him.

Conclusion

However, if you decide not to support any of her fantasies, she very well **may** use her desire to indulge with another king because you decided not to be supportive. As kings and princes, it's encouraged to be the best man you can be. Reminder is that not every woman's fantasy is vanilla but of a different loving. The fantasies are all derived from the wanting desire of craving affection or control on their part because they indulge that you admire their beauty to the point of enticement to merge forbidden, naughty, and uncontrollable behaviors. All in all, love your submissive the best ways you can!

---

[96] A realism assertion us heterosexual men would often language we're a "Three-Hole" man as a way of saying subliminally or straightforward we're interested in a being with a natural born Vagina, a woman, and fulfilled in utilizing all three penetrative holes, the "Three-Hole Par."

Chapter XVII:
Intimate Investment

"Observation is the key to a wise approach before diving into temptation and discovering infinite deceptions."

Protocol: "Priorities, gentlemen" is important. Some may wonder like I have. How many men have this woman slept with? Will she remain committed and supportive? Is she an ethical slut or a decent queen? Is she a willing submissive as Lord of Most High created or rebellious? Will she satisfy sexual desires? Does she take good care of her health and capable of breeding? Does she have acceptable housekeeping discipline? Is she investing in love or money? Would she be suitable for a good wife? Has she experienced trauma in life? If so, is she willing to accept healing from a more deserving man, or is she bound? What are her spiritual beliefs and expectancies? Does she have the personality that you hope for, or are you just lusting after her beauty and ignoring the facts of pre-anguishing you'll afflict upon yourself because of disturbing personality? Is she willing to accept a new legacy, or is she attracted to drama? And many other questions we ask ourselves before we take relations deeper or pursue. **Preselection** phase should be more progressed for us kings, for women preselection is women observing social approval of their choice. For men, this is observing social, maiden, and intimate approval of their choice.

A woman is destined to be a man's companion, bloodline carriers, and blissful lovers. Among the common men thinking that women are sex subjects and baby makers, actually, it's much deeper than that, for they are our hope of divine bliss and comforter. They're also the evolutionary strong hold of man's existence, so much more love should be acknowledged toward our queens. Queens and princesses are the treasure, and kings and princes are the prize.

𝔐ature 𝔄cknowledgment

Speculating relationship is like an expensive investment in wine. In connection of two individuals, both must make effort to fill the glass of wine. One can't contribute to everything, while the other does nothing. Emotional connections go stale when there's neither communication nor trust of faithfulness, but the only way to gather it is through *emunah* from your significant other and orientation of *emunah* from within your *personage*. In comparison, when wine is left open, the savoring aromatics and flavors fade away then are no longer cherishable just as the relationship went from sacred to an open relationship, which investment demolishes or depolarizes. In a relationship or an assumed relationship has to be mature acknowledgment.

Addressed/Shared Principles + True Intentions
+ Resolutions + Confessions =

Mature Acknowledgment

Below are five important investing relationship questions:

- ❖ Where we stand in this relationship on a serious stature? *(Question asked within three to five weeks)*
- ❖ What are your compromises and dismissals? *(Question asked within six to eight weeks)*
- ❖ Any heavy burdens you like to get off your mind or something I should be aware of? *(Question asked within nine to twelve weeks)*
- ❖ What are your truest intentions and nature? (Question asked within thirteen to fifteen weeks)
- ❖ Are you open to a transformation and divinity (or ask where does faith reside)? *(Question asked within sixteen to twenty weeks)*
- ❖ *Testing Emunah!* (Test within twenty-one plus weeks)

These questions are essential toward determinism, for various individuals have a strong possibility of wearing hearts on their sleeves and even the individuals who never thought they would be capable of heartfelt sentiment. A few wise elderly people once told me that in this millennium, "wear your mentality outbound and heart inbound," basically permanently use the ark of rationalism, sensibility and noetic thinking before you blossom heartfelt sentiments. The Word discerns this, "keep thy heart with all diligence; for out of it are the issues of life," (Proverbs 4v23 KJV) Yahawah (Ahayah) warned us of the diligence of the heart. Thereby, you'll be guiding yourself with clarity of discernment before you've been deceived even though deception is inevitable. The positive possibilities are better evaluated then without evaluation. Unfortunately, there's large proportion of individuals who love to act on free love, ludic and manic loving; however, if our great ancestors from the nineteenth century and below were alive today, a large proportion of them would hit free lovers and ludic and manic lovers with a cane and say. "Stay committed" or "Confront the truth before you twain." In addition, because of infidelity and contempt, many suffer with dolorous temptation for revenge through sexual immorality (*see* Sacred Marriage Truth, for sexual immorality causes). Remember this, "Lies carry more contempt and dolor, while emunah carries more loyalty and integrity," for this means more than you'll know and a savior to your personage.

Most important of all is test her *emunah*, for everyone that's had an unsuccessful relationship develops trust issues. The only way to let go of this is testing her **emunah** *"faith, truth, faithfulness, fidelity, stability."* Many would say if you love them, then trust comes with it, but the truth is love is feed from *emunah*, so *emunah* builds up to love and not the other way around. However, it's important to not insinuate that she won't test you back because in time she more likely will. Although as you're testing her loyalty, so is she, for kings/princes need to acknowledge their relationship is similar to spy intelligence, for our will, mentality, and emotion is often being tested. She'll do these things to test a man's *emunah* and to determine union in your livelihood—the character and traits of the individual Adon's manhood. The royal thinking method is solidity while sensible. The man who is solid in *emunah* availeth much more because she is often determined to learn a king's/prince's strengths and weaknesses to better know who you are and the truth of you.

Conversely, sometimes various individuals become caught up in tangled emotions. Defining tangled emotions would be a double-minded person with a choice to make wisely between varieties of partners. Tangled emotions are driven by the stature of the person's personality, intimacy, figures, and legacy. Emotions that are tangled come with boundaries of being tolerant and fair and finding clarity in oneself to make the right decision. A tangled emotion derives from unfaithfulness, being unsure of the actions made and regrets of who made. —J.S.J.

Mankind and womankind are not built like machines, programmed as captives. Without awakening to their hedonistic and Ahavah, there's no spirituality and livelihood when it's captive and suffocated within human mind.

Aesthetic Love for Muses

Every brethren I know (including myself) looks for a woman that is of creative artistry. These type of women are known as muses. A muse is a woman of artistry. Artistry can range from her beauty, being a very good cook, stylish in fashion, an interior and exterior decorator, singer, musician, poetic, an erotic dancer, comedian, pioneer in lovemaking or strong romancer, oracle gifts, a historian or storyteller, therapist, to simply intelligent.

A muse can always be very special to us kings and princes, for she'll uplift him in the times of stress, give insight of beauty among nature, and support in the times of difficulties. In the world, there's also a proportion of drama queens. This can be a hazard to the faith if an Adon is a Christian individual because my Christendom brothers, drama queens often like to be affiliated with wild environments (such as clubs, home parties filled with alcohol, private sex clubs). Many drama queens indulge in stirring up havoc and contention, though contention in reality works for some couples for love is made up in the bedroom or spontaneous environments that's a preserver of anonymity to create momentum of feisty and Thanatos behaviorism to fulfil sexual ecstasy, similar to film *About Last Night* (2014). Certain drama queens are manic lovers, free lovers, or ludic lovers, so there would more likely be invokes of jealousy, Ra, persuasion of drugs and liquor to induce a sober man to a drunkard, brawling or throwing of dangerous objects at the Adon, stealing of money, whoring, lying, and heartaches in time. No queen is so beautiful that she has the right to withdraw the Adon's liberated conscience to abyss filled with attrition and contempt because of not being conducted to Adon Olam's Word and harm to Adon externally and internally.

𝕾acred 𝕸arriage 𝕿ruth

"Marriage ought to be based primarily on affection—love if you like—and only if this is present does marriage offer something that is . . . sacred."

"That's exactly what I'm talking about, the preference for one man or for one woman above all others, but what I'm asking is a preference for how long?"

—Leo **Tolstoy**, *The Kreutzer Sonata*

Clarifying the word "marriage" means an intimate or close union of the opposite sex. In biblical times, marriage was completely perceived different from modest society. Marriage wasn't a civil matter but considered a union that was **consummated** (means *completion by sexual intercourse*), then laws were strongly given against **adultery** (means *sex outside of marriage* [someone that you're not married to]) and providence of physical and financial support. In sexual relations, "mating is an *innate propensity* (means *natural tendency of behavior*), and marriage is its evolutionary social *repercussion* (means *unintended/sudden consequence presumed after action or event*),"[97] meaning the prime nature is sexual union, but then an obligation is consequential on our part. Ancient marriages were traditionally planned by the parent or arranged members of the family. In primitive agapic marriage that hold emunah many choose who they'll marry without conceit or social pressure but agapic, a blessing from YHWH for the admiration of His Word, "let love be <u>without</u> dissimulation . . ." (Romans 12v9) *Dissimulation* means an individual(s) conceals and deceitfully give false truth about, motive or persona in feelings, thoughts and character. The common insinuation from individuals is that you have to be married through a priest and inside a church. The church is the sacred union with Yahawah and Christ Yahawashi church and nowhere in the Bible does it say you have to marry through a priest. The truth is marriages from biblical age are completely different from this millennium. In biblical age, marriage is a possession (1 Peter 3v7, state heirs), keeper of covenant, and union. Reason for possession is because the man has invested in marriage, and

---

[97] Paper 82 The Evolution of Marriage page 913, *The Urantia Book.*

the wife is his treasure. Nowhere in the Bible does it explain or clarify that marriage is only justified through governmental documentation nor ordained through a licensed priest (or someone similar, such as a minister, apostle, etc.). The Adon Olam established marriage as a union of one flesh, commitment, ownership, and vows (Num. 30). The governance of a lawful betroth is through a signet and vow, then after consummation, unifies marriage. **Signet** "token, seal" means a symbolic ring or signature of agreement (cf. Genesis 38v18). Do you really think Adon Olam cares about a piece of paper or your vows from your tongue giving consent?

Do you really think Adon Olam care about a typed document or your signature of agreeable principalities to what is given? Adon Olam expects us be agreeable to what we vowed and signed off to. The truth is when we twain (coition) with another you have already validated one flesh. The repercussion is your long-term commitment, the marriage itself. For once twain vows are the *repercussion*, only privileged to divorce the vows if it's *prudent* to the divine law for the sake to manifest your *liberation*. Marriage is part of intimate spirituality communed with the Trinity. According to Numbers 30, marriage is a union of vows to unite male and female along with consummation (Matt. 19v6). I believe marriage is about really loving each other or a strong sense of bond that an individual don't want to let go because that person is part of you. In the film *Seven Pounds*, Ben (Will Smith) fell in love with Emily (Rosario Dawson), a queen that had heart deficiency who was soon to give out on her, but Ben couldn't bear the thought of her dying, so he made the sacrifice to donate his heart (literally) through his suicide for her and others.

Marriage in this era of intimacy somehow became restrictive on how we should have sex, derived from social construction and perceived doctrine from others who don't approve of certain heterosexual acts. This type of construction is labeled taboos, or unnatural, something created to tarnish union relations with regulations. Personally, I would say rebuke them all. The reason for this is because sex is a natural innate propensity, and your emotions are going to provide the action you so desire, and if it's done with prudence and sensibility from the Bible, then there's nothing neither restrictive nor taboo on your part, just naturalism. How about we end this philosophy of restriction in husband and wife intimacy with one scripture thereby neither priest, minister, apostle, nor any position of Christian or Jew can argue on because it's Yahweh's Word.

[4]Marriage (is) honourable in all, and the bed undefiled: but whoremongers and adulterers God will judge. (Hebrews 13v4 King James Version)

[4]Let the marriage Chuppah (**canopy** [means *covering*]) have respect in the eyes of all, and let the marriage bed be undefiled, for those guilty of gilui arayot (**sexual immorality** [means *promiscuity and prostitution*]) and no'afim (adulterers), Hashem (God) will judge. (Yehudim [Hebrews] 13v4 Orthodox Jewish Bible)

Take a closer look in notice the word *"undefiled"* means *pure ceremonially, physically, and/or morally unrestricted*, meaning it's not judged because of vows from Adon Olam's Word. However, this doesn't mean treat her scornful, for husbands are supposed to love their wives as much as they love themselves (Ephesians 5v28). Because marriage is undefiled, this gives the celebration of liberation towards each other in actions of libidinous, naughty, salacious, carnal, amorous, and concupiscence behaviorism. The Lord granted us three types ministries: the *conjugal love "devotees," priesthood*, and *Ahavah*—all communions; all of which services each other and Adon Olam, which gives communion of the Holy Spirit. For reason Adon Olam condemns whoremongers is because *sexual immorality causes* havoc to family life, crumbles a person's potential to love, plagues of diseases, and builds contempt to human beings, making them feel like objects. The film *Unfaithful* gave a visual example of how sexual immorality can create a broken home and crumble potential emotional love that another had for their significant other because of tangled emotions. Therefore, Adon Olam warned us because of protection of our longevity, protected us from being treated less than royal due to unfaithfulness, trained us to treat each other with real love instead of rent or layaway cycles, and prevented massive divorces and plague of STD's due to sexual immorality.

Adon Olam despises men and women not remaining obligated and not remaining *emunah* to each other because it creates those sexual immoral causes. This is why it's called *sin* because of the causes. Your sins are your repercussion, for if you twain with someone and treat them as rent, rent will follow your body. If men fornicate with men, then blood cells will form a plague in time, and HIV will procreate then would have committed suicide among themselves . . . Karma is in sin, but Christ has the power to remove karma and the power to allow karma from vile affections of the flesh. It all depends on the individual seeking for mercy and transformation or the individual who seeks to continue.

I've kept monogamy very short because I've covered much on couple relation throughout the preceding chapters of Part III of this book, plus monogamy is more basically expected. One woman can be more than enough when blessed with the right one. For one of the best women point of view books that's well informative I highly recommend *Monogamy: The Untold Story* by Marianne Brandon, cultivate Adonim that being a Master lover is articulated from wisdom, knowledge and truth; while lovemaking is all a form of cultivated art, therefore Adonim don't be bitterly disdained on cultivating what's helpful from the beautiful woman Marianne Brandon giving discernment with the *principle of utility.*

The Polygamy Revelation

In this criteria, were going to approach polygamy in biblical notion because many believers believe polygamy to be a sin. Partial of this is true in the reference to *a woman having multiple husbands* known as **polyandry** (2 Corinthians 11v2) but not necessarily true for *a man to have multiple wives* known as **polygyny**. Before we begin looking at the polygamist lifestyles, let's clarify what Christ spoke about the Old Testament in Matthew 5v17. "Think not that I am come to destroy the law, or the prophets: I am not come to destroy, but to fulfill." This means the Old Testament is still valid.

The polygyny institution has a framework of four differential wives, according to the history of Urantia (World) from *The Urantia Book* page 926.

I.   The ceremonial or legal wives.
II. Wives of affection and permission.
III. Concubines, contractual wives.
IV. Slave wives.

Abram (Abraham) Polygamist Lifestyle

Sarai, the *wife* of Abram, *gave permission and initiative* for a polygamist marriage to Abram and her Egyptian maiden, Hagar, to bear children (Genesis 16v1–11).

Jacob Polygamist Lifestyle

Laban gave his two daughters, Leah (the eldest) and Rachel (the youngest), to Jacob. Laban gave both his daughters to Jacob to marry, commonly known as *sororal polygyny*, which are cowives that are siblings married to one man which are forethought to be sensible to one another and less contentious among each other. Leah's handmaid, Zilpah, and Rachel's handmaid, Bilhah, (Genesis 29v14–30) became intimate companions to Jacob *from wives agreement and initiative*, which was *given to* Jacob to have intercourse with both of the handmaidens for promise of children (Genesis 30v1–24, 31v17, 32v22), and they also became wives of Jacob (Genesis 37v2).

Other Biblical Men Who Were in Polygamist Marriage

Gideon had many wives and a concubine according to Judges 8v30–31, and Ephraim had two wives (1 Samuel 1v2). David[98] married Abigail and Ahinoam and others at Jerusalem (1 Samuel 25v42–43, 30v18; 1 Chron. 14v3), Ashur married Helah and Naarah (1 Chron. 4v5), and Shaharaim had two wives named Hushim and Baara (1 Chron. 8v8). Rehoboam had eighteen wives and three concubines (2 Chron. 11v21), Abijah married fourteen wives (2 Chron. 13v21), King Solomon married seven hundred princesses/wives and had three hundred concubines (1 Kings 11v1–8), and Jehoiada married two women (2 Chron. 24v3).[99] These polygamist marriages weren't clarified to rend permission to the husband from the wife/wives but were possibly done on their own will.

Biblical Law of Polygamist Marriage

A husband must provide fruitful lovemaking, food, and clothing (Exodus 21v10). Kinswomen such as mother with daughter, sister with sister . . . to be wives to the same man are outlawed (Leviticus 18v17, 20v14). My

---

[98]   Another scripture in reference to David on polygamy: 2 Sam. 12v7–8.

[99]   Other scriptures referring to polygamist marriages: Dan. 5v2–3, Isaiah 4v1.

belief is this law was brought upon after experience of Jacob having trouble with contenting two sisters because it derives envy. El Elyon expressed prudential suffering of King Solomon losing his way through foreign women worshipping other gods and goddesses while provoking him to join their beliefs. It wasn't that foreign women were the problem, but the religion they carried to vex another's mind that was the problem (1 Kings 11v4–5, v8–10). King Solomon's example is a law that men should not turn beliefs for heathen women who don't carry equal faith because Adon Olam is a jealous God and don't indulge in His saints worshipping other gods and goddesses. (cf. 2 Corinthians 6v14)

Polygamy may perhaps be of good treasure to kings and princes, but the alternative negatives can become anguish itself if not domestically disciplined with fair share of love, for polygamy may cause *envy* (means feeling/expressing annoyance provoked of craved desire by another's affections and possessions), *laziness* (means unwilling to put more energy into relations), *gluttony* (means intense desire for something), and craved *lust* (means intensely strong sexual appetite) that's dissatisfied. Conversely, as I was reading **Rollo Tomassi's** *The Rational Male* book, in chapter 3, "The Honor System," the message was of great importance, for in ancient times, men were empowered Adonim. Now feminism has intelligently altered the primal purpose of a man's position to challenge and covertly exchange to feminisms purpose. In the Ten Commandments, we are told not to commit *adultery* but wasn't a problem with polygyny because men were more satisfied in marriage with wives and because *harem*—means wives or concubines, were signified as *wealth*—means abundance of desirable and valuable possessions.

The biblical times were men who were blessed with submissive wives were more agreeable to polygyny. The amount of wives in biblical notion was only accommodated from ability to provide physiological stability (as confirmed in *The Urantia Book*,[100] *see footnote*) (taking care of expenses, sexually satisfying the harem, affection of love and *emunah* to the harem and younglings, the *Maslow theory* stability [presented in Chapter I]) and providing *amorous* virtues and awakening the Adon *personage*). In *The Kolbrin Bible*, the law says a man can have no more than three wives ([Book of Sons of Fire (SOF:9v69]). The analogy is since in the Bible,

---

[100] The Marriage Institution, from *The Urantia Book*, pg. 927, stated, "The number of wives was only limited by the ability of the man to provide for them."

many biblical men had multiple wives would be limited on how many wives bedrooms can an Adon supply or can sleep comfortably on the master's bed provides the limit (there are only so many size beds to buy. This limits the available room for the Adon and his wives), food, shelter, and finance and overall how much the Adon can provide for them equally along with liberation. Many men may have this hidden desire to have a polygyny conjugal love, for it's an innate propensity of fruitfulness from times of old along with testosterone concupiscence.

Wedding Understanding

A wedding clarification to the Adon is the acknowledgment of its novelty for the treasures queen, not brought upon selfishness from the Adon because of expense. A wedding can be very important to your queen, an engagement can be very important to your queen, *emunah* can be very important to your queen, and an Adon's ardency toward the queen can be very important. In the film ***Baggage Claim*** (starting approximate runtime of 00:26:30 to 00:28:07), William (Derek Luke) openly expressed to Montana (Paula Patton) that the essence of marriage is to preserve the *emunah* and *Ahavah* within the covenant. Marriage is not the temperance of falsifying image of others through social pressures but being true to what you desire. This ignites the *Ahavah*, so make no rush but discover oneself in its significance toward another determining *emunah*. Weddings are the admiration of a queen's enchanted grace and because of this its valued, but when emunah and love is fair, the admiration becomes a aspiration for women and also men that hope to receive such honorable and fair beauty.

Conscious Caution

Women can be Dangerous Beings

In reality, rebuke all social media that implement all women are angels because these philosophies are not true, for majority of women are not of purity, innocence, nor loyalist but perhaps of a loving personality. There's a common misconception of what loyal really is, for **loyal** means ***giving or demonstrating firm allegiance and support to another person***, for various individuals mistake this for **one-flesh loyal-heirs** "devotee," and for this means *being an ownership of their flesh which your flesh is also theirs now with a loyalist personage*. In addition, many individuals really want the *emunah*, but they mistake this as only loyalty. Many men as it is common have this one-flesh loyal-heirs demand from their woman, but this is natural as the Bible also demands this. Truth is when this is engraved in the mind, it gives foolish ones a full understand of don't fornicate or the common street word "cheat." Some fellow brethren of mine told me that there are women who don't understand what loyal is because loyalty was never explained clearly to them.

Honestly, women are living beings like us and capable of becoming great manipulators and liars and can be very jealous beings. Jealousy leads to negative commotion, and negative commotion leads to hate, and hate leads to suffering. They portray this by using their sexuality to taunt and give off the illusion of power while causing mental anguish on the king to provoke the mind to submit toward the misery of losing them through something more appealing to them. Various women are commonly brainwashed by idols, family, friends, and strangers, influencing them it's justified to play or use men for money, even in their feminist studies. Empirical reality is variously neither majority nor a moderation of women feel empathetic at all when they break up with you, nor do they feel regret, this is the sadly truth, but there's always hope and faith promised by Yahawah in your prayers for someone more loving in the *emunah* way and loyal-heir. Empirically, given between the two sexes, females are the most judgmental and prejudice. Then there are women who carry themselves with false confidence and deceitfulness, who enjoy manipulating men and seduce other men outside of relationship projected to satisfy curiosity. A variety of individuals will become ignorant and accept enslaving themselves to deceitful temptations, breaking down their mentality and acceptance of partner to loose fornications when it's revealed true. It's clearly stated in Matthew 19v8–9 that a husband may dismiss his wife if she has fornicated to relieve the burden of a heavy heart although you'll have difficulties dismissing a wife if you've fruitfully bestowed youngling(s) from your loins.

In biblical scriptures, God warns considerable investigation in a woman before being caught up in her webs of anguish and deception. In *Proverbs Chapter 5*, promiscuous woman doesn't bring anything good, only misery. To emphasis the main point, Proverbs 23v27 clarifies this message when stated, **"A prostitute is a dangerous trap; a promiscuous woman is as dangerous as falling into a narrow well."** In reflection, this doesn't mean they're not capable of love. There's a common quote from the streets that "you can't turn an ethical slut into a housewife," but practically, you can but requires a lot more affection on your part and a transformation with divinity on her part. Shelley Lubben, ex-porn star, President of Pink Cross Foundation, who received her Theology Doctrine degree, has made a huge impact on deliverance from pornography, giving her testimony to many through transformation and divinity, for she is living proof that women who lived on unfortunate darker pathways can be delivered, but much patient and affection is required. However, to all husbands, it's important to acknowledge infidel women have evolved the intelligence of their time frame of reproduction to predetermine a more convenient time to commit an affair through their ovulatory cycle and evaluating when more likely to conceive, thereby trying to cover up their infidelity[101] in holistic (raw natural) sex.

Empirically, there are women who preserve their *emunah* to their potential, the real loving wives and single women looking for prolonged commitment. The women who are real loving wives who sustain *emunah* and have a husband who doesn't sustain his *emunah* will secretly crave vengeance because the husband filled her with contempt, gave communion "Serere Medicine and Love Muscle" to another woman without approval, and left her sexually unsatisfied. For instance, in TV series *True Detective Season 1 Episode 6 Hunted Houses* (starting runtime of 00:44:23 to 00:52:12), the wife endured a cheating husband for some years, so she decided to have Hershey Highway loving with his detective partner to break him because of his unfaithfulness because she never approved of him having concubines. The wife's action was strictly vengeance than after from the following episode was inferenced his immediate separation of any kind of communication for two years after she told him. Often in life, it's always sex outside of the covenant that leads to a heartbreak or a broken covenant of Ahavah between couples. Adultery out of malice or retribution to make up for love doesn't quench love, "*many waters* cannot quench love . . ." nor the "floods drown it," as a way of overwhelming tears or emotions to heal or mitigate burdens of love, for God warns of improvidence and contempt among ourselves for love from one that doesn't love back that "if a man would give all the substance of his household for love, it would utterly be contemned" (Song of Solomon 8v7 KJV). Even when its unintended, one of my favorite films on this criterion is *Barney's Version* and a favorable film called

---

[101] David M. Buss, *The Evolution of Desire*, page 76.

Forgetting Sarah Marshall when Peter tries to get over Sarah, and a new woman becomes his savor in companionable love.

Wolves Seeking to Devour

Adonim and submissive queens, be skeptical on who you allow to live in your home, for your palaces were meant for you and your consort and younglings. Everyone else, regardless if family, friends, or associates, may provoke your loving to fornicate with your consort, causing repercussion of plagues in your home. Wolves can confidingly sneak into your boudoir, play a communicative role to inflame a love map, or try seducing your consort just to have a treasure/prize that belongs to you. "Catch the shu'alim (**foxes**), the shu'alim ketanim (**little foxes**), that spoil the kramim (**vines**); for krameinu (**our [*blooming*] vines**) have tender grapes."[102] For instance, I will provide a film for visual learners so you'll understand the importance of it.

1. In the film *Soul Food* (Ravera, Beach and Williams 1997) (starting approximate runtime of 01:06:20 to 01:13:01), Miles (Michael Beach) was devoting himself to writing his songs, and Faith (Gina Ravera) walked into the house smiling because she had a breakthrough in fulfilling her dreams. Miles and Faith both have in common of seeking to fulfill their dreams, so they both communicated for a good while in the dining room, drinking some beer. Miles left Faith in the dining room to practice on his music, Faith craved affection from Miles than a love map opened, the erotic desire between them both built up, then they shared sexual communion and healing against the wall (Miles wife, Teri, wasn't providing sex often). Then Teri (Vanessa L. Williams) walked into the house with Ahmad (Brandon Hammond) calling Miles, and Teri and Ahmad went to the studio, while Ahmad didn't notice Teri saw her husband Miles and Faith (Teri's cousin) having intercourse, then she felt betrayed and emotional suffering, so she left with Ahmad. After Miles and Faith finished fulfilling their erotic desires, they both realized the shame of it. Later, the love that Teri and Miles had was

---

[102] Shir Hashirim (Song of Songs [Solomon]) 2v15, Scripture taken from Orthodox Jewish Bible.

divorced. Teri made the mistake of offering her cousin, Faith, who is another beautiful woman (Teri is beautiful as well) to temporarily live in her house and husband, Miles, causing Miles to be sexually repressed and suppressed because she often rejected sex from being a workaholic!

The foxes keep a persistence of covetous, lascivious, envious, and gluttonous behavior because they simply desire another individual's treasure or prize. The biblical scripture speaks the truth for our blooming vines have tender grapes. Grapes is symbolic for a fruitful sexual appetite, and our vines is the adulthood of our foundation, which is our sexual chambers that ignite us and our primitive nature. The mind, the strength holds of faith, the emunah, and Ahavah are the only ways to prevent such tenderness from igniting the sexual fire unto something we will regret. This is the common thing foxes (wolves) prey on, the tender vines filled with grapes to feed on. After they've taken all that can satisfy their appetite, they move on sniffing for another tree, leaving the past tree with lesser fruit that makes that tree unattractive or emptier in fruits.

The Realism of Adolescents

~ 2013   Adolescent Females Provocation Encounter   Journal

The realism I've come to encounter is that in 2013 when I brought some groceries at Food Lion, there was this adolescent female that I thought was a grown woman, so I initiated a conversation. Then the conversation became in interrogation from the female asking me what my name is, how old am I, and what I do for a living, so I told her I go to FTCC, and then she asked about my major while another woman was smiling at me with her son. Then I interrogated her asking if she was in school. She told me she's finishing up school at Douglas Byrd Senior and that she's thinking about applying for FTCC. Then I assumed she must be a senior; therefore, I asked if she's looking for help registering at FTCC. She told me she's a freshman (this flipped all switches of courting, then I immediately felt embarrassed) and turned out that other woman was her mother. The mother looked at me and smiled and said, "She really doesn't look her age, does she?" then I was puzzled and told her, "No, she doesn't," then remained silent, but the mother and the daughter seem to attempt to initiate a conversation even when I try to play the decent role to prevent accusations of pedophilia and keep from further embarrassment. Then they waved good-bye to me during me checking out my groceries and again outside. I told my mother about it. She told me some mothers don't really care about the age system. They just care about a man providing stability and love to their daughter and having a little financial assistance for the mother, but she let me know I did the right thing to protect myself from accusations by ending the conversation. —J.S.J.

During my experience, I've come to realize that in reality, there are some single mothers who provoke or train their daughter(s) very well to maidenhood and romancing when they figure they've reached a certain age of growing into novice levels of womanhood (this is empirical realism!). Then I began to understand a systematic clarity of this, and that's traditionalism or a primitive ancestral principality; nor is it right or wrong, but it is reality that certain individuals don't obey the U.S. government's regulations to legalism of age. Some adolescent girls are intentionally searching for males in their eighteens or older. The reason it's not entirely wrong is because the law is governed by philosophy, control and issuing illusion of fairness that's insinuated justice. Therefore, it's practically a way of saying the government makes choices for the people not the people making choices for themselves so a proportion of the people outlaw secretly. Furthermore, this is a matter of social construction, for its governed by authorities, but in Paul's teaching in Romans 13v6 said be a subject unto "official governing authorities, higher powers," but none is "official governing authorities, higher powers" except given by God.

In addition, the biblical testaments are different from the modest living in the United States according to scriptures on ages of legal marriage, for it was more so judged upon bodily form of womanhood. In accordance to the Hebrew Bible and New Testament, marriage as a natural state that of which "most women marry quite young, usually soon after the onset of menstruation, which of course, heralds fertility" and in traditional or ancient marriages men are normally the older or venerable among women (Wray 2011, p. 146). Furthermore, this is the same with ancient Israelites biblical times for the order of increasing descendants within the household (Lowery 2000, p. 8). In reality, certain individuals are so quickly to judge, but I've overheard some say to the other, "Shut up, for you don't understand." The reason I've come to acknowledge what this individual means is the realism of their sufferings, for some live in a household of a sadistic step-father, blood-father, or kin who constantly rapes them and beats on them, and certain mothers would allow it to happen; however, this is not the case for all young females, for certain young females want to aggress adulthood. On the contrary, the analogy is surely, certain individual forecast judgment, but they're not living their struggle, they're not helping, and offering a map is not too much of a useful help; meaning when an individual says there are places you can go but not willing to provide finance or transportation or job. Some fathers and mothers, in reality, are prostituting their daughters, so technically, it's not entirely wrong for them to not care about their age when pursuing older king because some adolescent princesses are seeking deliverance. A centric Christian will say deliverance is from God, but how do they know if that older king is not from the vocation of God?

This is why I've had a transformative analogy on princesses who seek kings; however, the case is in relation to the analogies I've just given. The questions adults must ask are, are you willing to do right by them to prevent princesses from going that way, or are you just judgmental without works to change their struggle? "Faith without works is dead" just like speculation without help is dead. Certain older queens forecast judgments often on kings who are with younger women because they secretly have envy, but certain woman who contains this is sometimes the woman who was in that same position once. In adolescent princes yet finding their way in life, sometimes a wiser older woman who still has a beautiful appearance can captivate a younger prince and train him in intros to lovemaking and companionship. This can be a savior as well to certain young princes. However, momentarily the young prince can have an *emotional suffering* behind a wiser older woman, but it makes them stronger when they make it through the suffering. A visual film that's similar to this criterion would be ***The Reader*** (2008) starring Kate Winslet and David Kross. Younger princes that are becoming venerable sometimes receives favor or bliss from the poise or venerable woman through her experience, submission, agape-eroticisms, maturity, passionate spoilage to please aggressively, skilled in companionship and romancing.

Sometimes there's a persistent pattern persisting in a way where younger women seek older men and sometimes leaving the younger man in their age-group abandoned, then the younger man grows wise, and that same woman he used to pursue is no longer pursuing. Then, she chases after growing young prince because the older man abandoned her, but the one who became wise can sometimes be the one to reject the old and start new because nature looks for the unfertilized or the new fish that preserved symbolically more chastity much like Solomon looking for the eloquent, honorable, undefiled, beauty —aesthetically which is based upon discernment and rationalism of fair, or virgin (cf. Song of Solomon 6v7–10). Solomon's quest for woman reflects many of us men modernity today for prudent intimate investment for possession of a potential submissive treasury wife. In accordance to the former woman the growing young prince was once infatuated for, she becomes judgmental and accuses the wise growing prince with a construction of immaturity or pedophile because desire for her from him has declined. Realism is certain growing wise young man may still have the innate propensity for that certain woman, but the choice for the growing wise young man is an innate nature of seeing her as a concubine or a preservative wife that discernably may become *treasures woman*. For a *treasures woman* is sensible, fair and of *good works*. In reality, sometimes life gives lemons on both sides—for young prince abandon because of an older man in his places of current desire to the princess, and the older man gets the princess, then younger prince grows envious and seek to rise in perseverance, and younger princess becomes older, fertilized, and depending, certain women libido change drastically to better or worse in sexual interest which includes Valley of Joy becoming less vigorously youthful in sexual appetite or more vigorous. Though to be fair as certain women have sexual dysfunctions so can certain men, thereby certain males seek sexual investments. Moreover, the young man who grow wise begins to search for a younger woman, while the one he once was passionate about seeks him, but he declines because of searching for a woman younger or symbolically more chastity, then she grows envious and either attempt to bring upon contempt or guilt to the one no longer clinging to her or passive and attempt to find another older man or seek a younger man who doesn't know her while she intelligently projects false innocence. There's karma in this!

Virgin Mary's Pregnancy Revelation

The daughter of Judah, and of Anna (Virgin Mary's mother). The Virgin Mary was left at the temple as an orphaned child at the age three, in accordance, she was very pious and a prayer warrior being without dissimulation. Yahawah took care of her along with angels who ministered to her, and her perfections increased throughout growing years. Virgin Marry was trained in the ways of maidenhood, her virginity remained impregnable to men and preserved for the Yahawah in righteousness. During the fourteenth age, she was stable of perfect age according to Yahawah and the high-priest within the temple; fourteenth age of adolescent females in biblical language is considered maturity, of womanhood and lawful to matrimony and consummation. Certain individual scholar's will disagree with me and probably say Virgin Mary was pregnant with Yahawashi between ages eleven to fourteen but in contextual it's fourteen. In accordance, Yahawah impregnated Virgin Mary with a prodigious light among her chamber during her age of fourteen, overshadowing her without heats of lust, her conception was unordinary to bring forth the Son of the Highest, Lord of Lords, and King of Kings. (Platt 2011, p. 1–5)

("The Gospel of the Birth of Mary," from *The Lost Books of the Bible*)

Therefore, in *conjugal love*, age fourteen and above is considered prudent, the consumation is lawful in God's law because that's the age God sowed seed to Virgin Mary. This explains the essence of God's law different from governing authorities law, and because there are many followers of the Christendom or Islam faith (Muslim's follow Muhammed who consummated A'isha at the age nine, before than A'isha was married to Muhammed at the age six; though I find this disturbing), not all individuals are governing law abiding citizens but God's law abiding citizens. Pedophilia in accurate biblical language is thirteen and below, although others individuals would protest dissensions between ages eleven to fourteen.

Excelling throughout Investment

For kings and princes that sometimes or maybe often pursue the female occasionally may become trapped in the web of friction. *Friction* is when a woman finds you attractive, but she perceives a value of differences or external circumstances that prevent further acting on attraction basis or sexual escalation, thereby she's suddenly no longer interested. Basically, she's sizing you up before she knows your depths. Sometimes friction can turn into a friend-zone complex, thereby enlisting a male on reserves listing and ignoring male pursuit. True confidence empowers journey prolong without acceptance of friction zone by moving forward and removal of bondage (not being a slave to friend zone). Learning to administer care to your mentality by not being bound but flowing like water without hindrance through emotional bondage that been established as friction.

The empirical reality is the unfortunate circumstance of choosing a woman who is very argumentative and abusive woman, "it is better to dwell in a corner of the housetop, than with a brawling woman in a wide house."[103] "It is better to dwell in the wilderness, than with a contentious and an angry woman."[104] Deliverance from a woman who you love dearly who has more **contentious** (means *an individual who indulges in provoking arguments or often causes an argument*) personality. Perhaps this prayer below may bring a relief and blessing to your contentious sufferings when you recite this prayer occasionally, pray for her or clarity:

Contentious Relief Prayer

Brethren (full name) calls upon Yahawah and Yahawashi,
From the Earthily Trinity: The Spirit, and the water, and the blood,
I come before you troubled with a contentious woman (full name),
Please grant serenity in this relationship for sake, so covenant may not break,
And give clarity to understand the anger while enlightening me to fix what I can,
In this covenant we call upon Adon Olam power to rebuke all evil spirits that provokes animosity,
And if it's not enough remove me from this union, let your will be done,
For you promised benevolence and a contentious woman is not benevolence;
In the covenant of the Trinity: The Father, the Son, and the Holy Spirit.
In the covenant of the Heaven Trinity: The Father, the Word, and the Holy Spirit. Amen.

---

[103]   Proverbs 21v9 King James Version.

[104]   Proverbs 21v19 King James Version.

Understanding Your Queen's Sexuality

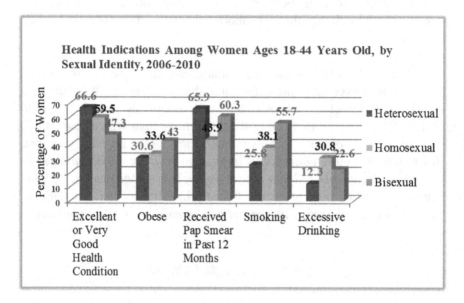

Figure 13-1 Indications of Effects on Women through Sexual Identity

Source: Chandra A, Copen CE, Stephen EH. "Infertility and impaired fecundity in the United States, 1982–2010: Data from the National Survey of Family Growth." National Health Statistics reports; no 67. Hyattsville, MD: National Center for Health Statistics. 2013.

According to the article "Why Are So Many Girls Lesbian or Bisexual?" the common estimation of women's sexual identity is 85.1 percent of young women are heterosexual, 0.5 percent reported nothing, and the remaining 14.4 percent sexually open to bisexual or lesbian intimacy. What I've learned from the Bible is that women are companions for men, and God intends on them marrying to a king, so truth is there's not a scripture but one that may give a rejection to bisexual women in Romans 1v26: "for this cause God gave them up unto vile affections: for even their women did change the natural use into that which is against nature," but these against natures can be bestiality, orgies, and prostitution. In addition, because there were many biblical men who were in polygyny marriage, there may have been often amorous lovemaking between wives who were lift unsatisfied or had lack of intimacy in eager moments. In my research and encounters, I come to understand that many women turn to bisexual or homosexuals because biologically, women investment paradox of men turned downward for them. Another reason is because women feel that no sex know the most pleasurable ways to fulfill satisfactions like another female do. Women lately all over media testify that they're more sexually fulfilled by the intimacy of another woman than a man. Third, some are just naturally attracted toward the female anatomy or been deviated by men influencing them with abuse or threats of leaving them to having sexual relations with another woman against their principality. Last but not least, child hood trauma or incarceration for long periods.

So is bisexual woman condemned of sin? Probably not, probably so, but the Bible didn't give an absolute certainty, only an absolute certainty on man-with-man condemnations; the optimistic investment on a bisexual woman is their more susceptible to submit to polygynous agreement. Lesbian is another story because it conflicts with procreation or having a covenant with a Adon as Adon Olam intended. Insight from my mother to me is that bisexual and lesbian women are still condemned of sin, and in context (Romans 1v26) God is referring to that, in her discernment. Conversely, I would debate on bisexual women because secretly there was once a woman that I was infatuated with that was bisexual at the time along with my thoughts that it was a benefactor to a potential polygynous relations (I confessed, please don't hold it against me!) and I disagreed that it was contextual, my opinion was the scripture (Romans 1v26) is a direct concordance with Leviticus 18v22 KJV: *"Thou shalt __not lie__ with __mankind__, as with __womankind__: it is abomination"* and by placing woman on thou, wouldn't condemn.

"__Woman__ shalt __not lie__ with __mankind__, as with __womankind__: it is abomination"

This made me think, "this doesn't add up." For how can woman not have sex with man as with woman, when indeed woman is made for man so what is the missing linkage, for woman has mouth, a Honey Pot, and a Hershey Highway. In context, God doesn't condemn husband to have his wife sexed upon a *Three-Hole Par*. In addition, during ancient times women didn't have dildos, all they had was the use of their mouth for kissing and oral intercourse of the Honey Pot and mankind doesn't biologically have a Honey Pot so in context it states what both men and women possess and nowhere in biblical context was there mentioned not to kiss. The unnatural in Leviticus 18v23: "Neither shalt thou lie with any beast to defile thyself therewith: neither shall any woman stand before a beast to lie down thereto: it is confusion." As contextual it clear that

Intimate Investment

women are condemned in the acts of bestiality. On the contrary, don't think all those biblical men and women would share their sex lives with you like Solomon, for they obviously weren't all like that, so excelled loving a woman that's bisexual is a personal sensibility and investment.

Shelley Lubben spoke of childhood trauma and lack of affection is the reason most princesses and queens turn to prostitution and because of abuse, they literally hate men. The only love they give because of this hate is pragmatic which most like to discern persona as gold diggers, and ludic love is another persona as long as the logic of financial profit is within the favor.

Empirically, there are women who have been treated like rent and objects and molested in early childhood, some predicaments the parent/'s were even aware and allowed it.

In the film *Black Snake Moan*, Lazarus (Samuel L. Jackson) played the *idol father* and *mentor* roles in *DD*, without the sexual intercourse to demonstrate Christian polyamory, love, and sensibility for Rae's (Christina Ricci) soul and sufferings. He helped her through her sexual addiction by showing resistance to her seduction and applying *Domestic Discipline (DD)* through chaining around her waist to prevent her from being a *nymphomaniac* and introducing her to faith through his best friend (who is a priest) then (starting approximate runtime of 01:15:14 to 01:50:20) removed the chains, giving her decision in freedom, and Rae asked Lazarus to play the guitar, during him playing the guitar she reminisced her traumatic rape experience, then later on, she developed a transformation by inspiration of Lazarus suffering and Ahavah and sympathize that everyone has a suffering they're trying to overcome, and Lazarus was her inspirer and adopted father. Lazarus gave Ronnie a symbolic wedding gift of gold chain to go around Rae's waist for symbolism of commitment for announced husband Ronnie (Justin Timberlake) to put around her as a symbolism for marriage, loyalty, faith, and transformation.

The lesson of this film is there are women who need love more intellectual, emotional, and spiritual than physical when they're in need of a transformation from within; otherwise, they'll think the Adon is an original, basically like all other men. If sensibility is given, she may develop a transformation.

Articulate Investment

Internalizing Loving Behaviors and Values

Choosing complementary opposites with important similarities gives stronger connections that may become everlasting.

Our companion for love is fueled by beauty, variety, pleasure principality, voluptuous nurturing Blossomed Pomegranates, Honey Pot, Sweet Mouth and Hershey Highway, mystery, and connection. According to **Felice Dunas** (Dunas, Ph.D. and Goldberg 1997), author of *Passion Play: Ancient Secrets for a Lifetime of Health and Happiness through Sensational Sex*, she discussed the common turn-on qualities for women are what "endures, such as stability, loyalty, and integrity." A treasures submissive's love is fueled by intimate capacities from Eros, with a spice of Thanatos, ardency, Storge love, and agapic loving, creativity of arts: the romance and masterful sexual positions, and revelations and desirable novelties. A potent aphrodisiac is for the queen to show her desire for the king in return because it motivates and inspires his position as a king. A common myth is that a man's heart is through his belly. The empirical reality is this is completely false. Truth is sexual satisfaction and loving gestures precede the primary of a man's heart because we're more visual beings and thrive coitus sensation, and this stimulates the sensibility that conveys the majority but also rationality. The bonus is when a woman can cook and perform housewife duties, but the revelation is chamber of intimacy. There's a common conception that power thrives from confidence. This is partly true, but the contrast is

> *Love is sacred, and sex is sacred too. The two things are not a part; they belong together.*
>
> *—Lame Deer, Lakota Indian holy man (1903–1976)*

between the false and the true, holding on to your *emunah* availeth much in confidence, not deceptions.

> **Sex is a holy thing, and one of the most marvelous revelations of the divine. (Alan Watts)**

Sex enhances the capacity for loving, allowing for a better determination of judgment. This revelation exchanges from what's agitating to what's bearable. In reverence, sociobiological view is beneficial in lovemaking because sex plays a huge role in our lives. Tangled emotions can evolve from lack of lovemaking, and this can make determinism difficult and prolong union difficult. Commonly for males, this ignites the *pleasure principle* and manic loving because the Weapon of Love urges to be nourished and feed, and without that satisfaction, it can go astray, looking for another woman. Then the Weapon of Love merges to swigging that of which is sex outside of commitment and fornicating with strange women, such as, prostitutes and promiscuous women outside of marriage. Say you as a man are having common stress issues that causes may cause heart problems. For instance, of a bad wife investment:

Prologue: *Angelo has a doctor's appointment with Dr. Douglas to receive diagnoses on the issue. His wife, Anastasia, insisted on being there with him to support him.*

Dr. Douglas: Mr. Angelo, I'm going to prescribe you a nerve relaxer. Do you mind waiting outside in the car while I address the nerve relaxer to your wife?

Mr. Angelo: Sure, Doctor, thanks for taking the time out to diagnose me.

Mrs. Anastasia: What's the formula doctor?

Dr. Douglas: Your husband is suffering from sexual depression, and this is interfering with his heart. Anastasia, in order for you to save your husband's life, you'll need to perform a blow job three times a day or have sexual intercourse three times a day. (*Anastasia leaves his office, walking toward the car.*)

Mr. Angelo: (*Anastasia gets in the car, while Angelo observed her expression.*) So, honey, what did Dr. Douglas say?

Mrs. Anastasia: I'm sorry honey, but it looks like you're going to die. Let's make sure your life insurance policy is well funded, and why where at it, let's upgrade it.

The sad truth is Mr. Angelo would be better off searching for a new wife or marrying another sacredly without the government affairs.

Empirically, many individuals would say that sex is not everything, and indeed, this is true, and anyone who says this should be applauded, for there is nothing that is everything but the Adon Olam. However, the importance of sex may not be the most important to various people, but it is the internal and external foundation (part of the Kabbalistic Tree of Life) of intimacy. On the contrary, our mentality should not be similar to James Bond (Daniel Craig) —the philanderer, from *Casino Royale* (Green and Craig 2006), from the psychological speculation of thinking "of women as disposable pleasures rather than meaningful pursuits" (01:01:56–01:02:01), the truth is on pardon of magnetism will likely become disposable when she's made her vessel a brothel, therefore, honor has become broken. It's wise and prudent for mankind not to construct ourselves as dominates (philanderers) but become Adonim, for this is the appreciation of womankind, not renting or deflowering then abandon them similar to the film *Kids (1995)*, for this makes womankind bitter, unless certain women agreed to allow themselves to be a *free lover* or *ludic lover* for the sake of *reality principle.*

<u>Sex is equated overall to these words:</u>

"Hunger, communion, union, mystery, bliss, aromatic or pungent, jubilation, fervent, emunah, feisty, forthright, impassioned, concupiscent, rapturous, naughty, hedonism, alluring, one flesh, artful, Ching-chi union of yin and yang, love, novelty, perspiration, euphoric, effusive, desire, prize, piquant, addictive, ecstasy, sensational, healing (therapeutic), mesmerizing, sensualism, fruitfulness (implies vigorous, potent, virility, and loving), lust, Thanatos, deviant, Eros, amorous, affection, ardent, and eagerness."

Chart 17-1: Primitive Sexology Acquainted Words

Intimate Investment

In the Karezza Method, sex is a framework of three.[105]

> **I.** First: Feed and rejuvenate by contact-pressure and a mysterious generation, interchange, and mutual exchange of subtle processes and forces.
> **II.** Physical reproduction-child creation.
> **III.** Soul-union, the mystery of love, affection, spiritual companionship, mental inspiration.

There are possibly many men and women who end up saying "I love you" in the art of sex, but they fear the repercussion, abandonment, and power not being exchanged. The important thing is to know your foundation (genitals) spoke a truth, for every moment of penetrative coitus you become in union with the other. Rilke expressed the artistry of sex is grand when love map is expressed amorous and undefiled (Rilke 1962, 31). For some strange reasons, certain individuals who live by the faith and eagerly had sex with another seem fueled with contempt and attrition, but the truth is "love covers a multitude of sins," so God knows your heart, and if it's committed to the significant other, then you're free of sin. An individual can be in a relationship with another person for some years and governmentally never signed a government contract of marriage, but a liberated person of the faith, "the sensible beings," should question who are they really signing for, God or the world? And if the answer is God, then create a personal contract or use the contract I've created (*see* Marriage Agreement Lifestyle), buy ring(s) to symbolically show devotion, vow to Adon Olam Yahawah together, and hold on to the emunah vowed. Train the mind to be transformed from world social constructions and the social pressures. A governmental marriage is based on insurance and stability of wealth and governing rights. A true Adon knows he doesn't need governmental construction of initiation of child support because of divorce and doesn't need reconciliation of sharing wealth with his consort. For he knows his responsibilities, our aim is to strive to be one with Adon Olam. Do you honestly think that Adon Olam and Adonai Yahawashi had someone administer to them to marry us?

> *"Sometimes when humanity think they've figured everything out and think they know just, a graven dimension is actually the conscious, and that graven is an error when it should be true is sometimes substantially different from our Creator."*

---

[105] J. William Lloyd. *The Karezza Method: The Art of Connubial Love*, pg. 21.

Part IV:

Conclusion

Chapter XVIII:
Humane Conclusion

"Reality strikes through a course of humane touch,
and that touch rectifies a stronger understanding of
the correspondence of divinity and human."

H umane conclusion is that despite the brainwashing the world
inflicts on another individual, it's up to the individual to rectify
its change without the forbiddance of feeling contempt for
others' ideologies on how an individual should address themselves with
liberation. Tides won't live in the same environment regardless if an
individual is un-understandable on its criteria or another doesn't approve
of its criteria. None learn the exact measure of another regardless of how
science fabricates statistics, but being in touch with individuality is the
first step to become the prowess within its nature.

This book is simply a guide, a truth of human behaviorism or the humane
of our mind being contempt upon that I've corresponded to open an
exchange of dissensions to positive discernment on certain criterions.
This book contains the three primary stages of life, which is the mind,
spiritual and intimacies. These are how we evolve, how we create, how we
develop faith, challenges we see and experience in life, the clarification of
church, Christian anarchism's liberation, discovers of Ahavah and cores
of domination and submission, develop domestic discipline, and many
other essential portions that needs to be acknowledge. This volume and
the proceeding volumes will be what I classify as an essence of true
theology, from a mixture of liberation, hedonism, naturalisms, humanity

constructive acknowledgements and while breaking the barriers with prudence, Loveology and different proportions of loving, more unveiled ideologies, studies, and extras (no spoilers).

As you've read through this book, I have faith there were many interesting and captivating insights. The point of the book is the break construction within yourselves while being true to your primal along with intelligent coordination. Truth is I provided limited examples in Part I and II because no one can live your life but you. Surely, the relations can correspond with you readers, but the technical portions of this book provides a truer direction, for it's the humanity's way to find the portions of their own. There's a great deal of lovemaking in this book, the point is the truth of being real and free yourselves from the mental anguish of suppression, repression, and compression. While fully opening up to your primitive nature, many individuals will oppose another with contempt if they don't agree with its nature, but the nature being true to itself frees itself from a ghetto. This makes distinction. Kings, queens, princes, and princesses don't allow your mind to be constructed on how you should love if you have faith that is completely liberated in accordance to Adon Olam's word. Excelling in perseverance is a preservice to having a hedonistic life, a way of freeing oneself from construction, from the dissensions of negativity others try to cultivate within your psyche, and of all, an investment within. Make sure you read *Appendix I* for biblical conspiracies and *Appendix II* for the core of domination and submission as an expanded portion to "Part III: Sensual Adon Lovemaking."

Appendix J:
Bible Conspiracies

"As Christian, we must seek the truth in the truth is very narrow, but it's a constant hustle for truth from Yahweh's Word."

B ible conspiracies and faith warfare constantly surround Christians and Jews. Few true Bible against the many versions, the empirical realism is that Christianity and Jews are often in constant attack, but Christianity perhaps even more. Often, Christians may be questioned by heathens on the various conspiracies of the Bible. A question that often comes up is

How can you help spread the truth when your Bible has over fifty versions? How do you know which ones is true? Which is the one? And which are forged into negative deviance?

There are many alternative versions of insinuated Holy Bibles, but only very few with 95 to 100 plus percent accuracy (the reason for that 5 percent less is because there's always the theological pursuit of more hidden, grammar and fragment errors, or missing text scholars look for); however, Dr. Bart D. Ehrman would disagree with this because the fragments from which is was translated always has a possibility of not being the same as the original manuscript of the New Testament. Brilliant Dr. Bart D. Ehrman wrote about in his book, *Jesus Apocalyptic Prophet of the New Millennium*, discussed the different viewpoints along with distinction of the original text, which is unknown to the copied text. The reason for many Bible versions is to implement a New World Order agenda, mislead many from faith, and portray making new versions understandable while corrupting Yahawah manuscript. If you haven't noticed, almost every president or supreme leader or politician has mention a New World Order. Even in music, there's a constant portraying influence of a New World Order. The Authorized King James Version has not changed in literacy of the King James 1611 Version, only been perfected from the common misspells and punctuations, although I leave this to your determinism. Please keep in mind these scriptures through other versions are just a portion of forgery and corruption but used these common translations to make my point of the evil deity.

Biblical Verses	True Doctrines	Other Versions
2 Corinthians 5v17	**King James Version** "Therefore if any man be in Christ, He is a New Creature: Old Things Are Passed away; Behold All Things are Become new."	**New English Bible** "The old order is gone and a New Order has Begun."
Hebrews (Yehudim) 9v10	**King James Version** "until the time of Reformation." **Orthodox Jewish Bible** "until the time of the Tikkun (Restoration)."	**New International Version** "until the time of The New Order." **Good News Translation** "will establish the new order." **New English Translation** "until the new order came." **Common English Bible** "new order." **New American Bible (RE)** "time of the new order."

	King James Version	New Century Version
Romans (Rome) 13v1	"Let <u>every soul be</u> <u>subject unto the higher</u> <u>powers. For there is</u> <u>no power but of God</u>: the powers that be are ordained of God."	"All of you must <u>yield</u> <u>to the</u> <u>governing rules.</u> <u>No one rules unless</u> <u>God has given him</u> <u>the Power to rule,</u> no one rules . . ."
	Orthodox Jewish Bible	**New Living Translation**
	"Let <u>'every soul,</u> <u>person' be subject to</u> <u>the official governing</u> <u>authorities.</u> For there is <u>no 'government'</u> <u>except given by</u> <u>Hashem (God),</u> and the powers that be have been established by God."	"Everyone must <u>submit to governing</u> <u>authorities.</u> For All authority comes from God . . ."
		The Message
		Be a good citizen. <u>All - governments</u> <u>are under God . . ."</u>

We're going to focus on the popular version on the shelves setting aside the KJV. The New International Version (NIV), English Standard Version (ESV), New Living Translation (NLT), and other versions like Common English Bible (CEB), American Standard Version (ASV), Complete Jewish Bible (CJB), Darby Translation (DARBY), English Standard Version Anglicised (ESVUK), Lexham English Bible (LEB), and New Revised Standard Version, Anglicised Catholic Edition (NRSVACE) are missing thirteen verses that has been purposely been withdrawn from the true doctrine.

Scriptures Forged from YHWH's Doctrine

"Matt. 17v21, Luke 17v36, Matt. 23v14, John 5v4, Mark 7v16, Acts 8v37, Acts 15v34, Acts 24v7, Acts 28v29, Mark 9v44, Mark 9v46, Mark 11v26, Mark 15v28, Romans 16v24"

Those scriptures have all been purposely altered to reject the doctrine of Christology and prepare for a New World order (preparing for the *Anti-Christ* means son of perdition). Take great notice that there are fewer KJV

Bibles in common bookstores but much more NIV, ESV, and NLT. It's all part of the marketing strategy and deception to feed the minds in a matter of construction to form doubts and a new order.

New King James Version is the most dangerous for controversy of the New Testament portions, for it removes the word "Lord" sixty-six times, removes the word "God" fifty-one times, removes word "heaven" fifty times, removes the word "repent" forty-four times, removes the word "blood" twenty-three times, removes the word "hell" twenty-two times, and completely omits the words "Jehovah," "Damnation," "New Testament," and "Devils."

The caution of why it can be controversially dangerous is because, the word "hell," is changed to "Sheol" or "Hades." Though the word "Hades" not everyone is familiar with and causes a misleading study to others on the Greek god "Hades," who is also known as "Pluto," while "hell," is a spiritually rooted environment of an overall torment, fear, hopelessness and evil of an environment built of fire and brimstone, but Sheol validates the meaning of "hell" according to the Jewish Encyclopedia[106].

Verses were the word "hell" is removed:
2 Sam. 22v6, Job 11v8, 26v6, Psalm 16v10, 18v5, 86v13, 116v3, Isaiah 5v14, 14v15, 28v15 and 18, 57v9, Jonah 2v2, Matt. 11v23, 16v18, Luke 10v15, 16v23, Acts 2v27 and 31, Revelation 1v18, 6v8, 20v13 and 14

The word "repent" was changed to "relent," "remorseful," and "irrevocable" which don't all mean the same thing, so this cause a little misunderstanding of teleological mission the scriptures are pointing out and that's the yielding fervency to create a transformation within ourselves while turning from past transgressions; so on a personal determinism the word "repent" suffices, hopefully it will for you'll to.

Certain revisions of the scriptures created perversions for the purpose of equal dominion in sexism in all things, for instance Genesis 2v18 changed from "I will make a help meet" (KJV) to "I will make a helper comparable to him" (NKJV), giving an alteration that the woman is equivalent in all ways which revokes the law of God in matters of marital rights that the man is the head (1 Corinthians 11v3), denies submission for dominance (why because it forms competitiveness), and subverts femininity in woman to being capable of masculinity in woman because of perversion of altering scripture to proportionality (so it has become feminist friendly). However, if previous scripture is interpreted as a queen

---

[106] Jewish Encyclopedia source: http://www.jewishencyclopedia.com/articles/13563-sheol

that will make the king whole than it's good because there are edges were the woman is strong in than the man and vice versa, others would urge also it's a matter of physics (ontology) of the physiology as well. Another perversion is John 4v24 "God is a Spirit . . ." (KJV) to "God is Spirit . . ." (NKJV), this may not seem like much but the *a* is very important because without it, they're qualifying God as a mixture of all Spirits which would mean both of evil and good or that man himself is God, much like Freemasonry when stated in *The Lost Keys of Freemasonry* by Manly P. Hall, "Man is a God in the making . . ."

- Do you believe in the holy trinity, because how can there be three Gods in one? Is it possible that Lucifer is coordinator?

Higher-ups agenda is to promote an evil deity of reformation to hopelessness to become vulnerable to a new order and misguided minds through social construction. Newer translation in fact commits evil deity through implementing that Jesus Christ not born from a virgin but born like everyone else through Luke 2v33 (NIV, ESV, and NLT), recommend using the King James Version to contrast this; for it says in the KJV "And Joseph and his mother . . .," not "The child's father and mother . . ." (NIV), "And his father and his mother . . ." (ESV) nor "Jesus' parents . . ." (NLT). This has been altered to make the gospel a lie, insinuating he wasn't created without the mother's virginity given to Joseph or any man. It's crucial to the doctrine that he's from everlasting (Micah 5v2 KJV "have been from of old, from everlasting.") not created as an average man (Micah 5v2 NIV "whose <u>origins</u> are from of old, <u>from ancient times.</u>"), the illusion is that word "origins" and phase from ancient times means a place of birth or early beginnings, and from everlasting means, he is infinite (the omega).

Prime examples they've rejected Christ doctrine:
Acts 8v36–37
Kings James Version – "[36]And as they went on their way, they came unto a certain water: and the eunuch said, See, here is water; what doth hinder me to be baptized? [37]And Philip said, If thou believest with all thine heart, thou mayest. And he answered and said, I believe that Jesus Christ is the Son of God."
New International Version – "[36]As they traveled along the road, they came to some water and the eunuch said, "Look, here is water. What can stand in the way of my being baptized? (Verse 37 is omitted) [38]And he gave orders to stop the chariot. Then both Philip and the eunuch went

down into the water and Philip baptized him." (They have with driven the quantity of faith. You can't just go dip into the water and be baptized. You're required to believe who is the Son of God "Jesus Christ.")

1 John 5v7
Kings James Version – "For there are three that bear record in heaven, the Father, the Word, and the Holy Ghost: and these three are one."
New International Version – "For there are three that testify:" (look at the contrasting difference, and you will notice it implements uncertainty because it provides illusion on the trinity. Yet it doesn't even clarify who the three are, so this confuses newly Christian believers, causing doubt thereby they're more prone to convert their faith to Islam or Judaism).

Hebrews 1v8
Kings James Version – "But **unto the Son** *he saith,* Thy throne, O God, *is* for ever and ever . . ."
New International Version – "But about the Son he says, Your throne, O God, will last for ever and ever . . ." (This deity is forgery to believing that throne was not for the Son and resents his position as the Son of God. The KJV clarifies his position, while NIV gives an illusion and confusion.)
New World Translation – "But with reference to the Son: "God is your throne forever and ever . . ." (This deity rejects Christ position as the Son of God).

Evil deity claimed to be the Son of Morning Star in Isaiah 14v12 KJV "How art thou fallen from heaven, O Lucifer, son of the morning! *how* art thou cut down to the ground, which didst weaken the nations!" Lucifer tried to correlate this title in Isaiah 14v12–13 KJV, but his evil deity was discovered and was cast out of heaven Isaiah 14v14–23.
The New International Version, Isaiah 14v12 states "How you have fallen from heaven, **morning star,** son of the dawn! You have been cast down to the earth, you who once laid low the nations!" (Take notice that there calling Lucifer the son of God. This is blasphemy because there's only one who can carry the title Morning Star.)
In **Revelation 22v16 KJV,** Jesus announces his title.
"I Jesus have sent mine angel to testify unto you these things in the churches. I am **the root** and **the offspring of David,** and **the bright ~~and~~ morning star.**" The conjunction of another and word was actually mistakenly placed.
This is another big deception because some saints and others believe that Lucifer is the light bringer, the God of Intellect, thou it is actually Christ

that's the light (John 8v12 KJV). Higher-ups have projected confusion among the saints that know no better and the experienced ones to make people of faith defenseless. This is an agenda to cause confusion because the Luciferian agenda is to turn Christ's followers against one another by disarming them the true Word of God.

Versions that commit evil deity through self-flagellation:
The King James Version 1 Corinthians 9v27 says,
"But I keep under my body, and bring it into subjection: lest that by any means, when I have preached to others, I myself should be a castaway."
Contrasting from KJV, the NIV says, "I beat my body . . ."; Amplified version "But (like a boxer) I buffet my body (handle it roughly, discipline it by hardships) and subdue it . . ."; and the Common English Bible "Rather I'm landing punches on my own body and subduing it like a slave . . ."
The King James Version Galatians 5v12 Paul's Doctrine says,
"I would they were even cut off which trouble you."
Contrasting from the KJV Paul's Doctrine the NIV Galatians 5v12, says,
"As for those agitators, I wish they would go the whole way and emasculate themselves!"
Common English Bible Galatians 5v12 Paul's Doctrine says,
"I wish that the ones who are upsetting you would castrate themselves!"
Contemporary English Version Galatians 5v12 Paul's Doctrine says,
"I wish that everyone who is upsetting you would not only get circumcised, but would cut off much more!"

Prophecy warning:
2 Thessalonians 2v3 KJV "Let no man deceive you by any means: for that day shall not come, except there comes a **falling away first**, and that man of sin be revealed, the son of perdition." This implies a falling away of loss of hope and faith, confusion and havoc, and during this falling away, Lucifer is appealed to the nation as the new hope and savior while declaring he is God. Falling away is promoting a New World Order; a union controlled with the Luciferian philosophy and religion and Lucifer himself.

Times will eventually get worst when we think they'll become better. Look around, and you'll notice terrorism is growing worst on the East. Western individuals sometimes think they're safe, but gangs are becoming more dangerous and ruthless, prisons are overfilled now the government is allowing many reduced time (which can be good for the one's seeking redemption and changeable resolution to do right but havoc to many individuals who may become victim because of real malice felons that have the intention to repeat evil morals), and religion corrupting vessels to behead Christians and Jews.

Histories of Our Bibles
The first was the Erasmus' Greek/Latin New Testament written 1516 non-English translation, second was The New Testament translated by William Tyndale written 1534 from Greek/Hebrew to English but wasn't completed because the Higher-ups crucified him. Then Myles Coverdale finished Tyndale's translation and named the Bible, The Coverdale Bible. The reformers of John Calvin, such as, William Whitingham and others who created the Geneva Bible written in 1560. The *1599 Geneva Bible (GNV)*, which a vast amount of individuals preferred because it was translated without favorable admission of governing authorities but for the people; the pilgrims and puritans preferred GNV translation. During the time of Queen Elizabeth, she authorized The Bishops Bible, which was a constructive deity to be authoritative but was disapproving by the eyes of the people. Then King James the VI of Scotland brought upon a new translation with the 54 best scholars who knew a multitude of languages to translate perfection. The Old Testament was translated from Hebrew and New Testament from Greek, and the King James Version was the preceding of strong doctrine accuracy in proper English.

Determinism is left to you who read this!
Higher-ups have also not only removed certain verses. They have also commentary certain verses like John 7v53–8v11, and many other biblical exegeses have implemented that certain doctrines may not be true, causing people of faith to doubt. Hopefully, after everyone has read through this did some research on the Bible, you'll decide the King James Version is one superior for highest accuracy of true doctrine.

#1st Word-for-word English translations is the *King James Bible* (KJV or AKJV: Authorized King James Version) and The *Orthodox Study Bible* (however, I suggest being observant with the NKJV New Testament portion, the Old Testament portion defers because it's from Saint Athanasius Academy Septuagint). Originally, the Apocrypha was included when it was authorized by King James the VI of Scotland. This version was translated by Anglicans, Mainline/British, and conservative, and the deity of Christ is strongly informed. The KJV 1611 had many misspellings, punctuations, and grammar errors, but the revised version (1885) fixed those errors. In deeper research, you'll notice a very, a portion of errors for wording, but variation maybe more of errors, brilliant scholar Dr. James R. White informed in his book *The King James Only Controversy: Can You Trust Modern Translations,* such as the New Testament translators substituted Ahavah (Hebrew word) meaning <u>love,</u> <u>agape</u> (Greek word) to mean either <u>charity or love</u>. They commonly choose <u>charity</u> when the word "love" was highly prized best suited for certain parts of the doctrine. The **Orthodox Jewish Bible** (OJB) is considered extremely valued according to my discernment alongside the *KJV, GNV,* and *Orthodox Study Bible* for its strong accuracy and treasures of meanings (demonstrating there's more to the Hebrew and Aramaic words than what was chosen from the KJV translators along with identifying the errors) and belief that is conservatively translated as the discernable Bible, however this is left to an individual's determinism. Although I'm disagreeable with a small portion of the OJB, particularly on the *Book of Revelation (Hisgalus).* Therefore, I'm more in agreement with the *AKJV, GNV, Orthodox Study Bible,* and discernably *OJB.*

#2nd Word for word would be the *Holman Christian Standard Bible* (HCSB) **or** *New American Standard Bible* (NASB). Both versions were translated by Evangelicals and Conservatives.

#1st Intellectual-based English translation is the *New Living Translation* (NLT). The deity of Christ is strong, but an adjustment is needed, for there are fourteen scriptures missing. Although there are some errors with *NLT,* it still consists of strong accuracy and is a very strong measured Bible to study for beginners, children, and adolescent individuals, and makes a decent side study Bible when you're reading the *AKJV, GNV* or *Orthodox Study Bible* if you're having difficulty understanding, but I would recommend a dictionary and intensive research. *NLT* version was translated by Evangelicals and Conservatives.

Appendix II:
Core of Domination and Submission

"The preliminary to Adon and Submission is the humility to understand nature and the provocative proclivities it has to offer."

Warning! This appendix may be inappropriate for certain ages.

Section I: Loveology in its Nature

Based on what I've learned from my elders is that women are often evaluating through emotion and this makes them irrational mostly. Emotion is inevitably theoretical in any circumstance and those emotional responses are sometimes dramatic. The issue is why don't we theoretically know our structure in the most sensual matters, the matriarch of our primitive roots from the aesthetic realism prospective?

Majority of us men want our power play affirmed, while a great proportion of women want their submissive value affirmed. Thus, meaning mankind often wants the resurgence and reverence to feeling we're the dominions and noblemen. While womankind often wants the venerability and value of feeling they're treasury and graced. One is the prize and the other is the treasure. These two are differential, for mankind desires to be more so grand while womankind desires to be more so honored.

Only men need to be loved . . . women need to be wanted.

(Gemma Teller Morrow [Katey Sagal], from Sons of Anarchy)

Submission within wife toward the husband is the disposition of open love toward the Adon with honor and affirmation of his Adon path and priesthood amenable to her husband's will to the finest of her vessel's ability, sensibility, and gifts. The distinguishing of the primitive sexual reactance derives from the amount of estrogen in the woman that gives the psychological reactance of docility, meekness, and assent receptively; and the amount of testosterone in the man that gives psychological reactance of aggression, cardinality (these cardinalities are to breed, to govern, and to sanctify reality principle), and assent sensuality. Although both mankind and womankind desire communion amongst intimacy, though some of us men may be a keeper of solidity; however, we have the conscious tendency to open to communion as well when we fight our shadow. On the contrary, both womankind and mankind have the physiological and emotional reactance to sanctify themselves with passionate and companionate love, Ahavah, and breathe ardency. An individual may ask, what makes ardent loving so essential? Though to clarify reason one must understand what comes with that in its nature. Ardency is the feel of accepting another regardless of imperfections and admires beauty in the natures that sensualize mostly to the other. Testing the positivity and giving the other grace in ways of pleasure and love; these pleasures and loves can be the physical, emotional and spiritual in the most sensual matters. Take notice though that emotion come in many forms; for emotions are inevitable through passion, aggression, docility, and sexual. Sex is primitively boundless when it feels liberated between the beings and the divine; it's all on the matter of provocative proclivities, what generates arousal to sexual ecstasy and communion of love. **Provocative proclivity** is a potential arousing intimate desire with submission to Adon and assertive urge to merge desire into a continuous fervent action or discover if it's an approval or disapproval in sensuality of love. This intimate nature is a connection of sexual ecstasy. **Sexual ecstasy** is a difficult understandable love act to grasp because it's the nature of emotion, physiology and sensuality; sexual ecstasy is a redemptive and connective flow of coition thrusts, Arcanum desire, Eros, submissive servility or dominant-aggression of desire, a mixture of sadomasochism, sybaritic and addiction. Now, doesn't that classify as a little difficult? Sexual ecstasy is perhaps one of the true forms of sexual primitives.

All of this is the **gospel of intimate primitive humankind.**

In reality perhaps many of mankind have the hardened heart to give womankind their heart figuratively speaking so the important factor to note is a hardened heart is the subjective of shield when womankind long for the desire of vulnerability. Sensuality must be present in order for true love to take form; because there are many definitions of true love, I'll like to refer you'll to chart 12-1: *Loveology Acquainted Words* for the forms true love takes hold and for coitus portion of true love see chart 17-1: *Primitive Sexology Acquainted Words*; for the combination of both charts gives true love strong form. For true love, gives no occasional love but love frequently; truth is even in the mist of true love there are unsmooth edges in life that will more likely be tested from inevitable situations and all will depend on fidelity of the union. The clarity understands that all beings have imperfections, either or all, from the physical, mental, faith and emotional proportions, it's all on what form the imperfections take hold, but love does its best preserve emunah in these imperfections. Why emunah? Because the truth is first owning our own understanding of who we are in the mental, emotional and sexual, and then bringing it unto the opening rather its receptive or rejected from the viewpoint of another at least you've freed yourselves without sublimation.

For instance, back in 2014 there was a woman that told me her past sexual relations with her former boyfriend who she given implication of satisfaction from analingus stimulation done towards her. Though I was disgusted by this, a small sense of honor I've given to her experience on the matter of honest practice but the truth is even though I've found this disgusting I made a sincere dissension and that was no part a desire nor sexual arousal I'm willing to perform. Though a woman may not want to hear non-negotiable dissensions and actions don't mean it should be sublimated, for if you don't give truth then she would expect its acceptable or an allowed construction on your behalf. This is true in everything, for if an individual doesn't oppose the dissensions and actions then it manifests already a personal consent another's mind. A man may encounter a woman that's a strong masochist that desired to be slapped on the face; however, the man may not feel comfortable performing such act and may feel a personal conviction. The essence of truth is not everyone in an exclusive relationship is going to live up to the desires of the one they're in an intimate relationship with. Women are more likely to submit than a man in such matters but for the most part it's important to focus on the sensualism attraction (see chart 12-1 *Flow of Attraction*), to know what you tolerate before engaging.

Conversely

Be skeptical of subversive brainwashing from influences, persuading sexual immoral sins, for those influences cause more damage than good when in an intimate relationship. One of the famous shows that brings about a subverting influence of sexual immorality would be shows like *Sex and the City* for it **creates a subverting mentality from ancestry traditionalism of fidelity and biblical authority into a modernity of opening brainwashed women up into infidelity and use of glamor to seduce men to what seems pragmatic to the mind while disregarding the honor of the sexual exclusive relationship** (meaning the one-flesh loyal-heirs) **for the impulse of sexual fluidity thereby deeming themselves as potential courtesans (concubines) or paramour.** In addition, the reality is it's not always the woman but the man that receives these subverting brainwash ideologies, thereby becoming courtesans, womanizers or infidels as well. Subversively some shows offer another type of sexual orientation, such as lesbian sexuality, shows like *The L Word.* Pragmatic is simply a way of saying what's disregarding from the heart to what's regarded more for the mind, loving in a way based on another's wealth, company (based on amount of friends or important individuals in the other's atmosphere; popularity) and importance.

Doctrine of Honor

Honor is a misleading subject because what an individual hears today as honor is the submission to obey and provide servility without thinking but action to what is asked. Honor in intimacy is what the submissive is regarded to provide servility but not so in everything else outside of marriage (or intimate relationship). Although honor for womanhood, woman is not honored by modest appeal of expensive ornaments and clothing but through her decency and sobriety, with prudency of *good works* and meekness in submission toward the Adon (cf. 1 Timothy 2v9–12). Furthermore, Adon Olam expects this same order from manhood toward Adonai Christ Yahawashi and Adon Olam Yahawah, order of not valued by modest appeal but love of the heart in humbles of the Spirit to honor God (cf. 1 Peter 3v3–4). Honor in the Bible was specifically given in context of giving a strong warm approval with the conscience of determinism to best evaluate if what's asked, what's positioned, what's charitable and what's rationally best of interest liberated or typically loving to the best of that person's interest or legally titled through vows to preserve ourselves fidelity [marital *dharma*(s)]. Honour is also the regard of ardency because of the consistence of favor with good works, which is the fondness, support, and assent to another. Honor is sensible. Conjugal honor is *sybaritic*. Honor is perceiving a purpose of challenging an ardency of seeing another as important or special, being honest, perceiving high principle, regarding a privilege of pleasure with fulfilled obligation and kept agreement, an expression of sincerities and overall emunah through verb context which is to be faithful to, comply with, be true to, act in accordance with, and effectuation. Honour in an intimate sense is being a keeper of discretion to sanctify our transgressions (Proverbs 19v11) and making much effort to humble ourselves to achieve wisdom (Proverbs 14v29); otherwise, the adversary will attempt to take a man's or woman's honour. Think in this way; say a man brags about his queen's performance in the bedroom to an insinuated male friend and the supposedly friend is looking after his own pleasure to attempt to aggress to fornicate with that man's queen. What do you think the man did wrong? The answer is he provoked a lascivious behavior in the other man about the woman he was already secretly curious about; then actions of sexual immorality take place, such as the possibility of infidelity, provocative lust and deceptions, thereby pre-creating a snake to attempt to steal your possessions. And vice versa with women, for women can experience this same type of deception.

Doctrine of Aggression (Thanatos)

Aggression is somewhat a complicated emotional impulse for its what form it takes that can lead to a little badness or assertion, but that's what forms interest at moments and then when aggressive tension is released it sanctifies itself or a repercussion of guilt forms. Aggression is a direct link to three portions; the physical, verbal, and mental. The purpose of aggression is to assert dominance, to subdue another, to initiate desire, to guard, to possess, and to fulfil sexual ecstasy. Aggression is also impulsively an *innate propensity* of *reality principle*. The evolution of desire is mostly derived from the aggression and aggression (Thanatos) is a part of love and death. The negative exergy is when an individual uses wealth to buy love; this is a form of negative aggression. Love has a great *vehement* flame and has a natural tendency of jealousy; this is a form of aggression (cf. Song of Solomon 8v6–7). **Vehement** means revealing strong emotions; forceful, passionate, or penetrating (piercingly intense). Mankind is more likely to engage in aggression than womankind, however, as I previously stated in *Becoming Lord of Sexual Roots*, certain women are prone to unleashing their sexual aggression to achieve sexual ecstasy. Thereby, the aggressive woman is not prone to relying on their intimate partner, for their assertion is more erotic satisfaction. For instance, if an aggressive woman doesn't achieve sexual satisfaction from a man she's intimate with she'll assert female dominance by taking sexual control; normally, she'll transform herself unto a passionate fellatrix than create a *switch* (*see The Switch Philosophy*) with cowgirl position to fulfill her sexual ecstasy. Mankind and womankind are all capable of aggression, sometimes aggression is used to sustain relationship, for instance, when passion is not invested in a relationship anymore and the man is slowly withdrawing from the covenants of intimacy and the woman becomes impulsive, demanding quality time and intimacy for the sake of love and reality principle, while at the same time she's making effort to save her lover from adultery and the sexual immorality *causes* (p. 304); this is a form of liberated aggression. A man being protective of his queen by giving her a curfew or asserting a demand that she has to wear presentable clothing to prevent lascivious behavior around men in public; this is an act of liberated aggression. In moments of aggression, sometimes there's audacity but audacity can be genuinely of good works or ineptitudes. When sex life becomes an impulsive power play in unexplainable tensions; this is an act of undefiled aggression. When an individual defends their mate's viewpoint for the sake of ardent approval, this is an act of liberated aggression. Aggression is the sheer form of evolution by a way of saying you know where you stand, what you want, who you're fighting for, the motive of audacity, a faith, a confidence, an assertion of hope and a love. Intimate love itself is a prelude of ownership for both man and woman that are relational with fair intimacy in primitive emotions, much like the authority of Song of Solomon 6v3, "I am my beloved's, and my beloved is mine; . . ." for this is a sheer form of aggression. So the question is why is aggression blown out of context into something of battering, when truly aggression can be a liberated emotion of the physical, verbal, and mental but also the spiritual? The answer is construction and to bring contempt up. Its spiritual in a way of saying in an intimate relationship that the, "we," need to assert prayer and study from the Word to develop stronger council, communicate, elevate love lifestyle, or study on ways to obtain sensibility.

Prophecy, Reason Why I've Discussed Primitives

During one of my momentarily studies of *The Kolbrin Bible* (note: *The Kolbrin* and *The Gospel of Kailedy* are the complete authorized versions according to Culdian), I've come across a prophecy from Adonai Christ Yahawashi and what was said had to be from him because it's happening currently. Adonai Christ Yahawashi foretold how the end of times will be with the Spirits captured by the revelation of truth, when he prophesized saying;

> Brotherhood shall lose its stronghold. Men will become effeminate, while women will become like men. Adultery will not be frowned upon nor fornication. Men will not honor their country and discrimination will be ended, and no purity of race will be maintained. Father's and mother's will be disregarded as honored, and sons and daughters will be mentored to become wayward. Perversions will be influenced, and lawbreakers will ridicule the law. There will be incest and defiling sexual assaults, making it dangerous to walk abroad. Floods, scarcity of food and water and earthquakes will cause havoc and death: Unusual sicknesses will plague on individuals and individuals will reject the existence of God. Infants will be murdered in the womb. Men will act lascivious after the wives of other men and marriage shall disorder its purpose. Women will pursue ordination of marriage "unchaste with deceit in their hearts." While their husbands' pity from poor discernment of *fair* woman in choice, while other men manipulate husbands of pity with delight of their pity. Priest will profane priesthood with disregard of prudency, governing authorities will be positioned with little regard. Mankind and womankind progressively creates the abyss for themselves, shaping end of times, not God.

(BRT [The Britain Book]: 3v55–56, from *The Kolbrin Bible*)

When I look around my environment and hear news from masses of media, this is exactly matching the prophecy of what Adonai Christ Yahawashi foretold. Thou, not all prophecy is bad, particularly "nor maintain the purity of their races" because their many parts in the Bible that discussed interracial marriages and the fact that we should not discriminate but follow the heart. One biblical example would be Moses, when he married an Ethiopian woman, Moses sister, Miriam and brother, Aaron, were both discriminative on the interracial marriage and Adon Olam Yahawah was displeased with they're prejudices, so brought upon a disease of leprosy upon Miriam to teach them a lesson (Numbers 12v1–6). Adonai Christ Yahawashi didn't give that portion of prophecy as an act of discrimination or prejudices conceit but a simple primitive of saying a proportion of men won't desire their same ethnicity but will desire a different ethnicity; it's simply agape fulfilling its nature. However, I've encountered certain Israelites who will protest to their race purity but live in the illusion of purity, for truth is many of our ancestral women were raped or perhaps willing to intermingle and disregarding the skin, and looking into the bloodline perhaps the majority will discover theirs no purity of a complete ethnicity or Israelite tribe, even when us certain individuals carry the bloodline of Israelites.

Faithful Love Slave and Submissive

Certain women are natural *faithful love slaves* or grand submissive's in intimacy because of the servility nature, for certain women, servicing their lover is more gratifying to them then servicing themselves so in essence they'll have the innate nature of agape and ardency. The nature of slave is servicing better rather than vindictive actions for personal liberation and authority. The submission desires the novelty of devotional acceptance (the ardent) and privacy in the euphoria of lovable actions she's yielding to surrender. Slave and submissive women can have in inducing coping psychological reactance of similar *Stockholm Syndrome* "capture-bonding," in a way were they'll be very empathic and sympathize from emotional attachment of their sovereign, manipulate as if their defenseless—the inner persona of guilt-free loving, gives acceptance and love through giving receptivity, passiveness and openness towards the aggressor thereby making the aggressor feel liberated. *Stockholm syndrome* is psychological reactance of captives giving empathy and sympathy with positive emotion towards their captors thereby defending the captors' (aggressors) philosophy and actions making them liberated. Certain individual submissive's with capture-bonding trait has deemed themselves as masochist. The important portion is for the submissive or love slave to know her value, for its wrong for her to induce that type of psychological reactance with the aggressor who is not her devotee (Adon), forced into real sexual slavery or who has been brutally beating her or bring contempt upon her.

Submissive women and *faithful love slaves* are very prudent to the divine conduct as a ministry of *conjugal love* for servility for they've induced themselves to become completely receptive, passive, and open for the mate's needs, thereby obeying the divine word:

> *Doing nothing according to anochiyut (selfishness) nor according to empty ga'avah (conceit, haughtiness, arrogance), but in anavah (humility), fergin (graciously grant) each other esteem above yourselves. (Philippi [Philippians] 2v3 OJB)*

The clarity of this message is not making the mate suffer in mating needs, proves they are individual that cares about the fidelity of the union and preserving another's soul from prevention of sexual immorality. Submissive's and *faithful love slaves* are keepers of remaining menpleasers for the sake of sensibility (cf. Colossians 3v22–24). Though this doesn't guarantee that the submissive or faithful love slave will obey every demand and whims of the Adon, she's more honored for giving grace of servility with expressing agape, amorous, ardency, companionate and passionate love toward the Adon that makes her cherished. In accordance the individual proves humility because they've receptively granted their intimate partner the *gospel of intimate primitive humankind* honored servility. This scripture above can be very difficult to perhaps many of us men and women because sexual satisfaction is often a selfish motive of eagerness to grasp connection, love, and to fulfill reality principle. Certain misogynists may have difficulty with this scripture if the individual's philosophy is to discipline a woman through treating them as sex objects, or egocentric because of not rewarding their woman with loving gestures in return momentarily or casually: loving gestures can be certain intimate acts she finds awarding like eloquent dates, gentleness and aftercare of communication; depending on financial situation, awards can be also precious jewels. Furthermore, certain misogynist has sadism of vain conceits that influences disposability of women, and vice versa, for certain feminist have this vain conceit toward men. Conversely, as men we must realize not all women are materialistic, which is an abundant blessing from Yahawah to have such a woman because not all thrive on the returning rewards of precious jewels, constant investment of expensive furniture and clothing when already wealthy in those criterions, or technological enthusiast (for instance, every year seeking to buy a new IPhone or Android). Alternatively, certain submissive women desire rewards of spiritual love investments such as incenses, casual wine and dining lifestyle, oils or perfumes, flowers, paid spa arrangements, and natural or organic esthetic cosmetic beauty supplies.

The Adon reward purpose is to make known casually his affection for the submissive or *faithful love slave* through beautifying her verbally, charitably or physically. In the feminist agenda, it's about a controlling power of seeking submissiveness in motions of selfish ambition or vain conceit from men through rejection of passiveness, openness and receptivity with strife toward the man through *negative reinforcement*, through creating sexual intercourse waiting periods while the male mate suffers with *suppression effect* to give an illusion of power or the need of worshipping her to receive favor. What makes it negative reinforcement is because the more build-up of *suppression effect*, there's a high probability that the man is going to swing because man's nature can't be programed to be submissive above the *reality principle* no matter how many books or other masses of media alter a false illusion of mankind being completely submissive and controlled to female dominance. A submissive and faithful love slave woman takes heed to the "do not deprive each other" (1 Corinthians 7v5). Why? Because of the *reality principle, prudency* and men itself connects love with sex and without love, sex is the urgency left to grasp for a piece of sensual passion.

The power of submission from a woman to her Adon, graces her as treasure because of her docility, meekness, amenable masochism favors and assent receptivity because of the heart and mentality of will for love to meet the demands of the Adon. Submission from the queen is 90 to 100 percent plus emunah base for the sexual intimacy portion; the remaining 10 percent is for the woman to make the choice of leaving if he's traumatizing her scornfully through beatings or usage of harmful objects to inflict flagellation or if there's been a long-term rejection of her favor of fruits (such as her Valley of Joy, Hershey Highway, and Sweet Mouth) and captivating affection for her company with Adon's refusal to spark the fruitfulness that was once there. The factor of an Adon that doesn't fervently have intercourse momentarily or often with his queen gives the denial of honor for her. Furthermore, because of denial of honor in queen, often or sometimes a queen will strive to recapture that honor by glamorizing themselves, changing hair and nails style, losing excessive weight, attempt to read love scriptures from the Bible to the Adon with hope it'll ignite sexual dharma, watch cinematic films or shows with the Adon that consist of sensual sexual scenes and(or) create romantic events or use lingerie or her nudity to grasp her Adon affection. A queen's submission from 50 to 85 percent plus emunah for moralities and companionship of how she should dress, how she should communicate with the Adon to throne honor and admiration for the Adon, how she should yield to authority of the Adon, how she should drink, regulate her curfew, how she should make time from work (if she's working), and other things that the Adon may address for the covenant sake of the relationship. However, never should submissive nor *faithful love slave* give up their faith in Adon Olam and Adonai Christ Yahawashi for their Adonai.

Submission is more so of a treasury appeal by how the woman conducts herself in a femininity nature, how she communicates in public with meekness but profoundly sexually carnal in privacy with only her Adon, convey a little aggression for sake of sustaining fidelity by giving more loving in ways that gratify her Adon most and her sensuality. The more openness and receptivity a submissive woman gives the more empathy, compassion, passion and impassion flows of love from that submissive will grow on the Adon. On the contrary, even if an unfortunate relationship separation happened her sensuality will always be part of the Adon because of how much she offered compared to another woman who offers can't even compare, he'll still miss his best desert by admiring and reminiscing the woman that was most charitable to his intimate needs and companionship. This is a portion of *spiritual BDSM* from profound attachment, for her charity lingers on the Adon. These are also the ways of the *faithful love slave* as well, contrarily, *faithful love slaves* apply submission at a 100 percent plus emunah level on intimacies' of passion, compassion, impassion, servility, companionate, masochism favors to sadism nature of the Adon, assent receptively nonconsensual consent, and overall a giver of her king's novelties with the consent of her prudency. The important portion an Adon needs to know is to honor her by remembering she has needs, desires, a Spirit, and vulnerable to trust so don't go far into humiliation, for humiliation should be done on privacy moment's or spontaneities of affection that will make her feel graced or desired. Exploiting personal favors, a submissive or faithful love slave offers devalues the beauty of openness, trust, and covenant for the Adon would make it a brothel if exploited. An important portion to a submissive is knowing to be passive to the Adon's demands but aggressive to the Adon's sexual needs for a submissive or *faithful love slave* queen's mentality should be charitable in intimate servility lovingly, naughtily, and undefiled desire to her Adon's sensuality overall.

Section II: Core Practices

Overview of BDSM

Certain individuals characterize others that are practitioners of sensual BDSM as abnormal but there only validating there lack of adventure into certain practices. According the Journal of Sexual Medicine, BDSM practitioners were "less neurotic, more extraverted, more open to new experience, more conscientious, less rejection sensitive," and concluded to be a notion of "recreational leisure, rather than" the articulation of psychopathological phases (AA & MA, 2013). The issue with individuals that are skeptical to try certain BDSM practices is because of the criterion of pain, the mystery partners gravitates for, the intellectual procedure of the sexual Arcanum of the other, which is the hesitation of deviance of the other. In addition, the deviances of nonconsensual consent, of aggression, of sadomasochism, and of surrendering control. All of which is a natural phase of self-protection, which is a natural human response of safety, and what ignites fear becomes a defense mechanism within the individual. For a woman to form the submission the issue is determining if her dominator (or master) giving the emunah proportions she's hoping for, or if she's comfortable with his philosophy and loving of the dominator's (or master's) power play, artistry which includes: bondage, role-play, spiritual love, and seductive instructions, and code to his love, family and emunah. As of today sensual BDSM is becoming a more wide-spread intimate and recreational leisure of sexual experimentation. All of this is somewhat primitive because of the natural nature of kink for it allures novelties and sexual ecstasy into forming a will to become practitioners for sanctifying amorous sensual naughtiness for freedom of eroticism, avowing Arcanum's, to seek connection and prolong relationship through recreational leisure, atonement for caged emotions and desires, and overly senses.

Sensual BDSM gives sensible actions and spirited force of profoundness of the undefiled, uncensored, unrated intimate lifestyle with the sustainment of fidelity from the investment of connection, *CDD* framework and *emunah* that was sensibly built and agreed between lovers.

To become of practitioner of sensual BDSM and (or) arts of Domestic Discipline, the individual is not required to attend munch(s) which are BDSM social gatherings, nor required to exploit themselves with collars that seem ineloquent or practice every single thing BDSM has to offer, it's all on what seems sensual and sensible to the individual(s) that defines the practitioner arts, neither do you need diplomacy of society to be qualified as a Adon, Submissive, Faithful love slave, or Dominant, nor do you need admission from a priest, pope, or any other branch of minister nor council; these personification is simply identity revealed into your eyes of who you are as a being and your desires and sensuality. Collars in the BDSM lifestyle are determined based on style, for a submissive may find a vague of contempt because of others or insecure based on fashion disapproval but the important portion is the submissive eloquence to the collar, for if its stylish with modernity she may feel more comfortable wearing one, but another portion on her part is the will to break construction of how others judge and become hedonistic to her sensuality. An eloquent collar that perhaps will be one of the best for the novice individuals would be *EternityCollars.com* or *MySecretHeartJewelry* from Etsy.com.

Sadism and Masochism

In chapter XIII, the dominator (man) of a submissive (woman) is the root of sexual life, but what's often censored is sadism and masochism as one of the main projectiles of domination and submission for the fear of exposure and being an outcast from others. In reality sadism and masochism is more of contemptuous when exposure has reached other individuals that don't agree with its deviance. In reality sadism can be the exposure of noticing when defloration is in action, certain women I've overheard instated that once a man penetrates a woman he doesn't want to stop thrusting even when she's in pain during coitus until he climaxes (the reality principle fulfills in orgasm or ejaculation). Although there is a certain amount of men that would have sensibility during her defloration phase, there's an innate truth to this, and that truth is that various men has yang fuel of assertiveness and superego and that assertive superego doesn't always compromise but further its inclination, in a way it's power play. Another is sadism of *"riding the crimson tide,"* which is the eagerness of a man being sexually aroused and desires sex and aggress *impact play* while the woman is on her period (menstruating). Mankind's primitive sexual aggression is based on his testosterone and the essential truth to this is testosterone is not always stable nor has the desire to be altered. The sadist can be classified as, "the seducer," because the seduction is drawing another into amorous or deviant intimate acts through taking advantage of another's mentality and physiology of their sexual intellectual nature as an investment to carryout inclinations with persuasions. Sadism methodology is about thrusting another's limits to a *resting potential* to justify what's liberated, compromising, acceptable, receptive to the other for an understandable notion of consensual consent which later evolves to nonconsensual consent after a relationship grows in trust because that individual acts according to knowledge for the sadist knows *resting potential* of the masochist. *Resting potential* simply means how far of tolerance the individual is willing to accept or compromise to. These are the innate primitive stages of **sadism (sadist)**. The important portion of an Adon sadist is to carryout desires with sensibility, though important to know every man is capably brutish (Jeremiah 51v17), therefore are predominately sadist as well.

The reason I'm giving this information is because many young individuals are not often educated in this criterion but many sensible mothers would sometimes tell the truth of this to their daughters for in understanding capacity. The woman would naturally become the masochist through defloration, because of the receptivity of submission and opening up to penetration while the Honey Pot and(or) Hershey Highway accommodates the man's member (Love Muscle) even during pain. The masochist can be classified as, "the amenable," for their servility and nourishing nature to heal another in the most submissive potential to sanctify another's inclination. These are the innate primitive stages of **masochism (masochist)**. A masochist can induce their own pain by pushing their limits, for instance a masochist can search for a man with the largest member and submit to intercourse that may possibly friction from intensified pain or receive intensified pleasure, but she induced herself to it. The character traits of **sadomasochism** which is the duality of sadism and masochism, is a natural tendency that can derive from pure sexual arousal on what's naturally a turn-on. These turn-ons can derive from sensual erotic spankings, grappling, lip biting, sensual hair pulling, power play, Hersey Highway loving, gentle to moderate nails-to-back scratching, bondage, sensual—gently aggressive choke hold on receiver (masochist) end being ravished by the giver (sadist), and controlling director (sadist) or yielding servant (masochist) desire. When a man takes advantage of a woman that seems to be naughty, licentious and(or) sexually carnal, he'll seduce her based on the intellectual, mental and physiological advantages of the woman's persona. The persona of the submissive of what she considers weakest or deemed liberated by what's she's yielding to without protestation on her persona that clarifies to the Adon she's a masochist; therefore, it's a suffering for connection and love from the masochist while the sadist became the convincer and seducer.

Sadomasochism is a natural impulsive desire, not something of a disease or disorder, however if an individual is chaotic with the impulse it can be an issue. Sadomasochism is closely correlated with Domestic Discipline, from the use of erotic spankings for it creates confessions, builds emunah, and induces kink. Pain is the core component of *sadomasochism*. The perception of pain in oneself or another is a recognizable empathy in another or oneself creating a nursey to oneself or another. This empathy can form a loveable attachment for others and oneself through the use of—affection, caressing, a kiss, a huge, sensibility, and solace with copulation: when there's *emotional suffering* and the other has innate concupiscence of taking advantage of the other in a vulnerable stage seeking a healing investor, this can be a *sadism* behavior. Pain can induce a coping strategy. In the essence of good pain, this is not always pleasant but can accommodate a conditioning within the physiology and mind. For instance, good pain comes from defloration because the woman's anatomy eventually accommodates to pleasure, the exception is the women who suffer from the agony of vaginismus, exercising conditions the muscles that can be beneficial in the long run, eroticisms like sensual spankings, mellow bites, sensual hair pulling and sensual chokes and aggression which can be sexually banging against objects during lovemaking, grabbling, rough sex; basically, *power play*. In analogy to sadomasochism is when receiving a tattoo an individual self-teaches themselves to honor the pain so that the artist doesn't make error, the individual that receives the tattoo is sometimes not even aware that it's closely correlated to a *masochism* trait while the artist smile or gives a sarcastic statement with delight has a closely correlated trait of *sadism*, just not sexually, or do they? My guess is depending on the person the artist is tattooing and where there tattooing.

On the contrary, individuals that have the sadomasochistic characters of cutting, harshly beating, and using devices to torment another or themselves should have psychiatric assistance but this is just my dissension, for those individuals are prequels of sadomasochistic bad pain. Bad pain is complex, for it ranges from medical issues to abuse. Bad pain comes from chronic issues such as arthritis, headaches, cancer, and other health related problems, torture from devices, cuts and burns; basically after the pain was over the individual has no delight for a reoccurrence or a type of pain that's difficult to cope and has no type of pleasure or honor for, or going above levels of pain tolerance. Hopefully, this gives individuals some enlightenment on the criterion of sadism and masochism.

Shibari Arts

The bondage portion is cultivated from the ancient Japanese marital art called *Hojo-jutsu*, the martial arts of restraining captives which has been altered to an erotic sexual artistry called **Shibari** means "to bind," next level is known as *Kinbaku* "tight binding." The discipline of Shibari is **Kokoro**, means "heart; mentality; spirit" as a way of giving power exchange of sensualism, serenity, capitulation, masochism and servility from the submissive queen to the Adon, giving the Adon the sovereignty undefiled, consent to immobilize, sensualism, and sadism. The important philosophic portions of Shibari is the aspirations symbolizing art in flexible and comfortable manner for the submissive, meaning not tying her up in a way were its difficult to cope but sensibly. Another is using luxury quality ropes; perhaps many women that are looking to indulge in Shibari would feel more comfortable with softer ropes like natural Silk, Mohair, or Bamboo rope. Other ropes that are commonly used in the art Shibari are natural Hemp and Jute ropes. However, Hemp and Jute ropes according to *Shibari-nation.com* requires treatment of three phases; washing, boiling, and oiling—baby oil or jojoba oil for smoother rope on the skin. These ropes can be found at mauikink.com and other sources. Shibari artistry is considered aesthetic because of the stylish appeals and sensuality.

Chastity devices discipline

The chastity belt (CB) devices in the DD and sensual BDSM lifestyle is a harvest of preserving an intimate relationship and build harmony through fidelity being honored through acceptance of this type of discipline. The reason is because it gives the ability of willful discipline on either the Adon or the Submissive as in act of increasing the assurance of fidelity through preventing masturbation so that it may heighten sexual energy and preventing unfaithfulness through granting the significant other with key to the padlock(s) to withdraw from inevitable temptations. For CB devices on women are to give the assurance to the Adon that she's only allowed her Adon to penetrate her only. The factors of CB devices are the mere diagnosis of curing the significant others insinuated thoughts of infidelity, prevent nymphomaniac behavior and "rape shield" preventing an outsider eager man's actions of unwanted coition towards the woman. CB device is a way of preserving honor or virginity, or demonstrating character of a *devotee*. CB device is manifested for empowerment, stability and privacy; used on women from adolescent to venerable adult stage. In hope, adolescent to venerable adult women will apply the CDD and BDSM, CB device discipline throughout the living on the earth, the kindred, the nations, and many tongues for manifestation. The reason why CB device wouldn't be worn in intimate relationships is because sexual intimacy is supposed to be rendered unto each other but outsiders, the non-exclusive partners or swinging are the sinful and sexual immoral in regards of prudency. Stainless steel CB is more so recommended for hygienic and body friendly. For quality and customizable stainless steel CB for your treasures queen, *fancysteel.com.au* is perhaps one of the best. In addition to CB discipline, there are male CB devices but concerns must be acknowledged on this criterion for a woman's anatomy erects from the inside so there's no pressure for them to wear a CB device, but mankind erects from the outside which may bring upon painful tension, nerve damage, penile disfigurement or create atrophy; so I'm simply persuading I wouldn't recommend men wearing this even if you'll have a woman that's probing the man to wear one, unless it's can accommodate erection without painful suspensions. Male CB device is commonly used for preventing masturbation and insuring fidelity towards there treasures woman. However, male CB device discipline is left to your determinism.

(Note: All sites or products I've recommended out of this book give me no profit; I'm just simply saving you'll time and expense from buying the unnecessary and ineffective)

Section III: Marriage Agreement Lifestyle

Marital Agreement Lifestyle

Special Note:

Note: Every time I said Yahawah or Yahawashi, I considered the respect of their true name but if you'll feel disagreeable upon the ancient names feel free to change the names to names that's common to you'll. For Yahawashi, an individual may feel comfortable with saying Jesus, Yeshua, Yashiyah, Iesus, Yehoshua, Yahoshua, or Iesous. For Yahawah, an individual may feel comfortable with saying Yahweh, Jehovah, Elohim, Hashem, Yahveh, Ahayah or El Shaddai.

The Adon and Submissive Marital Contract

On the grace of Adon Olam Yahawah and Adonai Christ Yahawashi, we (*recite name individually*, Groom full name) and (*recite name individually*, Bride full name), cleanse all our impurities and give sake of fervent mercy for our impulses for our vessels and Spirits call upon for the ordination to the vows of becoming husband and wife, a covenant of one-flesh loyal-heirs with Christ Yahawashi in the center. To prevent adultery and fornication we're permitting to your Word to keep the law. Thou flaws, pressures, trails and uncertainties of the future may be of hindrance and our imperfections faultier a little we (*recite full names individually*) call upon your strength and Ahavah to council us, grace us, and rapture us with Ahavah. We (*recite name individually*, Groom full name) and (*recite name individually*, Bride full name) promise to preserve our faith in the "grace of the Lord Jesus Christ, and the love of God, and the communion of the Holy Spirit" (2 Corinthians 13v14 KJV). Through emunah (truth, faith, fidelity, stability), hope and love, we acknowledge that love gives the greater (1 Corinthians 13v4–7 and 13); though we promise to live to the best of prudent expectations with honors to emunah, hope and love in this marriage, and by your grace be our guardian throughout the covenant that you've allowed so that Ahavah remain in union. Our love is what's vocation to our heart and by this discovery we've chosen to become one covenant from vessel's—"the Spirit, and the water, and the blood" (1 John 5v8 KJV), with the embodiment of Adonai Christ Yahawashi church to intercede to the Father Adon Olam Yahawah in this marriage for ordination, for we have grace that on this day love is *teleological* and fair and rendered onto each other without fear and dissimulation (cf. 1 John 4v18, Romans 12v9). Yahawah reverence providence within this *conjugal love* among our vessels to provide the matrimony a ministry of sensibility toward one another. Through the grace of wedded lifestyle, Adon Olam Yahawah grant us fertility, virility, vigor, and overall primitive embrace of each other for the fulfillment of undefiled marriage, and by the omniscient love of Adon Olam Yahawah and Adonai Christ Yahawashi grant us fair child(ren), and of intelligence, and of prudence. Throughout sickness and health, allow the gift of intimacies' impassionate, compassionate, passionate and companionate love become a baptism of resilience from sufferings and tribulations to subvert to the angelic touch of a sound mind (***Yahawah's farming***, page 94) and healing amongst the covenant.

𝔈𝔫𝔤𝔞𝔤𝔢𝔪𝔢𝔫𝔱 𝔞𝔫𝔡 𝔚𝔢𝔡𝔡𝔦𝔫𝔤 𝔦𝔦𝔫𝔤 𝔓𝔩𝔞𝔠𝔢𝔪𝔢𝔫𝔱

According to certain scholar's a wedding and engagement ring are considered pagan from the lessons from ancient times of Moses because God commended a removal of ornaments, because they were not of Him (cf. Exodus 33v4–6). However, ornaments are built on modest wearable fashion that gives eloquence, purpose, no purpose or is flourished from wealth, so the question is a simple wedding and (or) engagement ring going to deport you to Sheol "hell" in the afterlife? Answer is no, because engagement and wedding ring has an advantage of telos "purpose" for it rectifies a symbol and signet of love and fidelity, plus Israelites were slave's to the Pharaoh, so I'm certain God didn't won't his beloved children to wear what was invented or under the Pharaoh's captive nation. Certain individual mistake "round tires," as symbolism for ring and assuming it belongs to *Ouroboros*, but God was speaking of necklaces according to the Orthodox Jewish Bible (cf. Yeshayah [Isaiah] 3v18), not all ornaments are unnecessary or not purposeful, for example, bedsheets or covers for the bed are considered an ornament, if we don't have them in cold nights we'll be shivering. Biblical examples would be Rebekah having a necklace and erring to symbolically show favor (Genesis 24v22–30), another would be giving a charitable gesture of ornaments is from the abundance of the heart is proven to be non-heathen (cf. Luke 15v20–24). A wedding band and engagement ring is only symbolic with nothing of evil but a constant reminder of marriage, only evil on how you value it in your heart and motive. The eye opening is why in western civilization is the rings commonly worn on the left hand, the answer is because of the adoption of Greco-Roman and ancient Egyptian mythology that on the left hand of the index finger belief theirs a vein that connects directly to the heart, however, science proves this a myth wrong, plus it's heathen. Truth is the rings are better placed on the right hand index finger because it's meaningful of the blessed side of power, fidelity, strength, and honor and subvert what's considered enemy (cf. Exodus 15v6, Psalms 16v11, Psalms 73v23, Isaiah 41v13, and Hebrews 12v2).

Recognition

For Bride:

Do you acknowledge and hereby become prudent to Adon Olam Yahawah Word to love your husband (recite his full name), and future or current child(ren) regardless if they're your blood or not, provide *good works*, be a keeper of the household, provide Ahavah, provide submission toward the husband (Titus 2v4–5), and submit to him as Adon (Adonai) and honor his laws until his vessel departs earth (1 Corinthians 7v39, Romans 7v2) and remain a keeper of the faith to have Adon Olam Yahawah and Adonai Christ Yahawashi a keeper of your Spirit?
The flesh is what's submitted to the Adon but remember the Spirit is what's in submission to the Adon Olam Yahawah and Adonai Christ Yahawashi (Colossians 3v22–24).

A Guided Exergy of Transformation

As wife that comes to unifying of marriage without the preserving of her virginity and deflowered long ago, must come to the unifying of marriage with repentance to Adon Olam, seeking transformation through Adon Olam Yahawah and actions. For what's done in the past of fornications Adon Olam Yahawah calls it whoring, for woman to deem themselves as courtesan for wealth, vain conceit of continuous infidelity and give desire of flesh without love of Spirit for the other is considered creating a brothel for themselves in acts of prostitution. *On the Prostitution of the Soul (129,5–131,13)*, stated a Adon must not associate himself upon such a woman if she doesn't seek transformation for she'll bring shame upon future or current child(ren) and Adon (husband), and beauty will fade because honor is not given to the woman's vessel and Spirit; therefore, the Adon will not honor the woman as treasure if she's whoring because the conception of beauty is how a woman carries herself not just glamorous looks. The process of transformation is given from the directions from *Restoration of the Soul (131,13–132,27)*, a woman must withdraw from "former whoring and cleansed herself of the pollution of adulterers," meaning a turning point of her disconnecting from former partners and no longer carry vain conceit of whoring for new beginning of restoration. *Marriage of the Soul to Her Beloved (132,27–133,31)*, woman who becomes wife must devote herself to husband in honors of accepting him as her king, real master, and amend to her husbands will but professor to Adon Olam Yahawah. Yahawah adores a wife that remains impregnable as a kingdom, against surroundings of other wolves (men) in the forest abroad. (Meyer & Pagels, 2007, p. 228-231)

Yea, yea: _____ (initial and say) or Nay, nay: _____ (initial and say)

(Special Note Journal)

Adon's agreement to special note: _____ Authorized Husband Initial

For Groom:

    Do you acknowledge and hereby become prudent to Adon Olam Yahawah Word to love your wife (recite her full name), and future or current child(ren) regardless if they're your blood or not, to dwell in accordance of knowledge and grant honor towards her, as heirs together of grace, and grant her to be your Submissive vessel and remain a keeper of the faith to have Adon Olam Yahawah and Adonai Christ Yahawashi a keeper of your Spirit?

Yea, yea: _____ (initial and say) or Nay, nay: _____ (initial and say)

(Special Note Journal)

Submissive's agreement to special note: _____ Authorized Wife Initial

Note, review together your completed journal homework assigned on chapter XIV, Solidity Discipline, "Homework Assignment," then apply it to this marital agreement before commencement.

Commencement

We place a seal with vows from our hearts (Song of Solomon 8v6) to provide emunah, hope and love toward each other with the Adonai Christ Yahawashi as our Great High Priest (Hebrews 4v14–16), propitiator (1 John 4v10) and intercessor (John 10v7) to Father Yahawah the Omniscient All-Loving El Shaddai, and Savior to ordain this marriage. I (*recite name, individually*, Groom full name), to be wedded to wife (Bride full name), and I, wife (*recite name individually*, Bride full name), to be wedded to husband (Groom full name). Holy El Elyon, we conceal with your laws and after we consummate we are wedded through the authority of the Adon Olam Yahawah and Adonai Christ Yahawashi. Amen and Shalom (*recite together*).

Adon (Husband) Authorized Signature

_____

(Format example: Sabbath, December 24, 2016) *Note: The month could be honorably addressed from the Hebrew calendar instead of the Gregorian or Caesar calendar; so instead of December it would be Teiveith = Goodness, the tenth month on Hebrew calendar (There are thirteen months in the Hebrew calendar so months and dates varies from modest calendars).*

Date Agreed Upon _____, _____ _____, _____

Submissive (Wife) Authorized Signature

_____

Date Agreed Upon _____, _____ _____, _____

After agreements between both, you'll have given the consent of will and in intimate law and to know what's expected, permissible and dismissible, and desired amongst each other. When finished, place signet agreements within an envelope and place inside this book or a private chest, cabinet or clothing drawer; for this is your allegiance to God and your spouse.

Part I: Ark of Mentality, Pahawashi Anarchism, Realism, and Church

Notes – Chapter I: Discovery Within

Books

Davis, Stephen F., Joseph J. Palladino, and Kimberly M. Christopherson. *Psychology.* New Jersey: Pearson, 2013.

Greene, Robert. *Mastery.* New York: Viking Penguin, 2012.

Mansfield, Stephen. *Mansfield's Book of Manly Men: An Utterly Invigorating Guide To Being Your Most Masculine Self.* Nashville, Tennessee: HarperCollins Christian Publishing, Inc., 2013.

Marley, Bob. "Three Little Birds." *Legend.* Cond. Bob Marley. Comp. Bob Marley, 2002.

Maxwell, John C. *The 360 Degree Leader: Developing Your Influence from Anywhere in the Organization.* Nashville, Tennessee: Thomas Nelson, 2005, 2011.

Milosz, Czeslaw. *New and Collected Poems Czeslaw Milosz.* New York, New York: HarperCollins Publishers, 2001, 1995, 1991, 1988.

Tyndale House Publishers. "Chronological Life Application Study Bible." In *Chronological Life Application Study Bible*, by Tyndale House Publishers, translated by Wycliffe Bible Translators. Carol Stream, Illinois, 2012.

Urantia Foundation. *The Urantia Book: Revealing the Mysteries of God, the Universe, World History, Jesus, and Ourselves.* 4th. Chicago, Illinois: Urantia Foundation, 1955–2013.

Warren, Rick. *The Purpose Driven Life: What On Earth Am I Here For?* 1st. Grand Rapids, Michigan: Zondervan, 2002.

Notes

Scriptures

1 Thessalonians 4:11–12 Authorized King James Version

Galatians 6:4–5 King James Version

Philippians 3:13–14

Notes – Chapter II: The Prowess of the Mind through Hypnosis

Books

Alcorn, Randy. *If God Is Good: Faith in the Midst of Suffering and Evil.* 1st. Colorado Springs, Colorado: WaterBrook Multnomah, 2009.

Davis, Stephen F., Joseph J. Palladino, and Kimberly M. Christopherson. *Psychology.* New Jersey: Pearson, 2013.

Engler, Barbara. *Personality Theories.* 7th. Boston: Houghton Mifflin Company, 2006.

-Transcendence, page 82. Persona, page 75.

Meyer, Marvin, and Elaine H. Pagels. *The Nag Hammadi Scriptures* XE *"Nag Hammadi Scriptures".* New York: HarperOne, 2007.

Porter, Burton F. "The Purpose of Living: Ethics." Chap. 6 in *What the Tortoise Taught Us: The Story of Philosophy*, by Burton F. Porter, 146–147. Lanham, Maryland: Rowman & Littlefield Publishers, Inc., 2011.

Tyndale House Publishers. "Chronological Life Application Study Bible." In *Chronological Life Application Study Bible*, by Tyndale House Publishers, translated by Wycliffe Bible Translators. Carol Stream, Illinois, 2012.

Urantia Foundation. *The Urantia Book: Revealing the Mysteries of God, the Universe, World History, Jesus, and Ourselves.* 4th. Chicago, Illinois: Urantia Foundation, 1955–2013.

Notes

Websites

Gruber, Tom. *Ontology.* 2009. http://tomgruber.org/writing/ontology XE "ontology" -definition-2007.htm (accessed March 13, 2015).

Films

The Dark Knight Trilogy. Directed by Christopher Nolan. Performed by Christian Bale, Michael Caine, and Gary Oldman. 2005–2012.

The Town. Directed by Ben Affleck. Produced by Graham King and Basil Iwanyk. Performed by Ben Affleck, Rebecca Hall, Jeremy Renner, and Jon Hamm. 2010.

Man of Steel. Directed by Zack Snyder. Performed by Henry Cavill, et al. 2013.

Unleashed. Directed by Louis Leterrier. Performed by Jet Li, Morgan Freeman, and Bob Hoskins. 2005.

Antwone Fisher. Directed by Denzel Washington. Performed by Denzel Washington, Derek Luke, and Joy Bryant. 2002.

Scriptures

Proverbs 24:5 Authorized King James Version

Philippians 4:8 King James Version

Notes – Chapter III: Adversaries among Kings and Princes

Books

Alcorn, Randy. *If God Is Good: Faith in the Midst of Suffering and Evil.* 1st. Colorado Springs, Colorado: WaterBrook Multnomah, 2009.

Davis, Stephen F., Joseph J. Palladino, and Kimberly M. Christopherson. *Psychology.* New Jersey: Pearson, 2013.

Diehl, Ulrich. 2009. "Human Sufferings as a Challenge for the Meaning of Life." *Existenz An International Journal in Philosophy, Religion, Politics, and the Arts* IV, no. 2: 36–44.

Engler, Barbara. *Personality Theories.* 7th. Boston: Houghton Mifflin Company, 2006.

Mansfield, Stephen. *Mansfield's Book of Manly Men: An Utterly Invigorating Guide to Being Your Most Masculine Self.* Nashville, Tennessee: HarperCollins Christian Publishing, Inc., 2013.

Meyer, Marvin, and Elaine H. Pagels. *The Nag Hammadi Scriptures* XE "*Nag Hammadi Scriptures*". New York: HarperOne, 2007.

Milosz, Czeslaw. *New and Collected Poems Czeslaw Milosz.* New York, New York: HarperCollins Publishers, 2001, 1995, 1991, 1988.

Philokalia text St. Isaiah the Solitary, "On Guarding the Intellect" vol. 1.

Swenson XE "Swenson, Chris", Chris. *Rhino Mentality Is Your Armor against Negativity.* February 14, 2015. http://www.journal-advocate.com/columnist_chrisswenson/ci_27525211/rhino-mentality-is-your-armor-against-negativity (accessed April 29, 2015).

Tyndale House Publishers. "Chronological Life Application Study Bible." In *Chronological Life Application Study Bible*, by Tyndale House Publishers, translated by Wycliffe Bible Translators. Carol Stream, Illinois, 2012.

Urantia Foundation. *The Urantia Book: Revealing the Mysteries of God, the Universe, World History, Jesus, and Ourselves.* 4th. Chicago, Illinois: Urantia Foundation, 1955–2013.

Warren, Rick. *The Purpose Driven Life: What On Earth Am I Here For?* 1st. Grand Rapids, Michigan: Zondervan, 2002.

Films

Antwone Fisher. Directed by Denzel Washington. Performed by Denzel Washington, Derek Luke, and Joy Bryant. 2002.

Notes

Keller, Jason. *Machine Gun Preacher.* Directed by Marc Forster. Produced by Robbie Brenner, Gary Safady, and Marc Forster. Performed by Gerard Butler, Michelle Monaghan, and Michael Shannon. 2011. Based on the life of Sam Childers (accessed May 16, 2015).

McKenna, David. *American History X.* Directed by Tony Kaye. Produced by John Morrissey. Performed by Edward Norton, Edward Furlong, Avery Brooks, Beverly D'Angelo, and Paul Short. 1998.

The Dark Knight Trilogy. Directed by Christopher Nolan. Performed by Christian Bale, Michael Caine, and Gary Oldman. 2005–2012.

Training Day. Directed by Antoine Fuqua. Performed by Denzel Washington, Ethan Hawke, and Eva Mendes. 2001.

Scriptures

1 Peter 5:8 King James Version

Matthew 5:25 King James Version

Proverbs 21:1 Authorized King James Version

Proverbs 22:3 King James Version

Ecclesiasticus 30:21–24, Apocrypha King James Version

Deuteronomy 31:6

2 Corinthians 5:7 King James Version

Psalms 133:1 King James Version

Ephesians 6:12 King James Version

Galatians 4:7 King James Version

1 Corinthians 15:33 King James Version

Notes

Psalms 1:1 King James Version

Music

Walk, Christopher "Citizen Aim." "I Am Legend." *A Music Manifesto.* Cond. Citizen Aim. Comp. Citizen Aim. 2011.

Notes – Chapter IV: Awakening the Royalty

Websites

Channah, Devorah. *Hebrew Glossy.* 2012. http://www.headcoverings-by-devorah.com/ (accessed April 15, 2015).

Books

Mansfield, Stephen. *Mansfield's Book of Manly Men: An Utterly Invigorating Guide to Being Your Most Masculine Self.* Nashville, Tennessee: HarperCollins Christian Publishing, Inc., 2013.

Meyer, Marvin, and Elaine H. Pagels. *The Nag Hammadi Scriptures* XE *"Nag Hammadi Scriptures".* New York: HarperOne, 2007.

Tyndale House Publishers. "Chronological Life Application Study Bible." In *Chronological Life Application Study Bible*, by Tyndale House Publishers, translated by Wycliffe Bible Translators. Carol Stream, Illinois, 2012.

Urantia Foundation. *The Urantia Book: Revealing the Mysteries of God, the Universe, World History, Jesus, and Ourselves.* 4th. Chicago, Illinois: Urantia Foundation, 1955–2013.

Scriptures
Proverbs 16:21 King James Version

Notes – Chapter V: Empirical Realities

Films

Crash. Directed by Paul Haggis. Performed by Sandra Bullock, et al. 2004.

Books

Diehl, Ulrich. 2009. "Human Sufferings as a Challenge for the Meaning of Life." *Existenz An International Journal in Philosophy, Religion, Politics, and the Arts* IV, no. 2: 36–44.

Greene, Robert. *Mastery*. New York: Viking Penguin, 2012.

Meyer, Marvin, and Elaine H. Pagels. *The Nag Hammadi Scriptures* XE *"Nag Hammadi Scriptures"*. New York: HarperOne, 2007.

Thomas, Pradip Ninan. *Political Economy of Communications in India: The Good, the Bad, and the Ugly*. Thousand Oaks, California: SAGA Publications Inc., 2010.

Tyndale House Publishers. "Chronological Life Application Study Bible." In *Chronological Life Application Study Bible*, by Tyndale House Publishers, translated by Wycliffe Bible Translators. Carol Stream, Illinois, 2012.

Urantia Foundation. *The Urantia Book: Revealing the Mysteries of God, the Universe, World History, Jesus, and Ourselves*. 4th. Chicago, Illinois: Urantia Foundation, 1955–2013.

Pacheco, Henry R. *Gangs 101: Understanding the Culture of Youth Violence*. Philadelphia, PA: Esperanza, 2010.

Notes - Chapter VI: Life's Formulas

Books

Tyndale House Publishers. "Chronological Life Application Study Bible." In *Chronological Life Application Study Bible*, by Tyndale House Publishers, translated by Wycliffe Bible Translators. Carol Stream, Illinois, 2012.

Notes

Part II: Medicine and Spiritual Reading

Notes - Chapter VII: Intro of Soulful Medicines

Books

Tyndale House Publishers. "Chronological Life Application Study Bible."
In *Chronological Life Application Study Bible*, by Tyndale House
Publishers, translated by Wycliffe Bible Translators. Carol
Stream, Illinois, 2012.

Notes – Chapter VIII: Our Kingdom, Our Vessel, One Church

Books

Charles Hodge. *Systematic Theology*. Grand Rapids, Michigan:
Eerdmans, 1952.

Karl Barth. *Evangelical Theology: An Introduction*. Grand Rapids,
Michigan: Eerdmans, 1963.

Mansfield, Stephen. *Mansfield's Book of Manly Men: An Utterly
Invigorating Guide to Being Your Most Masculine Self.* Nashville,
Tennessee: HarperCollins Christian Publishing, Inc., 2013.

Maxwell, John C. *The 360 Degree Leader: Developing Your Influence
from Anywhere in the Organization.* Nashville, Tennessee:
Thomas Nelson, 2005, 2011.

Meyer, Marvin, and Elaine H. Pagels. *The Nag Hammadi Scriptures.* New
York: HarperOne, 2007.

- Faith and Love (61,36–62,6).

- The Gospel of Philip – Jesus's names (62,6–17).

Milosz, Czeslaw. *New and Collected Poems Czeslaw Milosz.* New York,
New York: HarperCollins Publishers, 2001, 1995, 1991, 1988.

Notes

Tyndale House Publishers. "Chronological Life Application Study Bible." In *Chronological Life Application Study Bible*, by Tyndale House Publishers, translated by Wycliffe Bible Translators. Carol Stream, Illinois, 2012.

Urantia Foundation. *The Urantia Book: Revealing the Mysteries of God, the Universe, World History, Jesus, and Ourselves.* 4th. Chicago, Illinois: Urantia Foundation, 1955–2013.

Viegas, Jennifer. 2011. *Did God have a wife? Scholar says that he did.* March 18. Accessed 2015. http://www.nbcnews.com/id/42154769/ns/technology_and_science-science/t/did-god-have-wife-scholar-says-he-did/.

Weor, Samuel Aun. *The Gnostic Bible the Pistis Sophia Unveiled: The Secret Teachings of Jesus Recorded by His Disciples*, Third Book, Chapter 102.
Websites
Channah, Devorah. *Hebrew Glossy.* 2012. http://www.headcoverings-by-devorah.com/ (accessed April 15, 2015).

Scriptures from Biblegateway.com

Romans 12:2 King James Version

Notes – Chapter VIV: Christ Inspires, Christian Outlaws

Books

Channah, Devorah. *Hebrew Glossy.* 2012. http://www.headcoverings-by-devorah.com/ (accessed April 15, 2015).

Meyer, Marvin, and Elaine H. Pagels. *The Nag Hammadi Scriptures.* New York: HarperOne, 2007.

Tyndale House Publishers. "Chronological Life Application Study Bible." In *Chronological Life Application Study Bible*, by Tyndale House Publishers, translated by Wycliffe Bible Translators. Carol Stream, Illinois, 2012.

Urantia Foundation. *The Urantia Book: Revealing the Mysteries of God, the Universe, World History, Jesus* XE "Jesus", *and Ourselves.* 4th. Chicago, Illinois: Urantia Foundation, 1955–2013.

Wallis Budge, Sir E. A., trans. *The Queen of Sheba and Her Only Son Menyelek.* Cambridge, Ontario: Ethiopian Series. 2000.

Scriptures

Matthew 22:37 and 39 King James Version

Matthew 7:12 Authorized King James Version

Luke 6:45 Authorized King James Version

Matthew 5:11 King James Version

Notes – Chapter X: Spiritual Reading Truth

Books

Freud, Sigmund. *Beyond the Pleasure Principle.* Translated by James Strachey. New York, New York: W.W. Norton & Company, 1961.

Meyer, Marvin, and Elaine H. Pagels. *The Nag Hammadi Scriptures.* New York: HarperOne, 2007.

- Spiritual Love (77,35–78,12)

Thomas, Kirk, and Kamini Thomas. *The Modern Kama Sutra: The Ultimate Guide to the Secrets of Erotic Pleasure.* Hong Kong: Da Capo Press, 2005.

Tyndale House Publishers. "Chronological Life Application Study Bible." In *Chronological Life Application Study Bible*, by Tyndale House Publishers, translated by Wycliffe Bible Translators. Carol Stream, Illinois, 2012.

Notes – Chapter XI: True Essence of Prayer

N/A

Part III: Sensual Adon Lovemaking

Notes – Chapter XII: Loveology Unfolds

Books

Byrne, Donn E. *The Attraction Paradigm*. New York: Academic Press, 1971.

Fromm, Erich. *The Art of Loving*. New York: Harper & Row, 1956.

Scriptures

1 Corinthians 13v4-7 and 13

Meyer, Marvin, and Elaine H. Pagels. *The Nag Hammadi Scriptures*. New York: HarperOne, 2007.

–Spiritual Love (77,35–78,12)

Notes – Chapter XIII: Awakening Arts of Domination and Mastery Within

Ferrer, Dr. Charley. *BDSM The Naked Truth*. Staten Island, New York: The Institute of Pleasure, 2011.

Meyer, Marvin, and Elaine H. Pagels. *The Nag Hammadi Scriptures*. New York: HarperOne, 2007.

Thernstrom, Melanie. *The Pain Chronicles: Cures, Myths, Mysteries, Prayers, Diaries, Brain Scans, Healing, and the Science of Suffering*. 1st. New York: Farrar, Straus and Giroux, 2010.

Tyndale House Publishers. "Chronological Life Application Study Bible." In *Chronological Life Application Study Bible*, by Tyndale House Publishers, translated by Wycliffe Bible Translators. Carol Stream, Illinois, 2012.

Vatsyayana. *The Complete Kama Sutra: The First Unabridged Modern Translation of the Classic Indian Text by Vatsyayana.* Translated by Alain Danielou. Rochester, Vermont: Park Street Press, 1994.

Yarber, William L., and Barbara W. Sayad. *Human Sexuality: Diversity in Contemporary America.* 8th. New York, New York: McGraw-Hill Companies, Inc., 2013, 2010, 2008, 2005, 2002, 1999, 1997, 1996.

Film

A History of Violence. Directed by David Cronenberg. Produced by Chris Bender and JC Spink. Performed by Viggo Mortensen, Maria Bello, Ed Harris, and William Hurt. 2005. Rough Sex Scene: 01:07:20.

Niccol, Andrew. *Lord of War.* Directed by Andrew Niccol. Produced by Philippe Rousselet and Andrew Niccol. Performed by Nicolas Cage and Bridget Moynahan. 2005.

Scriptures

1 Corinthians 7:3–4 Authorized King James Version, New Living Translation.

Notes – Chapter XIV: Art of Domestic Discipline

Books

Em & Lo. *The Bottom Line.* October 25, 2007. http://nymag.com/nightlife/mating/25988/ (accessed May 18, 2015).

Isidore Twersky, *Introduction to the Code of Maimonides (Mishneh Torah),* Yale Judaica Series, vol. XII (New Haven and London:

Yale University Press, 1980). Passim and especially Chapter VII, "Epilogue," 515–538.

Payne, Anthony G. 2012. "Osteoporosis in Women: Seminal Fluid Compounds Absorbed through Mucosal Tissues Help Protect Against & Remediate Bone Loss." *Idea/Hypothesis*, 1–15.

Lumpkin, J. B. *The Books of Enoch: The Angels, The Watchers and The Nephilim* (Vols. The Book of Fallen Angels, The Watchers, and the Origins of Evil). Blountsville, Alabama: Fifth Estate Publisher, 2011.

Markham, Jules. *Domestic Discipline.* Toronto, Canada: Lightningsource, 2007.

Meyer, Marvin, and Elaine H. Pagels. *The Nag Hammadi Scriptures.* New York: HarperOne, 2007.

Rosenau, Dr. Douglas E. *A Celebration of Sex: A Guide to Enjoying God's Gift of Sexual Intimacy.* Revised & Updated. Nashville, Tennessee: Thomas Nelson, Inc., 2002.

Tomassi, Rollo. *The Rational Male.* 1st. Nevada: Counterflow Media LLC, 2013.

Vatsyayana. *The Complete Kama Sutra: The First Unabridged Modern Translation of the Classic Indian Text by Vatsyayana.* Translated by Alain Danielou. Rochester, Vermont: Park Street Press, 1994.

Weor, Samuel Aun. *The Gnostic Bible the Pistis Sophia Unveiled: The Secret Teachings of Jesus Recorded by His Disciples,* Sixth Book – Chapter 147.

Scriptures

Leviticus 18:22 King James Version Romans 7:2 King James Version

Ephesians 5:22–24 King James Proverbs 16:24 King James Version
Version

Ephesians 5v22

Notes

Romans 7v2 KJV   Song of Solomon 5v4 KJV

Proverbs 16v24 KJV   Proverbs 12v4 KJV

Colossians 3v18-19 KJV   1 Corinthians 11v19 NLT

John 4v14 KJV   1 Corinthians 11v3 NLT

Song of Solomon 2v3 KJV   Titus 2v4-5 NLT

Notes – Chapter XV: Sacred Penetrative Roots and Revelation of Ancient to Modest Remedies

Books

Chia, Mantak. *The Multi-Orgasmic Man: Sexual Secrets Every Man Should Know.* New York, New York: HarperCollins, 1996.

Engler, Barbara. *Personality Theories.* 7th. Boston: Houghton Mifflin Company, 2006.

Hilsman, Gordon J. *Intimate Spirituality: The Catholic Way of Love & Sex.* Lanham, Maryland: Rowman & Littlefield Publishers, Inc., 2007.

Kerner, PhD, Ian. *She Comes First: The Thinking Man's Guide to Pleasuring a Woman.* New York, New York: HarperCollins Publishers, 2004.

Meyer, Marvin, and Elaine H. Pagels. *The Nag Hammadi Scriptures.* New York: HarperOne, 2007.

Rosenau, Dr. Douglas E. *A Celebration of Sex: A Guide to Enjoying God's Gift of Sexual Intimacy.* Revised & Updated. Nashville, Tennessee: Thomas Nelson, Inc., 2002.

Tyndale House Publishers. "Chronological Life Application Study Bible." In *Chronological Life Application Study Bible*, by Tyndale House

Publishers, translated by Wycliffe Bible Translators. Carol Stream, Illinois, 2012.

Yarber, William L., and Barbara W. Sayad. *Human Sexuality: Diversity in Contemporary America.* 8th. New York, New York: McGraw-Hill Companies, Inc., 2013, 2010, 2008, 2005, 2002, 1999, 1997, 1996.

Trudeau, Kevin. *Natural Cures "They" Don't Want You to Know About.* Elk Grove Village, Illinois: Alliance Publishing Group, Inc., 2004.

Websites

Collins, John. 2012. "Penis Enlargement Bible." *Penis Enlargement Bible.* www.penisenlargementbible.com (accessed March 2015).

Livescience.com. 2011. *The long and short of penile extenders.* http://www.cbsnews.com/news/the-long-and-short-of-penile-extenders/ (accessed March 30, 2015).

Mayo Clinic Staff. 2012. *Penis-enlargement products: Do they work?* http://www.mayoclinic.org/healthy-living/sexual-health/in-depth/penis/art-20045363 (accessed March 30, 2015).

Seeker, The. 2014. "Satisfy a Harem." *Learn How to Satisfy a Harem.* www.satisfyaharem.com.

Stone, Isabelle. 2013. *Her Fantasy Lover Formula.* http://www.herfantasylover.com (accessed February 2015).

Worth, Tammy. 2011. *Does Vagina Size Matter?* Edited by Laura J Martin, MD. http://www.webmd.com/women/features/vagina-size (accessed April 09, 2015).

Notes – Chapter XVI: Master Lover

Scholarly Journals

Notes

Bivona, J. and J. Critelli. 2009. "The Nature of Women's Rape Fantasies: An Analysis of Prevalence, Frequency, and Contents," *Journal of Sex Research*, 46:33.

Books

Porter, Burton F. *What the Tortoise Taught Us: The Story of Philosophy.* Lanham, Maryland: Rowman & Littlefield Publishers, Inc., 2011.

- Authoritarian personality – "highly controlled, rational, and deliberate."

Glass, PhD, Shirley P., and Jean Coppock Staeheli. *Not "Just Friends": Rebuilding Trust and Recovering Your Sanity After Infidelity.* New York, New York: Free Press, 2003, 2004.

Hilsman, Gordon J. *Intimate Spirituality: The Catholic Way of Love & Sex.* Lanham, Maryland: Rowman & Littlefield Publishers, Inc., 2007.

Kerner, PhD, Ian. *She Comes First: The Thinking Man's Guide to Pleasuring a Woman.* New York, New York: HarperCollins Publishers, 2004.

Lee, John. "Love Styles." In Barnes MH, Sternberg RJ. *The Psychology of Love.* New Haven, Connecticut: Yale University Press.

Lee, John. *Colours of Love: An Exploration of the Ways of Loving.* Toronto: New Press.

Meyer, Marvin, and Elaine H. Pagels. *The Nag Hammadi Scriptures.* New York: HarperOne, 2007.

- *Eros (109,1–100,1),* **On the Origin of the World.**

- *The Creation of Plants, Animals, and Heavenly Bodies (111,8– 112,25),* **On the Origin of the World.**

Romeo, Felicia F. 2010. "Acquaintance Rape on College and University Campuses," AAETS. Web.

Notes

Rosenau, Dr. Douglas E. *A Celebration of Sex: A Guide to Enjoying God's Gift of Sexual Intimacy.* Revised & Updated. Nashville, Tennessee: Thomas Nelson, Inc., 2002.

Tomassi, Rollo. *The Rational Male.* 1st. Nevada: Counterflow Media LLC, 2013.

Trudeau, Kevin. *Natural Cures "They" Don't Want You to Know About.* Elk Grove Village, Illinois: Alliance Publishing Group, Inc., 2004.

Vatsyayana. *The Complete Kama Sutra: The First Unabridged Modern Translation of the Classic Indian Text by Vatsyayana.* Translated by Alain Danielou. Rochester, Vermont: Park Street Press, 1994.

Yarber, William L., and Barbara W. Sayad. *Human Sexuality: Diversity in Contemporary America.* 8th. New York, New York: McGraw-Hill Companies, Inc., 2013, 2010, 2008, 2005, 2002, 1999, 1997, 1996.

Websites

Snow, Isabella. n.d. *Top 10: Female Sex Fantasies.* http://www.askmen.com/dating/heidi_200/214_dating_girl.html (accessed June 1, 2015).

Toglia, Michelle. 2014. *30 Sex Fantasies To Turn Into Reality.* http://www.womenshealthmag.com/sex-and-relationships/sex-fantasies (accessed June 1, 2015).

Elam, Paul. 2011. *Study Reveals Female Rape Victims Enjoyed the Experience.* http://www.avoiceformen.com/feminism/study-reveals-female-rape-victims-enjoyed-the-experience/ (accessed May 27, 2015).

Scriptures

Proverbs 5:19 King James Version

Romans 8:1–2 King James Version

Ecclesiastes 9:9 King James Version

Notes

Matthew 7:1–2 King James Version

Genesis 2:25 King James Version

Films

Lawson, Josh. *The Little Death.* Directed by Josh Lawson. Produced by Jamie Hilton, Michael Petroni, and Matt Reeder. Performed by Bojana Novakovic and Josh Lawson. 2014.

Notes – Chapter XVII: Intimate Investment

Books

Dunas, Felica. *Passion Play: Ancient Secrets for a Lifetime of Health and Happiness through Sensational Sex.*

Glass, PhD, Shirley P., and Jean Coppock Staeheli. *Not "Just Friends": Rebuilding Trust and Recovering Your Sanity After Infidelity.* New York, New York: Free Press, 2003, 2004.

Hilsman, Gordon J. *Intimate Spirituality: The Catholic Way of Love & Sex.* Lanham, Maryland: Rowman & Littlefield Publishers, Inc., 2007.

Lowery, Richard H. 2000. *Sabbath and Jubilee (Understanding Biblical Times).* St. Louis, Missouri: Chalice Press.

Meyer, Marvin, and Elaine H. Pagels. *The Nag Hammadi Scriptures.* New York: HarperOne, 2007.

Platt, Rutherford H. 2011. *The Lost Books of the Bible.* Pacific Publishing Studio.

Rosenau, Dr. Douglas E. *A Celebration of Sex: A Guide to Enjoying God's Gift of Sexual Intimacy.* Revised & Updated. Nashville, Tennessee: Thomas Nelson, Inc., 2002.

Notes

Tomassi, Rollo. *The Rational Male*. 1st. Nevada: Counterflow Media LLC, 2013.

Urantia Foundation. *The Urantia Book: Revealing the Mysteries of God, the Universe, World History, Jesus, and Ourselves.* 4th. Chicago, Illinois: Urantia Foundation, 1955–2013.

Vatsyayana. *The Complete Kama Sutra: The First Unabridged Modern Translation of the Classic Indian Text by Vatsyayana.* Translated by Alain Danielou. Rochester, Vermont: Park Street Press, 1994.

Wray, T. J. 2011. *What the Bible Really Tells Us: The Essential Guid to Biblical Literacy.* Lanham, Maryland: Rowman & Littlefield Publishers.

Scriptures

Proverbs 12:4 King James Version

Proverbs 21:9 King James Version

Proverbs 21:19 King James Version

Proverbs 23:27 King James Version

Chart

Figure 13-1 Indications of Effects on Women through Sexual Identity

Source: Chandra, A., Copen, C. E, Stephen, E. H. 2013. "Infertility and impaired fecundity in the United States, 1982–2010: Data from the National Survey of Family Growth." National Health Statistics Reports; no 67. Hyattsville, MD: National Center for Health Statistics.

Films

Casino Royale. Directed by Martin Campbell. Performed by Eva Green and Daniel Craig. 2006.

Notes

𝔓art 𝔍𝔙: Conclusion

Appendix I: Bible Conspiracies

Revelation 22:18–19 King James Version

Ephesians 2:18–19 Authorized KJV

James 5:16 King James Version

Matthew 6:7 King James Version

2 Corinthians 5:17 King James Version

Hebrews 9:10 King James Version

Romans 13:1 King James Version

Luke 2:33 King James Version, New International Version, English Standard Version, New Living Translation

Micah 5:2 King James Version, New International Version

Acts 8:36–37 King James Version, New International Version

1 John 5:7 King James Version, New International Version

Hebrews 1:8 King James Version, New International Version, New World Translation

Isaiah 14:12 King James Version, New International Version

1 Corinthians 9:27 King James Version, New International Version, Amplified Version, Common English Bible

Galatians 5:12 King James Version, New International Version, Common English Bible, Contemporary English Bible

2 Thessalonians 2:3 King James Version

Notes

Appendix II: Core of Domination and Submission

AA, Wismeijer, and van Assen MA. 2013. "Psychological characteriestics of BDSM practitioners." *Journal of Sexual Medicine* 1943-52. Accessed October 23, 2015. doi:10.1111/jsm.12192.

Index

Index

Index

Index

Index

Urge and Merge 163

V

vicarious reinforcement 187, 191
Vicarious reinforcement (VR) 187
vocation 7, 10, 16, 29, 38, 48, 98, 101,
    120, 130
Vocation 7

W

Waxman, Jamye 214, 219
wealth 307
White, James R. 337
Whitingham, William 336
William Lloyd, J. 253, 254, 324
Winfrey, Oprah 142
Winslet, Kate 277, 314
writing erotica 179

Y

Yahawah 7, 31, 39, 49, 54, 60, 66, 70,
    79, 80, 89, 94, 95, 100, 102,
    103, 105, 109, 110, 113, 115,
    121, 122, 127, 128, 129, 131,
    199, 212, 224, 309, 330
Yahawashi 7, 9, 35, 39, 40, 49, 51, 52,
    54, 66, 74, 77, 84, 89, 94, 95,
    97, 100, 102, 109, 110, 111, 113,
    114, 121, 127, 128, 129, 131,
    212, 271, 324, 362
Yahushua 29, 40, 42, 43, 91, 103, 104,
    112, 130, 179
Yeshua xix, 9, 103
YHWH 40, 70, 80, 81, 97, 98, 103,
    104, 105, 113, 123, 213, 219,
    221, 231, 331
    Yahawah 103
    Yahawashi 102, 103
    Yahushua 104
    Yahuwah 103

Z

Zalman King
    Pleasure or Pain 171

Printed in the United States
By Bookmasters